Porsche
911
Source Book

Porsche

911

Source Book

The full specification history, 1963 to 2009

Jörg Austin • Sigmund Walter

© Motorbuch Verlag 2011

English-language translation © Haynes Publishing 2011

German-language version first published in 2008 by
Motorbuch Verlag as *Porsche 911: Die technische
Dokumentation von 1963 bis 2009*

Jörg Austen and Sigmund Walter have asserted their
right to be identified as the authors of this work.

British Library cataloguing-in-publication data:
A catalogue record for this book is
available from the British Library.

This edition published by Haynes Publishing,
Sparkford, Yeovil, Somerset BA22 7JJ, UK

Tel: 01963 442030 Fax: 01963 440001
Int. tel: +44 1963 442030 Fax: +44 1963 440001

E-mail: sales@haynes.co.uk
Website: www.haynes.co.uk

ISBN 978 1 84425 969 4

Library of Congress catalog card number 2010927382

Haynes North America Inc.
861 Lawrence Drive, Newbury Park,
California 91320, USA

Translation by Elke Smale

Design and layout by James Robertson

Printed in the USA by Odcombe Press LP, 1299
Bridgestone Parkway, LaVergne, TN 37086

Contents

Foreword

The aim of this book is to provide a reference source for the technical changes that have been made to the Porsche 911, 912 and 911 Turbo production cars from the model's introduction in 1964 through to 2009.

The sections into which the text is divided, such as 'Engine', 'Fuel and ignition system' and 'Suspension', follow the arrangement established in Porsche's repair service manuals, parts catalogues and technical information leaflets.

The complete 911 development team, including Ferry Porsche nearest the camera., photographed with a prototype car.

In order to document any changes as completely as possible, without any omissions, publications by the Porsche factory as well as the personal notes of co-author Jörg Austen were used. For many years Jörg Austen was responsible for the Porsche Sales Department's technical literature, especially for training purposes.

The model years at Porsche start in August of the year before the listed model year. The allocation of a modification or an innovation to a certain model year is not always easy, as changes were often introduced either before or after the start of a new model year, or were launched in specific foreign markets. In this book, special

attention has been paid to models intended for the German market, but modifications for particular countries are also mentioned when these were subsequently applied to the entire range worldwide.

We considered the following 911 criteria especially important:

- Continuing development of Porsche's air-cooled boxer engines.
- Emissions controls worldwide.
- Self-shifting transmission development, from four-speed Sportomatic through to Tiptronic and PDK.
- Wheels and tyres, from steel wheels to three-part light-alloys, and from hollow-spoke technology to friction welding.
- Corrosion protection and Porsche's industry-leading warranties.
- Passive security features.
- Development stages of vehicle heating and air conditioning.
- The electrical system, from direct current to on-board computer.
- Individual style modifications.

All technical data has been compiled from a variety of factory documents – for example, annual Service Information records and the brochure 'Model, Measurements and Tolerances' – as well as from the cars' handbooks.

Special attention has been paid to the oils and fluids for the engine and transmission, as in the earlier 911 generations these often need to be replaced with modern products. Generally it can be said that modern multi-grade engine oils with a broad viscosity range are suitable for the slightly older models. However, the single-grade oils of the past – if you can get them – can still be used today, although it is best to be cautious when changing an unknown engine oil in an older model to modern oils, which have properties that dissolve and bind oil carbon and dirt in the engine. This could lead to an oil blockage after an oil change and cause engine damage due to an obstruction in the pipes, and increased abrasion between the engine's moveable parts. In such cases one should change the oil and the filter a number of times during the first 1,000km.

As for transmission oils, the situation is slightly different but still critical when modern oils are used in older vehicles. The Porsche 911's manual transmission incorporates the synchromesh mechanism and final drive with highly stressed bevel gears in one common housing. From about 1970 the oil industry supplied a new high-alloy transmission oil which had a vastly improved 'compressive strength of the oil film' at critical lubrication points. Additives reduced the friction in

The 2009-model 911 GT3 RS shows just how far the 911 has developed over almost 50 years, while maintaining an obvious family resemblance to the original prototype.

the oil, and the lifespan of highly stressed gears was lengthened significantly. However, the improved lubrication properties led to chemical smoothing at the friction surfaces of the synchromesh, causing it to fail without any warning signs. Porsche reacted very quickly to this new generation of transmission oil and adjusted its own synchromesh system to allow for the reduced friction. Starting with model year 1972, Porsche's gearboxes were filled with the new high-alloy transmission oil GL 5 (US standard MIL-L 2105 B). Until the end of 1973 both oil specifications were still permissible during servicing, but as from model year 1974 only the high-alloy oil was allowed.

With brake fluids also, the latest generation of fluid should be used for older vehicles, as great strides have been made in performance at high temperatures and longevity.

The listing of chassis numbers (later renamed as Vehicle Identification Numbers or VINs) has been done exactly according to Porsche factory specifications. The digits at the end of the chassis/VIN sequences were assigned as follows: …0001 to …0050 denote test vehicles; …0051 to …0060 denote special vehicles; and production car numbers start with the number …0061.

Noticeable are partly amended number sections for cars intended for the American and Canadian markets. Here, models are included in the *subsequent* model year, due to the start of production often being later than that of cars for the so-called 'rest of the world'. Porsche introduced new regulations from 1970.

The Authors, February 2011

Introduction

In 1960 I joined Porsche as a young engineer in its engine development department, and I was fortunate to be able to be involved in the initial development of the air-cooled six-cylinder boxer engine.

Dr Ferry Porsche was then himself fully involved with the future six-cylinder car and he decided that this engine-gearbox unit was going to be built according to a future-proof concept which has been proved right to this very day: a dry sump lubrication system, overhead camshafts and wide use of light-alloy. However, it was not only the engine whose benchmarks were set high, but also the transmission (which had five forward gears), Porsche's very own synchromesh system, MacPherson front suspension, rack-and-pinion steering and a split safety steering column – all trailblazers in their time. Right at the beginning of production, the 911 was a sports car that not only represented the latest state-of-the-art technology but also had tremendous future potential, and it still boasts cutting-edge technology as a result of constant modifications and enhancements. Furthermore, the simple and timeless design by Ferdinand Alexander Porsche has always been key to this car's success.

Through the years, the initial 2.0-litre car has developed into a legend, right up to its most extreme forms with twin turbochargers and 3.8-litre displacement. The 911 model range at the time of writing includes nine versions (excluding USA variants) and 28 models. 104 examples of the 911 are produced every day, and hardly ever do two identical vehicles leave the production facility in Stuttgart-Zuffenhausen on the same day. That is virtually unique in the motor industry.

I am very happy to see that this book chronologically and systematically follows the path of the 911's success, and not only shows through the many technical specifications how

the various models have changed and improved but also supplies the background information necessary to understand the reasons behind these modifications.

The fact that more than 70% of the 400,000-plus 911 vehicles produced still survive demonstrates the need for such a book.

Horst Marchart
Porsche Executive Board Member for Research and Development

9

911 Prototypes 1963/4

Porsche 901

In total Porsche produced 13 prototypes of its future 911 before starting full production in November 1964. These 13 cars had the chassis numbers 13,321 to 13,330, 13,352, 300,001 and 300,002. The models with the numbers 13,330 and 13,352 were the forerunners of the four-cylinder 912. They were used partly for exhibitions and partly as test cars, were continually modified, and differed from the production cars in some basic details. No two prototypes were exactly the same. The 911 was previewed at the IAA international motor exhibition in Frankfurt, Germany, in September 1963.

Engine

The first six-cylinder horizontally opposed (boxer) engine was given the type designation 745, and started development at the beginning of 1960. At this stage it was still a pushrod unit, rotating in four journal bearings, using two fans driven via a V-belt by the crankshaft. The next development phase was the 821 that was much closer to the eventual production version. The main difference was that the engine-gearbox unit did not as yet have a dry sump lubrication system. After extensive testing in the 911's forerunner, the T7, which had a 745 engine, Ferry Porsche decided to abandon pushrod motors.

Fuel and ignition system

Solex downdraught carburettors were already being used in the 745. Up until the completion of the

The engine cover opened to reveal the 821 six-cylinder boxer engine used on all Porsche 901 models.

production versions, Solex 40 PI designs from Lancia (type 40 PBIC) were used. The Solex overflow-type carburettors had been engineered at tremendous expense, while at the same time Porsche was experimenting with Italian Weber carburettors.

Transmission

Both four- and five-speed transmissions were tested, but as driving comfort was paramount it was decided to go with five forward gears. First gear was engaged by moving the lever to the left and back, and reverse gear to the left and forward, as it was important to Porsche that the layout of the gears should also be suited to race cars. The development of the gearbox did not pose any problems, as Porsche not only had tremendous know-how in the design of high-performance

A 1963-model Porsche 901 Coupé. The classic lines of the Porsche 911 are already very evident.

gearboxes but was also the inventor of the locking synchromesh system.

Suspension
During the early stages of development, Porsche was already experimenting with new suspension in the 356. Both 901 prototypes had the chassis subframe of the 356 at the front and its axles at the rear. It was decided only at the last minute to use a new rear axle system. If it had not been for the numerous road tests carried out with the 356 in the mid-1950s it would have been impossible to develop a completely new suspension for the 911. The fuel tank capacity was a generous 62 litres in order to emphasise the car's touring potential.

Body
The blueprint for the type 695 was developed for the most part by Graf (Earl) Goertz in 1957; Ferdinand Alexander Porsche created the 754 T7 with its slightly sloping tail in 1959, while the head of the body development team, Erwin Komenda, devised an ostentatious version, the 754 T9. The 901 finally evolved out of the preliminary design by Ferdinand Porsche, the 644 T8, on which the wheelbase was changed. The prototypes had no overriders and no sill trim on the sides but were fitted with two exhaust tailpipes. Many people were not ready to accept any type of Porsche other than the 356, which is why the new styling initially met with some criticism.

Equipment and fittings
The new Porsche had large windows and 2+2 seats (the rear ones split and folding), very much like the 356. Initially the large round main instruments (as in the 356) were used, and the combination of five round gauges with green printed dials was only introduced just before the 911 hit the market in 1964. The interior of the prototype shown at the Frankfurt IAA show in 1963 was very different from the subsequent production run.

Interior fittings
Porsche wanted to bring out the new model with an all-leather interior, but ultimately it used a combination of imitation leather and fabric. It experimented a great deal with seat heights, as it was important to Porsche that this sports touring car be a comfortable one.

Heating
As the heating system was speed- and load-dependent, Porsche did trials with fuel-driven auxiliary heating. This was later introduced as an optional extra for the 911, positioned in a cavity in the front luggage compartment on the right-hand side hidden by the dashboard, which was the location originally reserved for the battery.

The interior of prototype No7 already featured the hallmark 911 layout of five circular gauges and the steering wheel of the 356.

The prototypes did not have any heating operated by engine waste heat, as heat exchangers were only developed much later; this is why some versions only had auxiliary heating in the luggage compartment.

Electrical system
It was decided at an early stage that a powerful 12-volt installation should be used. The generator produced 360W, while later production cars produced 490W. The arrangement of the wiper arms was discussed extensively and in the first models they were positioned on the right-hand side in order to enlarge the field of vision.

The Porsche 911 2.0 Coupé went into production in 1964. The 356C models in the background were produced until 1965.

Model year 1965

Porsche 901/911

It was not until 1964 that production started of the successor to the Porsche 356, which had been built for 14 years with the same basic concept of a compact air-cooled boxer engine with clutch, manual transmission and final-drive assembly all located behind the rear axle. Peugeot's tradition of using model numbers with zero in the middle persuaded Porsche to change its designation 901 to 911 before the new model's introduction in November 1964, although this first model range is also referred to as the 'zero model range'. The Porsche 901/911 was the logical progression of a line of cars that had originated with the VW Beetle. Porsche's design fundamentals were an air-cooled boxer engine in the rear, wide use of light-alloy, suspension through torsion bars on both axles, proven transmission using Porsche's own synchromesh system, and boot and fuel tank sited in the front.

Engine

Six-cylinder boxer engine 901/01 with 1,991cc displacement. Air cooling by means of a fan mounted on the driveshaft of the generator. Dry

A 1964 Porsche 911 2.0 Coupé – one of the first 911 production models. This example is fitted with front foglights.

sump circulation lubrication with separate oil tank, engine performance 130hp (96kW) at 6,100rpm. Oversquare dimensions with bore of 80mm, stroke 66mm, total displacement 1,991cc. Compression ratio 9.0:1. Crankcase made from die-cast magnesium, cylinder from grey cast iron, and pistons cast from light-alloy. The crankshaft rotated in eight journal bearings. One camshaft per cylinder bank, camshaft driven by two drive chains.

Right from the start the six-cylinder boxer engine was designed with a view to future increases in performance. The crankshaft-driven cooling fan not only cooled the cylinders and cylinder heads but also the engine oil via a separately mounted oil cooler. The overhead camshafts enabled high engine revs right from the start of production, which was important for subsequent racing and sports engines. Also interesting was the advanced dry sump lubrication system, which prevented power loss from the crank splashing through the oil, especially at high revolutions.

Fuel and ignition system

Six individual Solex 40 PI overflow carburettors. The early system of two rows of three Solex carburettors was a very short-lived solution, as it was very difficult to keep them all synchronised. The ignition functioned as a conventional coil system with ignition breaker contact in the distributor. Firing order: 1-6-2-4-3-5. Distributor: Marelli S 112 AX.

Transmission

Type 901 five-speed manual transmission and differential in combined housing. Shift pattern: first gear left backwards, reverse gear left forwards, spring-loaded lock on first and second gears. Porsche locking synchromesh on all forward gears. Final-drive assembly: spiral bevel gears. Bevel gear differential optional extra: ZF limited-slip differential.

Drive to the rear wheels was via Nadella-jointed half-shafts; the outer universal joint was of the usual shape, while the inner 'Nadella' joint allowed axial movement between the connection of the two joints. Porsche also used an improved version of its synchromesh system in the 901/911 that it patented worldwide; it has since been used in all models of Alfa Romeo, Simca and Audi, as well as certain models of Fiat, Ferrari, Maserati and Lamborghini, plus trucks from Fiat-OM, Unic, Berliet and various diesel-engined forklifts.

Suspension

Sheet steel box sections were welded to the body. The basic suspension layout was independent front suspension by wishbones and MacPherson struts, and independent rear suspension by semi-trailing arms. Porsche stuck with its proven torsion bar set-up, but the installation of a round longitudinal

An early Porsche 911 2.0 Coupé (right) parked next to its 356C predecessor outside the Porsche factory at Zuffenhausen in 1964.

torsion bar at the front end was completely new. The rear suspension included one round, transverse torsion bar per wheel. Dampers: front double-action dampers as per MacPherson system, rear double-action telescopic dampers. It was not possible to adjust track and camber in the first model year. Wheels: perforated steel disc wheels, available chrome-plated as an optional extra, drop-centre design 4.5Jx15; tyres 165 HR 15. Brakes: hydraulic single-circuit brake system, front discs 282mm, rear discs 285mm. Handbrake operated mechanically as a drum brake on both rear wheels.

The ZF rack-and-pinion steering (steering ratio 1:16.5) was new in the 901/911. This was pioneering technology introduced by Porsche, while the rest of the automobile industry was still generally using worm-and-nut steering. Porsche's attention to safety was evident in the split steering column, which used two universal joints to reach the steering rack.

Four disc brakes on the 901/911 were quite a luxury in the 1960s, but they used outboard discs rather than the inboard disc brakes developed by

13

Porsche and tested in the 356 Carrera 2 and Porsche Formula 1 car. The single-circuit brake system acted on all four wheels.

Body
The Coupé was an all-steel design. The 911 was prepared for the introduction of safety belts and had extensive instrumentation. Oil level at idle speed was indicated for the first time. The idle position of the wiper arms was on the right-hand side. Compared to the Porsche 356 there was significantly more space in the boot and in the cabin.

The classic Porsche silhouette was clearly discernible in the 911's classically distinctive body shape. Slanted headlights were positioned in the front wings, while air intake ducts were sited not only in the engine cover at the rear but at the front next to the indicators in a compact, chromed design. There was gold-plated 911 lettering on the engine cover at the rear, and chromed overriders without rubber stops as well as door trim strips.

Equipment and fittings
The windscreen was made of laminated safety glass and the car had circular wing mirrors. Curved laminated safety glass was virtually unknown in 1963/4, but Porsche used this safety feature right from the beginning of 911 production.

Interior fittings
The concept and execution of the 911's interior was completely new to Porsche, with elegant and functional interior trim and seats, covered partly in imitation leather. The steering wheel was

A works-prepared Porsche 911 2.0 Coupé ready to compete in the 1965 Monte Carlo rally.

made from wood, as was the dashboard, which carried silver '911' script. The door sills were rubber-clad.

Heating
The 911 was heated by waste heat from the engine: the engine fan carried fresh air through the heat exchanger and delivered heated air into the passenger cabin. In addition, a petrol-powered Webasto independent heater (type P1018) could be supplied as an optional extra but it was not particularly reliable. This heating system was much improved compared to the one in the Porsche 356 and complied with the regulations that prevailed during the 1960s. Air conditioning was not available at the start of production.

Electrical system
Sophisticated 12-volt electrical system, asymmetrical dipping headlights, three wiper speeds and an electric windscreen washer system made the 901/911 one of the most modern vehicles of its day.

Additional information
Initially a luxury version of the 911 was planned, but this was later dropped. By the standards of the era, there was a relatively wide range of optional extras available from launch, but this number would grow significantly in later years.

Model range	Total production
Porsche 901	13
Porsche 911	230

Model range	911
Engine	
Engine type, manual transmission	901/01
Number of cylinders	6
Bore (mm)	80
Stroke (mm)	66
Displacement (cc)	1991
Compression ratio	9.0:1
Engine output (kW/hp)	96/130
at revolutions per minute (rpm)	6100
Torque (Nm)	174
at revolutions per minute (rpm)	4200
Output per litre (kW/l)	48.6 (65PS/l)
Max. engine speed (rpm)	6500
Engine weight (kg)	184

Carburation, ignition, settings	
Fuel system	Solex downdraught overflow carburettor 40PI
Type of fuel (RON)	96
Ignition system	Conventional battery coil ignition
Firing order of all 911 engines	1-6-2-4-3-5
Distributor	Marelli S 112 AX
Spark plugs	
Bosch	W225T7. W 200T35
Beru	P 225/14
Spark plug gap (mm)	0.6–0.7
Idle speed (rpm)	850–950

Model range	911
Transmission	
Clutch, pressure plate	M 215K
Clutch plate (mm)	215
Manual transmission	901/02
Gear ratios	
1st gear	3.091
2nd gear	1.888
3rd gear	1.318
4th gear	1.000
5th gear	0.758
Synchromesh system gears 1–5	POSY
Final drive	4.4285
Limited-slip differential	Option
Lock-up factor under load/ coasting (%)	40/40

S Standard
POSY Porsche Locking synchromesh system, synchroniser rings, mo-coated

Suspension, steering and brakes	
Front axle	
Anti-roll bar dia. (mm)	–
Steering ratio	17.87
Turning circle dia. (m)	10.7
Rear axle	
Anti-roll bar dia. manual transmission (mm)	–
Brake system:	Single-circuit brake system
Brake master cylinder dia. (mm)	19.05
Brake calliper piston diameter	
front (mm)	48
rear (mm)	35
Brake disc diameter	
front (mm)	282
rear (mm)	285
Brake disc thickness	
front (mm)	12.7 U
rear (mm)	285
Effective brake disc area (cm²)	185
Handbrake	Operating mechanically on both rear wheels
Brake drum diameter (mm)	180
Contact area (cm²)	170

Wheels and tyres	
Standard tyre specification, front	165-15 (radial)
wheel	4½ J x 15
Standard tyre specification, rear	165-15 (radial)
wheel	4½ J x 15
Tyre pressure	
front (bar)	2.0
rear (bar)	2.4

Key: 12.7 U = non-ventilated full brake disc thickness 12.7 mm

Model range	911
Body and interior (dimensions at kerb weight)	
Length (mm)	4163
Width (mm)	1610
Height (mm)	1320
Wheelbase (mm)	2211
Track	
front (mm)	1367
rear (mm)	1335
Ground clearance at permissible gross weight (mm)	150

Electrical system	
Generator output (W/A)	490/30
Battery (V/Ah)	12/45

Weight according to DIN 70020	
Kerb weight (kg)	1080
Permissible gross weight (kg)	1400

Performance	
Maximum speed (kmh/mph)	
Manual transmission	210/130
Acceleration 0–62mph/100kmh (sec)	
Manual transmission	9.1
Measured kilometre from standing start (sec)	
Manual transmission	29.9

Fluid capacities	
Engine oil quantity 1* (l)	9
Oil change quantity 1* (l)	8–9
Manual transmission 2* (l)	2.5
Fuel tank (l)	62
Brake fluid reservoir 3* (l)	0.20

* Key to numerals
1* Approved API SE/SF with combinations API SE/CC - SF/CC - SF/CD - SE/CD
   Multigrade engine oil factory recommended (SAE 10 W/50 or 15 W/40 or 20 W/50).
   Single-grade engine oils were also permissible (branded HD oils). Summer SAE 30. Winter SAE 20.
2* Single-grade transmission fluid SAE 90 acc. MIL-L 2105 and GL 4
   Not permissible: transmission fluid SAE 90 acc. MIL-L 2105 B and API-classified GL 5
3* Use only brake fluid acc. SAE J 1703. DOT 3 or 4

Chassis numbers (six digits)						
Model year	From	To	Production period	Type	Model	Body manufacturer
1964	300 001	300 232	Production from September 1964	911	Coupé	Body Porsche
1965	300 233	303 390	Production to July 1965	911	Coupé	Body Porsche
	350 001	351 970	Production to July 1965	912	Coupé	Body Porsche
	450 001	454 470	Production to July 1965	912	Coupé	Body Porsche
1966	303 391	305 100	Production Aug. 1965 to July 1966	911	Coupé	Body Porsche
	351 971	353 000	Production Aug. 1965 to July 1966	912	Coupé	Body Porsche
	454 471	485 100	Production Aug. 1965 to July 1966	911	Coupé	Body Karmann
1967	305 101	308 522	Production Aug. 1966 to July 1967	911	Coupé	Body Porsche
	305 101S	308 522	Production Aug. 1966 to July 1967	911S1	Coupé	Body Porsche
	354 001	355 601	Production Aug. 1966 to July 1967	911	Coupé	Body Porsche
	458 101	463 204	Production Aug. 1966 to July 1967	911	Coupé	Body Karmann
	500 001	500 718	Production Aug. 1966 to July 1967	911	Targa	Body Porsche
	500 001S	500 718S	Production Aug. 1966 to July 1967	911S	Targa	Body Porsche
	550 001	550 544	Production Aug. 1966 to July 1967	911	Targa	Body Porsche

Model year 1966

Porsche 911 Coupé
Porsche 912 Coupé

The major news for Porsche's 1966 model range was the arrival of the new 'junior' Porsche 912. This was fitted with the four-cylinder engine of the 356 SC, albeit detuned to 90hp (66kW). The 912 was intended as a model to entice newcomers to the Porsche marque. In the US especially, where road speed checks were carried out from 1965, the reasonably priced and economical Porsche 912 proved very popular.

A sectional view of the 2-litre, six-cylinder boxer engine used in early Porsche 911 models.

A period promotional photograph of a 1966 Porsche 911 2.0 Coupé.

Engine
Engines 901/01 and 901/05 were used for the six-cylinder 911, while engine type 616/36 was for the 912. The engine housing was made of magnesium alloy.

Fuel and ignition system
There was a change to the Solex carburettors for cars equipped with engine 901/01 at the venturi, which was now open at the bottom. A new version of the engine, Type 901/05, was fitted with two triple-choke Weber carburettors (type 40 IDA 3L and 3C1). This change over to Weber carburettors arrived quickly because these were much easier to adjust and did not suffer from the same flat spot as the Solex carbs. All other technical details of both engines were identical.

Transmission
Five-speed manual transmission Type 901/02 for the whole 911 range. A four-speed gearbox was standard in the 912 with a five-speed transmission (Type 902/01) available as an optional extra. Simplified driveshafts with ball joints were also used in the 912.

Porsche recognised that cars with a top speed of over 124mph (200kmh) required a five-gear transmission as with only four gears, it could not make sure each gear ratio was matched to the performance. That is why five-speed manual transmission was offered as an optional extra for the 912.

Suspension
Modified brake callipers.

A cutaway view of the 2.0-litre six-cylinder boxer engine. The camshaft drive mechanism can be seen at the front of the engine.

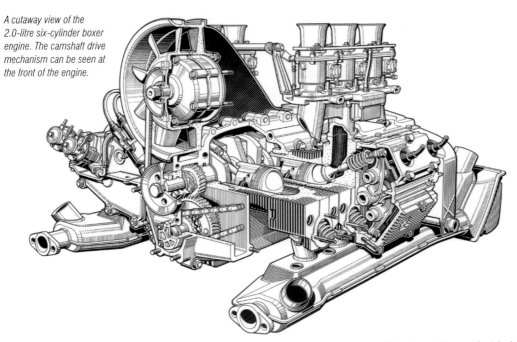

Body
The angled gold-plated '911' script at the rear was replaced by horizontal silver-plated script.

Equipment and fittings
Instead of the wooden steering wheel, a leather-covered one was now fitted, and it was decided to abandon exotic wood on the dashboard. The carpets were made of soft felt.

Electrical system
More powerful 490W alternator.

A view showing the surprisingly spacious luggage compartment on a Porsche 911 2.0 Coupé.

The Porsche 912, with the flat-four 1.6-litre engine from the 356, was introduced to the Porsche range in 1966.

17

Model range	Total production
911 Coupé	3155 + 1710 USA
912 Coupé	6401

Model range	911
Engine	
Engine type, manual transmission	901/01 and 901/05
Number of cylinders	6
Bore (mm)	80
Stroke (mm)	66
Displacement (cc)	1991
Compression ratio	9.0:1
Engine output (kW/hp)	96/130
at revolutions per minute (rpm)	6100
Torque (Nm)	174
at revolutions per minute (rpm)	4600
Output per litre (kW/l)	48.6 (65PS/l)
Max. engine speed (rpm)	6500
Engine weight (kg)	184

Carburation, ignition, settings	
Fuel system	
Engine 901/01	Solex downdraught overflow carburettor 40PI
Engine 901/05	Weber carburettor 40IDA 3L and 3C1
Type of fuel (RON)	96
Ignition system	Conventional battery coil ignition
Distributor	Marelli S 112 AX
Spark plugs	
Bosch	W225T7. W 200T35
Beru	P 225/14
Spark plug gap (mm)	0.6–0.7
Idle speed (rpm)	850–950

Transmission	
Clutch, pressure plate	M 215K
Clutch plate (mm)	215
Manual transmission	901/02
Gear ratios	
1st gear	3.091
2nd gear	1.888
3rd gear	1.318
4th gear	1.000
5th gear	0.758
Synchromesh system gears 1–5	POSY
Final drive	4.4285
Limited-slip differential	Option
Lock-up factor under load/coasting (%)	40/40

Key:
S   Standard
POSY Porsche Locking synchromesh system, synchroniser rings, mo-coated

Suspension, steering and brakes	
Front axle	
Anti-roll bar dia. (mm)	–
Steering ratio	17.87
Turning circle dia. (m)	10.7
Rear axle	
Anti-roll bar dia. (mm)	–
Brake system:	Single-circuit brake system
Brake master cylinder dia. (mm)	19.05
Brake calliper piston diameter	
front (mm)	48
rear (mm)	35

Model range	911
Suspension, steering and brakes (continued)	
Brake disc diameter	
front (mm)	282
rear (mm)	285
Brake disc thickness	
front (mm)	12.7 U
rear (mm)	10.0 U
Effective brake disc area (cm²)	185
Handbrake	Operating mechanically on both rear wheels
Brake drum diameter (mm)	180
Contact area (cm²)	170

Wheels and tyres	
Standard tyre specification, front	165-15 (radial)
wheel	4½ J x 15
Standard tyre specification, rear	165-15 (radial)
wheel	4½ J x 15
Tyre pressure	
front (bar)	2.0
rear (bar)	2.4

Key: 12.7 U = non-ventilated full brake disc thickness 12.7 mm

Body and interior (dimensions at kerb weight)	
Length (mm)	4163
Width (mm)	1610
Height (mm)	1320
Wheelbase (mm)	2211
Track	
front (mm)	1367
rear (mm)	1335
Ground clearance at permissible gross weight (mm)	150

Electrical system	
Generator output (W/A)	490/30
Battery (V/Ah)	12/45

Weight according to DIN 70020	
Kerb weight (kg)	1080
Permissible gross weight (kg)	1400

Performance	
Maximum speed (kmh)	
Manual transmission	210
Acceleration 0–62mph/100kmh (sec)	
Manual transmission	9.1
Measured kilometre from standing start (sec)	
Manual transmission	29.9

Fluid capacities	
Engine oil quantity 1* (l)	9
Oil change quantity 1* (l)	8–9
Manual transmission 2* (l)	2.5
Fuel tank (l)	62
Brake fluid reservoir 3*	0.20

* Key to numerals
1* Approved API SE/SF with combinations API SE/CC - SF/CC - SF/CD - SE/CD
   Multigrade engine oil factory recommended (SAE 10 W/50 or 15 W/40 or 20 W/50).
   Single-grade engine oils were also permissible (branded HD oils). Summer SAE 30. Winter SAE 20.
2* Single-grade transmission fluid SAE 90 acc. MIL-L 2105 and GL 4
   Not permissible: transmission fluid SAE 90 acc. MIL-L 2105 B and API-classified GL 5
3* Use only brake fluid acc. SAE J 1703. DOT 3 or 4

Model year 1967
Targa and 911 S

Porsche 911 Coupé and Targa
Porsche 911 S Coupé and Targa
Porsche 912 Coupé and Targa

At customers' request Porsche introduced a new model, the high-performance 911 S, while continuing to build the standard 911 and 912. The new S boasted 160hp. Suspension and brake systems were adjusted accordingly.

Furthermore, a new Targa body style expanded the 911 model line-up. This was a convertible but it featured a fixed safety roll-over bar. After the success of the 356 Cabriolet, Roadster and Speedster, the Targa was another convertible body style for Porsche. The Targa concept (*targa* is Italian for 'shield') was immediately adopted by other car manufacturers worldwide, but only the removable roof of the 911 was allowed to be called by the Targa name, which Porsche copyrighted as a reminder of the company's racing successes at the Targa Florio in Sicily.

Porsche carried out its first emission test in 1966 in order to comply with Californian emission regulations, while in Germany a value of 4.5% CO at idle speed was still being debated.

Engine
There was an improved engine (Type 901/06) for the standard 911 with modified camshafts and improved heat exchangers. However, the big news this year was the new higher performance engine (Type 901/02)

with the same 1,911cc displacement, fitted to the new 911 S. Maximum output was 160hp (118kW) at 6,600rpm, specific power output was 80hp per litre, maximum engine speed was 7,200rpm. The improvement in performance of the 'S' engine was achieved by increasing the compression ratio to 9.8:1. Other technical details included soft nitrided forged steel con rods, forged aluminium pistons, altered cam profiles, 42mm inlet valves, 38mm exhaust valve diameter, and two valve springs per valve.

The 911 S engine was developed from the basic unit without compromising durability. The high compression ratio of 9.8:1 was remarkable considering the fuel types available at that time. The cylinders used Biral, a proprietary name for the process of making cylinders with a grey cast iron liner contact surface on to which cooling fins were 'sleeved'. This improved heat dissipation.

Fuel and ignition system
The high-performance 911 S engine was fitted with two triple-choke Weber carburettors (type IDA (S), 40 IDS 3C and 3C 1). The distributor used was the Bosch 0231159002 type, yellow label. The spark plugs had a heat value of 260 and the octane rating requirement was 98RON (premium fuel).

All six-cylinder engines were now fitted with Weber carburettors. The ignition system was made by Bosch, with the distributor, ignition coil and spark plugs all coming from the Stuttgart-Feuerbach manufacturer.

The 2.0 Targa was a new addition to the Porsche 911 range to supplement the Coupé for 1967.

A 1967-model Porsche 911 S Targa. The S models used the 160hp 2.0-litre engine, with uprated suspension and brakes.

Transmission

The 901/03 five-speed manual transmission was fitted as standard in the 911 S. Apart from the standard transmission, which varied only very slightly from the prototype one, a variety of special competition transmissions were offered to sports enthusiasts for the first time. The following transmissions were available as optional extras: 901/51 (sports transmission), 901/52 (for hill

A Porsche 911 2.0 Targa modified for use as a police car in Düsseldorf during 1967.

racing), 901/53 (for airfield racing), 901/54 (for fast races) and 902/0 (Nürburgring transmission).

Suspension

New on the 911 S were transverse anti-roll (stabiliser) bars front and rear, Koni dampers all round, forged drop-centre 4.5Jx15 light-alloy wheels from Fuchs, and front and rear ventilated brake discs.

The light-alloy wheels were a first for Porsche. The forged, or rather pressed, light-alloy five-spoke wheel remained well known and much loved even into the 1990s. Today it is often incorrectly known as the 'Fuchs wheel', but in fact the Porsche Studio (with Ferdinand Alexander Porsche at the helm) designed it. The manufacture of the wheel was carried out by Fuchs in Meinerzhagen, strictly in accordance with Porsche's drawings.

Body

The inside rear-view mirrors of all cars were glued to the windscreen. A new addition to the Porsche range was the Targa, a convertible body style which boasted an emphasis on safety. The B-pillar was designed as a fixed roll bar. The removable roof between the windscreen and the roll bar could be folded like a concertina and stowed away in the luggage compartment at the front, without taking up all of the space. The section behind the roll bar was soft, rather than glass, and could be folded down.

While in the past there had been little concern regarding open-top safety, Porsche recognised at an early stage the importance of protecting both passenger and driver. The Targa offered three open-top driving configurations: with the roof in place but the rear window open; completely open to the elements; or without the roof but with the rear window closed. This enabled Porsche to preserve the open-air driving experience even with the roof in place. This was a flexible arrangement in more ways than one: while the fixed bar offered

some strength, the Targa was not as rigid overall as the standard Coupé.

A 1967 Porsche 911 2.0 Targa poses in a snowy setting for a publicity photograph.

Equipment and fittings

A leather-covered steering wheel was standard in the 911 S. The Targa had a flexible rear window (between the roll bar and the rear body), which, as explained opposite, could be folded down or completely removed with the help of a zip. A racing version – the 911 R – also marked the first time that a fuel tank made from plastic was installed. This safety novelty only became a standard feature in 1973.

Heating

A petrol/electrical external heating system could be supplied as an optional extra.

Electrical system

In the 911 S an additional gauge was installed to display the oil pressure in analogue format. This completed what was admittedly a confusing state of affairs for the non-technically minded, since the engine oil condition was now displayed on four separate analogue gauges: oil temperature (in degrees Centigrade), oil pressure (atmospheric pressure, later in bar), oil level indicator (which only read correctly at idle speed, under hot running conditions, and on level ground), and a yellow oil pressure warning light that would come on when the pressure dropped below 0.8bar.

The compact dimensions of the 2.0-litre six-cylinder boxer engine and its ancillaries are clearly illustrated in this view.

21

Model range	Total production
912 Coupé	9325
912 Targa	N/A
911 Coupé	3155 + 1710 USA
911 Targa	N/A
911 S Coupé	523
911 S Targa	N/A

Model range	911	911 S
Engine		
Engine type, Manual transmission	901/06	901/02
Number of cylinders	6	=
Bore (mm)	80	=
Stroke (mm)	66	=
Displacement (cc)	1991	=
Compression ratio	9.0:1	9.8:1
Engine output (kW/hp)	96/130	118/160
at revolutions per minute (rpm)	6100	6600
Torque (Nm)	174	179
at revolutions per minute (rpm)	4600	5200
Output per litre (kW/l)	48.6	59.2
Max. engine speed (rpm)	6500	7200
Engine weight (kg)	184	184

Carburation, ignition, settings		
Fuel system	WV 401DA	WV 401DS
Type of fuel (RON)	96	98
Ignition system	Conventional battery coil ignition	
Distributor	Bosch	Bosch
Spark plugs		
Bosch	W230T30	W250P21
Beru	P 225/14	–
Spark plug gap (mm)	0.6–0.7	0.35
Idle speed (rpm)	850–950	=

Key:
WV = Weber carburettor 40 IDT P

Transmission		
Clutch, pressure plate	M 215K	=
Clutch plate (mm)	215	=
Manual transmission	901/02	901/03
Gear ratios		
1st gear	3.091	=
2nd gear	1.888	=
3rd gear	1.318	=
4th gear	1.000	=
5th gear	0.758	=
Synchromesh system gears 1–5	POSY	=
Final drive	4.4285	=
Limited-slip differential	Option	Option
Lock-up factor under load/ coasting (%)	40/40	=

Key:
S   Standard
POSY Porsche Locking synchromesh system, synchroniser rings, mo-coated

Suspension, steering and brakes		
Front axle		
Anti-roll bar dia. (mm)	Option	14
Steering ratio	17.87	=
Turning circle dia. (mm)	10.7	=
Rear axle		
Anti-roll bar dia (mm)	Option	14
Brake system:	Dual-circuit brake system	
Brake master cylinder dia. (m)	19.05	=
Brake calliper piston diameter		
front (mm)	48	=
rear (mm)	35	38

Model range	911	911 S
Suspension, steering and brakes (continued)		
Brake disc diameter		
front (mm)	282	=
rear (mm)	285	=
Brake disc thickness		
front (mm)	12.7 U	20. intern. vented
rear (mm)	10.0 U	20. intern. vented.
Effective brake disc area (cm²)	185	=
Handbrake	Operating mechanically on both rear wheels	
Brake drum		
diameter (mm)	180	=
Contact area (cm²)	170	=

Wheels and tyres		
Standard tyre specification, front	165-15 (radial)	=
wheel	4½ J x 15	=
Standard tyre specification, rear	165-15 (radial)	=
wheel	4½ J x 15	=
Tyre pressure		
front (bar)	2.0	=
rear (bar)	2.4	=

Key:
12.7U = non-ventilated full brake disc thickness, 12.7 mm

Body and interior (dimensions at kerb weight)		
Length (mm)	4163	=
Width (mm)	1610	=
Height (mm)	1320	=
Wheelbase (mm)	2211	=
Track		
front (mm)	1367	=
rear (mm)	1335	1339
Ground clearance at permissible gross weight (mm)	150	=

Electrical system		
Generator output (W/A)	490/30	=
Battery (V/Ah)	12/45	=

Weight according to DIN 70020		
Kerb weight (kg)	1080	1030
Permissible gross weight (kg)	1400	=

Performance		
Maximum speed (kmh)		
Manual transmission	200	225
Acceleration 0–62mph/100kmh (sec)		
Manual transmission	9.1	7.6
Measured kilometre from standing start (sec)		
Manual transmission	32.1	27.55

Fluid capacities		
Engine oil quantity 1* (l)	9	=
Oil change quantity 1* (l)	8–9	=
Manual transmission *2 (l)	2.5	=
Fuel tank (l)	62	=
Brake fluid reservoir 3* (l)	0.20	=

* Key to numerals
1* Approved API SE/SF with combinations API SE/CC - SF/CC - SF/CD - SE/CD Multigrade engine oil factory recommended (SAE 10 W/50 or 15 W/40 or 20 W/50).
   Single-grade engine oils were also permissible (branded HD oils). Summer SAE 30. Winter SAE 20.
2* Single-grade transmission fluid SAE 90 acc. MIL-L 2105 and GL 4 Not permissible: transmission fluid SAE 90 acc. MIL-L 2105 B and API-classified GL 5
3* Use only brake fluid acc. SAE J 1703. DOT 3 or 4

Key:
SPM Sportomatic

Model year 1968

A Series, Sportomatic and 911 T

Porsche 911 T, L, S, Coupé and Targa
Porsche 912 Coupé and Targa

In 1968, semi-automatic 'Sportomatic' transmission was introduced for the 911 only (the four-cylinder 912 would never be offered with Sportomatic). The 1968 model year also marked the moment when the first cars with exhaust emission control were delivered to the USA.

The previous 'regular' 911 was now badged as the 911 L and was fitted with the carburettor-fed 901/06 engine (130hp). A slightly different 901/07 engine was prepared for Sportomatic transmission. A new model for 1968 was the 911 T, a six-cylinder version with less power than the standard L (110hp), also available with Sportomatic. This car was intended for the first-time Porsche buyer, and was especially aimed at the female market; the even less powerful 912 continued in production.

Engine

Exhaust-controlled engines (US type 901/14 for manual transmission and 901/17 for Sportomatic cars) were offered for the first time in the US market. Six-cylinder engines with reduced power – type 901/03 for manual transmission models and type 901/13 for Sportomatics – were made for the 911 T. The compression ratio of these 110hp engines (81kW) was reduced to 8.6:1 while peak power was reached at 5,800rpm. The cylinders of

these engines were made from grey cast iron, as used on the original 901 prototypes.

As concerns USA cars with exhaust emission control, since over half of Porsche's cars were exported to the USA, it had done pioneering work right from the start and was able to comply with the strict regulations in place in California without compromising performance, and still offer almost the same driving comfort. Exhaust emission control in the cars, which still had carburettors, was achieved through exhaust gas recirculation (into the inlet manifold) and thermal reactors. In those days Porsche was able to boast the first exhaust test rig in Europe.

Fuel and ignition system

The engine of the 911 T was fitted with two Weber triple-choke carburettors, and Marelli S 112 AX distributors were used. The heat value of the spark plugs was 230.

Transmission

No changes to the manual transmission this year, but semi-automatic four-speed transmission was available for all six-cylinder cars, the Sportomatic 905/00 for the four-cylinder 912 cars, and 905/01 for the 911 T, L and S. The difference between the two transmissions was the ratio of the fourth gear, which was suited to the differing performances of the models.

Sportomatic was a drive system that consisted of a hydraulic torque converter fixed to the engine flywheel, and a manual transmission that operated with vacuum assistance from the induction

A Porsche 911 S 2.0 Coupé fitted with the black wiper arms and blades introduced for 1968.

Dr Ferry Porsche, who was closely involved with the development of the 911, poses with a 1968-model Porsche 911 Coupé.

An interior view of a 1968 Porsche 911 S fitted with the four-speed semi-automatic Sportomatic transmission.

manifold. It was a four-speed transmission with Porsche synchromesh system and a lower crown wheel and pinion ratio of 7:27.

Sportomatic cars did not have a clutch pedal. In order to change gears the driver would touch the gear lever, which initiated a vacuum-operated servo to open the clutch coupling within a split second;

A Porsche 911 2.0 Coupé competing on the 1968 East African Safari Rally.

the power flow from engine to gearbox was interrupted, and the chosen gear could then be engaged using the lever. Once the gear had shifted and after releasing the lever, the clutch would once again work automatically.

Market research had shown that a generation of buyers was being raised in the USA that had never learnt how to use a clutch pedal. Furthermore, the scale of stop-and-go traffic all over the world had increased to such an extent that even a sports car was more comfortable to drive with a torque converter.

The drive system of the Sportomatic contained torque converters and a manual transmission from Fichtel & Sachs (F&S). As the longitudinal installation space within the 911 was very limited due to its rear-engined design, Porsche developed an elongated clutch release system. This type of clutch operation, in which the clutch release bearing ran concurrently with engine revs, required less space and became accepted worldwide in the years that followed, for manual transmissions too. The hydraulic torque was supplied with oil from the engine's oil reservoir. A ZF-Eaton oil-feed pump, driven by one of the camshafts, created an oil flow to the converter that was responsible for filling and cooling during operation. Engine damage through loss of oil in the converter or at the inlet pipes or return lines was very unlikely, as the intake to the converter supply in the oil reservoir was installed high up so that the supply of oil to the motor was always guaranteed.

Suspension

Boge dampers were now standard for the 912, 911 T and L as well as all Targas; in contrast, the 911 S had Koni dampers. The diameter of the anti-roll (stabiliser) bar at the front was 11mm for the

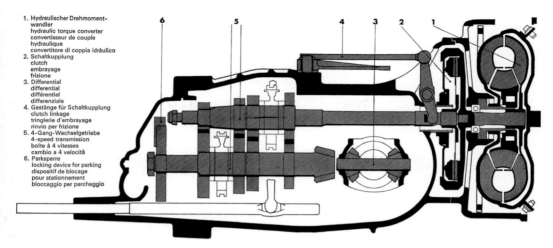

1. Hydraulischer Drehmoment-
   wandler
   hydraulic torque converter
   convertisseur de couple
   hydraulique
   convertitore di coppia idràulico
2. Schaltkupplung
   clutch
   embrayage
   frizione
3. Differential
   differential
   différentiel
   differenziale
4. Gestänge für Schaltkupplung
   clutch linkage
   tringlerie d'embrayage
   rinvio per frizione
5. 4-Gang-Wechselgetriebe
   4-speed transmission
   boîte à 4 vitesses
   cambio a 4 velocità
6. Parksperre
   locking device for parking
   dispositif de blocage
   pour stationnement
   bloccaggio per parcheggio

The Sportomatic gearbox made for a more comfortable driving experience and was the precursor of today's Tiptronic S gearbox.

911 L and 15mm for the 911 S, and at the rear was 15mm for the 911 S. Wider 5.5Jx15 wheels were fitted, as well as a dual-circuit brake system for six-cylinder cars. Research at Porsche showed that wider wheels in conjunction with adjustments to the chassis and suspension tuning significantly improved handling.

An interesting view of a sectioned Sportomatic transmission, illustrating its compact design.

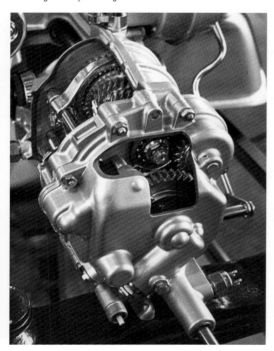

Body

Chromed windscreen wipers were nice to look at but could dazzle the driver when the sun was shining, and were therefore changed over to black wiper arms and wiper blades. Rubber inserts for the overriders front and rear were now standard.

Model range	Total production
912 Coupé	5501
912 Targa	N/A
911 T Coupé	473 + 742 USA
911 T Targa	268 + 521 USA
911 L Coupé	720 + 5449 USA
911 L Targa	307 + 5134 USA
911 S Coupé	1267
911 S Targa	442

Model range	911 T	911 L	911 S
Engine			
Engine type, Manual transmission	901/03	901/06	901/02
Number of cylinders	6	=	=
Bore (mm)	80	=	=
Stroke (mm)	66	=	=
Displacement (cc)	1991	=	=
Compression ratio	8.6:1	9.0:1	9.8:1
Engine output (kW/hp)	81/110	96/130	118/160
at revolutions per minute (rpm)	5800	6100	6600
Torque (Nm)	157	174	179
at revolutions per minute (rpm)	4200	4600	5200
Output per litre (kW/l)	40.7	48.2	59.2
Max. engine speed (rpm)	6500	6500	7200
Engine weight (kg)	184	184	184

Carburation, ignition, settings			
Fuel system	WV 401DT P	WV 401DA	WV 401DA
Type of fuel (RON)	98	98	98
Ignition system	Conventional battery coil ignition		
Firing order	All 911 engines – 1-6-2-4-3-5		
Distributor	Marelli	Bosch	Bosch
Spark plugs			
Bosch	W230T30	W250P21	W26521
Beru	P 225/14	–	–
Spark plug gap (mm)	0.6–0.7	0.35	0.35
Idle speed (rpm)	850–950	=	=

Key:
WV = Weber carburettor

Model range	911 T	911 L	911 S
Transmission			
Clutch, pressure plate	M 215K	=	=
Clutch plate (mm)	215	=	=
Manual transmission	901/03	901/50	901/50
Gear ratios			
1st gear	3.091	=	=
2nd gear	1.888	=	=
3rd gear	1.318	=	=
4th gear	1.000	=	=
5th gear	0.758	=	=
Synchromesh system gears 1–5	POSY	=	=
Final drive	4.4285	=	=
Limited-slip differential	Option	Option	Option
Lock-up factor under load/coasting (%)	40/40	=	=
Sportomatic	905/00	=	–
Torque converter (mm)	F&S 190	=	
Stall speed (rpm)	2500–2700	=	
Gear ratios			
1st gear	2.400	=	
2nd gear	1.631	=	
3rd gear	1.217	=	
4th gear	0.926	=	
Synchromesh system forward gears	POSY	=	
Final drive	3.857	=	

Key:
S Standard
F&S Manufacturer Fichtel & Sachs
POSY Porsche Locking synchromesh system, synchroniser rings, mo-coated

Suspension, steering and brakes			
Front axle			
Anti-roll bar dia. (mm)	Option	14	14
Steering ratio	17.87	=	=
Turning circle dia. (m)	10.7	=	=
Rear axle			
Anti-roll bar dia. (mm)	Option	14	14
Brake system:	Dual-circuit brake system		
Brake master cylinder dia. (mm)	19.05	=	=
Brake calliper piston diameter			
front (mm)	48	=	=
rear (mm)	35	38	38
Brake disc diameter			
front (mm)	282	=	=
rear (mm)	285	=	=
Brake disc thickness			
front (mm)	12.7 U	20. intern. vented	
rear (mm)	10.0 U	20. intern. vented	
Effective brake disc area (cm²)	185	=	=
Handbrake	Operating mechanically on both rear wheels		
Brake drum diameter (mm)	180	=	
Contact area (cm²)	170	=	

Wheels and tyres			
Standard tyre spec., front	165HR15	165VR15	=
wheel	4½ J x 15	5½ J x 15	5½ J x 15 LM
Standard tyre spec., rear	165HR15	165VR15	=
wheel	4½ J x 15	5½ J x 15	5½ J x 15 LM
Tyre pressure			
front (bar)	2.2	=	=
rear (bar)	2.4	=	2.2

Key:
12.7 U = non-ventilated full brake disc thickness 12.7 mm
LM = forged light-alloy wheels, manufacturer Fuchs

Model range	911 T	911 L	911 S
Body and interior (dimensions at kerb weight)			
Length (mm)	4163	=	=
Width (mm)	1610	=	=
Height (mm)	1320	=	=
Wheelbase (mm)	211	=	=
Track			
front (mm)	1367	=	=
rear (mm)	1335	=	=
Ground clearance at permissible gross weight (mm)	150	=	=

Electrical system			
Generator output (W/A)	490/30	=	=
Battery (V/Ah)	12/45	=	=

Weight according to DIN 70020			
Kerb weight (kg)	1080	=	1030
Permissible gross weight (kg)	1400	=	=
Permissible trailer weight			
unbraked (kg)	480	=	=
braked (kg)	600	=	=

Performance			
Maximum speed (kmh)			
Manual transmission	200	215	225
Acceleration 0–62mph/100kmh (sec)			
Manual transmission	10.0	9.0	8.0
Measured kilometre from standing start (sec)			
Manual transmission	32.1	29.8	28.8

Fluid capacities			
Engine oil quantity 1* (l)	9	=	10
Engine oil quantity with SPM (l)	+2	=	–
Oil change quantity 1* (l)	8–9	=	=
Manual transmission 2* (l)	2.5	=	=
Sportomatic 2* (l)	2.5	=	=
Fuel tank (l)	62	=	=
Brake fluid reservoir 3* (l)	0.20	=	=

* Key to numerals
1* Approved API SE/SF with combinations API SE/CC - SF/CC - SF/CD - SE/CD
   Multigrade engine oil factory recommended (SAE 10 W/50 or 15 W/40 or 20 W/50).
   Single-grade engine oils were also permissible (branded HD oils). Summer SAE 30. Winter SAE 20.
2* Single-grade transmission fluid SAE 90 acc. MIL-L 2105 and GL 4
   Not permissible: transmission fluid SAE 90 acc. MIL-L 2105 B and API-classified GL 5
3* Use only brake fluid acc. SAE J 1703. DOT 3 or 4

Key:
SPM Sportomatic

Chassis numbers (eight digits)				
Cars	Model year	Model	Sequence	Summary
11	8	0	0001–9999	911 S Coupé
11	8	1	0001–9999	911 L Coupé
11	8	2	0001–9999	911 T Coupé
11	8	3	0001–9999	911 Coupé USA
11	8	5	0001–9999	911 S Targa
11	8	6	0001–9999	911 L Targa
11	8	7	0001–9999	911 T Targa
11	8	8	0001–9999	911 Targa USA

From 1968 until 1969 (inclusive), chassis numbers started with '11', and not '911'; but as from 1970 chassis numbers began with '911' (later '930' for the Turbo)
Model year: 8 = 1968. 9 = 1969

Model year 1969

B Series, mechanical fuel injection

Porsche 911 T, E Coupé and Targa
Porsche 911 S Coupé and Targa
Porsche 912 Coupé and Targa

Model year 1969 saw major changes to the 911, principally in the body and engine departments. A longer wheelbase was able to accommodate changes to the chassis geometry this year and for future years. The extensive body changes started with the so-called B-series, chief among which were a longer wheelbase, modified wings (fenders) and altered lights.

The 911 L badge was dropped in favour of the 911 E, denoting the arrival of fuel injection engines for the first time (in the 911 E and 911 S). The power output of the 911 S increased to 170hp (125kW) at this time. Carburettor induction remained for the 912 and 911 T. In order to avoid a mix-up internally, Porsche assigned letters to the respective model years: A for 1968, B for 1969, and so on.

Engine
Both the 911 E (for *Einspritzung* = fuel injection) and the 911 S were fitted with mechanical Bosch fuel injection. The engine for the 911 E – 901/09

(or 901/11 for cars with Sportomatic) – had a power output of 140hp (103kW) at 6,500rpm, and a compression ratio of 9.1:1. The 911 S (engine 901/10) was fitted with a second oil cooler in the right front wing (fender), in addition to the oil cooler sited in the engine compartment.

The fuel-injected engines for the 911 E and S formed the basis of future performance increases and improved exhaust emission characteristics. Sodium-filled exhaust valves were normally only used in race engines in order to transmit the heat of the valve disc along the valve shaft and across the valve guide to the cylinder head. In order to ensure engines that could cope with high speeds, all six-cylinder units were now fitted with these complex sodium-filled exhaust valves with additional steel-plated valve seat reinforcement.

Fuel and ignition system
The era of carburettors was almost at an end for Porsche: the 911 T touring model and the 912 were the only Porsches still delivered with carburettors. Two Weber triple-choke downdraught carburettors (40 IDT3 C) were fitted to the 911 T, while there were twin-row Bosch fuel injection pumps for the 911 E and 911 S. Capacitive-discharge ignition (CDI) was standard for all six-cylinder engines, which helped prevent spark plugs oiling up in traffic.

A Sportomatic Targa with hydropneumatic spring struts and the rare 14in rims; the chromed wheelarch was available as an optional extra.

Drivers Kremer/Gall piloted this 911 S 2.0 during the 1969 Spa 24 Hours race.

A rare accessory on a 911 S Targa: the panel underneath the rear end. The rubber on the overriders was already standard.

Transmission

Clutch pressure was increased (530 to 590kp) in the 911 S, using the M 215 KL clutch, but there were no other noteworthy modifications to the transmission. The 911 T was fitted with a five-speed gearbox as standard.

Suspension

Longer wheelbase (2,268mm). Hydropneumatic spring struts were fitted only to the 911 E, while the torsion bars at the front were left out in the E model. These hydropneumatic self-levelling struts were a new joint development by Boge and Porsche. The front brake callipers were made from light-alloy in the 911 E and S, which were both equipped with 6Jx15 light-alloy wheels and 185/70 VR 15 tyres. Also available for the 911 T and 911 E Sportomatic were 5.5Jx14 wheels and 185/70 HR 14 tyres.

Body

The edges of the 911 wings (fenders) were outward-sloping and this year saw enlarged front indicators and a smaller horn grille. The wiper arms now parked on the left side.

Instead of the earlier flexible rear window, the Targa was fitted with a rigid one made of safety glass with integral heating wires, which greatly improved rearward vision. The Targa also now had vent slots on the side of the stainless steel roll bar.

Equipment and fittings

The 911 E also came with an analogue oil pressure indicator.

Interior fittings

Inside rear-view mirror had a day/night adjustment. Smaller steering wheel with padded horn button. Ashtray flipped downwards from lower dashboard padding. Interior door panels fitted with larger storage compartments and door release integrated in the armrest in the form of a pull lever. Improved backrest locking.

Heating and air conditioning

Improved Behr heating system, or optional air conditioning.

Electrical system

Modifications to the cable loom. Fuse box in the front part of the luggage compartment. The single 45Ah battery of previous models was replaced in all cars by two separate 36Ah batteries, one mounted in each of the front wings (fenders), which brought an increase in electrical output. Their positioning ahead of the front wheels also improved handling, as the two masses stabilised the car substantially. The alternator now delivered 770W. Halogen lamps with two reflectors (H1). Modified rear lamps. Hazard warning lights as standard. The glove compartment was now lit.

A 1969 Porsche 911 S 2.0-litre engine with Bosch mechanical fuel injection. This engine also featured sodium-filled exhaust valves.

Model range	Total production
912 Coupé	2579
912 Targa	N/A
911 T Coupé	7615
911 T Targa	2879
911 E Coupé	954
911 E Targa	N/A
911 S Coupé	1492
911 S Targa	614

Model range	911 T	911 E	911 S
Engine			
Engine type, Manual transmission	901/03	901/09	901/10
Number of cylinders	6	=	=
Bore (mm)	80	=	=
Stroke (mm)	66	=	=
Displacement (cc)	1991	=	=
Compression ratio	8.6:1	9.1:1	9.9:1
Engine output (kW/hp)	81/110	103/140	125/170
at revolutions per minute (rpm)	5800	6500	6800
Torque (Nm)	157	175	182
at revolutions per minute (rpm)	4200	4600	5500
Output per litre (kW/l)	40.7	51.5	62.5
Max. engine speed (rpm)	6500	6800	7200
Engine weight (kg)	176	182	182

Carburation, ignition, settings			
Fuel system	WV 401DT P	MSE	MSE
Type of fuel (RON)	96	98	98
Ignition system	BZ	BHZK	=
Distributor	Marelli	Bosch	Bosch
Spark plugs			
Bosch	W230T30	W265P21	W265P21
Beru	P 240/14/3	265/14/3P	265/14/3P
Spark plug gap (mm)	0.6	=	=
Idle speed (rpm)	850–950	=	=

Key:
BZ   Conventional battery coil ignition
BHKZ   Battery, capacitive-discharge ignition system (CDI)
WV   Weber carburettor 40 IDT P
MSE   Mechanical Bosch induction manifold fuel injection using
        6-element twin-row fuel injection pump

Model range	911 T	911 E	911 S
Transmission			
Clutch, pressure plate	MFZ 215KSph	=	M 215 KL
Clutch plate (mm)	215	=	=
Manual transmission	901/13	=	=
Gear ratios			
1st gear	3.091	=	=
2nd gear	1.888	=	=
3rd gear	1.318	=	=
4th gear	1.040	=	=
5th gear	0.7931	=	=
Synchromesh system gears 1–5	POSY	=	=
Final drive	4.4285	=	=
Limited-slip differential	Option	Option	Option
Lock-up factor under load/coasting (%)	40/40	=	=
Sportomatic	905/13	=	=
Torque converter dia. (mm)	F&S 190	=	=
Stall speed (rpm)	2600	=	=
Gear ratios			
1st gear	2.400	=	=
2nd gear	1.631	=	=
3rd gear	1.217	=	=
4th gear	0.926	=	=
Synchromesh system forward gears	POSY	=	=
Final drive	3.857	=	=

Key:
S   Standard
F&S   Fichtel & Sachs
POSY   Porsche Locking synchromesh system, synchroniser rings,
        mo-coated

A 1969-model Porsche 911 T 2.0 Coupé. The 901/03 engine fitted to this model produced 81kW (110hp) at 5800rpm.

Model range	911 T	911 E	911 S
Suspension, steering and brakes			
Front axle			
Anti-roll bar dia. (mm)	Option	Option	Option
Steering ratio	17.87	=	=
Turning circle dia. (m)	10.7	=	=
Rear axle			
Anti-roll bar dia. (mm)	Option	Option	Option
Shock absorber	Boge	HPF*	Koni
Brake system:	Dual-circuit brake system		
Brake master cylinder dia. (mm)	19.05	=	=
Brake calliper piston diameter			
front (mm)	48	=	=
rear (mm)	35	38	38
Brake disc diameter			
front (mm)	282	=	=
rear (mm)	285	=	=
Brake disc thickness			
front (mm)	12.7 U	20. intern. vented	=
rear (mm)	10.0 U	20. intern. vented	=
Effective brake disc area (cm²)	185	=	=
Handbrake	Operating mechanically on both rear wheels		
Brake drum			
diameter (mm)	180	=	
Contact area (cm²)	170	=	

Wheels and tyres			
Standard tyre specification, front	165HR15	185/70VR15	=
wheel	5½ J x 15	6J x 15	6J x 15 LM
Standard tyre specification, rear	165HR15	185/70VR15	=
wheel	5½ J x 15	6J x 15	6J x 15 LM
Tyre pressure			
front (bar)	2.2	=	=
rear (bar)	2.4	=	=

Key:
HPF* = hydro-pneumatic spring struts, self-adjusting
12.7 U = non-ventilated full brake disc thickness 12.7 mm
LM = forged light-alloy wheels, manufacturer Fuchs

Body and interior (dimensions at kerb weight)			
Length (mm)	4163	=	=
Width (mm)	1610	=	=
Height (mm)	1320	=	=
Wheelbase (mm)	268	=	=
Track			
front (mm)	1362	1374	=
rear (mm)	1343	1355	=
Ground clearance at permissible gross weight (mm)	150	=	=

Model range	911 T	911 E	911 S
Electrical system			
Generator output (W/A)	770/55	=	=
Battery (V/Ah)	x 2 12/36	=	=

Weight according to DIN 70020			
Kerb weight (kg)	1020	=	=
Permissible gross weight (kg)	1400	=	=
Permissible trailer weight			
unbraked (kg)	480	=	=
braked (kg)	600	=	=

Performance			
Maximum speed (kmh)			
Manual transmission	200	215	225
Acceleration 0–62mph/100kmh (sec)			
Manual transmission	10.0	9.0	8.0
Measured kilometre from standing start (sec)			
Manual transmission	30.35	28.5	27.5

Fluid capacities			
Engine oil quantity 1* (l)	9	=	10
Engine oil quantity with SPM (l)	+ 2	=	–
Oil change quantity 1* (l)	8–9	=	=
Manual transmission 2* (l)	2.5	=	=
Sportomatic 2* (l)	2.5	=	=
Fuel tank (l)	62	=	=
Brake fluid reservoir 3* (l)	0.20	=	=

* Key to numerals
1* Approved API SE/SF with combinations API SE/CC - SF/CC - SF/CD - SE/CD
  Multigrade engine oil factory recommended (SAE 10 W/50 or 15 W/40 or 20 W/50).
  Single-grade engine oils were also permissible. Summer SAE 30. Winter SAE 20.
2* Single-grade transmission fluid SAE 90 acc. MIL-L 2105 and GL 4
  Not permissible: transmission fluid SAE 90 acc. MIL-L 2105 B and API-classified GL 5
3* Use only brake fluid acc. SAE J 1703. DOT 3 or 4

Key:
SPM Sportomatic

Chassis numbers (nine digits)					
Car	Model year	Engine	Body	Sequence	Summary
11	9	1	0	0001–9999	911 T Coupé
11	9	1	1	0001–9999	911 T Targa
11	9	2	0	0001–9999	911 E Coupé
11	9	2	1	0001–9999	911 E Targa
11	9	3	0	0001–9999	911 S Coupé
11	9	3	1	0001–9999	911 S Targa

From 1968 until 1969 (inclusive), chassis numbers started with '11', and not '911'; but as from 1970 chassis numbers began with '911'
Model year: 8 = 1968. 9 = 1969
Engine: 1 = 911 T; 2 = 911 E; 3 = 911S
Body: 0 = Coupé; 1 = Targa; 2 = Coupé Karmann

Model year 1970
C Series, 2.2-litre engines

Porsche 911 T, E and S Coupé and Targa

All 911 engines now had a larger 2.2-litre displacement (2,195cc) which offered greater flexibility in driving, especially at low revs. The larger capacity would also push the 911 into the more senior GT class in competition.

Production of the Porsche 912 was finally suspended, its role as the entry-level Porsche having been taken over by the new VW-Porsche 914. This newcomer was the only product ever to be distributed by the joint company founded by Volkswagen and Porsche. The two-seater VW-Porsche was available in four-cylinder form or, as the 914/6, powered by the old 911 T's 2.0-litre six-cylinder engine.

A Porsche 911 E 2.2 Coupé, featuring the new 2.2-litre, 114kW (155hp) engine introduced for 1970.

Engine
By increasing the cylinder bores to 84mm, displacement was enlarged from 1,991cc to 2,195cc. The performance of all three engines was increased: the 911 T had 92kW (125hp), the 911 E 114kW (155hp) and the 911 S 132kW (180hp). From this model year onwards the crankcase was made of aluminium alloy, which benefited the stiffness of the case. The crankshafts were of forged steel and, in the case of the 911 S, were treated with Tenifer afterwards. Pistons were made from die-cast light-alloy or, on the 911 S, from forged light-alloy. The 911 E and S were fitted with Biral cylinders, while the 911 T's were cast iron. All engines received modified cylinder heads with enlarged valve diameters (intake 46mm and exhaust 40mm).

A 1970-model 911 T 2.2 Targa, fitted with the 2.2-litre, 92kW (125hp) engine.

Using magnesium for the crankcases helped reduce the DIN kerb weight, alongside further lightweight construction measures: the 911 E now weighed 1,020kg compared to 1,080kg in model year 1968. This development undoubtedly bore the signature of the new head of the development team, Ferdinand Piëch.

Fuel and ignition system
The 911 T remained non-fuel-injected, having two triple-choke downdraught carburettors; the new manufacturer from this year was Zenith (although some cars were still fitted with Webers). For the 911 E and S, mechanical twin-row fuel injection pumps came from Bosch. The ignition system for all engines was BHKZ (breakerless high-tension capacitive-discharge ignition) from Bosch.

Transmission
The Fichtel & Sachs clutch was enlarged to a diameter of 225mm for all 911s. The increased clutch size was not only a boost for reliability but

allowed further performance increases without any problems. The force of the pressure plate (MFZ 225 KL) was 600–670N. The 911 T had a 911/00 four-speed manual transmission as standard, while the 911 E and S had the 911/01 five-speed. The 911 T and the 911 E could also be ordered with the four-speed 905/20 Sportomatic transmission.

Suspension
Ventilated brake discs were now fitted to the 911 T.

Equipment and fittings
The interior of the 911 E was identical to the 911 S. 'Skai' leatherette was used.

Electrical system
Improved safety of electrical components for the driver: additional fuse box in the engine compartment. Rear window wipers were an optional extra.

Model range	Total production
911 T Coupé	2418 + 4126 USA
911 T Targa	2545
911 E Coupé	1304 + 667 USA
911 E Targa	993
911 S Coupé	1744
911 S Targa	729

Model range	911 T	911 E	911 S
Engine			
Engine type, Manual transmission	911/03	911/01	911/02
Bore (mm)	84	=	=
Stroke (mm)	66	=	=
Displacement (cc)	2195	=	=
Compression ratio	8.6:1	9.1:1	9.8:1
Engine output (kW/hp)	92/125	114/155	132/180
at revolutions per minute (rpm)	5800	6200	6500
Torque (Nm)	176	191	199
at revolutions per minute (rpm)	4200	4500	5200
Output per litre (kW/l)	41.9	51.9	60.1
Max. engine speed (rpm)	6500	6700	7200
Engine weight (kg)	176	182	182

Model range	911 T	911 E	911 S
Carburation, ignition, settings			
Fuel system	WV 40IDT3C	MSE	MSE
Type of fuel (RON)	98	=	=
Ignition system	BHKZ	=	=
Distributor	Bosch	=	=
Spark plugs			
Bosch	W230T30	W265P21	=
Beru	240/14/3P	265/14/3P	=
Spark plug gap (mm)	0.6	=	=
Idle speed (rpm)	850–950	=	=
Standard fuel consumption (litres/100 km)	9.0	9.5	10.2

Key:
BHKZ   Battery, capacitive-discharge ignition system (CDI)
WV   Weber carburettor 40 IDT3C
MSE   Mechanical Bosch induction manifold fuel injection using 6-element twin-row fuel injection pump

Transmission	911 T	911 E	911 S
Clutch, pressure plate	G MFZ 225KL	=	=
Clutch plate (mm)	225	=	=
Manual transmission	911/01	=	=
Gear ratios			
1st gear	3.091	=	=
2nd gear	1.777	=	=
3rd gear	1.217	=	=
4th gear	0.926	=	=
5th gear	0.758	=	=
Synchromesh system gears 1–5	POSY	=	=
Final drive	4.4285	=	=
Limited-slip differential	Option	Option	Option
Lock-up factor under load/coasting (%)	40/40	=	=
Sportomatic	905/20	=	=
Torque converter dia. (mm)	F&S 190	=	=
Stall speed (rpm)	2600	=	=
Gear ratios			
1st gear	2.400	=	=
2nd gear	1.555	=	=
3rd gear	1.125	=	=
4th gear	0.857	=	=
Reverse gear	2.533	=	=

The top-of-the-range 911 S 2.2 Coupé, featuring the 2.2-litre, 132kW (180hp) engine. This car also has additional driving lights.

Model range	911 T	911 E	911 S
Transmission (continued)			
Synchromesh system, forward gears	POSY	=	=
Final drive	3.857	=	=

Key:
S   Standard
F&S   Manufacturer Fichtel & Sachs
POSY   Porsche Locking synchromesh system, synchroniser rings, mo-coated

Suspension, steering and brakes			
Front axle			
Anti-roll bar dia. (mm)	Option	Option	15
Steering ratio	17.87	=	=
Turning circle dia. (m)	10.7	=	=
Rear axle			
Anti-roll bar dia. (mm)	Option	Option	15
Shock absorber	Boge	HPF*	Koni
Brake system:	Dual-circuit brake system		
Brake master cylinder dia. (mm)	19.05	=	=
Brake calliper piston diameter			
front (mm)	48	=	=
rear (mm)	35	38	38
Brake disc diameter			
front (mm)	282	=	=
rear (mm)	285	=	=
Brake disc thickness			
front (mm)	20. intern. vented	=	
rear (mm)	20. intern. vented	=	
Effective brake disc area (cm²)	185	=	=
Handbrake	Operating mechanically on both rear wheels		
Brake drum			
diameter (mm)	180	=	
Contact area (cm2)	170	=	

Wheels and tyres			
Standard tyre specification, front	165HR15	185/70VR15	=
wheel	5½ J x 15	6J x 15	6J x 15 Light alloy
Standard tyre specification, rear	165HR15	185/70VR15	=
wheel	5½ J x 15	6J x 15	6J x 15 Light alloy
Tyre pressure			
front (bar)	2.2	=	=
rear (bar)	2.4	=	=

Key:
HPF* = hydro-pneumatic spring struts, self-adjusting

Model range	911 T	911 E	911 S
Body and interior (dimensions at kerb weight)			
Length (mm)	4163	=	=
Width (mm)	1610	=	=
Height (mm)	1320	=	=
Wheelbase (mm)	2268	=	=
Track			
front (mm)	1362	1374	=
rear (mm)	1343	1355	=
Ground clearance at permissible gross weight (mm)	150	=	=

Electrical system	911 T	911 E	911 S
Generator output (W/A)	770/55	=	=
Battery (V/Ah)	2 x 12/36	=	=

Weight according to DIN 70020	911 T	911 E	911 S
Kerb weight (kg)	1020	=	=
Permissible gross weight (kg)	1400	=	=
Permissible trailer weight			
unbraked (kg)	480	=	=
braked (kg)	600	=	=

Performance	911 T	911 E	911 S
Maximum speed (kmh)			
Manual transmission	200	215	225
Acceleration 0–62mph/100kmh (sec)			
Manual transmission	9.5	9.0	7.0
Measured kilometre from standing start (sec)			
Manual transmission	30.35	28.5	27.5

Fluid capacities	911 T	911 E	911 S
Engine oil quantity 1* (l)	9	=	10
Engine oil quantity with SPM (l)	+ 2	=	–
Oil change quantity 1* (l)	8–9	=	=
Manual transmission 2* (l)	2.5	=	=
Sportomatic 2* (l)	2.5	=	=
Fuel tank (l)	62	=	=
Brake fluid reservoir 3* (l)	0.20	=	=

* Key to numerals
1* Approved API SE/SF with combinations API SE/CC - SF/CC - SF/CD - SE/CD Multigrade engine oil factory recommended (SAE 10 W/50 or 15 W/40 or 20 W/50).
    Single-grade engine oils were also permissible. Summer SAE 30. Winter SAE 20.
2* Single-grade transmission fluid SAE 90 acc. MIL-L 2105 and GL 4 Not permissible: transmission fluid SAE 90 acc. MIL-L 2105 B and API-classified GL 5
3* Use only brake fluid acc. SAE J 1703. DOT 3 or 4
Key:
SPM   Sportomatic

Chassis numbers (ten digits)					
Car	**Model year**	**Engine**	**Body**	**Sequence**	**Summary**
911	0	1	0	0001–9999	911 T Coupé
911	0	1	1	0001–9999	911 T Targa
911	0	2	0	0001–9999	911 E Coupé
911	0	2	1	0001–9999	911 E Targa
911	0	3	0	0001–9999	911 S Coupé
911	0	3	1	0001–9999	911 S Targa

Model year: 0 = 1970. 9 = 1969
Engine: 1 = 911 T; 2 = 911 E; 3 = 911S
Body: 0 = Coupé; 1 = Targa

Model year 1971

D Series, minor changes

Porsche 911 T, E and S Coupé and Targa

There were hardly any modifications to the Porsche 911 during this model year.

Fuel and ignition system

Due to more stringent exhaust emission rules in several export markets, the fuel injection system was modified: the pressure sensor, ignition distributor, throttle body and ignition control unit were all changed. The fuel pump was installed between the transverse pipe and the rear axle radius arm.

Body

The 911 S had a profiled rubber strip on front and rear bumpers.

Heating and air conditioning

The 911 S system was changed to an engine heater.

Electrical system

The wiper system now had three speed ranges.

Model range	Total production
911 T Coupé	583 + 1934 USA
911 T Targa	3476
911 E Coupé	1088
911 E Targa	935
911 S Coupé	1430
911 S Targa	788

Model range	911 T	911 E	911 S
Engine			
Engine type, Manual transmission	911/03	911/01	911/02
Bore (mm)	84	=	=
Stroke (mm)	66	=	=
Displacement (cc)	2195	=	=
Compression ratio	8.6:1	9.1:1	9.8:1
Engine output (kW/hp)	92/125	114/155	132/180
at revolutions per minute (rpm)	5800	6200	6500
Torque (Nm)	176	191	199
at revolutions per minute (rpm)	4200	4500	5200
Output per litre (kW/l)	41.9	51.9	60.1
Max. engine speed (rpm)	6500	6700	7200
Engine weight (kg)	176	182	182

Carburation, ignition, settings			
Fuel system	SZV	MSE	MSE
Type of fuel (RON)	98	=	=
Ignition system	BHKZ	=	=
Distributor	Bosch	=	=
Spark plugs			
Bosch	W230T30	W265P21	=
Beru	250/14/3P	265/14/3P	=
Spark plug gap (mm)	0.6	=	=
Idle speed (rpm)	850–950	=	=
CO-content (%)	2.5–3.5	=	=
Standard fuel consumption (litres/100 km)	9.0	9.5	10.2

Key:
BHKZ   Battery, capacitive-discharge ignition system (CDI)
SZV   Solex-Zenith Carburettor 40TIN
MSE   Mechanical Bosch induction manifold fuel injection

A 1971-model 911 S 2.2 Targa, showing the profiled rubber strip on the front and rear bumpers.

911s featuring prominently on the Porsche stand at the 1971 International Auto Show at New York Coliseum.

OPPOSITE: A 1971 Porsche 911 S 2.2 Coupé ready to take part in the East African Safari Rally.

Model range	911 T	911 E	911 S
Transmission			
Clutch, pressure plate	G MFZ 225	=	=
Clutch plate (mm)	225	=	=
Manual transmission	911/01	=	=
Gear ratios			
1st gear	3.091	=	=
2nd gear	1.777	=	=
3rd gear	1.217	=	=
4th gear	0.926	=	=
5th gear	0.7586	=	=
Reverse gear	3.325	=	=
Synchromesh system gears 1–5	POSY	=	=
Final drive	4.4285	=	=
Limited-slip differential	Option	Option	Option
Lock-up factor under load/coasting (%)	40/40	=	=
Sportomatic	905/20	=	=
Torque converter dia. (mm)	F&S 190	=	=
Stall speed (rpm)	2600	=	=
Gear ratios			
1st gear	2.400	=	=
2nd gear	1.555	=	=
3rd gear	1.125	=	=
4th gear	0.857	=	=
Reverse gear	2.533	=	=
Synchromesh system forward gears	POSY	=	=
Final drive	3.857	=	=

Key:
M   Optional extras
S   Standard
F&S   Manufacturer Fichtel & Sachs
POSY Porsche Locking synchromesh system, synchroniser rings, mo-
          coated

Model range	911 T	911 E	911 S
Suspension, steering and brakes			
Front axle			
Anti-roll bar dia. (mm)	Option	Option	15
Steering ratio	17.87	=	=
Turning circle dia. (m)	10.7	=	=
Rear axle			
Anti-roll bar dia. (mm)	Option	Option	15
Shock absorber	Boge	HPF*	Koni
Brake master cylinder dia. (mm)	19.05	=	=
Brake calliper piston diameter			
front (mm)	48	=	=
rear (mm)	38	=	=
Brake disc diameter			
front (mm)	282.5	=	=
rear (mm)	290	=	=
Brake disc thickness			
front (mm)	20. vented	=	=
rear (mm)	20. vented	=	=
Effective brake disc area (cm²)	210	=	257
Handbrake	Operating mechanically on both rear wheels		
Brake drum diameter (mm)	180	=	
Contact area (cm²)	170	=	

Wheels and tyres			
Standard tyre specification, front	165HR15	185/70VR15	=
wheel	5½ J x 15	6J x 15	=
Standard tyre specification, rear	165HR15	185/70VR15	=
wheel	5½ J x 15	6J x 15	=
Space-saver spare wheel	Space-saver wheel 5½ J x 15		
Tyre pressure			
front (bar)	2.0	=	=
rear (bar)	2.4	=	=
Space-saver spare wheel (bar)	2.0	=	=

Body and interior (dimensions at kerb weight)			
Length (mm)	4163	=	=
Width (mm)	1610	=	=
Height (mm)	1320	=	=
Wheelbase (mm)	2268	=	=
Track			
front (mm)	1362	1374	=
rear (mm)	1355	=	=
Ground clearance at permissible gross weight (mm)	150	=	=

Model range	911 T	911 E	911 S
Electrical system			
Generator output (W/A)	770/55	=	=
Battery (V/Ah)	2 x 12/36	=	=

Weight according to DIN 70020			
Kerb weight (kg)	1020	=	=
Permissible gross weight (kg)	1400	=	=
Permissible trailer weight			
unbraked (kg)	480	=	=
braked (kg)	600	=	=

Performance			
Maximum speed (kmh)			
Manual transmission	200	215	225
Acceleration 0–62mph/100kmh (sec)			
Manual transmission	9.5	9.0	7.0
Measured kilometre from standing start (sec)			
Manual transmission	30.35	28.5	27.5

Model range	911 T	911 E	911 S
Fluid capacities			
Engine oil quantity 1* (l)	9	=	10
Engine oil quantity with SPM (l)	+ 2	=	–
Oil change quantity 1* (l)	8–9	=	=
Manual transmission 2* (l)	2.5	=	=
Sportomatic 2* (l)	2.5	=	=
Fuel tank (l)	62	=	=
Brake fluid reservoir 3* (l)	0.20	=	=

* Key to numerals

1* Approved API SE/SF with combinations API SE/CC - SF/CC - SF/CD - SE/CD Multigrade engine oil factory recommended (SAE 10 W/50 or 15 W/40 or 20 W/50).
Single-grade engine oils were also permissible. Summer SAE 30. Winter SAE 20.

2* Single-grade transmission fluid SAE 90 acc. MIL-L 2105 and GL 4 Not permissible: transmission fluid SAE 90 acc. MIL-L 2105 B and API-classified GL 5

3* Use only brake fluid acc. SAE J 1703. DOT 3 or 4
Key:
SPM Sportomatic

Chassis numbers (ten digits)					
Car	Model year	Engine	Body	Sequence	Summary
11	1	1	0	0001–9999	911 T Coupé
11	1	1	1	0001–9999	911 T Targa
11	1	2	0	0001–9999	911 E Coupé
11	1	2	1	0001–9999	911 E Targa
11	1	3	0	0001–9999	911 S Coupé
11	1	3	1	0001–9999	911 S Targa

Model year: 1 = 1971. 0 = 1970   Engine: 1 = 911 T; 2 = 911 E; 3 = 911S   Body: 0 = Coupé; 1 = Targa

Model year 1972

E Series, 2.4-litre engines and front spoilers

Porsche 911 T, E and S Coupé and Targa

The major change this year was the enlargement of the engine yet again – it grew to 2.4 litres (actually 2,341cc) and offered much improved performance as a result. All Porsche cars were now able to use regular-grade petrol, as ever-tightening exhaust emission rules, especially in the USA, required a total rethink of the way engines were built. High-octane fuel with a high level of tetraethyl lead was no longer available in many export markets in 1972, so the conversion of engines to regular-grade petrol worldwide was necessary.

There were also changes to the body. For the first time Porsche applied aerodynamic knowledge gained from racing to its production car bodies. The 911 S was fitted with a front spoiler to deflect airflow around the sides of the car and thus reduce front-end lift; this spoiler was initially optional on the T and E but would become standard across the

The aerodynamic age begins: a 1972-model 911 S with front spoiler, which had a recess in the middle for the towing eye.

range the following year. An engine oil filler lid was also added on the right rear wing (fender) as a result of the relocation of the oil tank, which improved weight distribution.

Engine

The engines were modified: a displacement of 2,341cc was achieved through a modified crankshaft with a longer 70.4mm stroke and a single counterweight per cylinder, while the crank pin diameter was reduced from 57 to 52mm. The compression ratio was reduced to enable the use of regular-grade fuel (91RON). The engine oil tank that was required for the dry sump lubrication system was now positioned in front of the right rear wheel and was filled via a separate lid positioned under the right rear side window. The aluminium oil cooler was located in the right front wheelarch.

Despite the lowering of the compression ratio, the increased 2.4-litre engine displacement boosted the 911's performance significantly; a rise in peak torque of about 10% was remarkable. Not only was outright acceleration improved, the 911 now responded better from low engine revs.

Fuel and ignition system

Because of more stringent exhaust emission rules in several export markets, the fuel injection system was modified.

Transmission

This year saw a new manual transmission generation (Type 915) whose gearbox housing, gear wheels and final-drive ratios were strengthened. More stable positioning of the shafts, improved heat flow and gearbox lubrication through the use of an additional pump. An altered gearchange pattern saw the old 'dog-leg' first gear consigned to history: first was now to the left and forward, reverse gear to the right and back, fifth gear to the right and forward. This amended gearchange pattern came at the request of racing and rally drivers: they wanted the first and the second gears on a single plane, as it was often required to change from second gear to first and up again in tight curves. It was also more convenient for town use. The clutch was now an MFZ 225 dry single-plate unit, and limited-slip differential was an optional extra.

The new 915 transmission would be able to cope with performance increases without any problems for many years to come. Experience gained from the Type 908 racing transmission was incorporated as much as possible: positioning of the driveshaft with two anti-friction bearings directly behind the bevel gear, a cylindrical roller bearing transferred the radial forces, while a large four-point ball bearing transferred the axial forces. The thermal expansion of the light-alloy casing no longer influenced the bevel gears. As the highly stressed bevel gears were placing great demands on the lubricant, a high-alloy GL5 transmission oil (MIL-L 2105B) was approved. This was only possible because the Porsche synchromesh system was able to incorporate the reduced friction very easily.

An increase in performance was also taken into

A Porsche 911 S 2.4 Coupé, featuring the new-for-1972 2.4-litre, 140kW (190hp) engine.

consideration with respect to the semi-automatic Sportomatic transmission (Type 925): this had a modified torque converter with improved mounting, bigger low-pressure servo motor, and adapted synchromesh on the four forward gears.

Body

Because the engine oil tank had been moved to a new position in front of the right rear wheel (to improve the front/rear axle weight distribution), body changes had to be made. A colour-coded flap near the B-pillar on the right-hand side allowed access to the oil filling nozzle. The 911 S had profiled rubber strips on front and rear bumpers. Exterior rear-view mirrors were now square. New '2.4' script appeared on the air intake grille of the engine lid. The new front spoiler (standard on the 911 S, optional on T and E) was made from plastic, with the sill trim made from aluminium.

Equipment and fittings

The interior door panels and the dashboard insert were finished in the same colour as the rest of the interior.

Model range	Total production
911 T Coupé	1963 + 2931 USA
911 T Targa	1523 + 1821 USA
911 E Coupé	1124
911 E Targa	861
911 S Coupé	1750
911 S Targa	989

39

A 1972 911 E 2.4 Coupé. This model featured the 2.4-litre, 121kW (165hp) engine.

Model range	911 T	911 E	911 S
Engine			
Engine type, Manual transmission	911/57	911/52	911/53
Bore (mm)	84	=	=
Stroke (mm)	70.4	=	=
Displacement (mm)	2341	=	=
Compression ratio	7.5:1	8.0:1	8.5:1
Engine output (kW/hp)	96/130	121/165	140/190
at revolutions per minute (rpm)	5600	6200	6500
Torque (Nm)	196	206	216
at revolutions per minute (rpm)	4000	4500	5200
Output per litre (kW/l)	41	52	60
Max. engine speed (rpm)	6500	7000	7300
Engine weight (kg)	176	183	182

Carburation, ignition, settings			
Fuel system	SZV	MSE	MSE
Type of fuel (RON)	91	=	=
Ignition system	BHKZ	=	=
Spark plugs			
Bosch	W230T1	W265P21	=
Beru	225/14/3	235/14/3P	
Spark plug gap (mm)	0.7	0.5–0.6	=
Idle speed (rpm)	850–950	=	=
CO-content (%)	2.5–3.5	=	=
Standard fuel consumption (litres/100 km)	9.2	9.0	9.5

Key: BHKZ = Battery, capacitive-discharge ignition system (CDI)
           SZV = Solex-Zenith Carburettor 40TIN
           MSE = Mechanical Bosch induction manifold fuel injection

Model range	911 T	911 E	911 S
Transmission			
Clutch, pressure plate	G MFZ 225	=	=
Clutch plate (mm)	GUD 225	=	=
Manual transmission	915/03	=	=
Gear ratios			
1st gear	3.181	=	=
2nd gear	1.833	=	=
3rd gear	1.261	=	=
4th gear	0.9615	=	=
5th gear	0.7586	=	=
Reverse gear	3.325	=	=
Synchromesh system gears 1–5	POSY	=	=
Final drive	4.4285	=	=
Limited-slip differential	Option	Option	Option
Lock-up factor under load/coasting (%)	40/40	=	=
Sportomatic	905/21	925/00	925/01
Torque converter dia. (mm)	F&S 190	=	=
Stall speed (rpm)	2600	2600	3000
Gear ratios			
1st gear	2.400	=	=
2nd gear	1.555	=	=
3rd gear	1.125	=	=
4th gear	0.857	=	=
Reverse gear	2.533	=	=
Synchromesh system forward gears	POSY	=	=
Final drive	3.857	=	=

Key:
S   Standard
F&S   Manufacturer Fichtel & Sachs
POSY Porsche Locking synchromesh system, synchroniser rings, mo-coated

Model range	911 T	911 E	911 S
Suspension, steering and brakes			
Front axle			
Anti-roll bar dia. (mm)	Option	Option	20
Steering ratio	17.87	=	=
Turning circle dia. (m)	10.80	=	=
Rear axle			
Anti-roll bar dia. (mm)	Option	Option	15
Brake master cylinder dia. (mm)	19.05	=	=
Brake calliper piston diameter			
front (mm)	48	=	=
rear (mm)	38	=	=
Brake disc diameter			
front (mm)	282.5	=	=
rear (mm)	290	=	=
Brake disc thickness			
front (mm)	20	=	=
rear (mm)	20	=	=
Effective brake disc area (cm²)	210	=	257
Handbrake	Operating mechanically on both rear wheels		
Brake drum diameter (mm)	180	=	
Contact area (cm²)	170	=	

Wheels and tyres			
Standard tyre specification, front	165HR15	185/70VR15	=
wheel	5½ J x 15	6J x 15	=
Standard tyre specification, rear	165HR15	185/70VR15	=
wheel	5½ J x 15	6J x 15	=
Space-saver spare wheel	Space-saver wheel	5½ J x 15	
Tyre pressure			
front (bar)	2.0	=	=
rear (bar)	2.4	=	=
Space-saver spare wheel (bar)	2.0	=	=

Body and interior (dimensions at kerb weight)			
Length (mm)	4227	=	4147
Width (mm)	1610	=	=
Height (mm)	1320	=	=
Wheelbase (mm)	2271	=	=
Track			
front (mm)	1360	1372	=
rear (mm)	1342	1354	1354
Ground clearance at permissible gross weight (mm)	150	=	=

Model range	911 T	911 E	911 S
Electrical system			
Generator output (W/A)	770/55	=	=
Battery (V/Ah)	12/66	=	=

Weight according to DIN 70020			
Kerb weight (kg)	1050	1075	=
Permissible gross weight (kg)	1400	=	=
Permissible trailer weight			
unbraked (kg)	480	=	=
braked (kg)	600	=	=

Performance			
Maximum speed (kmh)			
Manual transmission	205	220	230
Acceleration 0–62mph/100kmh (sec)			
Manual transmission	9.5	7.9	7.0
Measured kilometre from standing start (sec)			
Manual transmission	30.35	28.5	27.5

Fluid capacities			
Engine oil quantity 1* (l)	11	13	=
Engine oil quantity with SPM (l)	+ 2	=	=
Oil change quantity 1* (l)	10	=	=
Manual transmission 2* (l)	3.0	=	=
Sportomatic 2* (l)	2.5	=	=
Fuel tank (l)	62	=	=
Brake fluid reservoir 3* (l)	0.20	=	=

* Key to numerals
1* Approved API SE/SF with combinations API SE/CC - SF/CC - SF/CD - SE/CD
Multigrade engine oil factory recommended (SAE 10 W/50 or 15 W/40 or 20 W/50).
Single-grade engine oils were also permissible. Summer SAE 30. Winter SAE 20.
2* Single-grade transmission fluid SAE 90 acc. MIL-L 2105 B and API-classified GL 5
Also permissible: transmission fluid SAE 90 acc. MIL-L 2105 and API-classified GL 4
3* Use only brake fluid acc. SAE J 1703. DOT 3 or 4

Key:
SPM Sportomatic

Chassis numbers (ten digits)					
Car	Model year	Engine	Body	Sequence	Summary
911	2	1	0	0001–9999	911 T Coupé
911	2	1	1	0001–9999	911 T Targa
911	2	2	0	0001–9999	911 E Coupé
911	2	2	1	0001–9999	911 E Targa
911	2	3	0	0001–9999	911 S-E Coupé
911	2	3	1	0001–9999	911 S-E Targa
911	2	5	0	0001–9999	911 T Coupé
911	2	5	1	0001–9999	911 T Targa

Model year: 2 = 1972. 1 = 1971
Engine: 1 = 911 T; 2 = 911 E; 3 = 911 S-E; 5 = 911 T Carburettor
Body: 0 = Coupé; 1 = Targa

Model year 1973
F Series, Carrera RS

Porsche 911 T, E and S Coupé
Porsche 911 Carrera RS Coupé

All 911s now came with front spoilers, and the 911 E and S now had bigger fuel tanks (85 litres). The oil tank was moved back to its original position, behind the right rear wheel. For the American market, cars were fitted with a K-Jetronic fuel injection system. Furthermore, a brand new six-cylinder model, the 911 Carrera RS (RennSport), was launched with a 210hp 2.7-litre engine.

Inspired by wind tunnel studies with the 908 and 917 racing cars, Porsche also carried out aerodynamic modifications on the 911's bodywork this year. The front spoiler was standard for all 911s, reducing front-end lift, the advantages being better directional stability and better controllability.

The Carrera RS featured a 'ducktail' rear spoiler that reduced aerodynamic lift over the rear axle and achieved higher terminal velocities. Porsche

Possibly the most desirable 911 ever produced, the legendary 911 Carrera RS 2.7, first appeared in 1973.

built four versions of the RS: Homologation (basic), Sport (with some concessions to road use), and Touring (trimmed like a 911 S) and finally a 2.8-litre Carrera RS racing version (the RSR lightweight). The latter featured lightweight construction throughout and wide use of light-alloy. The RS kerb weight varied according to model from 900kg to 1,075kg. Porsche improved the RS's lateral acceleration by means of different tyre dimensions front and rear.

Engine
There were no changes to the 2.4-litre engines but the exciting news this year was the Carrera RS powerplant. This was a 2,687cc engine which, despite its high state of tune (210hp) could also operate with regular-grade petrol (91RON). The enlarged displacement of the so-called 911/83 engine was made possible because of pistons with diameters of 90mm. For the first time, aluminium cylinders coated with Nikasil (nickel-silicon) were used in the Carrera RS engine.

The cylinders of the 911/83 engine were made entirely from aluminium alloy. As two light metal alloys with the same properties do not slide well against each other (so that a matching combination of piston/cylinder would normally fail), Porsche covered the cylinders with a nickel dispersion layer. The Nikasil cylinder design proved

to be the best solution with regards to fuel and oil consumption, and sliding properties, while the heat dissipation through the light-alloy cylinder wall to the cooling fins was greatly improved.

Fuel and ignition system
Apart from the USA, the 911 T was fitted with two triple-choke downdraught carburettors (type 40 TIN from Zenith). The 911 E, S and Carrera RS all had Bosch twin-row fuel injection pumps. It was common knowledge that road salt used in winter was destroying exhaust pipes through corrosion, so Porsche's answer was to introduce an exhaust system made of stainless steel for the first time.

Porsche was the first car manufacturer to use K-Jetronic from Bosch, a continuous-flow fuel injection system, able to measure the quantity of air aspirated by the engine with the aid of an air sensor plate, and then supply fuel to the injection nozzle accordingly. The first 911s with Bosch K-Jetronic were delivered to the US market. These were 2.4-litre cars with an output of 140hp (103kW) – more than the carburettor-equipped 911 T – and had emissions figures that were surprisingly good.

Transmission
There were no changes to the transmission for the 2.4-litre engine. The new Carrera RS had a

A 1973-model 911 E 2.4 Targa which featured hydropneumatic suspension as standard.

modified five-speed gearbox (Type 915/08), which featured polished gear sets as well as a transmission oil pump for cooling and lubrication in the works race cars. Third, fourth and fifth gear ratios were adapted to match the engine's improved performance. The gearshift bracket and the gear lever were modified in order to improve the shift quality, while a reverse-gear locking feature prevented the driver going into reverse accidentally.

Suspension
The wheelbase was lengthened again to 1,171mm. The hydropneumatic front suspension system that had been standard on the model year 1969 911 was relegated to the optional extras list (you could order it for the 911 T, E and S, but not the Carrera RS). That meant that front torsion bar suspension was once again standard for all models. The hydropneumatic system may have enhanced driving comfort, but it was never very popular with sports car fans, who generally preferred raw handling ability over comfort.

The 911 E was fitted with new and very distinctive 'cookie-cutter' 6Jx15 die-cast wheels from ATS with 185/70 VR 15 tyres. The 911 S continued to feature 6Jx15 forged light-alloy

A classic view – the unique rear detailing of the 911 Carrera RS 2.7, with prominent 'ducktail' rear spoiler.

wheels, which were optional for other models. A space-saver 5.5Jx15 spare wheel on a steel rim was used for the 911 E, S and Carrera RS.

Porsche was the first manufacturer to offer different tyre dimensions front and rear (for the Carrera RS). This resulted in an excellent lateral acceleration figure of over 0.9g. 6Jx15 cast light-alloy wheels and 185/70 VR 15 tyres were used at the front, 7Jx15 wheels with 215/60 VR 15 tyres at the rear.

Body

After only one year in its new position, the oil tank was moved again, back behind the rear axle, and was once again accessed via the engine compartment at the right rear. The previous relocation of the oil tank in front of the rear axle for 1972, even though it had improved the car's handling, had one major problem. The oil filler opening could be confused with the fuel tank flap, so the oil tank was often filled with petrol by mistake. The passenger sitting on the right-hand

side in the back also felt uncomfortable because of the heat generated in the seat area. An 85-litre plastic fuel tank was fitted to the 911 E, S and Carrera RS, the T retaining a 62-litre tank.

The so-called 'ducktail' spoiler (officially an option) on the engine lid of the Carrera RS caused quite a stir at the time, ranging from excited acceptance among the public to total rejection by the motoring authorities (because of the risk of injury to cyclists colliding with the car).

The rear wings (fenders) of the Carrera RS were widened to accommodate wider rear wheels. Various body parts, such as the front bonnet (hood), were made of thin sheet metal, and the engine lid at the rear with its 'ducktail' spoiler was made of fibreglass-reinforced plastic.

Equipment and fittings

The front horn grilles were made of black plastic. Plastic fuel tanks were now used in 911 production cars, which initially resulted in considerable difficulties in the manufacture of the tanks. Vivid 'Carrera' stripes were offered as an option to adorn the body sides of the RS.

Electrical system

While the RS Touring version had two 36Ah batteries, the racing Carrera RSR was fitted with a single 36Ah battery to keep weight down. The main headlights of all 911s were converted to H4 twin-filament bulbs, while all vehicles in the USA still had to be equipped with sealed-beam main headlights.

Additional information

The number of maintenance inspections up to a mileage of 40,000km (24,000 miles) was reduced from six to five. The number of points to be inspected was decreased from 43 to 23.

Model range	Total production
911 T Coupé	3819 + 1252 USA
911 T Targa	2843 + 781 USA
911 E Coupé	1366
911 E Targa	1055
911 S Coupé	1430
911 S Targa	925
911 Carrera RS Coupé	1580

Model range	911 T	911 E	911 S	911 RS 2.7
Engine				
Engine type, Manual transmission	911/57	911/52	911/53	911/83
Bore (mm)	84	=	=	90
Stroke (mm)	70.4	=	=	=
Displacement (cc)	2341	=	=	2687
Compression ratio	7.5:1	8.0:1	8.5:1	8.5:1
Engine output (kW/hp)	96/130	121/165	140/190	154/210
at revolutions per minute (rpm)	5600	6200	6500	6300
Torque (Nm)	196	206	216	255
at revolutions per minute (rpm)	4000	4500	5200	5100
Output per litre (kW/l)	41	52	60	57
Max. engine speed (rpm)	6500	7000	7300	7300
Engine weight (kg)	176	183	182	182

Carburation, ignition, settings				
Fuel system	SZV	MSE	MSE	MSE
Type of fuel (RON)	91	=	=	=
Ignition system	BHKZ	=	=	=
Spark plugs				
Bosch	W230TI	W265P21	=	W260P21
Beru	225/14/3	235/14/3P	265/14/3P	265P21
Spark plug gap (mm)	0.7	0.5–0.6	=	=
Idle speed (rpm)	850–950	=	=	=
CO-content (%)	2.5–3.5	=	=	2.0–3.0
Standard fuel consumption (litres/100 km)	9.2	9.0	9.5	10.2

Key:
BHKZ Battery, capacitive-discharge ignition system (CDI)
SZV Solex-Zenith Carburettor 40TIN
MSE Mechanical Bosch induction manifold fuel injection

Model range	911 T	911 E	911 S	911 RS 2.7
Transmission				
Clutch, pressure plate	G MFZ 225	=	=	=
Clutch plate (mm)	GUD 225	=	=	=
Manual transmission	915/03	=	=	915/08
Gear ratios				
1st gear	3.181	=	=	=
2nd gear	1.833	=	=	=
3rd gear	1.261	=	=	=
4th gear	0.9615	=	=	0.925
5th gear	0.7586	=	=	0.724
Reverse gear	3.325	=	=	=
Synchromesh system gears 1–5	POSY	=	=	=
Final drive	4.4285	=	=	=
Limited-slip differential	Option	Option	Option	Option
Lock-up factor under load/coasting (%)	40/40	=	=	=
Sportomatic	905/21	925/00	925/01	–
Torque converter dia. (mm)	F&S 190	=	=	–
Stall speed (rpm)	2600	2600	3000	–
Gear ratios				
1st gear	2.400	=	=	
2nd gear	1.555	=	=	
3rd gear	1.125	=	=	
4th gear	0.857	=	=	
Reverse gear	2.533	=	=	
Synchromesh system forward gears	POSY	=	=	
Final drive	3.857	=	=	

Key:
S Standard
F&S Manufacturer Fichtel & Sachs
POSY Porsche Locking synchromesh system, synchroniser rings, mo-coated

Suspension, steering and brakes				
Front axle				
Anti-roll bar dia. (mm)	Option	Option	20	15
Steering ratio	17.87	=	=	=
Turning circle dia. (mm)	10.80	=	=	=
Rear axle				
Anti-roll bar dia. (mm)	Option	Option	15	=
Brake master cylinder diameter (mm)	19.05	=	=	=
Brake calliper piston diameter				
front (mm)	48	=	=	=
rear (mm)	38	=	=	=
Brake disc diameter				
front (mm)	282.5	=	=	=
rear (mm)	290	=	=	=
Brake disc thickness				
front (mm)	20	=	=	=
rear (mm)	20	=	=	=
Effective brake disc area (cm²)	210	=	257	=
Handbrake	Operating mechanically on both rear wheels			
Brake drum diameter (mm)	180	=	=	=
Contact area (cm²)	170	=	=	=

Model range	911 T	911 E	911 S	911 RS 2.7
Wheels and tyres				
Standard tyre specification, front	165HR15	185/70VR15	=	=
wheel	5½ J x 15	6J x 15	=	=
Standard tyre specification, rear	165HR15	185/70VR15	=	215/60VR15
wheel	5½ J x 15	6J x 15	=	7J x 15
Space-saver spare wheel	Space-saver wheel	Space-saver wheel	5½ J x 15	
Tyre pressure				
front (bar)	2.0	=	=	=
rear (bar)	2.4	=	=	=
Space-saver spare wheel (bar)	2.0	=	=	=

Body and interior (dimensions at kerb weight)				
Length (mm)	4227	=	4147	=
Width (mm)	1610	=	=	1652
Height (mm)	1320	=	=	=
Wheelbase (mm)	2271	=	=	=
Track				
front (mm)	1360	1372	=	=
rear (mm)	1342	1354	1354	1394
Ground clearance at permissible gross weight (mm)	150	=	=	=
Electrical system				
Generator output (W/A)	770/70	=	=	=
Battery (V/Ah)	12/66	=	=	=

Weight according to DIN 70020				
Kerb weight (kg)	1050	175	=	=
Permissible gross weight (kg)	1400	=	=	=
Permissible trailer weight				
unbraked (kg)	480	=	=	=
braked (kg)	600	=	=	=

Model range	911 T	911 E	911 S	911 RS 2.7
Performance				
Maximum speed (kmh)				
Manual transmission	205	220	230	240
Acceleration 0–62mph/100kmh (sec)				
Manual transmission	9.5	7.9	7.0	6.3
Measured kilometre from standing start (sec)				
Manual transmission	30.35	28.5	27.5	26.5

Fluid capacities				
Engine oil quantity 1* (l)	11	13	=	=
Engine oil quantity with SPM (l)	+ 2	=	=	–
Oil change quantity 1* (l)	10	=	=	=
Manual transmission 2* (l)	3.0	=	=	=
Sportomatic 2* (l)	2.5	=	=	–
Fuel tank (l)	62	62	85	85
Brake fluid reservoir 3* (l)	0.20	=	=	=

* Key to numerals

1* Approved API SE/SF with combinations API SE/CC - SF/CC - SF/CD - SE/CD
  Multigrade engine oil factory recommended (SAE 10 W/50 or 15 W/40 or 20 W/50).
  Single-grade engine oils were also permissible. Summer SAE 30. Winter SAE 20.

2* Single-grade transmission fluid SAE 90 acc. MIL-L 2105 B and API-classified GL 5
  Also permissible: transmission fluid SAE 90 acc. MIL-L 2105 and API-classified GL 4

3* Use only brake fluid acc. SAE J 1703. DOT 3 or 4

Key:
SPM Sportomatic

Chassis numbers (ten digits)					
Car	Model year	Engine	Body	Sequence	Summary
11	3	1	0	0001–9999	Rest of world 911 TE Coupé
11	3	1	1	0001–9999	Rest of world 911 TE Targa
11	3	2	0	0001–9999	Rest of world 911 E Coupé
11	3	2	1	0001–9999	Rest of world 911 E Targa
11	3	3	0	0001–9999	911 S Coupé
11	3	3	1	0001–9999	911 Targa
11	3	5	0	0001–9999	911 T Coupé
11	3	5	1	0001–9999	911 T Targa
11	3	6	0	0001–9999	911 SC Coupé
11	3	6	1	0001–9999	911 SC Targa

Model year: 3 = 1973. 2 = 1972
Engine: 1 = 911 TE; 2 = 911 E; 3 = 911 S; 5 = 911 T Carburettor; 6 = 911 SC 2.7
Body: 0 = Coupé; 1 = Targa

Model year 1974

G Series, 2.7-litre engine and non-RS Carrera

Porsche 911 Coupé and Targa
Porsche 911 S Coupé and Targa
Porsche 911 Carrera Coupé and Targa
Porsche 911 Carrera RS 3.0 Coupé

The main features of model year 1974 were extensive body modifications, enhanced interior safety and another increase in engine displacement, this time to 2.7 litres. Power was up across the range as a result but emissions were down thanks to the adoption of Bosch K-Jetronic fuel injection for the 911 and 911 S.

The old model range of T, E and S was dispensed with, and the new range consisted of the 911, 911 S and 911 Carrera, the latter perhaps an unjustified marketing use of what had been up until then an illustrious badge.

The Carrera RS also continued in slightly different form with a larger engine displacement of 3.0 litres; only 111 examples of this Group 3 homologation model were built, all using heavier bodywork from the regular production 911.

In the USA new laws had come into effect requiring that no repair cost should be incurred at an impact speed of 5mph (8kmh). Porsche acted immediately worldwide and made its bumpers from strong light-alloy; these were attached to the frame in a flexible spring-loaded manner for the American market.

A cutaway illustration of a 1974-model 911 2.7-litre Coupé, showing the drivetrain, suspension and steering.

Manufacturers were faced with yet another challenge when they had to reduce the lead content of the fuel from 0.5g/litre to less than 0.15g/litre in Germany when designing their 'non-USA' engines. However K-Jetronic fuel injection, which was developed by Bosch in close cooperation with Porsche, enabled 911 engines worldwide to run at a low octane rating (91RON).

Engine
All engines in the mainstream range were now 2,687cc displacement, achieved by increasing the bore of the cylinders. All engines were also now fitted with light-alloy cylinders with Nikasil coating on the sliding surfaces. The 911 S and Carrera had oil cooling via additional cooling coils in the front right wheelarch. The power output of the base 911 engine was now 110kW (150hp), with the 911 S offering 129kW (175hp) and the Carrera having 154kW (210hp) – the same output as last year's Carrera RS.

Fuel and ignition system
The 911 and 911 S were now fitted with Bosch K-Jetronic injection system, while the Carrera had a mechanical Bosch twin-row fuel injection pump. All engines could run on regular-grade fuel (91RON), which proved that Porsche could produce environmentally friendly sports cars.

Transmission
USA market cars had a four-speed manual transmission as standard (915/16) or the 915/06 five-speed was optional. The gear ratios in the gearboxes were altered to match the increased engine performance. Sportomatic transmission (type 925/02) was available for the 911 and 911 S only (not the Carrera), and it had a revised fourth gear ratio of 0.821 to match the higher engine performance.

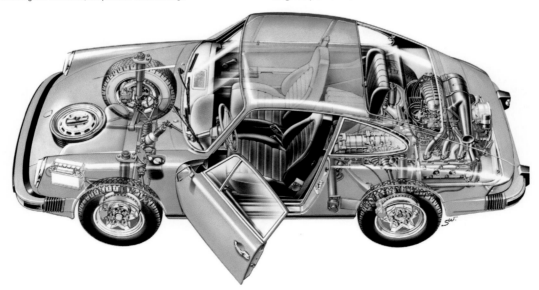

The 911 model line-up in 1974 – from left to right: 911 2.7 Targa (yellow), 911 S 2.7 Coupé (green), 911 Carrera 2.7 Coupé (red).

The foot pedals were also revised, being lengthened and made more user-friendly. The clutch pedal was supported by a helper spring, to assist the pressure applied by the foot when changing gears. This was situated near the clutch control lever at the transmission housing. The great counterforce of the clutch during the disengaging process was

A 1974-model 911 S 2.7 Coupé, showing the dark red panel between the rear lights featuring the Porsche signature.

considerably reduced, so that the gearchange could be performed without difficulty by less able drivers.

Suspension

The unpopular hydropneumatic self-levelling springs were no longer available, even as an option. The rear radius arms were now made from cast light-alloy, lighter and stronger than the original steel versions. All vehicles had standard anti-roll bars at the front (16mm for the 911 and 911 S, and 20mm for the Carrera). The 911 S was equipped with 6Jx15 die-cast light-alloy wheels.

The spare wheel was generally a 165x15 space-saver, since the standard fuel tank left little space for a full-size spare in the front luggage compartment.

Here again Porsche made good use of its racing experience, as spare wheels had been a requirement in sports car racing for many years. In competition, the 917 racer carried a light and non-bulky space-saver wheel fastened above the transmission.

A 1974 911 2.7 Coupé, with the collapsible front and rear bumpers, and their flexible bellows, clearly visible.

Body

Extensive exterior changes were carried out in model year 1974, mostly as a result of new crash impact laws. Compared with other manufacturers, Porsche's solution to the requirement for collapsible bumpers was undisputedly the most stylish and elegant. The bumpers were attached to the body without any visible gap, thanks to black flexible pleats between the bumper and body. In the USA, the bumpers compressed on impact using dampers. In other markets, the bumpers collapsed up to 50mm on impact via simpler (and cheaper) impact tubes; after an accident these economically priced tubes could be replaced easily. The compressible impact dampers used on 911s sold in the USA were also available worldwide as an optional extra. The front and rear bumpers were made of light-alloy, colour-coded with rubber trim across their length, and had integrated front indicators.

Various items on the Carrera were now colour-coded black: the larger square exterior rear-view mirrors, headlamp surrounds (previously chromed) and the rear-view mirrors. All cars were fitted with a new steel 80-litre fuel tank (of which eight litres was reserve). A dark red, non-reflecting panel with black Porsche lettering was located between the rear light clusters.

Equipment and fittings

Three-point inertia reel safety belts for driver and passenger were now standard. Padded steering-wheel rims arrived for the 911 and 911 S, with a leather sports steering wheel for the Carrera. Safety

steering wheels with large impact areas had been in use for years, but now another safety element was introduced: an energy/impact-absorbing damper between the steering wheel and the steering column. These dampers softened the impact of the body against the steering wheel during an accident, so that injuries could mostly be avoided.

The 2.7-litre 911/93 engine, fitted to 911 S models from 1974, produced 129kW (175hp) at 5,800rpm.

49

Interior fittings
New door panels and trim. New generation of seats with integrated fixed headrests.

Heating and air conditioning
Defroster vents for the side windows.

Electrical system
The 911 and 911 S were equipped with stronger 980W alternators. For weight reasons the 770W generator was kept for the Carrera. The two 36Ah batteries previously sited under the front wings (fenders) were replaced by one 66Ah battery in the luggage compartment. A headlamp cleaning system was available.

Additional information
The 911 Carrera RS 3.0 was the homologated road version of the Group 3 race car, and 111 units were built. It was fitted with wider wings (fenders), similar to the later 911 Turbo, to match the larger ATS wheels (8in front and 9in rear). The engine produced 230hp (169kW) from a displacement of 3.0 litres, an increase in size that was made possible by the larger 93mm cylinder bores. The compression ratio was 9.8:1 and the octane rating requirement of the fuel was 96RON.

Model range	Total production
911 Coupé	4889 + 1252 USA
911 Targa	4651
911 S Coupé	1359 + 898 USA
911 S Targa	
911 Carrera Coupé	1036 + 528 USA
911 Carrera Targa	433 + 246 USA

The Carrera RS 3.0 was built for homologation in Group 3 racing. Over 100 examples were built, including around 60 roadgoing versions.

Model range	911	911 S	911 Carrera
Engine			
Engine type, Manual transmission	911/92	911/93	911/83
Bore (mm)	90	=	=
Stroke (mm)	70.4	=	=
Displacement (cc)	2687	2687	2687
Compression ratio	8.0:1	8.5:1	8.5:1
Engine output (kW/hp)	110/150	129/175	154/210
at revolutions per minute (rpm)	5700	5800	6300
Torque (Nm)	235	235	255
at revolutions per minute (rpm)	3800	4000	5100
Output per litre (kW/l)	41	48	57
Max. engine speed (rpm)	6400	6400	7200
Engine weight (kg)	182	182	182

Carburation, ignition, settings			
Fuel system	K-Jetronic	K-Jetronic	MSE
Type of fuel (RON)	91	91	91
Ignition system	BHKZ	BHKZ	BHKZ
Spark plugs			
Bosch	W215T30	W225T30	W260T2
Beru	215/14/3	225/14/3A	260/14/3
Spark plug gap (mm)	0.7	=	=
Idle speed (rpm)	850–950	=	=
CO-content (%)	2.5	=	=
Fuel consumption for combined cycle (litres/100km)	12–14	13–15	15–18

Key:
BHKZ   Battery, capacitive-discharge ignition system
SLE   Secondary-air injection, ZLP = Auxiliary air pump
MSE   Mechanical Bosch induction manifold fuel injection

Transmission			
Clutch, pressure plate	G MFZ 225	=	=
Clutch plate (mm)	GUD 225	=	=
Manual transmission	915/06	915/40	915/06
Gear ratios			
1st gear	3.181	=	=
2nd gear	1.833	=	=
3rd gear	1.261	=	=
4th gear	0.9259	=	=
5th gear	0.7241	=	=
Reverse gear	3.325	=	=
Synchromesh system gears 1–5	POSY	=	=
Final drive	4.4285	=	=
Limited-slip differential	Option	Option	Option
Lock-up factor under load/coasting (%)	40/40	=	=
Sportomatic	952/02	=	–
Torque converter dia. (mm)	F&S 190	=	–
Stall speed (rpm)	2000	=	–
Gear ratios			
1st gear	2.400	=	–
2nd gear	1.555	=	–
3rd gear	1.125	=	–
4th gear	0.821	=	–
Reverse gear	2.533	=	–
Synchromesh system forward gears	POSY	=	–
Final drive	3.857	=	–

Key:
S   Standard
F&S   Manufacturer Fichtel & Sachs
POSY   Porsche Locking synchromesh system, synchroniser rings, mo-coated

Model range	911	911 S	911 Carrera
Suspension, steering and brakes			
Front axle			
Anti-roll bar dia. (mm)	16	16	20
Steering ratio	17.87	=	=
Turning circle dia. (mm)	10.80	=	=
Rear axle			
Anti-roll bar dia. (mm)	Option	Option	18
Brake master cylinder diameter (mm)	19.05	=	=
Brake calliper piston diameter			
front (mm)	48	=	=
rear (mm)	38	=	=
Brake disc diameter			
front (mm)	282.5	=	=
rear (mm)	290	=	=
Brake disc thickness			
front (mm)	20	=	=
rear (mm)	20	=	=
Effective brake disc area (cm²)	210	=	257
Handbrake	Operating mechanically on both rear wheels		
Brake drum diameter (mm)	180	=	=
Contact area (cm²)	170	=	=

Wheels and tyres			
Standard tyre specification, front	165HR15	185/70VR15	=
wheel	5½ J x 15	6J x 15	=
Standard tyre specification, rear	165HR15	185/70VR15	215/60VR15
wheel	5½ J x 15	6J x 15	7J x 15
Space-saver spare wheel	Space-saver wheel 5½ J x 15		
Tyre pressure			
front (bar)	2.0	=	=
rear (bar)	2.4	=	=
Space-saver spare wheel (bar)	2.0	=	=

Body and interior (dimensions at kerb weight)			
Length (mm)	4291	=	=
Width (mm)	1610	1610	1652
Height (mm)	1320	=	=
Wheelbase (mm)	2271	=	=
Track			
front (mm)	1360	1372	=
rear (mm)	1342	1354	1380
Ground clearance at permissible gross weight (mm)	150	=	=

Model range	911	911 S	911 Carrera
Electrical system			
Generator output (W/A)	770/70	=	=
Battery (V/Ah)	12/66	=	=

Weight according to DIN 70020			
Kerb weight (kg)	1075	=	=
Permissible gross weight (kg)	1440	=	1400
Permissible trailer weight			
unbraked (kg)	480	=	=
braked (kg)	800	=	=

Performance			
Maximum speed (kmh)			
Manual transmission	210	225	240
Acceleration 0–62mph/100kmh (sec)			
Manual transmission	8.5	7.6	6.3
Measured kilometre from standing start (sec)			
Manual transmission	29.0	28.0	26.5

Fluid capacities			
Engine oil quantity 1* (l)	11	13	=
Engine oil quantity with SPM (l)	+ 2	=	–
Oil change quantity 1* (l)	10	=	=
Manual transmission 2* (l)	3.0	=	=
Sportomatic 2* (l)	2.5	=	–
Fuel tank (l)	80	=	=
Brake fluid reservoir 3* (l)	0.20	=	=

* Key to numerals
1* Approved API SE/SF with combinations API SE/CC - SF/CC - SF/CD - SE/CD
   Multigrade engine oil factory recommended (SAE 10 W/50 or 15 W/40 or 20 W/50).
   Single-grade engine oils were also permissible. Summer SAE 30. Winter SAE 20.
2* Single-grade transmission fluid SAE 90 acc. MIL-L 2105 B and API-classified GL 5
3* Use only brake fluid acc. SAE J 1703. DOT 3 or 4

Key:
SPM Sportomatic

Chassis numbers (ten digits)					
Car	Model year	Engine	Body	Sequence	Summary
11	4	1	0	0001–9999	Rest of world 911 Coupé
11	4	1	1	0001–9999	Rest of world 911 Targa
11	4	3	0	0001–9999	Rest of world 911 S Coupé
11	4	3	1	0001–9999	Rest of world 911 S Targa
11	4	4	0	0001–9999	USA + California 911 Carrera Coupé
11	4	4	1	0001–9999	USA + California 911 Carrera Targa
11	4	6	0	0001–9999	Carrera Coupé
11	4	6	1	0001–9999	Carrera Targa

Model year: 4 = 1974. 3 = 1973
Engine: 1 = 911; 3 = 911 S; 4 = Carrera USA; 6 = Carrera
Body: 0 = Coupé; 1 = Targa

Model year 1975
H Series, Turbo debut

Porsche 912 E Coupé and Targa
Porsche 911 Coupé and Targa
Porsche 911 S Coupé and Targa
Porsche 911 Carrera Coupé and Targa
Porsche 911 Turbo Coupé

No major modifications were made to the 911, 911 S and 911 Carrera over the previous year. However, the 911 Turbo – the first production sports car in the world with an exhaust turbocharger – was completely new. Porsche was able to apply its vast racing experience with turbochargers to the production of a pioneering road car. At first only a short production run was planned, but demand for the Turbo was so great worldwide that it soon became the company's flagship model and the dream car of many sports car drivers, not just Porsche enthusiasts. The Turbo's 3.0-litre engine developed 260hp (191kW), which translated to a top speed of more than 155mph (250kmh). The Turbo, which was only available as a Coupé, was called the '930 Turbo' in-house because its engine and transmission design were listed under the 930 model designation.

Engine
All the stops were pulled out for Porsche's strongest performance production engine: all the

The 911 Turbo 3.0 Coupé made its debut in 1975 as Porsche's flagship model – the world's first turbocharged production sports car.

experience gathered during the company's relentless long-distance racing career greatly benefited the first production engine with an exhaust turbocharger. The 930/50 engine of the Turbo was based on the 2,992cc naturally aspirated unit used in the special 911 Carrera RS 3.0, but fitted with a single KKK exhaust turbocharger. The crankcase was made from a sturdy light metal-silicon alloy. Engine rigidity was achieved through forged light-alloy pistons and light-alloy cylinder heads from RR 350 alloy (GK AlCu5Ni1, 5CoSbZr). An additional oil cooler was positioned in the right front wing (fender).

There were no mechanical changes to the naturally aspirated engines, but improvements were made to the heat exchangers.

Fuel and ignition system
As the turbocharged engine used a lot of fuel at full throttle, Porsche played it safe by installing two electric roller-vane fuel pumps in series, a principle that had already been proven on the 917 race car. Induction was by Bosch K-Jetronic, ignition system by contactless high-performance condenser ignition (BHKZ).

Transmission
There were no changes to the gearboxes of the naturally aspirated engines, with one exception: cars for the USA received taller gear and axle ratios in order to reduce fuel consumption and therefore emissions. The 911 and 911 S were now available with Sportomatic.

As for the Turbo, from the crankshaft onwards its transmission was all-new. The four-speed manual gearbox (Type 930/30) was specific to the Turbo, and the shafts, bearings, gear sets and final-drive assembly were significantly reinforced

compared with the Type 915 transmission. A single-plate clutch was installed with a diameter of 240mm.

The 930/30 four-speed transmission took into consideration the limited space as well as the high stress created by torque and engine revs. The gear wheels were wider and the differential bevel wheel diameter of the final-drive assembly was bigger, so only a four-speed gearbox was possible. As it was envisaged to use the car in racing and high revs were anticipated, a newly developed Porsche synchromesh system, able to withstand such high revs, needed to be employed. Again, Porsche's racing experience served it well in this area, as it had developed a racing transmission for Matra France in 1973 that withstood up to 12,000rpm from the Matra 12-cylinder engine without any problems. Matra beat Porsche at Le Mans in 1973 and 1974 with this particular transmission. The new version of the Porsche all-synchromesh system was designed to cope with up to 10,000rpm.

ABOVE: Porsche's non-turbo 1975 line-up (all US-spec) – from left to right: 911 Carrera 2.7 Coupé, 911 2.7 Coupé, 911 2.7 Targa.

BELOW: The 'whale tail' rear spoiler first appeared on the 1975-model 911 Carrera 2.7 Coupé.

BELOW: A 1975-model 911 S 2.7 Targa. This model was equipped with the 911/42 engine, developing 129kW (175hp) at 5,800rpm.

The unmistakable 'whale tail' of the 911 Turbo, which featured grilles in the top to feed extra cooling air to the engine.

Suspension

The suspension of the 911 Turbo was completely reworked compared to that in naturally aspirated cars. The front transverse links with light-alloy subcarriers and the light-alloy rear semi-trailing arms were newly designed. Bilstein dampers, anti-

The interior trim options in 1975 included all-leather, or a combination of leather and tartan cloth.

roll bars front and rear (18mm diameter) with a securing bracket. Dual-circuit brake system with failure warning signal. Ventilated disc brakes front and rear. Front brake callipers in light-alloy, the rear ones in cast iron. Forged alloy wheels, 7Jx15 at the front with 185/70 VR 15 tubeless tyres, and 8Jx15 at the rear with 215/60 VR 15 tubeless tyres.

Body

The Turbo looked utterly different to other 911s. It had wider wings (fenders), a front spoiler made from polyurethane and a dramatic horizontal polyurethane-rimmed rear spoiler that was dubbed the 'whale-tail'. This rear spoiler initially had to be presented to the German transport authorities for approval separately 'as there was a danger that cyclists could hurt themselves when colliding with the car, especially children'. The engine lid was in reinforced fibreglass. Exterior rear-view mirrors and headlamp surrounds were colour-coded.

Equipment and fittings

A three-spoke, leather-covered steering wheel was standard for the 911 Turbo, as well as electrically adjustable and heated exterior rear-view mirrors. Electric windows arrived for the 911 Carrera as well as the Turbo. For the first time, the 911 Turbo featured a speedometer with an electronic odometer as standard. Inertia-reel safety belts in the front.

Porsche was probably the first car manufacturer to use electric pulses to measure distance and speed and display the result in the speedometer of a production car. Here too the know-how derived from racing experience was helpful. Ferry Porsche had been given a Porsche 914 with a fixed roof, a 3.0-litre eight-cylinder race engine and type 916 racing transmission for his birthday. However, in order to drive it on public.roads, he needed a speedometer. Porsche gave it some thought and came up with a distance counter consisting of a tiny bar magnet that rotated at the back end of the driveshaft, and a 15mm-long reed switch that was mounted on the outside of the gearbox cover at the rear. The reed switch was influenced by the changing magnetic field of the bar magnet, despite the light-alloy gearbox cover positioned in between, and registered two pulses per driveshaft revolution with the electronic speedometer, where the pulses were converted into a distance and speed value.

Interior fittings

All-leather interior or a combination of leather and tartan cloth.

Heating and air conditioning

The 911 Turbo had an automatically regulated air conditioning system, operated from the centre tunnel. Continuous adjustment of the heating in air-cooled cars is unavoidable, as full speed uphill generates lots of heat while no acceleration downhill generates none. In the 911 Turbo a temperature sensor was installed in the cabin for the first time, which notified an electric system of the temperature. This value was then compared with the desired value that the driver could set with the help of a rotary potentiometer. Depending on the situation, automatic control of the heater flaps allowed more or less hot air to enter the cabin.

Electrical system

Standard for the 911 Turbo: 66Ah battery, 980W generator, air conditioning, headlamp cleaning system, rear windscreen wiper, stereo system, two additional speakers in the rear, electric aerial.

Other information

A model with a four-cylinder engine, the 912 E, was offered once again, exclusively for overseas markets (especially the USA). The 2.0-litre engine was shared with the VW-Porsche 914 and was equipped with an electronically controlled fuel injection system with airflow sensing (L-Jetronic); it achieved 90hp (66kW). As the compression ratio was only 7.6:1, the 912 E could use regular-grade

petrol (91RON). Exhaust emission control was achieved through thermal reactors. The 912 E was fitted with a Type 923/02 five-speed transmission as standard. A ZF limited-slip differential with 40% lock-up was available as an optional extra.

Porsche's decision to re-enter the market with a four-cylinder model occurred because calls for an economical and reasonably priced sports car rose in the USA after the energy crisis of 1973–74. Even though the economical Porsche 924 was also first seen in 1975, as many as 2,092 Porsche 912 Es were sold in the USA.

On the occasion of the 25th anniversary of Porsche production beginning in Stuttgart, a special edition of the 911, 911 S and 911 Carrera was introduced. All 400 vehicles built were in metallic silver with a blue-black leatherette interior and a dash plaque on the glovebox lid.

Model range	Total production
912 E Coupé	873
912 E Targa	N/A
911 Coupé	1283 + 998 USA
911 Targa	N/A
911 S Coupé	385 + 2310 USA
911 S Targa	266 + 1517 USA
911 Carrera Coupé	518 + 395 USA
911 Carrera Targa	N/A
911 Turbo Coupé	284

Model range	911	911 S	911 Carrera	911 Turbo
Engine				
Engine type, Manual transmission	911/41	911/42	911/83	930/52
Bore (mm)	90	90	90	95
Stroke (mm)	70.4	=	=	=
Displacement (cc)	2687	2687	2687	2994
Compression ratio	8.0:1	8.5:1	8.5:1	6.5:1
Engine output (kW/hp)	110/150	129/175	154/210	191/260
at revolutions per minute (rpm)	5700	5800	6300	5500
Torque (Nm)	235	235	255	343
at revolutions per minute (rpm)	3800	4000	5100	4000
Output per litre (kW/l)	41	48	57	64
Max. engine speed (rpm)	6500	6500	7300	7000
Engine weight (kg)	195	200	200	207

Carburation, ignition, settings				
Fuel system	K-Jetronic	K-Jetronic	MSE	K-Jetronic
Type of fuel (RON)	91	91	91	96
Ignition system	BHKZ	BHKZ	BHKZ	BHKZ breakerless
Spark plugs				
Bosch	W215T30	W225T30	W260T2	W280P21
Beru	215/14/3	225/14/3A	260/14/3	–
Spark plug gap (mm)	0.7	=	=	=
Idle speed (rpm)	850–950	=	=	900–950
Exhaust/purification system	–	–	–	–
CO-content (%)	2.5	=	=	=
Fuel consumption for combined cycle (litres/100km)	12–14	13–15	15–18	14–18

Key:
BHKZ   Battery, capacitive-discharge ignition system (CDI)
MSE   Mechanical Bosch induction manifold fuel injection

Model range	911	911 S	911 Carrera	911 Turbo
Transmission				
Clutch, pressure plate	G MFZ 225	=	=	G MFZ 240
Clutch plate (mm)	GUD 225	=	=	GUD 240
Manual transmission	915/43	915/40	915/06	930/30
Gear ratios				
1st gear	3.181	=	=	2.250
2nd gear	1.833	=	=	1.304
3rd gear	1.261	=	=	0.893
4th gear	0.9615	1.000	0.9259	0.656
5th gear	0.7241	0.8214	0.7241	–
Reverse gear	3.325	=	=	2.437
Synchromesh system gears 1–5	POSY	=	=	POSY
Final drive	4.4285	=	=	4.222
Limited-slip differential	Option	Option	Option	Option
Lock-up factor under load/coasting (%)	40/40	=	=	=
Sportomatic	925/02	925/13	–	–
Torque converter dia. (mm)	F&S 190	=	–	–
Stall speed (rpm)	2000	=	–	–
Gear ratios				
1st gear	2.400	=	–	–
2nd gear	1.555	=	–	–
3rd gear	1.125	=	–	–
4th gear	0.821	=	–	–
Reverse gear	2.533	=	–	–
Synchromesh system forward gears	POSY	=	–	–
Final drive	3.857	=	–	–

Key:

S   Standard
F&S   Manufacturer Fichtel & Sachs
POSY   Porsche Locking synchromesh system, synchroniser rings, mo-coated

Suspension, steering and brakes				
Front axle				
Anti-roll bar diameter (mm)	16	16	20	20
Steering ratio	17.87	=	=	=
Turning circle diameter (m)	10.80	=	=	=
Rear axle				
Anti-roll bar diameter (mm)	–	–	18	18
Brake system				
Brake master cylinder diameter (mm)	19.05	=	=	=
Brake calliper piston diameter				
front (mm)	48	=	=	=
rear (mm)	38	=	=	=
Brake disc diameter				
front (mm)	282.5	=	=	=
rear (mm)	290	=	=	=
Brake disc thickness				
front (mm)	20	=	=	=
rear (mm)	20	=	=	=
Effective brake disc area (cm2)	210	=	257	257
Handbrake	Operating mechanically on both rear wheels			
Brake drum diameter (mm)	180	=	=	=
Contact area (cm^2)	170	=	=	=

Wheels and tyres				
Standard tyre specification, front	185/70VR15	=	=	205/50VR15*
wheel	6J x 15	=	=	7J x 15
Standard tyre specification, rear	185/70VR15	=	215/60VR15	225/50VR15*
wheel	6J x 15	=	=	7J x 15
Space-saver spare wheel	Space-saver wheel 5½ J x 15			
Tyre pressure				
front (bar)	2.0	=	=	=
rear (bar)	2.4	=	=	=
Space-saver spare wheel (bar)	2.0	=	=	=

*As per special request 185/70VR15 tyres front and 215/60VR15 rear

Model range	911	911 S	911 Carrera	911 Turbo
Body and interior (dimensions at kerb weight)				
Length (mm)	4291	=	=	=
Width (mm)	1610	1610	1652	1775
Height (mm)	1320	=	=	=
Wheelbase (mm)	2271	=	=	2272
Track				
front (mm)	1372	=	=	1438
rear (mm)	1354	=	1380	1511
Ground clearance at permissible gross weight (mm)	120	=	=	=
Electrical system				
Generator output (W/A)	980/70	=	=	=
Battery (V/Ah)	12/66	=	=	=
Weight according to DIN 70020				
Kerb weight (kg)	1075	=	=	1140
Permissible gross weight (kg)	1440	=	1400	1470
Permissible trailer weight				
unbraked (kg)	480	=	=	none
braked (kg)	800	=	=	none
Performance				
Maximum speed (kmh)				
Manual transmission	210	225	240	250
Acceleration 0–62mph/100kmh (sec)				
Manual transmission	8.5	7.6	6.3	5.5
Measured kilometre from standing start (sec)				
Manual transmission	29.0	28.0	26.5	24
Fluid capacities				
Engine oil quantity 1* (l)	11	13	=	=
Engine oil quantity with SPM (l)	+ 2	=	–	–
Oil change quantity 1* (l)	10	=	=	=
Manual transmission 2* (l)	3.0	=	=	3.7
Sportomatic 2* (l)	2.5	=	–	–
Fuel tank (l)	80	=	=	=
Brake fluid reservoir 3* (l)	0.20	=	=	=

* Key to numerals
1* Approved API SE/SF with combinations API SE/CC - SF/CC - SF/CD - SE/CD
   Multigrade engine oil factory recommended (SAE 10 W/50 or 15 W/40 or 20 W/50).
   Single-grade engine oils were also permissible. Summer SAE 30. Winter SAE 20.
2* Single-grade transmission fluid SAE 90 acc. MIL-L 2105 B and API-classified GL 5
3* Use only brake fluid acc. SAE J 1703. DOT 3 or 4

Key:
SPM Sportomatic

Chassis numbers (ten digits)					
Car	**Model year**	**Engine**	**Body**	**Sequence**	**Summary**
11	5	1	0	0001–9999	Rest of world 911 Coupé
11	5	1	1	0001–9999	Rest of world 911 Targa
11	5	2	0	0001–9999	USA + California 911 S Coupé
11	5	2	1	0001–9999	USA + California 911 S Targa
11	5	3	0	0001–9999	Rest of world 911 S Coupé
11	5	3	1	0001–9999	Rest of world 911 S Targa
11	5	4	0	0001–9999	USA + California Carrera Coupé
11	5	4	1	0001–9999	USA + California Carrera Targa
11	5	6	0	0001–9999	Carrera Coupé
11	5	6	1	0001–9999	Carrera Targa
30	5	7	0	0001–1000	911 Turbo

Car: 11 = all 911; 30 = 911 Turbo
Model year: 5 = 1975. 4 = 1974
Engine: 1 = 911; 2 = 911 S USA; 3 = 911 S; 4 = Carrera USA; 6 = Carrera; 7 - Turbo
Body: 0 = Coupé; 1 = Targa

Model year 1976
I Series, with galvanised body

Porsche 912 E Coupé and Targa
Porsche 911 Coupé and Targa
Porsche 911 Carrera 3.0 Coupé and Targa
Porsche 911 Turbo Coupé

Due to the availability of an all-new entry-level Porsche – the Porsche 924 with a 125hp (92kW) engine – the 911 range was now trimmed. The 911 with 2.7-litre displacement remained, but the 911 S was dropped and the Carrera's naturally aspirated engine grew in size to 3.0 litres and was fitted with K-Jetronic fuel injection. The semi-automatic Sportomatic transmission available for the naturally aspirated engines now had only three forward gears.

Hot-dip galvanised steel panels for the structural body parts represented a huge advance, a genuine milestone in the car manufacturing industry. It was now possible to issue a six-year warranty against floorpan rust. Previously extensive trials had been carried out using non-rusting stainless steel, and three stainless steel-bodied prototypes were built at great expense, one of which remains on display at the Deutsche Museum in Munich. The fact that these trials were terminated was due mainly to the tremendous difficulties encountered in deep-drawing and welding the steel parts.

A 1976-model 911 Carrera 3.0 Targa – one of the first cars to be manufactured using hot-dip galvanised steel panels.

Engine
Modifications to the Carrera 3.0-litre engine: apart from the increased displacement to 2,994cc and larger valves, K-Jetronic injection was employed. Despite the larger capacity, power actually fell to 147kW (200hp). The engine of the base 911 enjoyed the higher 8.5:1 compression of the now-defunct 911 S model and its power increased to 121kW (165hp). Both naturally aspirated engines were fitted with a cooling fan with only five blades. The fan gearing was altered, so that the alternator and fan rotated faster. This became necessary because the electrical consumption of cars running at low speeds in city traffic was higher than the alternator could supply.

Fuel and ignition system
The Turbo engine was fitted with an auxiliary air valve and air injection to reduce exhaust emissions, as well as a pressure tank in the fuel system between the fuel pumps and an improved distributor. With the Carrera also converted to use K-Jetronic, all of Porsche's cars, including the 924, were now for the first time equipped with the same fuel injection system. The fuel pumps of the 911 and 911 Carrera were moved to the front in the vicinity of the tank and steering. Certain components were added to the induction system of the Turbo engine to make both cold and hot starts easier.

Transmission
The 925/09 Sportomatic transmission for the 911 and the 925/13 for the 911 Carrera 3.0 lost a gear for 1976, now only having three forward gears. The reason for this lay in the stricter noise regulations in some major export markets: when driving along a measured section the vehicles that

were fitted with the four-speed Sportomatic reached the threshold revolution speed of 6,800rpm in second gear, when accelerating at full throttle. As a result the exhaust and noise thresholds were exceeded according to the new regulations. The gear ratios were adjusted to the engine output for the transmissions on the naturally aspirated engines.

Due to its wider tyres, there were two different transmissions available for the 911 Turbo, which differed only in their final drive ratio: transmission type 930/30 (final drive ratio 4.222:1) for normal tyres; and transmission type 930/32 (final drive ratio 4.000:1), for the lower profile 225/50 VR 15 tyres.

Suspension
No changes to the suspension of naturally aspirated cars. The 911 Turbo was now available with two different sets of tyres: front 185/70 VR 15, rear 215/60 VR 15 as before; or low-profile front 205/50 VR 15, rear 225/50 VR 15. This was the first time that Porsche had offered tyres with a height/width ratio of 50%. The demand was so great that the tyre industry struggled to keep pace with it.

Body
Hot-dip galvanised steel panels for structural body parts were introduced for all models and the surface and cavity treatment of the body and paintwork were improved. Porsche was the first car manufacturer to make production cars from hot-dip galvanised deep-draw steel. After trials building bodies from non-rusting steel, Porsche used hot-dip galvanised panels in Zuffenhausen (and at Audi-NSU in Neckarsulm for the 924). Through extensive preparation of the paintwork, Porsche succeeded in maintaining a high-quality finish on

'His and hers' 911 Turbo 3.0 Coupés. The 1976-model Turbo, with 3.0-litre engine, developed 191kW (260hp) at 5,500rpm.

the galvanised panels. Headlamp surrounds of the 911 Carrera 3.0 were now also colour-coded. Headlamp washer system for the 911 Carrera 3.0 and the 911 Turbo now standard.

Equipment and fittings
The 911 Carrera and 911 Turbo featured stitched door panels and carpet trim. Illuminated ignition/door key.

The 911 interior was becoming more refined, and for 1976 featured plush, stitched carpet trim. This is a USA-spec 911 2.7.

Electrical system

Electrically adjustable and heated exterior rear-view mirrors on all cars. The 911 and 911 Carrera 3.0 had two audio speakers in each door panel, while the Turbo also had two in the rear. Cruise control was available as an optional extra (but not for the 912 E).

The 911 and the 911 Carrera 3.0 were fitted with the first electronic speedometers; Porsche was again on the cutting-edge with its electronic speedometer. A light-alloy rotor, with eight small bar magnets around its periphery, rotated with the differential. A reed switch attached to the outside of the gearbox cover was influenced by the magnetic fields of the rotating bar magnets, despite the cover wall in between, and the switch then submitted the number of pulses to the speedometer.

Additional information

For production reasons, some 123 examples of the 911 Carrera 3.0 were fitted with a more powerful engine with 155kW (210hp).

Model range	Total production
912 E (for USA)	1216
911 Coupé	1868
911 Targa	1576
911 Carrera Coupé	1093 + 2079 USA
911 Carrera Targa	479 + 2175 USA
911 Turbo Coupé	644 + 530 USA

Model range	911	911 Carrera	911 Turbo
Engine			
Engine type, Manual transmission	911/81	930/02	930/52
Bore (mm)	90	95	95
Stroke (mm)	70.4	70.4	70.4
Displacement (cc)	2687	2994	2994
Compression ratio	8.5:1	8.5:1	6.5:1
Engine output (kW/hp)	121/165	147/200	191/260
at revolutions per minute (rpm)	5800	6000	5500
Torque (Nm)	235	255	343
at revolutions per minute (rpm)	4000	4200	4000
Output per litre (kW/l)	45	50	64
Max. engine speed (rpm)	6700	7000	7000
Engine weight (kg)	195	200	207

Carburation, ignition, settings			
Fuel system	K-Jetronic	K-Jetronic	K-Jetronic
Type of fuel (RON)	91	91	96
Ignition system	BHKZ	BHKZ	BHKZ breakerless
Spark plugs			
Bosch	W225T30	W260T2	W280P1
Beru	225/14/3	260/14/3	225/14/3A
Spark plug gap (mm)	0.7	=	=
Idle speed (rpm)	850–950	=	900–950
Exhaust/purification system	–	–	SLE+ZLP
CO-content (%)	2.5	2.5	2.5
Fuel consumption for combined cycle (litres/100km)	13–15	14–16	14–18

Key:
BHKZ   Battery, capacitive-discharge ignition system (CDI)
SLE   Secondary-air injection, ZLP = Auxiliary air pump

Model range	911	911 Carrera	911 Turbo
Transmission			
Clutch, pressure plate	G MFZ 225	=	G MFZ 240
Clutch plate (mm)	GUD 225	=	GUD 240
Manual transmission	915/44	915/44	930/33
Gear ratios			
1st gear	3.181	=	2.250
2nd gear	1.833	=	1.304
3rd gear	1.261	=	0.893
4th gear	1.000	=	0.656
5th gear	0.821	=	–
Reverse gear	3.325	=	2.437
Synchromesh system gears 1–5	POSY	=	POSY
Final drive	3.875	=	4.222 and 4.000
Limited-slip differential	Option	Option	Option
Lock-up factor under load/coasting (%)	40/40	=	=
Sportomatic	925/09	925/13	–
Torque converter dia. (mm)	F&S 190	=	–
Stall speed (rpm)	1900	=	–
Gear ratios			
1st gear	2.400	=	–
2nd gear	1.428	=	–
3rd gear	0.926	=	–
4th gear	–	–	–
Reverse gear	2.533	=	–
Synchromesh system forward gears	POSY	=	–
Final drive	3.375	=	–

Key:
S   Standard
F&S   Manufacturer Fichtel & Sachs
POSY   Porsche Locking synchromesh system, synchroniser rings, mo-coated

Suspension, steering and brakes			
Front axle			
Anti-roll bar dia. (mm)	16	20	18
Steering ratio	17.87	=	=
Turning circle dia. (m)	10.80	=	=
Rear axle			
Anti-roll bar dia. (mm)	–	18	18
Brake system			
Brake booster dia. (inch)	–	7	7
Brake master cylinder diameter (mm)	20.64	=	23.81
Brake calliper piston diameter			
front (mm)	48	=	=
rear (mm)	38	=	=
Brake disc diameter			
front (mm)	282.5	=	=
rear (mm)	290	=	=
Brake disc thickness			
front (mm)	20	=	=
rear (mm)	20	=	=
Effective brake disc area (cm2)	257	=	=
Handbrake	Operating mechanically on both rear wheels		
Brake drum diameter (mm)	180	=	=
Contact area (cm²)	170	=	=

Model range	911	911 Carrera	911 Turbo
Wheels and tyres			
Standard tyre specification, front	185/70VR15	=	205/50VR15*
wheel	6J x 15	6J x 15	7J x15
Standard tyre specification, rear	185/70VR15	215/60VR15	225/50VR15*
wheel	6J x 15	7J x 15	8J x15
Space-saver spare wheel	165-15 89P	=	=
Tyre pressure			
front (bar)	2.0	=	2.0
rear (bar)	2.4	=	3.0
Space-saver spare wheel (bar)	2.2	=	2.2

*As per special request 185/70VR15 tyres front and
215/60VR15 rear.

Body and interior (dimensions at kerb weight)			
Length (mm)	4291	=	=
Width (mm)	1610	1652	1775
Height (mm)	1320	=	=
Wheelbase (mm)	272	=	=
Track			
front (mm)	1369	=	1438
rear (mm)	1354	1380	1511
Ground clearance at permissible gross weight (mm)	120	=	=

Electrical system			
Generator output (W/A)	980/70	=	=
Battery (V/Ah)	12/66	=	=

Weight according to DIN 70020			
Kerb weight (kg)	1120	=	1195
Permissible gross weight (kg)	1500	1440	1525
Permissible trailer weight			
unbraked (kg)	480	=	none
braked (kg)	800	=	none

Performance			
Maximum speed (kmh)			
Manual transmission	210	230	250
Acceleration 0–62mph/100kmh (sec)			
Manual transmission	7.8	6.5	5.5
Measured kilometre from standing start (sec)			
Manual transmission	29.0	27.0	24.0

Model range	911	911 Carrera	911 Turbo
Fluid capacities			
Engine oil quantity 1* (l)	13	=	=
Engine oil quantity with SPM (l)	+ 2	=	–
Oil change quantity 1* (l)	10	=	=
Manual transmission 2* (l)	3.0	=	3.7
Sportomatic 2* (l)	2.5	=	–
Fuel tank (l)	80	=	=
Brake fluid reservoir 3* (l)	0.20	=	=

* Key to numerals
1* Approved API SE/SF with combinations API SE/CC - SF/CC - SF/CD - SE/CD Multigrade engine oil factory recommended (SAE 10 W/50 or 15 W/40 or 20 W/50).
   Single-grade engine oils were also permissible. Summer SAE 30. Winter SAE 20.
2* Single-grade transmission fluid SAE 90 acc. MIL-L 2105 B and API-classified GL 5
3* Use only brake fluid acc. SAE J 1703. DOT 3 or 4
Key:
SPM = Sportomatic

A 911 2.7-litre engine receives the finishing touches on the production line, prior to being installed in a car in 1976.

Chassis numbers (ten digits)					
Car	Model year	Engine	Body	Sequence	Summary
911	6	1	2	0001–9999	USA + California Coupé 911 S
911	6	1	2	0001–9999	USA + California Targa 911 S
911	6	2	3	0001–9999	Rest of world 911 S Coupé
911	6	2	3	0001–9999	Rest of world 911 S Targa
911	6	3	6	0001–9999	Carrera Coupé
911	6	3	6	0001–9999	Carrera Targa
930	6	4	7	0001–1000	Rest of world 911 Turbo
930	6	4	8	0001–1000	USA + California 911 Turbo

Car: 911 = all 911; 930 = 911 Turbo
Model year: 6 = 1976. 5 = 1975
Engine: 2 = 911 S USA; 3 = 911 S; 6 = Carrera; 7 = 911 Turbo; 8 = 911 Turbo USA
Body: 0 = Coupé; 1 = Targa

Model year 1977
J series, with brake servo

Porsche 911 Coupé and Targa
Porsche 911 Carrera 3.0 Coupé and Targa
Porsche 911 Turbo Coupé

There was little news in model year 1977, only modified heating and air conditioning operation for naturally aspirated models, while the Carrera 3.0 and 911 Turbo were fitted with brake servos and the 911 Turbo with larger 16in wheels. The 912 E was dropped.

Engine

Emissions regulations in the USA, Canada and Japan were tightened this year. That necessitated the introduction of an afterburn system through the intake of oxygen, partial recirculation of the exhaust gas in the induction system, and the use of thermal reactors in the exhaust stream, before cars could be exported to those countries. Engines destined for the USA were equipped with secondary air injection behind the outlet valves, with exhaust gas recirculation (EGR) in the induction system, and exhaust thermal reactors. For Japan, an additional optic exhaust temperature control was stipulated which alerted the driver when the normal exhaust temperature was exceeded (for example, 750°C in the Turbo). Turbo engines were fitted with a gauge displaying the turbo boost pressure.

A 1977-model 911 2.7 Targa. The 1977 models remained largely unchanged from the previous year.

Fuel and ignition system

New fuel pump type: Bosch EKP IV. This pump generated less noise and had a higher flow rate. The Turbo used two EKP IV pumps in series.

Transmission

In the 911 Carrera and 911 Turbo, disengaging the clutch was made more comfortable. The 915/60 transmission for the 911 and the 915/61 transmission for the 911 Carrera 3.0 were fitted with modified gearshift mechanism parts for the first gear. The introduction of asymmetrically pointed gear teeth on the clutch body of the first gear as well as on the gearshift sleeve made engaging first gear much easier.

Suspension

Vacuum brake servos were fitted to the 911 Carrera 3.0 as well as to the 911 Turbo and the 911 Sportomatic. This had become a necessity, as the cars were getting heavier with each passing year and their maximum speed was increasing. In order to keep the pedal forces low, vacuum brake servos from Teves (ATE) were installed. The brake system was adjusted to incorporate this modification. Further modifications to the Turbo: larger anti-roll bars (20mm at the front, 18mm at the rear), and a switch over to 16in wheels, 7Jx16 front and 8Jx16 rear, with 205/55 VR 16 front tyres and 225/50 VR 16 rear tyres.

Equipment and fittings

Car theft was on the increase worldwide. From 1977, therefore, Porsche made the front quarter-lights of the Targa fixed rather than movable, as this was a common place for thieves to break into cars. Door locking and unlocking from the inside

was by means of a knob which went up and down, and as a further anti-theft protection this now retracted entirely in the locked position and could not be lifted up manually.

The Turbo was equipped with a turbo boost pressure gauge which read up to 1.5bar and was positioned in the centrally located rev counter.

Interior fittings
Front and back seats could be covered with pinstripe cloth as an optional extra.

Heating and air conditioning
Two ventilation controls (one for the right and one for the left side of the car) were illuminated at

The 911 Carrera 3.0 had colour-coded headlamp surrounds and ATS die-cast rims in model year 1977.

night. For improved ventilation, two additional air vents were located in the centre of the dashboard. The automatic air conditioning system of the 911 Turbo was now installed in the 911 Carrera 3.0.

Electrical system
Safety belt warning lamp for all cars.

The interior of a 1977-model 911 Turbo 3.0 Coupé. The Turbo was fitted with a three-spoke sports steering wheel.

Model range	Total production
911 Coupé	2449 + 3388 USA
911 Targa	1724 + 2747 USA
911 Carrera Coupé	1473 + 646 USA
911 Carrera Targa	N/A
911 Turbo Coupé	695 + 727 USA

Model range	911	911 Carrera	911 Turbo
Engine			
Engine type, Manual transmission	911/81	930/02	930/52
Bore (mm)	90	95	95
Stroke (mm)	70.4	70.4	70.4
Displacement (cc)	2687	2994	2994
Compression ratio	8.5:1	8.5:1	6.5:1
Engine output (kW/hp)	121/165	147/200	191/260
at revolutions per minute (rpm)	5800	6000	5500
Torque (Nm)	235	255	343
at revolutions per minute (rpm)	4000	4200	4000
Output per litre (kW/l)	45	50	64
Max. engine speed (rpm)	6700	7000	7000
Engine weight (kg)	195	200	207

Model range	911	911 Carrera	911 Turbo
Carburation, ignition, settings			
Fuel system	K-Jetronic	K-Jetronic	K-Jetronic
Type of fuel (RON)	91	91	96
Ignition system	BHKZ	BHKZ	BHKZ breakerless
Spark plugs			
Bosch	W225T30	=	W280P1
Beru	225/14/3	=	225/14/3A
Spark plug gap (mm)	0.7	=	0.6
Idle speed (rpm)	850–950	=	900–950
Exhaust/purification system	ZLP+TR= EGR*	SLE+ZLP	
CO-content (%)	2.0–2.4	2.0–4.0	2.5
Fuel consumption for combined cycle (litres/100km)	13–15	14–16	14–18

Key:
BHKZ   Battery, capacitive-discharge ignition system (CDI)
SLE   Secondary-air injection, ZLP = Auxiliary air pump
TR   thermal reactors, EGR = exhaust-gas recirculation, * = only USA

Model range	911	911 Carrera	911 Turbo
Transmission			
Clutch, pressure plate	G MFZ 225	=	G MFZ 240
Clutch plate (mm)	GUD 225	=	GUD 240
Manual transmission	915/60	915/60	930/33
Gear ratios			
1st gear	3.181	=	2.250
2nd gear	1.833	=	1.304
3rd gear	1.261	=	0.893
4th gear	1.000	=	0.656
5th gear	0.821	=	–
Reverse gear	3.325	=	2.437
Synchromesh system gears 1–5	POSY	=	POSY
Final drive	3.875	=	4.222
Limited-slip differential	Option	Option	Option
Lock-up factor under load/coasting (%)	40/40	=	=
Sportomatic	925/15	925/16	–
Torque converter dia. (mm)	F&S 190	=	–
Stall speed (rpm)	1900	=	–
Gear ratios			
1st gear	2.400	=	–
2nd gear	1.428	=	–
3rd gear	0.926	=	–
4th gear	–	–	–
Reverse gear	1.81	=	–
Synchromesh system forward gears	POSY	=	–
Final drive	3.375	=	–

Key:
S   Standard
F&S   Manufacturer Fichtel & Sachs
POSY   Porsche Locking synchromesh system, synchroniser rings, mo-coated

1977-model 911 Turbo 3.0 Coupé (left) and 911 Carrera 3.0 Coupé (right). Note the black stone-chip protection on the Turbo.

Model range	911	911 Carrera	911 Turbo
Suspension, steering and brakes			
Front axle			
Anti-roll bar dia. (mm)	16	20	20
Steering ratio	17.87	=	=
Turning circle dia. (m)	10.95	=	=
Rear axle			
Anti-roll bar dia. (mm)	–	18	18
Brake system			
Brake booster dia. (inch)	–	7	8
Brake master cylinder diameter (mm)	20.64	=	23.81
Brake calliper piston diameter			
front (mm)	48	=	=
rear (mm)	38	=	=
Brake disc diameter			
front (mm)	282.5	=	=
rear (mm)	290	=	=
Brake disc thickness			
front (mm)	20	=	=
rear (mm)	20	=	=
Effective brake disc area (cm^2)	257	=	=
Handbrake	Operating mechanically on both rear wheels		
Brake drum diameter (mm)	180	=	=
Contact area (cm^2)	170	=	=

Wheels and tyres			
Standard tyre specification, front	185/70VR15	=	205/55VR16
wheel	6J x 15	6J x 15	7J x16
Standard tyre specification, rear	185/70VR15	215/60VR15	225/50VR16
wheel	6J x 15	7J x 15	8J x15
Space-saver spare wheel	165-15 89P	=	=
Tyre pressure			
front (bar)	2.0	=	2.0
rear (bar)	2.4	=	3.0
Space-saver spare wheel (bar)	2.2	=	2.2

Body and interior (dimensions at kerb weight)			
Length (mm)	4291	=	=
Width (mm)	1610	1652	1775
Height (mm)	1320	=	=
Wheelbase (mm)	2272	=	=
Track			
front (mm)	1369	=	1438
rear (mm)	1354	1380	1511
Ground clearance at permissible gross weight (mm)	120	=	=

Model range	911	911 Carrera	911 Turbo
Electrical system			
Generator output (W/A)	980/70	=	=
Battery (V/Ah)	12/66	=	=

Weight according to DIN 70020			
Kerb weight (kg)	1120	=	1195
Permissible gross weight (kg)	1500	1440	1525
Permissible trailer weight			
unbraked (kg)	480	=	none
braked (kg)	800	=	none

Performance			
Maximum speed (kmh)			
Manual transmission	210	230	250
Acceleration 0–62mph/100kmh (sec)			
Manual transmission	7.8	6.5	5.5
Measured kilometre from standing start (sec)			
Manual transmission	29.0	27.0	24.0

Fluid capacities			
Engine oil quantity 1* (l)	13	=	=
Engine oil quantity with SPM (l)	+ 2	–	–
Oil change quantity 1* (l)	10	=	=
Manual transmission 2* (l)	3.0	=	3.7
Sportomatic 2* (l)	2.5	–	–
Fuel tank (l)	80	=	=
Brake fluid reservoir 3* (l)	0.20	=	=

* Key to numerals

1* Approved API SE/SF with combinations API SE/CC - SF/CC - SF/CD - SE/CD

Multigrade engine oil factory recommended (SAE 10 W/50 or 15 W/40 or 20 W/50).

Single-grade engine oils were also permissible. Summer SAE 30. Winter SAE 20.

2* Single-grade transmission fluid SAE 90 acc. MIL-L 2105 B and API-classified GL 5

3* Use only brake fluid acc. SAE J 1703. DOT 3 or 4

Key:

SPM = Sportomatic

Chassis numbers (ten digits)					
Car	Model year	Engine	Body	Sequence	Summary
911	7	2	0	0001–9999	USA+California Coupé 911 S
911	7	2	1	0001–9999	USA+California Targa 911 S
911	7	3	0	0001–9999	Rest of world 911 S Coupé
911	7	3	1	0001–9999	Rest of world 911 S Targa
911	7	6	0	0001–9999	Carrera Coupé
911	7	6	1	0001–9999	Carrera Targa
930	7	7	0	0001–1000	Rest of world 911 Turbo
930	7	8	0	0001–1000	USA+California 911 Turbo

Car: 911 = all 911; 930 = 911 Turbo
Model year: 7 = 1977. 6 = 1976
Engine: 2 = 911 S USA; 3 = 911 S; 6 = Carrera; 7 = 911 Turbo; 8 = 911 Turbo USA
Body: 0 = Coupé; 1 = Targa

Model year 1978

K Series, SC and Turbo 3.3 with intercooler

Porsche 911 SC Coupé and Targa
Porsche 911 Turbo 3.3 Coupé

By 1978, Porsche's model range had grown substantially to include the front-engined 924 and the 928. That was why the 911 line-up of 1978 was trimmed back to only two. A single new 911 SC model with a 3.0-litre engine replaced the previous 2.7-litre 911 and 3.0-litre Carrera; and the 911 Turbo continued but with a larger engine. The SC

model designation was derived from 'S' for Super and 'C' for Carrera engine. The Turbo was now equipped with a bigger 3.3-litre engine which was intercooled for the first time. Since cooling the compressed air resulted in more oxygen in the combustion chamber, more fuel could therefore be injected and thus higher power and torque outputs could be achieved throughout the rev range. With the increased performance of the 911 Turbo 3.3, the gap to Porsche's 928 widened, even though the 928 had originally been intended to replace the 911.

Engine

Due to various exhaust regulations in Porsche's export markets there were six different naturally aspirated engines for the 911 SC alone:

Description	Type	Displacement (cc)	Compression	Octane rating (RON)	Performance (hp/kW)	Torque (Nm)	Notes
911 SC	930/03	2994	8.5:1	91	180/132	265	Manual transmission for RoW
911 SC	930/13	2994	8.5:1	91	180/132	265	Sportomatic for RoW
911 SC	930/04	2994	8.5:1	91*	180/132	265	Manual transmission for USA and Canada
911 SC	930/05	2994	8.5:1	91*	180/132	265	Manual transmission for Japan
911 SC	930/15	2994	8.5:1	91*	180/132	265	Sportomatic for Japan
911 SC	930/06	2994	8.5:1	91*	180/132	265	For California

* Unleaded petrol required
RoW = Rest of world excluding USA, Canada, Japan and California

OPPOSITE: A 1978-model 911 SC 3.0 Targa. The difference in width between the front and rear wheels can be clearly seen.

ABOVE: 1978 US models – 911 SC 3.0 Targa (brown), 911 SC 3.0 Coupé (blue), 911 Turbo 3.3 Coupé (silver).

Further modifications to the naturally aspirated engines: the crankshaft was reinforced, the main-bearing diameter was increased to 60mm, and the con rods were redesigned to match the crankshaft.

By increasing cylinder bore to 97mm and installing a new crankshaft with a 74.4mm stroke, displacement of the Turbo engine was increased to 3.3 litres. The comparison of the two engines shows how environmental demands influence performance.

Exhaust emission control of the various turbocharged engines was affected as follows:

Engine type	User country	Secondary air injection	Exhaust catalytic converter	Exhaust-gas recirculation	Grass fire protection
930/03	Manual transmission for RoW	Yes	–	–	–
930/13	Sportomatic for RoW	Yes	–	–	–
930/04	USA and Canada	Yes	Yes	–	–
930/05	Manual transmission for Japan	Yes	Yes	Yes	Yes
930/15	Sportomatic for Japan	Yes	Yes	Yes	Yes
930/06	California	Yes	Yes	Yes	Yes

RoW = Rest of world excluding USA, Canada, Japan and California

Motor	Type	Displacement (cc)	Compression	Octane rating (RON)	Performance (hp/kW)	Torque (Nm)	Notes
911 Turbo	930/60	3299	7.0:1	98	300/221	412	For RoW
911 Turbo	930/61	3299	7.0:1	96*	265/195	395	For USA and Canada
911 Turbo	930/62	3299	7.0:1	96*	265/195	395	For Japan
911 Turbo	930/63	3299	7.0:1	96*	265/195	395	For California

* Unleaded petrol required
RoW = Rest of world excluding USA, Canada, Japan and California

Measures taken for control of exhaust emissions:
930/60 (RoW)   secondary air injection
930/61 (USA and Canada) secondary air injection + thermal reactor + exhaust gas recirculation
930/62 (Japan)   secondary air injection + thermal reactor + exhaust gas recirculation + grass fire protection
930/63 (California)   secondary air injection + thermal reactor + exhaust gas recirculation + ignition timing adjustment

ABOVE: The 911 interior was becoming increasingly refined. This is a 1978-model 911 SC 3.0 Targa.

BELOW: The rear seats were well trimmed, although rather compact and better suited to children rather than adults.

Porsche abolished running-in instructions for all engines. Due to modern production methods and much-improved material combinations, the only requirement was not to exceed a maximum of 5,000rpm in any gear for the first 1,000km.

Fuel and ignition system

Bosch K-Jetronic was used in all engines. The 911 Turbo 3.3 with its turbocharger was now fitted with an air-to-air intercooler for the first time. All engines were now equipped with an HKZ 12V breakerless ignition system from Bosch. When the engine's rev limit was reached – for example, 6,800rpm for the 911 SC – the ignition was not interrupted in engines intended for the US, Canadian or Japanese markets; instead, the fuel feed was stopped by shutting down the fuel pump(s).

In emission-controlled engines with thermal reactors (or, later, catalytic converters), the ignition must under no circumstances be switched off and the fuel feed must be continued, as combustion could otherwise take place in the exhaust system, which could cause overheating and destroy the thermal reactor.

Transmission

The clutch plate of the 911 SC was fitted with a rubber damper system that was developed by Porsche to cure gear noise at low engine revs. This allowed for up to 28° angular movement, while the Turbo 3.3's rotational damper permitted up to

34° angular rotation. Rotational vibrations of the engine, when starting and at idle speed, cause natural resonance of the drivetrain, especially if the driver pulls away at low revs. The new damper in all six-cylinder cars helped to dampen the vibrations considerably and cut annoying rattles in the transmission almost completely. The manual transmission of the Turbo 3.3 (type 930/34) was fitted with a longer fourth gear to match the increase in power.

Suspension

The 911 SC was fitted with 20mm anti-roll bars at the front and 18mm at the rear. It had a brake servo as well as die-cast 6Jx15 wheels front and 7Jx15 rear. Tyres were 185/70 VR 15 front, 215/60 VR 15 rear; 16in wheels and tyres were an optional extra for the 911 SC. The Turbo 3.3 was equipped with a completely new brake system: wide, internally vented brake discs with perforated friction surfaces front and rear. The four-piston light-alloy fixed brake callipers were developed by Porsche itself and were derived from the 917 race car. The brake servo was adjusted to the new system. Forged 9Jx16 wheels at the rear were factory-approved.

In braking terms, Porsche was once again at the cutting edge due to its vast racing experience. A new brake system that had proved itself in long-distance racing at Le Mans and the Nürburgring was developed for the Turbo 3.3, which now had a top speed of 161mph (260kmh) and weighed 1,680kg. The brake callipers carried the name of the developer, Porsche, for the first time.

Body

For all vehicles, rear quarter-lights were now fixed in place. The front and rear spoilers were of a different shape for the Turbo 3.3 and the engine lid was made from steel, while the rear spoiler was partly made from plastic.

Equipment and fittings

Modified instruments were fitted to all cars, with revised calibration. The rev counter bore markings only up to 7,000rpm. In the Turbo 3.3 only, the speedometer read up to 300kmh and the turbo boost pressure gauge was improved.

Model range	Total production
911 SC Coupé	2438 + 2740 USA
911 SC Targa	1729 + 2609 USA
911 Turbo Coupé	735 + 522 USA

Model range	911 SC	911 Turbo
Engine		
Engine type, Manual transmission	930/03	930/60
Bore (mm)	95	97
Stroke (mm)	70.4	74.4
Displacement (cc)	2994	3299
Compression ratio	8.5:1	7.0:1
Engine output (kW/hp)	132/180	221/300
at revolutions per minute (rpm)	5500	5500
Torque (Nm)	265	412
at revolutions per minute (rpm)	4200	4000
Output per litre (kW/l)	50	67
Max. engine speed (rpm)	7000	7000
Engine weight (kg)	200	230

Carburation, ignition, settings		
Fuel system	K-Jetronic	K-Jetronic
Type of fuel (RON)	91	98
Ignition system	BHKZ	BHKZ breakerless
Spark plugs		
Bosch	W225T30	W280P21
Beru	225/14/3	225/14/3A
Spark plug gap (mm)	0.8	0.8
Idle speed (rpm)	850–950	950–1050
Exhaust/purification system	SLE+ZLP	SLE+ZLP
CO-content (%)	2.0–2.4	2.0–4.0
Fuel consumption acc. DIN 70 030. (litres/100km)		
A. at a constant 90kmh	9.2	8.1
B. at a constant 120kmh	11.4	15.3
C. EC urban cycle	17.3	20.0

Key:
BHKZ Battery, capacitive-discharge ignition system (CDI)
SLE Secondary-air injection, ZLP = Auxiliary air pump

Transmission		
Clutch, pressure plate	G MFZ 225	G MFZ 240
Clutch plate (mm)	TD 225	GUD 240
Manual transmission	915/62	930/34
Gear ratios		
1st gear	3.181	2.250
2nd gear	1.833	1.304
3rd gear	1.261	0.893
4th gear	1.000	0.625
5th gear	0.785	–
Reverse gear	3.325	2.437
Synchromesh system gears 1–5	POSY	POSY
Final drive	3.875	4.222
Limited-slip differential	Option	Option
Lock-up factor under load/coasting (%)	40/40	40/40
Sportomatic	925/16	–
Torque converter dia. (mm)	F&S 190	–
Stall speed (rpm)	1900	–
Gear ratios		
1st gear	2.400	–
2nd gear	1.428	–
3rd gear	0.926	–
4th gear	–	–
Reverse gear	1.81	–
Synchromesh system forward gears	POSY	–
Final drive	3.375	–

Key:
S Standard
F&S Manufacturer Fichtel & Sachs
POSY Porsche Locking synchromesh system, synchroniser rings, mo-coated

Model range	911 SC	911 Turbo
Suspension, steering and brakes		
Front axle		
Anti-roll bar dia. (mm)	20	20
Steering ratio	17.87	17.87
Turning circle dia. (m)	10.95	10.95
Rear axle		
Anti-roll bar dia.		
manual transmission (mm)	18	18
Brake system		
Brake booster dia. (inch)	7	8
Brake master cylinder dia. (mm)	20.64	23.81
Brake calliper piston diameter		
front (mm)	48	38+38
rear (mm)	38	30+30
Brake disc diameter		
front (mm)	282.5	304
rear (mm)	290	309
Brake disc thickness		
front (mm)	20.5	32
rear (mm)	20	28
Effective brake disc area (cm²)	257	376
Handbrake	Operating mechanically on both rear wheels	
Brake drum diameter (mm)	180	=
Contact area (cm²)	170	=

Wheels and tyres		
Standard tyre specification, front	185/70VR15	205/55VR16
wheel	6J x 15	7J x 16
Standard tyre specification, rear	215/60VR15	225/50VR16
wheel	7J x 15	8J x 16
Space-saver spare wheel	165-15 89P	=
Tyre pressure		
front (bar)	2.0	2.0
rear (bar)	2.4	3.0
Space-saver spare wheel (bar)	2.2	2.2

Body and interior (dimensions at kerb weight)		
Length (mm)	4291	4291
Width (mm)	1652	1775
Height (mm)	1320	1310
Wheelbase (mm)	2272	2272
Track		
front (mm)	1369 (1361)*	1432
rear (mm)	1379 (1367)*	1501
Ground clearance at permissible gross weight (mm)	120	120

* figures for the USA in brackets

Model range	911 SC	911 Turbo
Electrical system		
Generator output (W/A)	980/70	=
Battery (V/Ah)	12/66	=

Weight according to DIN 70020		
Kerb weight (kg)	1160	1300
Permissible gross weight (kg)	1500	1680
Permissible trailer weight		
unbraked (kg)	480	none
braked (kg)	800	none

Performance		
Maximum speed (kmh)		
Manual transmission	225	260
Acceleration 0–62mph/100 kmh (sec)		
Manual transmission	7.0	5.4
Measured kilometre from standing start (sec)		
Manual transmission	27.5	24.0

Fluid capacities		
Engine oil quantity 1* (l)	13	=
Engine oil quantity with SPM (l)	+ 2	–
Oil change quantity 1* (l)	10	=
Manual transmission 2* (l)	3.0	3.7
Sportomatic 2* (l)	2.5	–
Fuel tank (l)	80	80
Brake fluid reservoir 3* (l)	0.20	0.20

* Key to numerals
1* Approved API SE/SF with combinations API SE/CC - SF/CC - SF/CD - SE/CD
  Multigrade engine oil factory recommended (SAE 10 W/50 or 15 W/40 or 20 W/50).
  Single-grade engine oils were also permissible. Summer SAE 30. Winter SAE 20.
2* Single-grade transmission fluid SAE 90 acc. MIL-L 2105 B and API-classified GL 5
3* Use only brake fluid acc. SAE J 1703. DOT 3 or 4

Key:
SPM   = Sportomatic

Chassis numbers (ten digits)					
Car	Model year	Engine	Body	Sequence	Summary
911	8	2	0	0001–9999	USA+California Coupé 911 SC
911	8	2	1	0001–9999	USA+California Targa 911 SC
911	8	3	0	0001–9500	Rest of world 911 SC Coupé
911	8	3	1	0001–9500	Rest of world 911 SC Targa
911	8	3	0	9501–9999	Japan 911 SC Coupé
911	8	6	1	0501–9999	Japan 911 SC Targa
930	8	7	0	0001–1000	Rest of world 911 Turbo
930	8	8	0	9501–9999	Japan 911 Turbo
930	8	8	8	0001–1000	USA+California 911 Turbo

Car: 911 = all 911; 930 = 911 Turbo
Model year: 8 = 1978. 7 = 1977
Engine: 2 = 911 S USA; 3 = 911 S RoW; 7 = 911 Turbo RoW; 8 = 911 Turbo USA
Body: 0 = Coupé; 1 = Targa

Model year 1979
L Series

Porsche 911 SC Coupé and Targa
Porsche 911 Turbo 3.3 Coupé

There were no notable changes to the 911 series during the 1979 model year.

Suspension
Fixed-calliper brake system.

Body
The 911 Turbo 3.3 had tinted glass all round.

Equipment and fittings
Floor covering: short-pile carpeting.

Heating and air conditioning
Automatic control of warm air.

Electrical system
The standard radio in the 911 Turbo was deleted.

Model range	Total production
911 SC Coupé	5333
911 SC Targa	3607
911 Turbo Coupé	820 + 1232 USA

Model range	911 SC	911 Turbo
Engine		
Engine type, manual transmission	930/03	930/60
Bore (mm)	95	97
Stroke (mm)	70.4	74.4
Displacement (cc)	2994	3299
Compression ratio	8.5:1	7.0:1
Engine output (kW/hp)	132/180	221/300
at revolutions per minute (rpm)	5500	5500
Torque (Nm)	265	412
at revolutions per minute (rpm)	4200	4000
Output per litre (kW/l)	50	67
Max. engine speed (rpm)	7000	7000
Engine weight (kg)	200	230

Carburation, ignition, settings		
Fuel system	K-Jetronic	K-Jetronic
Type of fuel (RON)	91	98
Ignition system	BHKZ	BHKZ breakerless
Spark plugs		
Bosch	W225T30	W280P21
Beru	225/14/3	225/14/3A
Spark plug gap (mm)	0.8	0.8
Idle speed (rpm)	850–950	950–1050
Exhaust system	SLE+ZLP	SLE+ZLP
CO-content (%)	2.0–2.4	2.0–4.0
Fuel consumption acc. DIN 70 030. (litres/100km)		
A. at a constant 90kmh	9.2	8.1
B. at a constant 120kmh	11.4	15.3
C. EC urban cycle	17.3	20.0

Key:
BHKZ   Battery, capacitive-discharge ignition system (CDI)
SLE   Secondary-air injection, ZLP = Auxiliary air pump

A 1979-model 911 Turbo 3.3 Coupé. This view clearly shows the flared front and rear wheel arches unique to the Turbo.

Model range	911 SC	911 Turbo
Transmission		
Clutch, pressure plate	G MFZ 225	G MFZ 240
Clutch plate (mm)	TD 225	GUD 240
Manual transmission	915/62	930/34
Gear ratios		
1st gear	3.181	2.250
2nd gear	1.833	1.304
3rd gear	1.261	0.893
4th gear	1.000	0.625
5th gear	0.785	–
Reverse gear	3.325	2.437
Synchromesh system gears 1–5	POSY	POSY
Final drive	3.875	4.222
Limited-slip differential	Option	Option
Lock-up factor under load/ coasting (%)	40/40	40/40
Sportomatic	925/16	–
Torque converter dia. (mm)	F&S 190	–
Stall speed (rpm)	1900	–
Gear ratios		
1st gear	2.400	–
2nd gear	1.428	–
3rd gear	0.926	–
4th gear	–	–
Reverse gear	1.81	–
Synchromesh system forward gears	POSY	–
Final drive	3.375	–

Key:
S   Standard
F&S Manufacturer Fichtel & Sachs
POSY Porsche Locking synchromesh system, synchroniser rings, mo-coated

ABOVE: A technician in the process of fitting the ancillaries to a USA-spec 911 Turbo engine on the production line in 1979.

OPPOSITE: The interior of a 1979-model 911 Turbo 3.3 Coupé. Note the blanking plate to the right of the steering wheel where the standard radio was previously fitted.

Model range	911 SC	911 Turbo
Suspension, steering and brakes		
Front axle		
Anti-roll bar dia. (mm)	20	20
Steering ratio	17.87	17.87
Turning circle dia. (m)	10.95	10.95
Rear axle		
Anti-roll bar dia. (mm)	18	18
Brake system		
Brake booster dia. (inch)	7	8
Brake master cylinder dia. (mm)	20.64	23.81
Brake calliper piston diameter		
front (mm)	48	38+38
rear (mm)	38	30+30
Brake disc diameter		
front (mm)	282.5	304
rear (mm)	290	309
Brake disc thickness		
front (mm)	20.5	32
rear (mm)	20	28
Effective brake disc area (cm²)	257	376
Handbrake	Operating mechanically on both rear wheels	
Brake drum diameter (mm)	180	=
Contact area (cm²)	170	=

Model range	911 SC	911 Turbo
Wheels and tyres		
Standard tyre specification, front	185/70VR15	205/55VR16
wheel	6J x 15	7J x 16
Standard tyre specification, rear	215/60VR15	225/50VR16
wheel	7J x 15	8J x 16
Space-saver spare wheel	165-15 89P	=
Tyre pressure		
front (bar)	2.0	2.0
rear (bar)	2.4	3.0
Space-saver		
spare wheel (bar)	2.2	2.2

Body and interior (dimensions at kerb weight)		
Length (mm)	4291	4291
Width (mm)	1652	1775
Height (mm)	1320	1310
Wheelbase (mm)	2272	2272
Track		
front (mm)	1369 (1361)*	1432
rear (mm)	1379 (1367)*	1501
Ground clearance at permissible gross weight (mm)	120	120

* Figures for the USA in brackets

Electrical system		
Generator output (W/A)	980/70	=
Battery (V/Ah)	12/66	=

Model range	911 SC	911 Turbo
Weight according to DIN 70020		
Kerb weight (kg)	1160	1300
Permissible gross weight (kg)	1500	1680
Permissible trailer weight		
unbraked (kg)	480	none
braked (kg)	800	none

Performance		
Maximum speed (kmh)		
Manual transmission	225	260
Acceleration 0–62mph/100kmh (sec)		
Manual transmission	7.0	5.4
Measured kilometre from standing start (sec)		
Manual transmission	27.5	24.0

Fluid capacities		
Engine oil quantity 1* (l)	13	=
Engine oil quantity with SPM (l)	+ 2	–
Oil change quantity 1* (l)	10	=
Manual transmission 2* (l)	3.0	3.7
Sportomatic 2* (l)	2.5	–
Fuel tank (l)	80	80
Brake fluid reservoir 3* (l)	0.20	0.20

* Key to numerals

1* Approved API SE/SF with combinations API SE/CC - SF/CC - SF/CD - SE/CD Multigrade engine oil factory recommended (SAE 10 W/50 or 15 W/40 or 20 W/50).

2* Single-grade transmission fluid SAE 90 acc. MIL-L 2105 B and API-classified GL 5

3* Use only brake fluid acc. SAE J 1703. DOT 3 or 4

Key: SPM Sportomatic

Chassis numbers (ten digits)					
Car	**Model year**	**Engine**	**Body**	**Sequence**	**Summary**
911	9	2	0	0001–9999	USA+California Coupé 911 SC
911	9	2	1	0001–9999	USA+California Targa 911 SC
911	9	3	0	0001–9500	Rest of world 911 SC Coupé
911	9	3	1	0001–9500	Rest of world 911 SC Targa
911	9	3	0	9501–9999	Japan 911 SC Coupé
911	9	3	1	9501–9999	Japan 911 SC Targa
930	9	7	0	0001–1000	Rest of world 911 Turbo
930	9	8	0	9501–9999	Japan 911 Turbo
930	9	8	8	0001–1000	USA+California 911 Turbo

Car: 911 = all 911; 930 = 911 Turbo
Model year: 9 = 1979. 8 = 1978
Engine: 2 = 911 SC USA; 3 = 911 SC RoW; 7 = 911 Turbo RoW; 8 = 911 Turbo USA
Body: 0 = Coupé; 1 = Targa

Model year 1980

A Programme, lambda sensor for the USA

Porsche 911 SC Coupé and Targa
Porsche 911 Turbo 3.3 Coupé

This year saw an increase in performance for the 911 SC to 138kW (188hp), except in the USA and Japan where power was strangled a little by the introduction of a lambda sensor and catalytic converter for the first time. The 911 Turbo 3.3 received a dual-branch exhaust system as standard.

Engine

Modifications to the SC engine: larger cooling fan from the Turbo engine and improved oil scavenging in the crankcase, and for non-USA/Japan models a higher 8.6:1 compression ratio, offering more power and lower fuel consumption. Modifications to the SC and Turbo engines: the valve cover at the bottom was ribbed, and valve cover gaskets were improved. New front-mounted oil cooler. There were now three different 911 SC engines for distinct markets.

Motor	Type	Displacement (cc)	Compression	Octane rating (RON)	Performance (hp/kW)	Torque (Nm)	Notes
911 SC	930/07	2,994	9.3:1	91*	132/180	245	For USA and Canada
911 SC	930/08	2,994	9.3:1	91*	132/180	245	For Japan
911 SC	930/09	2,994	9.3:1	91	138/188	265	For RoW

* Unleaded petrol with minimum 91 RON octane rating absolutely essential
RoW = Rest of world excluding USA, Canada and Japan

Measures to control exhaust emissions:
930/07 (USA and Canada) secondary air injection + exhaust catalytic converter + lambda sensor
930/08 (Japan)   secondary air injection + exhaust catalytic converter + lambda sensor
930/09 (RoW)   secondary air injection
RoW = Rest of world excluding USA, Canada and Japan

The 1980-model 911 SC 3.0 Coupé was fitted with an uprated engine, now producing 138kW (188hp).

Fuel and ignition system

In 1980 Porsche built its first engines with G-Kat lambda sensors, the 930/07 and 930/08. Lambda sensors, the development of which was finalised by Bosch, measured the residual oxygen in exhaust gases. The lambda signals were converted in the control unit and sent as a clocked pulse to the fuel injection system, which either reduced the injected fuel quantity (made the mixture leaner) or enriched it (made the mixture richer).

In order to use the signals of the lambda sensors to improve exhaust emission control, the following additional components were fitted: timing/stroke valve at the distributor, throttle-valve switch, temperature sensor at the engine housing, and a control unit. The 911 Turbo 3.3 was fitted with a dual-branch exhaust system.

Equipment and fittings

Three-spoke steering wheel for the 911 SC, centre console and electric windows for all models. Speedometers of all six-cylinder cars were arranged differently, with calibrations every 20kmh.

Interior fittings

All Porsche models were fitted with standardised safety belts.

A 911 SC 3.0 Targa. The 1980 911 SC models featured various engine modifications, primarily to improve exhaust emissions.

Heating and air conditioning

Nippondenso air conditioning.

Electrical system

An alarm system was available on request that needed to be activated before the driver's door was shut. All cars had an illuminated engine compartment.

Additional information

In 1980 European and US legislative measures necessitated a change in the numbering of chassis. The aim of this international standardisation was to ensure that vehicles were marked in such a way that they could be identified over a period of 30 years. A 17-digit chassis number was devised from which the following could be determined: manufacturer, country/town of manufacture, vehicle type, vehicle specification, and year of manufacture. Up until the adoption of this worldwide standardisation, model year 1980 is seen as representing an interim solution with a ten-digit chassis number.

Model range	Total production
911 SC Coupé	5010
911 SC Targa	3603
911 Turbo Coupé	840

The rear seat cushions of a 911 SC 3.0 Targa folded down to provide useful luggage space.

Model range	911 SC	911 Turbo
Engine		
Engine type, Manual transmission	930/09	930/60
Bore (mm)	95	97
Stroke (mm)	70.4	74.4
Displacement (cc)	2994	3299
Compression ratio	8.6:1	7.0:1
Engine output (kW/hp)	138/188	221/300
at revolutions per minute (rpm)	5500	5500
Torque (Nm)	265	412
at revolutions per minute (rpm)	4200	4000
Output per litre (kW/l)	50	67
Max. engine speed (rpm)	6500	7000
Engine weight (kg)	190	230

Carburation, ignition, settings		
Fuel system	K-Jetronic	K-Jetronic
Type of fuel (RON)	91	98
Ignition system	BHKZ	BHKZ breakerless
Spark plugs		
Bosch	W260T2	W280P21
Beru	260/14/3	225/14/3A
Spark plug gap (mm)	0.8	0.8
Idle speed (rpm)	850–950	950–1050
Exhaust/purification system	SLE+ZLP	SLE+ZLP
CO-content (%)	2.0–2.4	2.0–4.0
Fuel consumption acc. DIN 70 030 (litres/100km)		
A. at a constant 90 kmh	9.2	8.1
B. at a constant 120 kmh	11.4	15.3
C. EC urban cycle	17.3	20.0

Key:
BHKZ Battery, capacitive-discharge ignition system (CDI)
SLE Secondary-air injection, ZLP = Auxiliary air pump

Model range	911 SC	911 Turbo
Transmission		
Clutch, pressure plate	G MFZ 225	G MFZ 240
Clutch plate (mm)	TD 225	GUD 240
Manual transmission	915/62	930/34
Gear ratios		
1st gear	3.181	2.250
2nd gear	1.833	1.304
3rd gear	1.261	0.893
4th gear	1.000	0.625
5th gear	0.785	–
Reverse gear	3.325	2.437
Synchromesh system gears 1–5	POSY	POSY
Final drive	3.875	4.222
Limited-slip differential	Option	Option
Lock-up factor under load/coasting (%)	40/40	40/40
Sportomatic	925/16	–
Torque converter dia. (mm)	F&S 190	–
Stall speed (rpm)	1900	–
Gear ratios		
1st gear	2.400	–
2nd gear	1.428	–
3rd gear	0.926	–
4th gear	–	–
Reverse gear	1.81	–
Synchromesh system forward gears	POSY	–
Final drive	3.375	–

Key:
S Standard
F&S Manufacturer Fichtel & Sachs
POSY Porsche Locking synchromesh system, synchroniser rings, mo-coated
BHKZ Battery, capacitive-discharge ignition system (CDI)

Model range	911 SC	911 Turbo
Suspension, steering and brakes		
Front axle		
Anti-roll bar dia. (mm)	20	20
Steering ratio	17.87	17.87
Turning circle dia. (m)	10.95	10.95
Rear axle		
Anti-roll bar dia. (mm)	18	18
Brake system		
Brake booster dia. (inch)	7	8
Brake master cylinder dia. (mm)	20.64	23.81
Brake calliper piston diameter		
front (mm)	48	38+38
rear (mm)	38	30+30
Brake disc diameter		
front (mm)	282.5	304
rear (mm)	290	309
Brake disc thickness		
front (mm)	20.5	32
rear (mm)	20	28
Effective brake disc area (cm²)	257	376
Handbrake	Operating mechanically on both rear wheels	
Brake drum diameter (mm)	180	=
Contact area (cm²)	170	=

Wheels and tyres		
Standard tyre specification, front	185/70VR15	205/55VR16
wheel	6J x 15	7J x 16
Standard tyre specification, rear	215/60VR15	225/50VR16
wheel	7J x 15	8J x 16
Space-saver spare wheel	165-15 89P	=
Tyre pressure		
front (bar)	2.0	2.0
rear (bar)	2.4	3.0
Space-saver spare wheel (bar)	2.2	2.2

Body and interior (dimensions at kerb weight)		
Length (mm)	4291	4291
Width (mm)	1652	1775
Height (mm)	1320	1310
Wheelbase (mm)	2272	2272
Track		
front (mm)	1369	1432
rear (mm)	1379	1501
Ground clearance at permissible gross weight (mm)	120	120

Model range	911 SC	911 Turbo
Electrical system		
Generator output (W/A)	990/70	=
Battery (V/Ah)	12/66	=

Weight according to DIN 70020		
Kerb weight (kg)	1160	1300
Permissible gross weight (kg)	1500	1680
Permissible trailer weight		
unbraked (kg)	480	none
braked (kg)	800	none

Performance		
Maximum speed (kmh)		
Manual transmission	225	260
Acceleration 0–62mph/100kmh (sec)		
Manual transmission	7.0	5.4
Measured kilometre from standing start (sec)		
Manual transmission	27.5	24.0

Fluid capacities		
Engine oil quantity 1* (l)	13	=
Engine oil quantity with SPM (l)	+ 2	–
Oil change quantity 1* (l)	10	=
Manual transmission 2* (l)	3.0	3.7
Sportomatic 2* (l)	2.5	–
Fuel tank (l)	80	80
Brake fluid reservoir 3* (l)	0.20	0.20

* Key to numerals

1* Approved API SE/SF with combinations API SE/CC - SF/CC -
SF/CD - SE/CD
Multigrade engine oil factory recommended (SAE 10 W/50 or
15 W/40 or 20 W/50).

2* Single-grade transmission fluid SAE 90 acc. MIL-L 2105 B and
API-classified GL 5

3* Use only brake fluid acc. SAE J 1703. DOT 3 or 4

Key:
SPM Sportomatic

Note:

In 1980 EU-legislative and USA-legislative measures necessitated a
change in the numbering of chassis.

The aim of this international standardisation was that vehicles needed
to be marked in such a way that they could be identified over a period
of 30 years. A seventeen-digit chassis number was devised from which
the following could be determined: manufacturer, country/town of
manufacture, vehicle type, vehicle specification and year of manufacture.

Up until the adoption of the worldwide standardisation, model year
1980 was seen as the interim solution with a ten-digit chassis number.

Chassis numbers (ten digits)						
Car	Model year	Manufacturer	Type	Engine design	Sequence	Summary
91	A	0	1	3	0001–9999	Rest of world+Japan Coupé 911 SC
91	A	0	1	3	0001–9999	Rest of world+Japan Targa 911 SC
91	A	0	1	4	0001–5000	USA 911 SC Coupé
91	A	0	1	4	5001–9999	USA 911 SC Targa
93	A	0	0	7	0001–1000	Rest of world+Japan 911 Targa

Car: 91 = all 911; 93 = 911 Turbo
Model year: A = 1980
Type: 1 = 911; 8 = 928; 0 = 911 Turbo
Engine design: 3 = RoW; 4 = USA; 7 = 911 Turbo

Model year 1981

B Programme, SC breaks the 200hp barrier

Porsche 911 SC Coupé and Targa
Porsche 911 Turbo 3.3 Coupé

There were no important changes for the 911 Turbo 3.3 this year but a further power increase arrived for the 911 SC: its engine now developed 150kW (204hp). Porsche extended its rust-proofing warranty to seven years, applying to the entire body. Sportomatic transmission was finally withdrawn after a long period of declining popularity.

Engine

Porsche's naturally aspirated engines for markets without unleaded petrol were reworked. 150kW (204hp) was achieved through increased compression ratios, altered valve timing, and the use of premium-rated petrol with 98RON. These changes also reduced fuel consumption as a side effect. Engines destined for the USA, Canada and Japan received new type designations (930/16 and 930/17), but their technical features and performance data did not change. Since premium-rated petrol was now available in almost all markets, Porsche did everything possible to increase the power of its engines.

A 1981-model 911 SC 3.0 Targa, now featuring the 930/10 engine, developing 150kW (204hp) at 5,900rpm.

Fuel and ignition system

The power increase for the 930/10 engine was achieved through a compression ratio increase to 9.8:1, as well as modified camshaft valve timing and altered ignition timing.

Transmission

Due to production problems with the rubber-damped clutch plates for the 911 SC, Porsche went back to using steel spring dampers for the naturally aspirated engine. The 911 Turbo 3.3 kept its rubber-damped clutch plate with a large torsional area. Sportomatic transmission was now no longer available.

Body

The entire steel body was now hot-dip galvanised on both sides, and the long-term warranty against rust perforation was extended to seven years – Porsche was the first car manufacturer in the world to offer such a long anti-rust warranty for the entire body. Galvanisation surely helped the statistic that 70% of all the Porsches ever manufactured are still on the road. One further small change was side-mounted indicators for all cars.

Equipment and fittings

Illuminated pull knobs.

Interior fittings

New sports seats were available as an optional extra, while seats could also be ordered in 'Berber' cloth.

Model range	Total production
911 SC Coupé	3181 + 1694 USA
911 SC Targa	1703 + 1417 USA
911 Turbo Coupé	698 + 63 CDN

Model range	911 SC	911 Turbo
Engine		
Engine type, Manual transmission	930/10	930/66
Bore (mm)	95	97
Stroke (mm)	70.4	74.4
Displacement (cc)	2994	3299
Compression ratio	9.8:1	7.0:1
Engine output (kW/hp)	150/204	221/300
at revolutions per minute (rpm)	5900	5500
Torque (Nm)	267	412
at revolutions per minute (rpm)	4300	4000
Output per litre (kW/l)	50.0	67
Max. engine speed (rpm)	6800	7000
Engine weight (kg)	190	245

Carburation, ignition, settings		
Fuel system	K-Jetronic	K-Jetronic
Type of fuel (RON)	91	98
Ignition system	BHKZ	BHKZ breakerless
Spark plugs		
Bosch	WR 4 C1	W 3 DP
Beru	14/4 C1	–
Spark plug gap (mm)	0.8	0.8
Idle speed (rpm)	800–950	900+-50
Exhaust/purification system	SLE+ZLP	SLE+ZLP
CO-content (%)	1.0–2.0	1.5–2.5
Fuel consumption acc. EC Standard, (litres/100km)		
A. at a constant 90kmh	9.2	8.1
B. at a constant 120kmh	11.4	15.3
C. EC urban cycle	17.3	20.0

Key:
BHKZ Battery, capacitive-discharge ignition system (CDI)
SLE Secondary-air injection, ZLP = Auxiliary air pump

A 911 SC 3.0-litre engine undergoing final assembly on the production line.

Always a stunning look – a 1981-model 911 Turbo 3.3 Coupé fitted with 16in Fuchs wheel rims.

Model range	911 SC	911 Turbo
Transmission		
Clutch, pressure plate	G MFZ 225	G MFZ 240
Clutch plate (mm)	TD 225	GUD 240
Manual transmission	915/62	930/34
Gear ratios		
1st gear	3.181	2.250
2nd gear	1.833	1.304
3rd gear	1.261	0.893
4th gear	1.000	0.625
5th gear	0.785	–
Reverse gear	3.325	2.437
Synchromesh system gears 1–5	POSY	POSY
Final drive	3.875	4.222
Limited-slip differential	Option	Option
Lock-up factor under load/ coasting (%)	40/40	40/40

Key:
S   Standard
POSY   Porsche Locking synchromesh system, synchroniser rings, mo-coated

Suspension, steering and brakes		
Front axle		
Anti-roll bar dia. (mm)	20	20
Steering ratio	17.87	17.87
Turning circle dia. (m)	10.95	10.95
Rear axle		
Anti-roll bar dia. (mm)	18	18
Brake system		
Brake booster dia. (inch)	7	8
Brake master cylinder dia. (mm)	20.64	23.81
Brake calliper piston diameter		
front (mm)	48	38+38
rear (mm)	38	30+30
Brake disc diameter		
front (mm)	282.5	304
rear (mm)	290	309
Brake disc thickness		
front (mm)	24	32
rear (mm)	24	28
Effective brake disc area (cm²)	257	376
Handbrake	Operating mechanically on both rear wheels	
Brake drum diameter (mm)	180	=
Contact area (cm²)	170	=

Model range	911 SC	911 Turbo
Wheels and tyres		
Standard tyre specification, front	185/70VR15	205/55VR16
wheel	6J x 15	7J x 16
Standard tyre specification, rear	215/60VR15	225/50VR16
wheel	7J x 15	8J x 16
Space-saver spare wheel	165-15 89P	=
Tyre pressure		
front (bar)	2.0	2.0
rear (bar)	2.4	3.0
Space-saver spare wheel (bar)	2.2	2.2

Body and interior (dimensions at kerb weight)		
Length (mm)	4291	4291
Width (mm)	1652	1775
Height (mm)	1320	1310
Wheelbase (mm)	2272	2272
Track		
front (mm)	1369	1432
rear (mm)	1379	1501
Ground clearance at permissible gross weight (mm)	120	120

Electrical system		
Generator output (W/A)	990/70	=
Battery (V/Ah)	12/66	=

Weight according to DIN 70020		
Kerb weight (kg)	1160	1300
Permissible gross weight (kg)	1500	1680
Permissible trailer weight		
unbraked (kg)	480	none
braked (kg)	800	none

Performance		
Maximum speed (kmh)		
Manual transmission	235	260
Acceleration 0–62mph/100kmh (sec)		
Manual transmission	6.8	5.4
Measured kilometre from standing start (sec)		
Manual transmission	26.8	24.0

Fluid capacities		
Engine oil quantity 1* (l)	13	=
Oil change quantity 1* (l)	10	=
Manual transmission 2* (l)	3.0	3.7
Fuel tank (l)	80	80
Brake fluid reservoir 3* (l)	0.20	0.20

* Key to numerals
1* Approved API SE/SF with combinations API SE/CC - SF/CC - SF/CD - SE/CD Multigrade engine oil factory recommended.
2* Single-grade transmission fluid SAE 90 acc. MIL-L 2105 B and API-classified GL 5
3* Use only brake fluid acc. SAE J 1703. DOT 3 or 4

Note:
As from model year 1981 all cars were issued with an internationally uniform 17-digit chassis number.

Chassis numbers (17 digits)											
World manufacturer code	Code body USA (A=Coupé, B=Targa, C=Cabriolet)	Code for engine variants (only USA)	Restraint system (0 = belt, 2 = airbag) only USA	First and second digit for car type	Fill character/check digit	Model year (B = 1981, C= 1982, etc.)	Manufacturing site (S = Stuttgart)	7th and 8th digit = car type	Code for body + engine	Sequence number	Summary
WPO	Z	Z	Z	91	Z	B	S	1	0	0001–5000	Rest of world, SC Coupé
WPO	Z	Z	Z	91	Z	B	S	1	2	9501–9999	Japan, SC Coupé
WPO	Z	Z	Z	91	Z	B	S	1	4	0001–5000	Rest of world, SC Targa
WPO	Z	Z	Z	91	Z	B	S	1	6	9501–9999	Japan, SC Targa
WPO	A	A	O	91	C*	B	S	1	2	0001–5000	USA/CDN, SC Coupé
WPO	E	A	O	91	C*	B	S	1	6	0001–5000	USA/CDN, SC Targa
WPO	Z	Z	Z	93	Z	B	S	0	0	0001–2000	Rest of world, 911 Turbo
WPO	J	A	O	93	-	B	S	0	5	0001–2000	CDN, 911 Turbo

C* = Check digit, can be 0–9 or X (only USA)   Z = Fill character for rest of world cars

Model year 1982
C Programme

Porsche 911 SC Coupé and Targa
Porsche 911 Turbo 3.3 Coupé

There were only slight changes in model year 1982. Porsche introduced a special model (200 cars) in time for its '50 Years of Porsche' anniversary. This was painted Meteor metallic grey with a luxury interior in a combination of burgundy leather and cloth.

Fuel and ignition system
No changes to the naturally aspirated engine. The Turbo 3.3 was fitted with an improved induction and ignition system. At a constant 120kmh (75mph), fuel consumption reduced considerably, from 15.3 litres per 100km (18.4mpg) to 11.8 (23.9mpg).

Transmission
The 911 SC received a reinforced differential.

Suspension
The 911 SC was fitted with die-cast wheels that now had bright rim flanges and black-painted centres.

Body
The 911 SC's optional 'whale-tail' rear spoiler now closely resembled that of the 911 Turbo. The Turbo

The 911 SC braking system featured ventilated front discs and twin-piston callipers, whereas the Turbo used four-piston alloy callipers.

became available with a special-order conversion at Zuffenhausen of a 'Flat-Nose' or 'Slant-Nose' front-end treatment inspired by Porsche's 935 racer. The

A 1982-model 911 SC 3.0 Coupé, featuring die-cast wheels with bright rim flanges and black-painted centres.

first examples had their headlamps in the front air dam but pop-up units were soon adopted.

Equipment and fittings

The oil temperature gauge was revised, with different calibration: the white area started at approximately 20°C and finished at 60°C, with two markings at 90°C and 120°C.

Interior fittings

Special children's seats were offered for the back.

Heating and air conditioning

The side vents now connected to the hot-air system and delivered warm air to the side windows.

Electrical system

An A 14 N11 alternator with 1,050W was used for all six-cylinder engines.

Additional information

A new roof-carrier system could carry loads of up to 75kg and was available as an optional extra. A special version of the Turbo 3.3 with a performance increase of 65hp/47kW was manufactured for Group B racing.

Model range	Total production
911 SC Coupé	3307 + 3085 USA
911 SC Targa	1737 + 2488 USA
911 Turbo Coupé	938 + 89 CDN

Model range	911 SC	911 Turbo
Engine		
Engine type, Manual transmission	930/10	930/66
Bore (mm)	95	97
Stroke (mm)	70.4	74.4
Displacement (cc)	2994	3299
Compression ratio	9.8:1	7.0:1
Engine output (kW/hp)	150/204	221/300
at revolutions per minute (rpm)	5900	5500
Torque (Nm)	267	412
at revolutions per minute (rpm)	4300	4000
Output per litre (kW/l)	50	67
Max. engine speed (rpm)	7000	7000
Engine weight (kg)	190	245

Carburation, ignition, settings		
Fuel system	K-Jetronic	K-Jetronic
Type of fuel (RON)	91	98
Ignition system	BHKZ	BHKZ
Spark plugs		
Bosch	WR 4 C1	W 3 DP
Beru	14/4 C1	–
Spark plug gap (mm)	0.8	0.8
Idle speed (rpm)	800–950	900+-50
Exhaust/purification system	SLE+ZLP	SLE+ZLP
CO-content (%)	1.0–2.0	1.5–2.5
Fuel consumption acc. EC Standard, (litres/100km)		
A. at a constant 90kmh	8.0	9.7
B. at a constant 120kmh	9.7	11.8
C. EC urban cycle	13.4	15.5

Key:
BHKZ Battery, capacitive-discharge ignition system (CDI)
SLE Secondary-air injection, ZLP = Auxiliary air pump

Model range	911 SC	911 Turbo
Transmission		
Clutch, pressure plate	G MFZ 225	G MFZ 240
Clutch plate (mm)	TD 225	GUD 240
Manual transmission	915/62	930/34
Gear ratios		
1st gear	3.181	2.250
2nd gear	1.833	1.304
3rd gear	1.261	0.893
4th gear	1.000	0.625
5th gear	0.785	–
Reverse gear	3.325	2.437
Synchromesh system gears 1–5	POSY	POSY
Final drive	3.875	4.222
Limited-slip differential	Option	Option
Lock-up factor under load/ coasting (%)	40/40	40/40

Key:
S Standard
POSY Porsche Locking synchromesh system, synchroniser rings, mo-coated

Suspension, steering and brakes		
Front axle		
Anti-roll bar dia. (mm)	20	20
Steering ratio	17.87	17.87
Turning circle dia. (m)	10.95	10.95
Rear axle		
Anti-roll bar dia. (mm)	18	18
Brake system		
Brake booster dia. (inch)	7	8
Brake master cylinder dia. (mm)	20.64	23.81
Brake calliper piston diameter		
front (mm)	48	38+38
rear (mm)	38	30+30
Brake disc diameter		
front (mm)	282.5	304
rear (mm)	290	309
Brake disc thickness		
front (mm)	24	32
rear (mm)	24	28
Effective brake disc area (cm²)	257	376
Handbrake	Operating mechanically on both rear wheels	
Brake drum diameter (mm)	180	=
Contact area (cm²)	170	=

Wheels and tyres		
Standard tyre specification, front	185/70VR15	205/55VR16
wheel	6J x 15	7J x 16
Standard tyre specification, rear	215/60VR15	225/50VR16
wheel	7J x 15	8J x 16
Space-saver spare wheel	165-15 89P	=
Tyre pressure		
front (bar)	2.0	2.0
rear (bar)	2.4	3.0
Space-saver spare wheel (bar)	2.2	2.2

Body and interior (dimensions at kerb weight)		
Length (mm)	4291	4291
Width (mm)	1652	1775
Height (mm)	1320	1310
Wheelbase (mm)	2272	2272
Track		
front (mm)	1369	1432
rear (mm)	1379	1501
Ground clearance at permissible gross weight (mm)	120	120

Model range	911 SC	911 Turbo
Electrical system		
Generator output (W/A)	1050/75	=
Battery (V/Ah)	12/66	=

Weight according to DIN 70020		
Kerb weight (kg)	1160	1300
Permissible gross weight (kg)	1500	1680
Permissible trailer weight		
unbraked (kg)	480	none
braked (kg)	800	none

Performance		
Maximum speed (kmh)		
Manual transmission	235	260
Acceleration 0–62mph/100kmh (sec)		
Manual transmission	6.8	5.4
Measured kilometre from standing start (sec)		
Manual transmission	26.8	24.0

'Flat-nose' or 'Slant-nose' conversion first arrived for 1982. This is a later example with pop-up headlamps.

Model range	911 SC	911 Turbo
Fluid capacities		
Engine oil quantity 1* (l)	13	=
Oil change quantity 1* (l)	10	=
Manual transmission 2* (l)	3.0	3.7
Fuel tank (l)	80	80
Brake fluid reservoir 3* (l)	0.20	0.20

* Key to numerals
1* Approved API SE/SF with combinations API SE/CC - SF/CC - SF/CD - SE/CD Multigrade engine oil factory recommended.
2* Single-grade transmission fluid SAE 90 acc. MIL-L 2105 B and API-classified GL 5
3* Use only brake fluid acc. SAE J 1703. DOT 3 or 4

Chassis numbers (17 digits)

World manufacturer code	Code body USA (A=Coupé, B=Targa, C=Cabriolet)	Code for engine variants (only USA)	Restraint system (0 = belt, 2 = airbag) only USA	First and second digit for car type	Fill character/check digit	Model year (B = 1981, C = 1982, etc.)	Manufacturing site (S = Stuttgart)	7th and 8th digit = car type	Code for body + engine	Sequence number	Summary
WPO	Z	Z	Z	91	Z	C	S	1	0	0001–3307	Rest of world, SC Coupé
WPO	Z	Z	Z	91	Z	C	S	1	0	9501–9628	Japan, SC Coupé
WPO	Z	Z	Z	91	Z	C	S	1	4	0001–1737	Rest of world, SC Targa
WPO	Z	Z	Z	91	Z	C	S	1	4	9501–9562	Japan, SC Targa
WPO	A	A	0	91	C*	C	S	1	2	0001–2457	USA/CDN, SC Coupé
WPO	E	A	0	91	C*	C	S	1	6	0001–2426	USA/CDN, SC Targa
WPO	Z	Z	Z	93	Z	C	S	0	0	0001–0938	Rest of world, 911 Turbo
WPO	J	A	0	93	C*	C	S	0	5	0001–0089	CDN, 911 Turbo

C* = Check digit, can be 0–9 or X (only USA)
Z = Fill character for rest of world cars

Model year 1983
D Programme, the Cabriolet

Porsche 911 SC Coupé, Targa and Cabriolet
Porsche 911 Turbo 3.3 Coupé

1983 brought no significant changes to the engine or power train. However, regulatory requirements to reduce noise were becoming more and more stringent. Model approval became much more difficult in countries like Switzerland, which was an important market for Porsche. But there were also positives in 1983: after a break of almost 20 years Porsche started to build Cabriolets again. In the USA, safety laws that would have banned convertibles had been under development for years but these proposals were finally dropped,

In 1983, the long-awaited 911 SC 3.0 Cabriolet was introduced to complement the Targa.

allowing Porsche to introduce the 911 Cabriolet – its first fully open 911 – at the 1983 Geneva Motor Show.

Fuel and ignition system
The 911 SC was fitted with pre-silencers and, for Switzerland, special silencers. The Turbo 911 received a revised exhaust system with a modified main silencer. The turbo wastegate pipe no longer led to the main silencer but to the tailpipe and into the atmosphere, while the pipe had its own silencer. There were detail engineering changes for K-Jetronic and the ignition system on the 911 Turbo.

Transmission
For Swiss cars the 930/34 (911 Turbo) transmission had a longer second gear ratio (1.25:1 rather than 1.304:1) in order to pass local noise laws.

Suspension
6Jx16 front and 7Jx16 rear wheels were available for the 911 SC.

Body

The 911 SC was also produced as a Cabriolet. Porsche pursued a different route in developing the Cabriolet than the old Targa. The missing Targa roll bar reduced body rigidity, so Porsche had to engineer in extensive floorpan reinforcements.

The design of the Cabriolet's soft top was governed by safety criteria. As a result of many trials Porsche developed a roof system that featured new cross-member technology, with 50% of the roof consisting of shaped sheet steel. Through the extensive use of metal sections, it spread like a cage above the occupants when closed. This meant the roof kept its shape at high speeds and offered protection for the occupants in the event of an accident. Opening and closing the roof by hand took only a few seconds, and the flexible rear window could be opened via a zip. Cabriolet models were equipped with two electrically adjustable and heated exterior rear-view mirrors.

Interior fittings

Static safety belts at the rear. All Cabriolets were equipped with leather seats as standard.

Heating and air conditioning

The 911 Turbo had two additional electric heating fans to provide more warm air, especially useful during the engine's warm-up phase. The 911 SC received automatic heat control but the Cabriolet stuck with a manually controlled system because of its open-top status.

Electrical system

New generation of radios: Blaupunkt SQR 22 Köln with ARI (traffic information system) for Germany; Atlanta without ARI for the rest of world (excluding America); and Monterey for the USA. The SQR 22 name derived from S for search, Q for quartz tuning (digital tuning with station memory), R for

The Cabriolet roof, cleverly designed with shaped sheet steel panels, could be opened or closed manually in a few seconds.

Above: The 911 Turbo 3.3 Coupé underwent minor detail changes for 1983, including a modified turbo wastegate system.

Below: The 911 SC 3.0 Coupé remained virtually unchanged for 1983, the only significant modifications being to the exhaust system.

reverse (allowing the cassette deck to play tapes continuously), the first 2 for 20W output, and the second 2 for 1982, which was the year it was first sold.

Additional information

The number of service inspections up to 40,000km (24,000 miles) was reduced from five to three. The inspection points were also reduced by seven to a total of 16.

Model range	Total production
911 SC Coupé	2995 + 2704 USA
911 SC Targa	1258 + 1492 USA
911 SC Cabriolet	2406 + 1871 USA
911 Turbo Coupé	1015 + 65 CDN

Model range	911 SC	911 Turbo
Engine		
Engine type, Manual transmission	930/10	930/66
Bore (mm)	95	97
Stroke (mm)	70.4	74.4
Displacement (cc)	2994	3299
Compression ratio	9.8:1	7.0:1
Engine output (kW/hp)	150/204	221/300
at revolutions per minute (rpm)	5900	5500
Torque (Nm)	267	430
at revolutions per minute (rpm)	4300	4000
Output per litre (kW/l)	50	67
Max. engine speed (rpm)	7000	7200
Engine weight (kg)	190	230

Carburation, ignition, settings		
Fuel system	K-Jetronic	K-Jetronic
Type of fuel (RON)	98	98
Ignition system	BHKZ	BHKZ, breakerless
Spark plugs		
Bosch	WR 4 C1	W 3 DP
Beru	14/4 C1	–
Spark plug gap (mm)	0.8	0.8
Idle speed (rpm)	800–950	900+-50
Exhaust/purification system	SLE+ZLP	SLE+ZLP
CO-content (%)	1.0–1.5	1.5–2.5
Fuel consumption acc. DIN 70 030 (litres/100km)		
A. at a constant 90kmh	8.0	9.7
B. at a constant 120kmh	9.7	11.8
C. EC urban cycle	13.4	15.5

Key:
BHKZ   Battery, capacitive-discharge ignition system (CDI)
SLE   Secondary-air injection, ZLP = Auxiliary air pump

Model range	911 SC	911 Turbo
Transmission		
Clutch, pressure plate	G MFZ 225	G MFZ 240
Clutch plate (mm)	TD 225	GUD 240
Manual transmission	915/62	930/34
Gear ratios		
1st gear	3.181	2.250
2nd gear	1.833	1.304
3rd gear	1.261	0.893
4th gear	1.000	0.625
5th gear	0.785	–
Reverse gear	3.325	2.437
Synchromesh system gears 1–5	POSY	POSY
Final drive	3.875	4.222
Limited-slip differential	Option	Option
Lock-up factor under load/ coasting (%)	40/40	40/40
Gearbox weight with oil (kg)	60	70.2

Key:
S   Standard
POSY   Porsche Locking synchromesh system, synchroniser rings, mo-coated

Suspension, steering and brakes		
Front axle		
Anti-roll bar dia. (mm)	20	20
Steering ratio	17.87	17.87
Turning circle dia. (m)	10.95	10.95
Rear axle		
Anti-roll bar dia. (mm)	18	18
Brake system		
Brake booster dia. (inch)	7	8
Brake master cylinder dia. (mm)	20.64	23.81
Brake calliper piston diameter		
front (mm)	48	38+38
rear (mm)	42	30+30
Brake disc diameter		
front (mm)	282.5	304
rear (mm)	290	309
Brake disc thickness		
front (mm)	24	32
rear (mm)	24	28
Effective brake disc area (cm²)	257	376
Handbrake	Operating mechanically on both rear wheels	
Brake drum diameter (mm)	180	=
Contact area (cm²)	170	=

Wheels and tyres		
Standard tyre specification, front wheel	185/70VR15	205/55VR16
	6J x 15	7J x 16
Standard tyre specification, rear wheel	215/60VR15	225/50VR16
	7J x 15	8J x 16
Space-saver spare wheel	165-15 89P	=
Tyre pressure		
front (bar)	2.0	2.0
rear (bar)	2.5	3.0
Space-saver spare wheel (bar)	2.2	2.2

Body and interior (dimensions at kerb weight)		
Length (mm)	4291	4291
Width (mm)	1652	1775
Height (mm)	1320	1310
Wheelbase (mm)	2272	2272
Track		
front (mm)	1369	1432
rear (mm)	1379	1501
Ground clearance at permissible gross weight (mm)	120	120

Model range	911 SC	911 Turbo
Electrical system		
Generator output (W/A)	050/75	=
Battery (V/Ah)	12/66	=

Weight according to DIN 70020		
Kerb weight (kg)	1160	1300
Permissible gross weight (kg)	1500	1680
Permissible trailer weight		
unbraked (kg)	480	none
braked (kg)	800	none

Performance		
Maximum speed (kmh)		
Manual transmission	235	260
Acceleration 0–62mph/100kmh (sec)		
Manual transmission	6.8	5.4
Measured kilometre from standing start (sec)		
Manual transmission	26.8	24.0

A 1983 publicity photograph featuring 911 SC 3.0 Targa and 911 SC 3.0 Coupé models.

Model range	911 SC	911 Turbo
Fluid capacities		
Engine oil quantity 1* (l)	13	=
Manual transmission 2* (l)	3.1	3.7
Fuel tank (l)	80	80
Brake fluid reservoir 3* (l)	0.20	0.20

* Key to numerals
1* Approved API SE/SF with combinations API SE/CC - SF/CC - SF/CD - SE/CD
   Multigrade engine oil factory recommended.
2* Single-grade transmission fluid SAE 90 acc. MIL-L 2105 B and API-classified GL 5
3* Use only brake fluid acc. SAE J 1703. DOT 3 or 4

Chassis numbers (17 digits)												
World manufacturer code	Code body USA (A=Coupé, B=Targa, C=Cabriolet)	Code for engine variants (only USA)	Restraint system (0 = belt, 2 = airbag) only USA	First and second digit for car type	Fill character/check digit	Model year (D = 1983, E= 1984, etc.)	Manufacturing site (S = Stuttgart)	7th and 8th digit = car type	Code for body + engine	Sequence number	Summary
WPO	Z	Z	Z	91	Z	D	S	1	0	0001–2995	Rest of world, SC Coupé
WPO	Z	Z	Z	91	Z	D	S	1	0	9501–9999	Japan, SC Coupé
WPO	Z	Z	Z	91	Z	D	S	1	4	0001–1258	Rest of world, SC Targa
WPO	Z	Z	Z	91	Z	D	S	1	4	9501–9645	Japan, SC Targa
WPO	Z	Z	Z	91	Z	D	S	1	5	0001–2406	Rest of world, SC Cabriolet
WPO	A	A	0	91	C*	D	S	1	2	0001–2599	USA/CDN, SC Coupé
WPO	E	A	0	91	C*	D	S	1	6	0001–1430	USA/CDN, SC Targa
WPO	E	A	0	91	C*	D	S	1	7	0001–1781	Rest of world, SC Cabriolet
WPO	Z	Z	Z	93	Z	D	S	0	0	0001–1015	Rest of world, 911 Turbo
WPO	J	A	0	93	C*	D	S	0	5	0001–0065	CDN, 911 Turbo

C* = Check digit, can be 0–9 or X (only USA)   Z = Fill character for rest of world cars

Model year 1984

E Programme,
3.2-litre engine

Porsche 911 Carrera Coupé, Targa and Cabriolet
Porsche 911 Carrera Coupé Turbo Look
Porsche 911 Turbo 3.3 Coupé

With the SC badge now dropped and the venerated Carrera badge reinstated, the main news for the 1984 model year was the release of a new generation of engines with 3.2-litre displacement and digital engine electronics. The naturally aspirated engines were again revised to meet new exhaust regulations, and the 911's brake system was boosted to match the increased power from the 3.2-litre engines. Although the 911 Turbo continued to be available in Canada, it was now no longer delivered to the USA, as its engine/gearbox assembly was not designed for catalytic converter technology. However, customers in the USA who were disappointed by this move at least had a new visual alternative: the 911 Coupé was now offered with a 'Turbo Look'.

1984 saw the introduction of the 3.2-litre engine for Carrera models. This engine featured electronic engine management.

Engine
The naturally aspirated engine of the 911 Carrera was reworked. Apart from enlarging the displacement to

This 1984-model 911 Carrera 3.2 Coupé is fitted with the Sport pack, which included stiffer suspension and front and rear spoilers.

3.2 litres by increasing the stroke to 74.4mm (the same as the 911 Turbo), the crankcase was reinforced and the chain tensioner was improved and connected to the lubrication system. With these hydraulically damped chain tensioners, Porsche finally eliminated the problem of the early 911's notoriously weak timing chain set-up.

Specifications of the Carrera engines:		
Engine used in	USA and Japan	Rest of world
Car type	911 Carrera	911 Carrera
Engine type	930/21	930/20
Displacement (cc)	3164	3164
Compression ratio	9.5:1	10.3:1
Octane rating requirement (RON)	91 unleaded	98
Output (kW/hp)	152/207	170/231
At revolutions (rpm)	5900	5900
Torque (Nm)	260	284
At revolutions (rpm)	4800	4800
No changes to the mechanics of the Turbo engine.		

While the naturally aspirated engines underwent substantial modifications, the mechanics of the Turbo remained untouched, except for the new pressure-fed camshaft timing chain tensioners, which boosted reliability substantially.

Fuel and ignition system
Fuel injection and mapped ignition were now controlled by a Digital Motor Electronics unit (DME or Motronic) on the Carrera engine. DME consisted of an electronically controlled fuel injection system plus an ignition system with an electronically stored

For 1984, the 911 Carrera 3.2 Cabriolet was available with a brown or blue roof (and cover) as well as the previous black.

map; both were controlled by a common digital microcomputer. The injection system was based on the familiar L-Jetronic. The DME had trailing throttle fuel cut-off and lambda control for the USA (including California), Canada and Japan. DME would recognise a trailing throttle and would cut off fuel injection completely if this occurred. Depending on the export market a lambda sensor could be inserted into the exhaust system, which delivered additional information to the controller to make immediate adjustments to the amount of injected fuel. All lambda sensors were electrically heated. There were no changes to the ignition system or induction of the Turbo engine.

Transmission
Manual transmission type 915/67 (Carrera, rest of the world) and 915/69 (Turbo Look, rest of the world) differed only in the output flanges. Both transmissions were fitted with a speed-dependent transmission oil pump and a finned-tube radiator mounted on the outside of the transmission housing. The transmission oil cooling provided an operational temperature of about 25°C less. Apart from the improved cooling effect, higher viscosity of the lubricants was achieved, leading to smoother running of the mechanical parts. Fourth and fifth gears were adapted to the increased engine output.

Suspension
The 911 Carrera was equipped with a more powerful brake system, with a brake pressure limiter, engine-driven vacuum pump and larger brake servo. New as standard were die-cast 'telephone-design' wheels, 6Jx15 at the front, 7Jx15 at the rear, with 185/70 VR 15 tyres at the front and 215/60 VR 15 at the rear. The Turbo Look was fitted with the front axle hub, rear axle transverse pipe, wishbones and brake system of the 911 Turbo, along with light-alloy wheels (7Jx16 with 205/55 VR 16 tyres at the front, 8Jx16 with 225/50 VR 16 tyres at the rear). All six-cylinder cars were equipped with brake pad wear sensors and wheel nut locks to prevent wheel theft. The service intervals were extended to a more customer-friendly 20,000km (12,000 miles).

Body
The fog lamps were integrated into the front spoiler on all vehicles. The 911 Coupé could be ordered in Turbo Look as an optional extra (code M 491), whose front and rear wings (fenders), as well as the front and rear spoilers, were identical to the 911 Turbo.

Equipment and fittings
Black 'Carrera' script on the engine lid; tinted, two-stage heated rear window in the Coupé

Twenty years after the prototype 911 first appeared, the lines of the 1984 911 Carrera 3.2 Coupé were still unmistakable.

Model range	Total production
911 Carrera Coupé	4033 + 2499 USA
911 Carrera Targa	1469 + 2324 USA
911 Carrera Cabriolet	1835 + 1268 USA
911 Turbo 3.3 Coupé	804 + 77 CDN
911 SC RS	20

Model range	911 Carrera	911 Turbo
Engine		
Engine type,	930/20	930/66
Manual transmission		
Bore (mm)	95	97
Stroke (mm)	74.4	74.4
Displacement (cc)	3164	3299
Compression ratio	10.3:1	7.0:1
Engine output (kW/hp)	70/231	221/300
at revolutions per minute (rpm)	5900	5500
Torque (Nm)	284	430
at revolutions per minute (rpm)	4300	4000
Output per litre (kW/l)	53.7	67
Max. engine speed (rpm)	6560	7200
Engine weight (kg)	210	253

Carburation, ignition, settings		
Fuel system	DME	K-Jetronic
Type of fuel (RON)	98	98
Ignition system	DME	BHKZ, breakerless
Spark plugs		
Bosch	R 4 CC	W 3 DP
Beru	14/4 CU	–
Spark plug gap (mm)	0.7	0.8
Idle speed (rpm)	800+-20	900+-50
Exhaust/purification system	–	SLE+ZLP
CO-content without cat. conv. (%)	1.0–1.5	1.5–2.5
Fuel consumption acc. EC Standard, (litres/100km)		
A. at a constant 90kmh	6.8	9.7
B. at a constant 120kmh	9.0	11.8
C. EC urban cycle	13.6	15.5
Euromix	9.8	12.3

Key:
BHKZ Battery, capacitive-discharge ignition system (CDI)
SLE   Secondary-air injection, ZLP = Auxiliary air pump

and Targa. The Targa roof and all its seals was modified. There was also a lockable bootlid pulley for the Coupé. Cabriolet roof colour now also available in brown or blue. A make-up mirror was now fitted on the sun visor on the driver's side as well. Was Porsche recognising the emancipation of the female sex, or did it perhaps anticipate that male drivers might also want to use a mirror?

Interior fittings
New cloth in matching shades with Porsche script. Door handles on the inside matched the interior.

Heating and air conditioning
Two additional fans in the heating ducts were added in the Carrera to improve heating performance. Change of the air conditioning system to a swash-plate compressor.

Electrical system
A 92amp generator with 1,260W output was installed.

Additional information
A small run of 20 units of the 911 SC RS was manufactured for use in motor sport (Group B): this had a 3.0-litre engine with 188kW (255hp) at 7,000rpm. The competition version of this engine used in races and rallies produced as much as 206kW (280hp).

Model range	911 Carrera	911 Turbo
Transmission		
Clutch, pressure plate	G MFZ 225	G MFZ 240
Clutch plate (mm)	TD 225	GUD 240
Manual transmission	915/67	930/34
Gear ratios		
1st gear	3.181	2.250
2nd gear	1.833	1.304
3rd gear	1.261	0.829
4th gear	1.965	0.625
5th gear	0.7631	–
Reverse gear	3.325	2.437
Synchromesh system gears 1–5	POSY	POSY
Synchromesh system reverse gear	no	no
Final drive	3.875	4.222
Limited-slip differential	Option	Option
Lock-up factor under load/ coasting (%)	40/40	40/40
Gearbox weight with oil (kg)	60	70.2

Key:
S   Standard
POSY   Porsche Locking synchromesh system, synchroniser rings, mo-
       coated
DME   Digital engine electronic system (fuel injection + ignition)

Suspension, steering and brakes		
Front axle		
Anti-roll bar dia. (mm)	20	20
Steering ratio	17.87	17.87
Turning circle dia. (m)	10.95	10.95
Rear axle		
Anti-roll bar dia. (mm)	18	18
Brake system		
Brake booster dia. (inch)	7	8
Brake master cylinder dia. (mm)	20.64	23.81
Brake calliper piston diameter		
front (mm)	48	38+38
rear (mm)	42	30+30
Brake disc diameter		
front (mm)	282.5	304
rear (mm)	290	309
Brake disc thickness		
front (mm)	24	32
rear (mm)	24	28
Effective brake disc area (cm²)	257	376
Handbrake	Operating mechanically on both rear wheels	
Brake drum diameter (mm)	180	=
Contact area (cm²)	170	=

Model range	911 Carrera	911 Turbo
Wheels and tyres		
Standard tyre specification, front	185/70VR15	205/55VR16
wheel	6J x 15	7J x 16
hump depth (mm)	23.3	
Standard tyre specification, rear	215/60VR15	225/50VR16
wheel	7J x 15	8J x 16
Space-saver spare wheel	165-15 89P	=
Tyre pressure		
front (bar)	2.0	2.0
rear (bar)	2.5	3.0
Space-saver spare wheel (bar)	2.2	2.2

Body and interior (dimensions at kerb weight)		
Length (mm)	4291	4291
Width (mm)	1652	1775
Height (mm)	1320	1310
Wheelbase (mm)	2272	2272
Track		
front (mm)	1372	1432
rear (mm)	1380	1501
Ground clearance at permissible gross weight (mm)	120	120

Electrical system		
Generator output (W/A)	1260/90	=
Battery (V/Ah)	12/66	=

Weight according to DIN 70020		
Kerb weight (kg)	1160	1300
Permissible gross weight (kg)	1500	1680
Permissible trailer weight		
unbraked (kg)	480	none
braked (kg)	800	none

Performance		
Maximum speed (kmh)		
Manual transmission	245	260
Acceleration 0–62mph/100kmh (sec)		
Manual transmission	6.1	5.4
Measured kilometre from standing start (sec)		
Manual transmission	26.8	24.0

Fluid capacities		
Engine oil quantity 1* (l)	13	=
Manual transmission 2* (l)	3.4	3.7
Fuel tank (l)	80	80
Brake fluid reservoir 3* (l)	0.20	0.20

* Key to numerals
1* Approved API SE/SF with combinations API SE/CC - SF/CC - SF/CD - SE/CD
   Multigrade engine oil factory recommended
2* Single-grade transmission fluid SAE 90 acc. MIL-L 2105 B and
   API-classified GL 5
3* Use only brake fluid acc. SAE J 1703. DOT 3 or 4

Chassis numbers (17 digits)													
World manufacturer code	Code body USA (A=Coupé, B=Targa, C=Cabriolet)	Code for engine variants (only USA)	Restraint system (0 = belt, 2 = airbag) only USA	First and second digit for car type	Fill character/check digit	Model year (E = 1984, F = 1985, etc.)	Manufacturing site (S = Stuttgart)	7th and 8th digit = car type	Code for body + engine	Sequence number	Summary
WPO	Z	Z	Z	91	Z	E	S	1	0	0001–4033	Rest of world, Carrera Coupé
WPO	Z	Z	Z	91	Z	E	S	1	0	9501–9717	Japan, Carrera Coupé
WPO	Z	Z	Z	91	Z	E	S	1	4	0001–1469	Rest of world, Carrera Targa
WPO	Z	Z	Z	91	Z	E	S	1	4	9501–9564	Japan, Carrera Targa
WPO	Z	Z	Z	91	Z	E	S	1	5	0001–1835	Rest of world, Carrera Cabriolet
WPO	Z	Z	Z	91	Z	E	S	1	5	9501–9577	Japan, Carrera Cabriolet
WPO	A	B	O	91	C*	E	S	1	2	0001–2282	USA/CDN, Carrera Coupé
WPO	E	B	O	91	C*	E	S	1	6	0001–2260	USA/CDN, Carrera Targa
WPO	E	B	O	91	C*	E	S	1	7	0001–1191	USA/CDN, Carrera Cabriolet
WPO	Z	Z	Z	93	Z	E	S	0	0	0001–0804	Rest of world, 911 Turbo
WPO	J	A	O	93	C*	E	S	0	5	0001–0077	CDN, 911 Turbo

C* = Check digit, can be 0–9 or X (only USA)   Z = Fill character for rest of world cars

Model year 1985

F Programme, catalytic converters in Germany

Porsche 911 Carrera Coupé, Targa and
  Cabriolet
Porsche 911 Carrera Coupé, Targa and
  Cabriolet Turbo Look
Porsche 911 Turbo 3.3 Coupé

Model year 1985 Porsches featured catalytic converters and lambda sensors for the first time in Germany, which had pioneered the switch to unleaded petrol in Europe. Although the availability of unleaded fuel was still limited, Porsche nonetheless offered the first cars with a catalytic converter on the European market. The Turbo Look Carrera was now offered in Targa and Cabriolet forms as well as Coupé.

Engine
For better engine oil cooling, all engines received finned oil coolers in the right front wing (fender) ahead of the wheel. The air intake was positioned underneath the front bumper, above the fog lamps.

Fuel and ignition system
M 930/20 and M 930/21 engines were already being built in 1984; however, the M 930/21 was now available with catalytic converter and lambda sensor, which was available as option M 298 in Germany but was compulsory in Austria, Australia and Switzerland. Because unleaded fuel in Europe was not premium-grade (only 95RON), the compression ratio of this engine was only 9.5:1, which meant its output was reduced to 152kW (207hp). Incidentally, petrol obtained from crude oil always has a naturally low amount of lead in it, but in order to increase its anti-knock properties it was common to introduce additives that had a high content of lead, which posed a health risk. The new generation of petrol should therefore technically be described as 'unleaded' petrol, rather than 'lead-free'.

Transmission
Gearbox housing reinforcement was carried out for the 911 Carrera with 915-type transmissions (dubbed 915/72 with gearbox oil pump and gearbox oil cooling for all engines without a catalytic converter, and 915/73 without oil cooling for engines with a catalytic converter). The synchromesh was reworked so that gearchanges were easier, especially engaging first gear. Gearshift travel became significantly shorter and sportier. The ratios were changed as well for the 915/73 'box: second, fourth and fifth were adapted to the lower engine output. Without these ratio changes, the lower-output engine would have suffered reduced maximum speed.

Suspension
Cars were fitted with dual-strut gas pressure GZ dampers from Boge. The suspension of the Turbo was recalibrated and fitted with stronger anti-roll bars, 22mm diameter at the front and 20mm at the rear. The brake servo for all Turbo Look cars was modified so that pedal forces were noticeably lower.

A cutaway view of a 1985-model 911 Carrera 3.2 Coupé, showing the drivetrain and suspension installations.

A 1985-model 911 Carrera 3.2 Cabriolet Turbo Look, featuring Turbo-spec suspension, flared wheel arches and wheels.

Body

Targa and Cabriolet body variants were also now available in Turbo Look guise, albeit without the Turbo rear spoiler. The open-top models had to be adapted to the Turbo suspension through modified sheet metal strengthening and additional reinforcements to the bodyshell.

For 1985, all 911 models featured a new four-spoke steering wheel and a new seat design.

Equipment and fittings

Four-spoke steering wheel; electric central locking which could be activated from the centre console; electrically heated windscreen washer nozzles. Sekuriflex windscreens were available as an optional extra, which had a clear, invisible film on the inside to protect the occupants of the car from sharp glass chips if their heads hit the windscreen or stones shattered it.

Interior fittings

A new generation of seats arrived for all vehicles: standard seats and sports seats featured partly electric adjustment, while comfort seats were all-electric. The handbrake lever was covered in

colour-coded leather, and for noise insulation a rubber collar was fixed underneath the lever.

Heating and air conditioning
Air conditioning in the 911 Turbo 3.3 came as standard.

Electrical system
Heated rear window. Front windscreen aerial on passenger side, plus aerial amplifier in boot. The windscreen aerial was designed using experience gained with systems tested on supersonic aeroplanes.

Model range	Total production
911 Carrera Coupé	3529 + 2181 USA
911 Carrera Targa	1435 + 2006 USA
911 Carrera Cabriolet	1583 + 2025 USA
911 Turbo 3.3 Coupé	1063 + 85 CDN

Model range	911 Carrera	911 Turbo
Engine		
Engine type, Manual transmission	930/20	930/66
Bore (mm)	95	97
Stroke (mm)	74.4	74.4
Displacement (cc)	3164	3299
Compression ratio	10.3:1	7.0:1
Engine output (kW/hp)	170/231	221/300
at revolutions per minute (rpm)	5900	5500
Torque (Nm)	284	430
at revolutions per minute (rpm)	4300	4000
Output per litre (kW/l)	53.7	67
Max. engine speed (rpm)	6560	7200
Engine weight (kg)	219	253

Carburation, ignition, settings		
Fuel system	DME	K-Jetronic
Type of fuel (RON)	98	98
Ignition system	DME	BHKZ, breakerless
Ignition	Single	Single
Spark plugs		
Bosch	WR 4 CC	W 3 DP
Beru	–	–
Spark plug gap (mm)	0.7	0.6

The 1985-model 911 Turbo 3.3 Coupé provided a purposeful presence in this all-black bodywork and interior livery.

Model range	911 Carrera	911 Turbo
Carburation, ignition, settings (continued)		
Idle speed (rpm)	800+-20	900+-50
Exhaust/purification system	–	SLE+ZLP
CO-content without cat. conv. (%)	1.0–1.5	1.5–2.5
Fuel consumption acc. EC Standard, (litres/100km)		
A. at a constant 90kmh	6.8	9.7
B. at a constant 120kmh	9.0	11.8
C. EC urban cycle	13.6	15.5
Euromix	9.8	12.3

Key:
DME   Digital engine electronic system (fuel injection + ignition)
BHKZ Battery, capacitive-discharge ignition system (CDI)
ZLP   Auxiliary air pump

Model range	911 Carrera	911 Turbo
Transmission		
Clutch, pressure plate	G MFZ 225	G MFZ 240
Clutch plate (mm)	TD 225	GUD 240
Manual transmission	915/72	930/36
Gear ratios		
1st gear	3.181	2.250
2nd gear	1.833	1.304
3rd gear	1.261	0.829
4th gear	1.965	0.625
5th gear	0.7631	–
Reverse gear	3.325	2.437
Synchromesh system gears 1–5	POSY	POSY
Synchromesh system r. gear	no	no
Final drive	3.875	4.222
Limited-slip differential	Option	Option
Lock-up factor under load/ coasting (%)	40/40	40/40
Gearbox weight with oil (kg)	60	70.2

Key:
S   Standard
POSY   Porsche Locking synchromesh system, synchroniser rings, mo-coated

Model range	911 Carrera	911 Turbo
Suspension, steering and brakes		
Front axle		
Anti-roll bar dia. (mm)	20	22
Steering ratio	17.87	17.87
Turning circle dia. (m)	10.95	10.95
Rear axle		
Anti-roll bar dia. (mm)	18	20
Brake system		
Brake booster dia. (inch)	8	8
Brake master cylinder dia. (mm)	20.64	23.81
Brake calliper piston diameter		
front (mm)	48	38+38
rear (mm)	42	30+30
Brake disc diameter		
front (mm)	282.5	304
rear (mm)	290	309
Brake disc thickness		
front (mm)	24	32
rear (mm)	24	28
Effective brake disc area (cm^2)	258	344
Handbrake	Operating mechanically on both rear wheels	
Brake drum diameter (mm)	180	=
Contact area (cm^2)	170	=

Wheels and tyres		
Standard tyre specification, front	185/70VR15	205/55VR16
wheel	6J x 15	7J x 16
hump depth (mm)	23.3	=
Standard tyre specification, rear	215/60VR15	245/45VR16
wheel	7J x 15	9J x16
hump depth (mm)	15	=
Space-saver spare wheel	165-15 89P	=
Tyre pressure		
front (bar)	2.0	2.0
rear (bar)	2.5	3.0
Space-saver spare wheel (bar)	2.5	2.5

Model range	911 Carrera	911 Turbo
Body and interior (dimensions at kerb weight)		
Length (mm)	4291	4291
Width (mm)	1652	1775
Height (mm)	1320	1310
Wheelbase (mm)	2272	=
Track		
front (mm)	1372	1432
rear (mm)	1380	1501
Ground clearance at permissible gross weight (mm)	120	120

Electrical system		
Generator output (W/A)	1260/90	=
Battery (V/Ah)	12/66	=

Weight according to DIN 70020		
Kerb weight (kg)	1160	1300
Permissible gross weight (kg)	1500	1680
Permissible trailer weight		
unbraked (kg)	480	none
braked (kg)	800	none

Performance		
Maximum speed (kmh)		
Manual transmission	245	260
Acceleration 0–62mph/100kmh (sec)		
Manual transmission	6.1	5.4
Measured kilometre from standing start (sec)		
Manual transmission	26.8	24.0

Fluid capacities		
Engine oil quantity 1* (l)	13	=
Manual transmission 2* (l)	3.4	3.7
Fuel tank (l)	80	80
Brake fluid reservoir 3* (l)	0.20	0.20

* Key to numerals
1* Approved API SE/SF with combinations API SE/CC - SF/CC - SF/CD - SE/CD
   Multigrade engine oil factory recommended
2* Single-grade transmission fluid SAE 90 acc. MIL-L 2105 B and
   API-classified GL 5
3* Use only brake fluid acc. SAE J 1703. DOT 3 or 4

Chassis numbers (17 digits)												
World manufacturer code	Code body USA (A=Coupé, B=Targa, C=Cabriolet)	Code for engine variants (only USA)	Restraint system (0 = belt, 2 = airbag) only USA	First and second digit for car type	Fill character/check digit	Model year (F = 1985, G= 1986, etc.)	Manufacturing site (S = Stuttgart)	7th and 8th digit = car type	Code for body + engine	Sequence number	Summary
WP0	Z	Z	Z	91	Z	F	S	1	0	0001–3529	Rest of world, Carrera Coupé
WP0	Z	Z	Z	91	Z	F	S	1	0	9501–9722	Japan, Carrera Coupé
WP0	Z	Z	Z	91	Z	F	S	1	4	0001–1435	Rest of world, Carrera Targa
WP0	Z	Z	Z	91	Z	F	S	1	4	9501–9564	Japan, Carrera Targa
WP0	Z	Z	Z	91	Z	F	S	1	5	0001–1583	Rest of world, Carrera Cabriolet
WP0	Z	Z	Z	91	Z	F	S	1	5	9501–9575	Japan, Carrera Cabriolet
WP0	A	B	0	91	C*	F	S	1	2	0001–1959	USA/CDN, Carrera Coupé
WP0	E	B	0	91	C*	F	S	1	6	0001–1942	USA/CDN, Carrera Targa
WP0	E	B	0	91	C*	F	S	1	7	0001–1050	USA/CDN, Carrera Cabriolet
WP0	Z	Z	Z	93	Z	F	S	0	0	0001–1063	Rest of world, 911 Turbo
WP0	J	A	0	93	C*	F	S	0	5	0001–0085	CDN, 911 Turbo

C* = Check digit, can be 0–9 or X (only USA)
Z = Fill character for rest of world cars

Model year 1986

G Programme, extended long-term warranty

Porsche 911 Carrera Coupé, Targa and
    Cabriolet
Porsche 911 Carrera Coupé, Targa and
    Cabriolet Turbo Look
Porsche 911 Turbo 3.3 Coupé, Targa and
    Cabriolet

The Porsche world was ablaze with the arrival of
the road going version of the spectacular 959 at
the 1985 Frankfurt Motor Show. This Group B rally
escapee had clear ancestry to the 911 but featured
four-wheel drive and a hugely impressive
specification. The 959 is however outside the scope
of this book.

There were no big changes to the 911 Carrera
this year. The Turbo was now available in Targa
and Cabriolet guises as well as the Coupé, and
1986 also marked the moment when the Turbo
returned to the USA market, fitted with a
controlled catalytic converter.

*Although there was little in the way of new development for 1986,
the 911 Turbo 3.3 Coupé was still the flagship of the 911 range.*

The warranty against body rust perforation was
extended to ten years (an industry first), the paint
warranty was three years, and the overall vehicle
warranty was two years with unlimited mileage.
Porsche also provided a 12-month warranty
on genuine Porsche parts bought from an
authorised dealer.

Engine

The turbo engine for the USA differed from the
rest of the world with respect to induction, ignition
and exhaust, meaning that it had less power
and torque.

Comparison of turbo engines:		
Engine for	USA	Rest of world
Description	911 Turbo USA	911 Turbo
Type	930/68	930/66
Displacement (cc)	3299	3299
Compression ratio	7.0:1	7.0:1
Octane rating requirement (RON)	96*	98
Output (kW/hp)	210/282	221/300
At rpm	5,500	5,500
Torque (Nm)	390	430
At rpm	4000	4000

* Unleaded petrol required.

Fuel and ignition system

While there were no changes to 911 engines for
most world markets, the 930/68 Turbo engine for
the USA was now fitted with a lambda sensor,
auxiliary air injection and three-way catalytic
converter. Auxiliary air was injected into the cold

ABOVE: 1985-model 911 Carrera 3.2 Convertible (red) and 911 Turbo 3.3 Coupé models flank Porsche's flagship 959.

BELOW: A cutaway view of the Porsche 959 which featured two turbochargers and all-wheel drive.

With the engine cover lifted, the intercooler, fed with cooling air from the grilles in the rear spoiler, can clearly be seen on this Turbo model.

911 Turbo models featured supportive sports seats – in this case leather and cloth-trimmed – in the well-appointed cabin.

engine behind the outlet valves, and into the exhaust gas catalytic converter under running conditions. The ignition system and K-Jetronic fuel injection system had been adapted to conform to strict exhaust regulations in the USA.

Transmission
No changes to the transmission for all world markets except the USA Turbo which was fitted with the 930/36 four-speed manual transmission.

Suspension
Suspension tuning of the Carrera was improved. The front anti-roll bar now had a thickness of 22mm (increased from 20mm), the rear anti-roll bar diameter increased from 18 to 21mm, and the rear torsion bar was now 25mm in diameter instead of 24mm. New wheel sizes arrived at the rear for the 911 Turbo and 911 Turbo Look: forged light-alloy rims 9Jx16 H2 ET 15 with 245/45 VR 16 tyres.

Body
An electrically operated Cabriolet roof was available as an optional extra. Slant-Nose bodywork was available for all three body variations of the Turbo.

Equipment and fittings
Cars for the USA were fitted with a third high-level brake light. New theft protection mechanism for wheel nuts. Intensive windscreen washer system for all vehicles. The make-up mirrors in both sun visors received sliding covers. Larger air vents. Front seats 20mm lower. Boot lining same design as interior.

Heating and air conditioning
New interior temperature sensor.

Electrical system
Modifications to the aerial amplifier, and new generation of Bremen SQR/Toronto SQR radios.

Although compact, the rear of the 911 Turbo was equally well appointed, with 'turbo' logos on the rear of the seat cushions.

Model range	Total production
911 Carrera Coupé	4031 + 2619 USA
911 Carrera Targa	1758 + 2055 USA
911 Carrera Cabriolet	1583 + 1125 USA
911 Turbo Coupé	1158 + 1512 CDN
911 Turbo Targa	1
911 Turbo Cabriolet	3

Model range	911 Carrera	911 Turbo
Engine		
Engine type,	930/20	930/66
Manual transmission		
Bore (mm)	95	97
Stroke (mm)	74.4	74.4
Displacement (cc)	3164	3299
Compression ratio	10.3:1	7.0:1
Engine output (kW/hp)	170/231	221/300
at revolutions per minute (rpm)	5900	5500
Torque (Nm)	284	430
at revolutions per minute (rpm)	4300	4000
Output per litre (kW/l)	53.7	67
Max. engine speed (rpm)	6570	7200
Engine weight (kg)	219	253

Carburation, ignition, settings		
Fuel system	DME	K-Jetronic
Type of fuel (RON)	98	98
Ignition system	DME	BHKZ, breakerless
Ignition	single	single
Spark plugs		
Bosch	WR 4 CC	W 3 DP
Beru	–	–
Spark plug gap (mm)	0.7	0.7
Anti-knock control	no	no
Idle speed (rpm)	880	900+-50
Exhaust/purification system		SLE+ZLP
CO-content without cat. conv. (%)	0.5–1.5	1.5–2.5
with cat. conv. (%)	0.4–0.8	
Fuel consumption acc. EC Standard, manual transmission (litres/100km)		
A. at a constant 90 kmh	6.8	9.7
B. at a constant 120 kmh	9.0	11.8
C. EC urban cycle	13.6	15.5
Euromix	9.8	12.3

Key:
DME   Digital engine electronic system (fuel injection + ignition)
BHKZ   Battery, capacitive-discharge ignition system (CDI)
SLE   Secondary-air injection
ZLP   Auxiliary air pump

Transmission		
Clutch, pressure plate	G MFZ 225	G MFZ 240
Clutch plate (mm)	TD 225	GUD 240
Manual transmission	915/72	930/36
Gear ratios		
1st gear	3.181	2.250
2nd gear	1.833	1.304
3rd gear	1.261	0.829
4th gear	0.965	0.625
5th gear	0.7631	–
Reverse gear	3.325	2.437
Synchromesh system gears 1–5	POSY	POSY
Synchromesh system reverse gear	no	no
Final drive	3.325	4.222
Limited-slip differential	Option	Option
Lock-up factor under load/ coasting (%)	40/40	40/40
Gearbox weight with oil (kg)	60	70.2

Key:
S   Standard
POSY   Porsche Locking synchromesh system, synchroniser rings, mo-coated

Model range	911 Carrera	911 Turbo
Suspension, steering and brakes		
Front axle		
Anti-roll bar dia. (mm)	20	22
Steering ratio	17.87	17.87
Turning circle dia. (m)	10.95	10.95
Rear axle		
Anti-roll bar dia. (mm)	21	20
Brake system		
Brake booster dia. (inch)	8	8
Brake master cylinder dia. (mm)	20.64	23.81
Brake calliper piston diameter		
front (mm)	48	38+38
rear (mm)	42	30+30
Brake disc diameter		
front (mm)	282.5	304
rear (mm)	290	309
Brake disc thickness		
front (mm)	24	32
rear (mm)	24	28
Effective brake disc area (cm²)	258	344
Handbrake	Operating mechanically on both rear wheels	
Brake drum diameter (mm)	180	=
Contact area (cm²)	170	=

Wheels and tyres		
Standard tyre specification, front	185/70VR15	205/55VR16
wheel	6J x 15	7J x 16
hump depth (mm)	23.3	=
Standard tyre specification, rear	215/60VR15	245/45VR16
wheel	7J x 15	9J x 16
hump depth (mm)	15	=
Space-saver spare wheel	165-15 89P	=
Tyre pressure		
front (bar)	2.0	2.0
rear (bar)	2.5	3.0
Space-saver spare wheel (bar)	2.5	2.5

Body and interior (dimensions at kerb weight)		
Length (mm)	4291	4291
Width (mm)	1652	1775
Height (mm)	1320	1310
Wheelbase (mm)	2272	=
Track		
front (mm)	1372	1432
rear (mm)	1380	1501
Ground clearance at permissible gross weight (mm)	130	120

Electrical system		
Generator output (W/A)	1260/90	=
Battery (V/Ah)	12/66	=

Weight according to DIN 70020		
Kerb weight (kg)	1210	1335
Permissible gross weight (kg)	1530	1680
Permissible trailer weight		
unbraked (kg)	480	none
braked (kg)	800	none

Performance		
Maximum speed (kmh)		
Manual transmission	245	260
Acceleration 0–62mph/100kmh (sec)		
Manual transmission	6.1	5.4
Measured kilometre from standing start (sec)		
Manual transmission	26.1	24.0

The fully trimmed luggage compartment was spacious enough to carry a full set of Porsche-designed luggage.

Model range	911 Carrera	911 Turbo
Fluid capacities		
Engine oil quantity 1* (l)	13	=
Manual transmission 2* (l)	3.4	3.7
Front axle 2* (l)	–	–
Fuel tank (l)	85	85
Brake fluid reservoir 6* (l)	0.24	0.24
Refrigerant 4* (g)	1350	1300
Refrigerant oil 5* (ml)	120	120

* Key to numerals
1* Approved API SE/SF with combinations API SE/CC - SF/CC - SF/CD - SE/CD
   Multigrade engine oil factory recommended
2* Single-grade transmission fluid SAE 90 acc. MIL-L 2105 B and API-classified GL 5
4* Refrigerant R 12
5* Commercially available refrigerant oils
6* Use only brake fluid acc. SAE J 1703. DOT 3 or 4

Chassis numbers (17 digits)

World manufacturer code	Code body USA (A=Coupé, B=Targa, C=Cabriolet)	Code for engine variants (only USA)	Restraint system (0 = belt, 2 = airbag) only USA	First and second digit for car type	Fill character/ check digit	Model year (G = 1986, H = 1987, etc.)	Manufacturing site (S = Stuttgart)	7th and 8th digit = car type	Code for body + engine	Sequence number	Summary
WPO	Z	Z	Z	91	Z	G	S	1	0	0001–4031	Rest of world, Carrera Coupé
WPO	Z	Z	Z	91	Z	G	S	1	0	9501–9733	Japan, Carrera Coupé
WPO	Z	Z	Z	91	Z	G	S	1	4	0001–1976	Rest of world, Carrera Targa
WPO	Z	Z	Z	91	Z	G	S	1	4	9501–9579	Japan, Carrera Targa
WPO	Z	Z	Z	91	Z	G	S	1	5	0001–1986	Rest of world, Carrera Cabriolet
WPO	Z	Z	Z	91	Z	G	S	1	5	9501–9580	Japan, Carrera Cabriolet
WPO	A	B	O	91	C*	G	S	1	2	0001–2619	USA/CDN, Carrera Coupé
WPO	E	B	O	91	C*	G	S	1	6	0001–1976	USA/CDN, Carrera Targa
WPO	E	B	O	91	C*	G	S	1	7	0001–1158	USA/CDN, Carrera Cabriolet
WPO	Z	Z	Z	93	Z	G	S	0	0	0001–5088	Rest of world, 911 Turbo
WPO	J	A	O	93	C*	G	S	0	5	5001–5088	CDN, 911 Turbo
WPO	J	B	O	93	C*	G	S	0	5	0001–1424	USA, 911 Turbo

C* = Check digit, can be 0–9 or X (only USA)   Z = Fill character for rest of world cars

Model year 1987

H Programme, new G50 gearbox

Porsche 911 Carrera Coupé, Targa and
  Cabriolet
Porsche 911 Carrera Coupé, Targa and
  Cabriolet Turbo Look
Porsche 911 Turbo 3.3 Coupé, Targa and
  Cabriolet

Due to the increasingly widespread availability of
unleaded petrol worldwide there were a number of
911 naturally aspirated engines on offer in 1987.
Although worldwide and within Europe the
introduction of unleaded petrol continued to
spread, the situation was very confusing since
many countries no longer offered premium-grade
petrol. New for the Carrera this year: Getrag G50
manual transmission and clutch.

Engine

Here is a comparison of 911 naturally aspirated
engines:

Engines for	Rest of world without cat Germany without cat	USA, Japan, Germany, Austria, Switzerland	Australia	Sweden
Description	911 Carrera	911 Carrera	911 Carrera	911 Carrera
Engine type	930/20	930/25	930/25	930/26
Displacement (cc)	3164	3164	3164	3164
Compression ratio	10.3:1	9.5:1	9.5:1	9.5:1
Octane rating (RON)	98 +/-	95*	91*	98 +/-
Output (kW/hp)	170/231	160/217	152/207	170/231
At rpm	5900	5900	5900	5900
Torque (Nm)	284	265	260	265
At rpm	4800	4800	4800	4800
Notes	Without cat	With cat (M 298)	With cat (DME)	Without cat (aux air)

+/-	= unleaded or leaded, note octane rating.
*	= unleaded petrol.
(M 298)	= Engine with G-kat available as optional extra.
(DME)	= Modifications to the digital engine electronics (*Digitale Motor Elektronik*): ignition mapping later.
(aux air)	= auxiliary air injection behind the outlet valves.

The Turbo Targa and Cabriolet models were popular alternatives to
the existing Turbo Coupé.

Vehicles with catalytic converters (naturally aspirated and turbocharged) were fitted with an electric cooling fan in front of the oil cooler in the right front wheelarch.

Fuel and ignition system
Six different DME control units were fitted to Carrera engines:

911.618.111.12	for highly compressed engines worldwide.
911.618.111.13	for countries with low-octane fuel rating (eg Belgium, France, Greece).
911.618.111.14	for USA, California, Japan, Canada, Austria, Switzerland and Europe/rest of world with cat.
911.618.111.15*	for highly compressed engines with 'Sports Package I'.
911.618.111.16*	for low-octane fuel with 'Sports Package I'.
911.618.111.17*	for USA etc with 'Sports Package I'.

* = with higher cut-off speed of 6840rpm (standard was 6520rpm).

Transmission
After 15 years, the 915 gearbox model range finally gave way to an all-new transmission in the form of Getrag's G50 five-speed manual. In many ways it was similar to that of the Porsche 959, and it featured many advances gained from experience in the 959's development, such as frictionless gearchange operation, the arrangement of the main bearings and clutch actuation. The G50 five-speed gearbox had shafts, spur gears, antifriction bearings and bevel gears that were significantly reinforced. The housing design was new and the gears were now actuated hydraulically. The new synchromesh system (by Borg Warner) now extended even to reverse gear: this was fully synchronised and could even be engaged while the car was still rolling forwards. The gearshift rods were arranged in longitudinal format and guided with the help of frictionless ball bearings. A new gearchange plane meant that reverse gear was now forward and to the left, fifth gear forward and to the right. This new arrangement allowed for an extension to turn it into a six-gear transmission at a later date. A hydraulically operated clutch (F&S MFZ 240) and a rubber-damped clutch plate (F&S 240 GUD) were now fitted to all Carrera models.

In 1987, the 911 Turbo 3.3 Cabriolet was offered with a standard electrically operated roof.

Suspension
Because of the new G50 transmission, a new rear axle tube was also required to clear the larger clutch bell housing.

Body
Electrical operation of the Cabriolet roof was now standard.

Equipment and fittings
All vehicles were fitted with a leather-covered gear lever and leather gaiter.

Interior fittings
The 911 Turbo now had fully adjustable electric seats.

Electrical system
Two rear fog lamps were integrated into the rear reflective strip on all cars. The operation of the electric exterior rear-view mirrors was modified.

Additional information
The 911 Carrera was available as a Club Sport version (Sports Package M637). This boasted an engine with a higher redline of 6,840rpm, shorter-throw gear lever, sports bumpers, 6J and 7J wheels (15in diameter at first, 16in later) and stronger engine mountings. Through the omission of fittings such as electric windows, power seat adjustment and radio, the kerb weight was reduced by 50kg to 1,160kg compared to the standard 911 Carrera. Many had 'Carrera CS' decals on the body sides.

Having been available as a special order conversion for several years, the 'Flat-Nose' body style was launched as an official option for 1987 in a limited edition. This was available on both Turbo and Carrera models. While maintaining the same technical specifications, modified flat front wings (fenders) were used into which the main headlights were incorporated as pop-up units, similar to Porsche's 944 model range. The package included pop-up headlights, wheelarch vents in the front wings (fenders), door trim left and right, air intake ducts with mesh on the rear wings (fenders), and an oil cooler with fan in the air intake duct at the right rear. Standard tyres were supplied by Bridgestone (RE 71 N0). The nose area and wing vents were copied from the successful Porsche 935 race car. Unlike the plastic parts offered by Porsche modifiers, the flat-nose design offered by the factory was made from fully galvanised steel panels, and the rust prevention measures as well as all the paintwork were carried out on the production line at Zuffenhausen, so that Porsche offered the usual long-term warranty. The flat-nose design proved to be a bit of a fad, remaining popular with Porsche customers only for a short time. In total, 948 Flat-Nose 911s were built up to model year 1992.

Model range	Total production
911 Carrera Coupé	3381 + 3224 USA
911 Carrera Targa	1354 + 2311 USA
911 Carrera Cabriolet	1464 + 2738 USA
911 Turbo Coupé	720 + 1693 USA
911 Turbo Targa	69 + 87 USA
911 Turbo Cabriolet	142 + 183 USA
911 Club Sport	81 + 300 USA

Model range	911 Carrera	911 Carrera Club Sport	911 Turbo
Engine			
Engine type, Manual transmission	930/20	=	930/66
Bore (mm)	95	=	97
Stroke (mm)	74.4	=	74.4
Displacement (cc)	3164	=	3299
Compression ratio	10.3:1	=	7.0:1
Engine output (kW/hp)	170/231	=	221/300
at revolutions per minute (rpm)	5900	=	5500
Torque (Nm)	284	=	430
at revolutions per minute (rpm)	4800	=	4000
Output per litre (kW/l)	53.7	=	67
Max. engine speed (rpm)	6570	6840	7200
Engine weight (kg)	219	=	253
Carburation, ignition, settings			
Fuel system	DME	=	K-Jetronic
Type of fuel (RON)	98	=	98
Ignition system	DME	=	BHKZ, breakerless
Ignition	single	=	single
Spark plugs			
Bosch	WR 4 CK	=	W 3 DP 0
Beru	–	–	–
Spark plug gap (mm)	0.7	=	0.7
Anti-knock control	no	no	no
Idle speed (rpm)	880	=	900+-50
Exhaust/purification system	–	–	SLE+ZLP
CO-content			
without cat. conv. (%)	0.5–1.5	=	–
with cat. conv. (%)	0.4–0.8	=	–

Model range	911 Carrera	911 Carrera Club Sport	911 Turbo
Carburation, ignition, settings (continued)			
Fuel consumption acc. EC Standard, manual transmission (litres/100km)			
A. at a constant 90kmh	6.8	=	9.7
B. at a constant 120kmh	9.0	=	11.8
C. EC urban cycle	13.6	=	15.5
Euromix	9.8	=	12.3

Key:
DME   Digital engine electronic system (fuel injection + ignition)
BHKZ   Battery, capacitive-discharge ignition system (CDI)
SLE   Secondary-air injection
ZLP   Auxiliary air pump

Transmission			
Clutch, pressure plate	G MFZ 240	=	=
Clutch plate (mm)	GUD 240	=	=
Manual transmission	G50/00	=	930/36
Gear ratios			
1st gear	3.500	=	2.250
2nd gear	2.059	=	1.304
3rd gear	1.409	=	0.829
4th gear	1.074	=	0.625
5th gear	0.861	=	–
Reverse gear	2.857	=	2.437
Synchromesh system gears 1–5	VK	=	POSY
Synchromesh system reverse gear	VK	=	no
Final drive	3.444	=	4.222
Limited-slip differential	Option	=	Option
Lock-up factor under load/coasting (%)	40/40	=	40/40
Gearbox weight with oil (kg)	66	=	70.2

Key:
S   Standard
VK   Full-cone synchromesh system with molybdenum-coated synchroniser rings
POSY   Porsche Locking synchromesh system, synchroniser rings, mo-coated

Suspension, steering and brakes			
Front axle			
Anti-roll bar dia. (mm)	22	=	22
Steering ratio	17.87	=	17.87
Turning circle dia. (m)	10.95	=	10.95
Rear axle			
Anti-roll bar dia. (mm)	21	=	18
Brake system			
Brake booster dia. (inch)	8	=	8
Brake master cylinder dia. (mm)	20.64	=	23.81
Pressure reducer			
Cut-in pressure (bar)	33	=	55
Reduction factor	0.46	=	0.46
Brake calliper piston diameter			
front (mm)	48	=	38+38
rear (mm)	42	=	30+30
Brake disc diameter			
front (mm)	282.5	=	304
rear (mm)	290	=	309
Brake disc thickness			
front (mm)	24	=	32
rear (mm)	24	=	28
Effective brake disc area (cm^2)	258	=	344
Handbrake	Operating mechanically on both rear wheels		
Brake drum diameter (mm)	180	=	=
Contact area (cm^2)	170	=	=

Model range	911 Carrera	911 Carrera Club Sport	911 Turbo
Wheels and tyres			
Standard tyre specification, front	185/70VR15	205/55ZR16	205/55VR16
wheel	6J x 15	7J x 16	7J x 16
hump depth (mm)	23.3	=	
Standard tyre specification, rear	215/60VR15	225/50ZR16	245/45VR16
wheel	7J x 15	8J x 16	9J x 16
hump depth (mm)	15	=	
Space-saver spare wheel	165-15 89P	=	=
Tyre pressure			
front (bar)	2.0	2.0	2.0
rear (bar)	2.5	2.5	3.0
Space-saver spare wheel (bar)	2.5	2.5	2.5

Body and interior (dimensions at kerb weight)			
Length (mm)	4291	=	4291
Width (mm)	1652	=	1775
Height (mm)	1320	=	1310
Wheelbase (mm)	2272	=	2272
Track			
front (mm)	1398	=	1432
rear (mm)	1405	=	1492
Ground clearance at permissible gross weight (mm)	130	=	120
Overhang angle			
front (degree)	12.3	=	11.7
rear (degree)	13.9	=	14.0

Electrical system			
Generator output (W/A)	1260/90	=	=
Battery (V/Ah)	12/66	=	=

Model range	911 Carrera	911 Carrera Club Sport	911 Turbo
Weight according to DIN 70020			
Kerb weight (kg)	1210	1160	1335
Permissible gross weight (kg)	1530	1530	1680
Permissible trailer weight			
unbraked (kg)	480	none	none
braked (kg)	800	none	none

Performance			
Maximum speed (kmh)			
Manual transmission	245	=	260
Acceleration 0–62mph/100kmh (sec)			
Manual transmission	6.1	5.9	5.2
Measured kilometre from standing start (sec)			
Manual transmission	26.1	25.9	24.0

Fluid capacities			
Engine oil quantity 1* (l)	13	=	=
Manual transmission 2* (l)	3.4	=	3.7
Fuel tank (l)	85	=	=
Brake fluid reservoir 6* (l)	0.24	=	=
Refrigerant 4* (g)	1350	=	1300
Refrigerant oil 5* (ml)	120	=	=

* Key to numerals
1* Approved API SE/SF with combinations API SE/CC - SF/CC - SF/CD - SE/CD Multigrade engine oil factory recommended
2* Multigrade transmission fluid 75 W 90 acc. MIL-L 2105 B and API-classified GL 5
4* Refrigerant R 12
5* Commercially available refrigerant oils
6* Use only brake fluid acc. SAE J 1703. DOT 3 or 4

Note: According to the 8th amendment of the STVZO* the term 'chassis number' was adapted to international regulations and was changed to vehicle identification number (VIN for short)

Vehicle Identification Numbers												
World manufacturer code	Code body USA (A=Coupé, B=Targa, C=Cabriolet)	Code for engine variants (only USA)	Restraint system (0 = belt, 2 = airbag) only USA	First and second digit for car type	Fill character/ check digit	Model year (G = 1986, H= 1987, etc.)	Manufacturing site (S = Stuttgart)	7th and 8th digit = car type	Code for body + engine	Sequence number	Summary
WPO	Z	Z	Z	91	Z	H	S	1	0	0001–3381	Rest of world, Carrera Coupé
WPO	Z	Z	Z	91	Z	H	S	1	0	5001–5081	Rest of world, Carrera Coupé (M637)
WPO	Z	Z	Z	91	Z	H	S	1	0	9501–9808	Japan, Carrera Coupé
WPO	Z	Z	Z	91	Z	H	S	1	4	0001–1354	Rest of world, Carrera Targa
WPO	Z	Z	Z	91	Z	H	S	1	4	9501–9579	Japan, Carrera Targa
WPO	Z	Z	Z	91	Z	H	S	1	5	0001–1464	Rest of world, Carrera Cabriolet
WPO	Z	Z	Z	91	Z	H	S	1	5	9501–9585	Japan, Carrera Cabriolet
WPO	A	B	0	91	C*	H	S	1	2	0001–2916	USA/CDN, Carrera Coupé
WPO	A	B	0	91	C*	H	S	1	2	5001–5300	USA/CDN, Carrera Coupé (M637)
WPO	E	B	0	91	C*	H	S	1	6	0001–2232	USA/CDN, Carrera Targa
WPO	E	B	0	91	C*	H	S	1	7	0001–2653	USA/CDN, Carrera Cabriolet
WPO	Z	Z	Z	91	Z	H	S	0	0	0001–0720	Rest of world , 911 Turbo
WPO	J	A	0	93	C*	H	S	0	5	5001–5008	CDN, 911 Turbo
WPO	Z	Z	Z	93	Z	H	S	0	2	0001–0142	Rest of world, 911 Turbo Cabriolet
WPO	E	B	0	93	C*	H	S	0	7	0001–0183	USA, 911 Turbo Cabriolet
WPO	E	A	0	93	C*	H	S	0	7	5000–7000	CDN, 911 Turbo Cabriolet
WPO	Z	Z	Z	93	Z	H	S	0	1	0001–0069	Rest of world, 911 Turbo Targa
WPO	E	B	0	93	C*	H	S	0	6	0001–0087	USA, 911 Turbo Targa
WPO	E	A	0	93	C*	H	S	0	6	5001–7000	CDN, 911 Turbo Targa
WPO	Z	Z	Z	95	Z	H	S	9	0	0001–1000	Worldwide, 959 Coupé

C* = Check digit, can be 0–9 or X (only USA)
STVZO* = Road Traffic Licensing Regulations in Germany

Z = Fill character for rest of world cars
M 637 (optional extra 637) is the 911 Coupe in Club Sport version

Model year 1988

J Programme, 250,000 cars built

Porsche 911 Carrera Coupé, Targa and
   Cabriolet
Porsche 911 Carrera Coupé, Targa and
   Cabriolet Turbo Look
Porsche 911 Turbo 3.3 Coupé, Targa and
   Cabriolet

There were no major changes to the 911 Carrera
or the 911 Turbo during this year. The only
noteworthy alteration was the conversion to an
asbestos-free clutch lining; Scandinavian countries
also received asbestos-free brake pads (no
materials containing asbestos had been allowed
there since 1 January 1988). On 5 June 1987 the
250,000th Porsche 911 rolled off the assembly line
and to celebrate this event, a special Diamond
Metallic limited edition of 875 cars was built.

Transmission
Asbestos-free clutch linings (Porter Thermoid
505/01) were introduced for all 911s worldwide.

Suspension
Conversion of brake pads to asbestos-free for
Scandinavia. The Carrera now had forged wheels,
front 7Jx15, rear 8Jx15 to a 'wing wheel' design
(by Fuchs). The forged light-alloy 'wing wheels'

A cutaway illustration of a 1988-model 911 Turbo 3.3 Coupé,
showing how the engine and ancillaries fill the engine compartment.

marked a return to the 911's roots, being the same
style as used in 1967.

Body
Reworked gas struts on engine lid and bootlid. The
windscreen trim strip, previously anodised
aluminium, was now made from plastic.

Equipment and fittings
An impact pad in the steering wheel also served as
the horn button, with a 'French horn' symbol. By
adding this Porsche was complying with a new
regulation in the USA that required a visually
identifiable button or lever able to sound an
acoustic warning signal.

Interior fittings
Electric height adjustment of seats was now fitted
to the Carrera as standard. Crushed leather seats
available as an optional extra.

Electrical system
Cruise control now available with sensitive electrical
adjustment (vacuum-controlled). Electromotive
central locking with a button on the centre console.
The 911 Turbo was fitted with an eight-speaker
sound package as standard equipment.

Additional information
The '25 years of 911' special edition offered during
model year 1988 was a 911 Carrera in Diamond
Blue metallic paint finish, with colour-coded Fuchs
five-star rims, metallic blue crushed leather interior
and 'F. Porsche' signatures embroidered in the
headrests. This was a limited edition of 875 cars
offered in all three body styles.
   A high-performance Turbo engine with 243kW
(330hp) was available for the European market.

The interior of a 1988-model 911 Turbo 3.3 Coupé, showing the electrically adjustable seats and the steering wheel impact pad.

Model range	Total production
911 Carrera Coupé	3580 + 2496 USA
911 Carrera Targa	1281 + 1586 USA
911 Carrera Cabriolet	1501 + 2197 USA
911 Turbo Coupé	677 + 701 USA
911 Turbo Targa	136 + 141 USA
911 Turbo Cabriolet	242 + 591 USA

Model range	911 Carrera	911 Turbo
Engine		
Engine type, Manual transmission	930/20	930/66
Bore (mm)	95	97
Stroke (mm)	74.4	74.4
Displacement (cc)	3164	3299
Compression ratio	10.3:1	7.0:1
Engine output (kW/hp)	170/231	221/300
at revolutions per minute (rpm)	5900	5500
Torque (Nm)	284	430
at revolutions per minute (rpm)	4800	4000
Output per litre (kW/l)	53.7	67
Max. engine speed (rpm)	6570	7200
Engine weight (kg)	219	253

Model range	911 Carrera	911 Turbo
Carburation, ignition, settings		
Fuel system	DME	K-Jetronic
Type of fuel (RON)	98	98
Ignition system	DME	BHKZ, breakerless
Ignition	single	single
Spark plugs		
Bosch	WR 4 CK	W 3 DP 0
Beru	–	–
Spark plug gap (mm)	0.7	0.7
Anti-knock control	no	no
Idle speed (rpm)	880	900+-50
Exhaust/purification system	–	SLE+ZLP
CO-content without cat. conv. (%)	0.5–1.5	1.5–2.5
with cat. conv. (%)	0.4–0.8	–
Fuel consumption acc. EC Standard, man. transm. (litres/100km)		
A. at a constant 90 kmh	7.9	10.7
B. at a constant 120 kmh	9.8	13.0
C. EC urban cycle	14.9	14.3
Euromix	10.9	12.7

Key:
DME   Digital engine electronic system (fuel injection + ignition)
BHKZ Battery, capacitive-discharge ignition system (CDI)
SLE   Secondary-air injection
ZLP   Auxiliary air pump

Transmission		
Clutch, pressure plate	G MFZ 240	=
Clutch plate (mm)	GUD 240	=
Manual transmission	G50/00	930/36
Gear ratios		
1st gear	3.500	2.250
2nd gear	2.059	1.304
3rd gear	1.409	0.829
4th gear	1.074	0.625
5th gear	0.861	–
Reverse gear	2.857	2.437
Synchromesh system gears 1–5	VK	POSY
Synchromesh system r. gear	VK	no
Final drive	3.444	4.222
Limited-slip differential	Option	Option
Lock-up factor under load/ coasting (%)	40/40	40/40
Gearbox weight with oil (kg)	66	70.2

Key:
S   Standard
VK   Full-cone synchromesh system with molybdenum-coated synchroniser rings
POSY Porsche Locking synchromesh system, synchroniser rings, mo-coated

Model range	911 Carrera	911 Turbo
Suspension, steering and brakes		
Front axle		
Anti-roll bar dia. (mm)	22	22
Steering ratio	17.87	17.87
Turning circle dia. (m)	10.95	10.95
Rear axle		
Anti-roll bar dia. (mm)	21	18
Brake system		
Brake booster dia. (inch)	8	8
Brake master cylinder dia. (mm)	20.64	23.81
Pressure reducer		
Cut-in pressure (bar)	33	55
Reduction factor	0.46	0.46
Brake calliper piston diameter		
front (mm)	48	38+38
rear (mm)	42	30+30
Brake disc diameter		
front (mm)	282.5	304
rear (mm)	290	309
Brake disc thickness		
front (mm)	24	32
rear (mm)	24	28
Effective brake disc area (cm^2)	258	344
Handbrake	Operating mechanically on both rear wheels	
Brake drum diameter (mm)	180	=
Contact area (cm^2)	170	=

Wheels and tyres	911 Carrera	911 Turbo
Standard tyre specification, front	195/65VR15	205/55VR16
wheel	7J x 15	7J x 16
hump depth (mm)	23.3	
Standard tyre specification, rear	215/60VR15	245/45VR16
wheel	8J x 15	9J x 16
hump depth (mm)	15	
Space-saver spare wheel	165-15 89P	=
Tyre pressure		
front (bar)	2.0	2.0
rear (bar)	2.5	3.0
Space-saver spare wheel (bar)	2.5	2.5

Body and interior (dimensions at kerb weight)	911 Carrera	911 Turbo
Length (mm)	4291	4291
Width (mm)	1652	1775
Height (mm)	1320	1310
Wheelbase (mm)	2272	2272
Track		
front (mm)	1398	1432
rear (mm)	1405	1492
Ground clearance at permissible gross weight (mm)	130	120
Overhang angle		
front (degree)	12.3	11.7
rear (degree)	13.9	14.0

Model range	911 Carrera	911 Turbo
Electrical system		
Generator output (W/A)	1260/90	=
Battery (V/Ah)	12/66	=

Weight according to DIN 70020		
Kerb weight (kg)	1210	1335
Permissible gross weight (kg)	1530	1680
Permissible trailer weight		
unbraked (kg)	480	none
braked (kg)	800	none

Performance		
Maximum speed (kmh)		
Manual transmission	245	260
Acceleration 0–62mph/100kmh (sec)		
Manual transmission	6.1	5.2
Measured kilometre from standing start (sec)		
Manual transmission	26.1	24.0

Model range	911 Carrera	911 Turbo
Fluid capacities		
Engine oil quantity 1* (l)	13	=
Manual transmission 2* (l)	3.4	3.7
Front axle 2*	–	–
Fuel tank (l)	85	=
Brake fluid reservoir 6* (l)	0.24	0.24
Refrigerant 4* (g)	1350	1300
Refrigerant oil 5* (ml)	120	120

* Key to numerals
1* Approved API SE/SF with combinations API SE/CC - SF/CC - SF/CD - SE/CD
   Multigrade engine oil factory recommended
2* Multigrade transmission fluid 75 W 90 acc. MIL-L 2105 B and API-classified GL 5
4* Refrigerant R 12
5* Commercially available refrigerant oils
6* Use only brake fluid acc. SAE J 1703. DOT 3 or 4

Vehicle Identification Numbers											
World manufacturer code	Code body USA (A=Coupé, B=Targa, C=Cabriolet)	Code for engine variants (only USA)	Restraint system (0 = belt, 2 = airbag) only USA	First and second digit for car type	Fill character/ check digit	Model year (J = 1988, K = 1989, etc.)	Manufacturing site (S = Stuttgart)	7th and 8th digit = car type	Code for body + engine	Sequence number	Summary
WPO	Z	Z	Z	91	Z	J	S	1	0	0001–3580	Rest of world, Carrera Coupé
WPO	Z	Z	Z	91	Z	J	S	1	0	5001–5148	Rest of world, Carrera Coupé M637
WPO	Z	Z	Z	91	Z	J	S	1	0	9501–9930	Japan, Carrera Coupé
WPO	Z	Z	Z	91	Z	J	S	1	4	0001–1281	Rest of world, Carrera Targa
WPO	Z	Z	Z	91	Z	J	S	1	4	9501–9586	Japan, Carrera Targa
WPO	Z	Z	Z	91	Z	J	S	1	5	0001–1501	Rest of world, Carrera Cabriolet
WPO	Z	Z	Z	91	Z	J	S	1	5	9501–9581	Japan, Carrera Cabriolet
WPO	A	B	O	91	C*	J	S	1	2	0001–2066	USA/CDN, Carrera Coupé
WPO	A	B	O	91	C*	J	S	1	2	5001–5082	USA/CDN, Carrera Coupé M637
WPO	E	B	O	91	C*	J	S	1	6	0001–1500	USA/CDN, Carrera Targa
WPO	E	B	O	91	C*	J	S	1	7	0001–2116	USA/CDN, Carrera Cabriolet
WPO	Z	Z	Z	93	Z	J	S	0	0	0001–0677	Rest of world, 911 Turbo
WPO	J	B	O	93	C*	J	S	0	5	5001–0701	USA/CDN, 911 Turbo
WPO	Z	Z	Z	93	Z	J	S	0	2	0001–0242	Rest of world, 911 Turbo Cabriolet
WPO	E	B	O	93	C*	J	S	0	7	0001–0591	USA/CDN, 911 Turbo Cabriolet
WPO	Z	Z	Z	93	Z	J	S	0	1	0001–0136	Rest of world, 911 Turbo Targa
WPO	T	O	E	93	C*	J	S	0	6	0001–0141	USA/CDN, 911 Turbo Targa

C* = Check digit, can be 0–9 or X (only USA)
Z = Fill character for rest of world cars
STVZO* = Road Traffic Licensing Regulations in Germany
M 637 (optional extra 637) is the 911 Coupe in CLUB SPORT VERSION

Model year 1989

K Programme, all-wheel drive, ABS and Speedster

Porsche 911 Carrera Coupé, Targa and
  Cabriolet and Speedster
Porsche 911 Carrera Coupé, Targa and
  Cabriolet and Speedster Turbo Look
Porsche 911 Carrera 4 Coupé
Porsche 911 Turbo Coupé, Targa and
  Cabriolet

The 911 Carrera continued to be manufactured
with few changes in 1989. The 911 Turbo finally
received a five-speed transmission, having made do
with just four speeds since 1975. A major new
arrival this year was the Speedster, an additional
body variant that evoked the style of the 356
Speedster of the 1950s.

*The 1989-model 911 Turbo 3.3 Coupé was the first 911 Turbo
model to be fitted with a five-speed gearbox.*

From January 1989, an important new
development for the 911 was all-wheel drive,
offered in the new 911 Carrera 4. This was
powered by a 3.6-litre engine and was visually
quite different to the then-current Carrera, and
was produced in a new body plant on the other
side of Bundesstrasse 10. The 911 Carrera and
Turbo were still produced in parallel with the
Carrera 4 until the end of the model year (July
1989). After that the 'old' body plant was
temporarily shut down. The new body of the
Carrera 4 would be transported across an enclosed
bridge with the aid of a conveyor belt to the paint
shop, where the surface treatment was carried out.
The last vehicle with the then-current body was the
911 Speedster.

After a brief renovation phase the 'old' body
plant, which still incorporated buildings from
the former Reutter company, was used to
rework and reinforce some 20 Mercedes-Benz
500 E bodyshells farmed out by Mercedes.
In the so-called 'Rößlebau', where Porsche
had previously built its 959, the 500 E bodies,
already painted and equipped by Mercedes,
were fitted with engines and chassis and
then finished.

*A cutaway illustration of a 911 Carrera 4 3.6 Coupé, showing the
new body styling and all-wheel drive system.*

*The 911 Speedster was added to the range in 1989. It was based
on the 911 Carrera 3.2 Turbo Look.*

For the Carrera 4 models launched in 1989, Porsche introduced a heavily revised engine with a capacity of 3.6 litres.

Engine

The following engines continued to be built without any significant changes: the 930/20 and 930/25 for the 911 Carrera, and the 930/66 and 930/68 for the 911 Turbo. Development of the 911 Carrera 4 engine (type M64/01) was based on these well-known engines. It was a 3.6-litre unit, built with or without catalytic converters, producing 184kW (250hp). Special features were two spark plugs per combustion chamber (dual ignition); knock control system; exhaust ducts in the cylinder head as ceramic port liners; camshaft drive system with double roller chains; hydraulic chain tensioners; separate drives for engine cooling fan and alternator; oil cooler with two-stage fan in the front of the car on the right; and two-stage resonance intake system.

Even though the proven crankcase made from light aluminium-silicon alloy remained mostly intact, the crankshaft was almost entirely new. The new engine was designed for exhaust emission control and catalytic converter technology. With a 100mm piston diameter, the simultaneous firing in the combustion chamber at two opposite points had stood the test: a more uniform combustion produced fewer pollutants in the exhaust gas already heading to the catalytic converter.

Fuel and ignition system

The new engine made use of expanded Motronic digital engine electronics: sequential fuel injection; anti-knock control, one sensor per cylinder row; adaptive lambda control; new metal catalytic converter; electronically controlled fuel-tank ventilation; dual ignition distributor with Hall sensor; exhaust system made completely from stainless steel. The new air-cooled engine's anti-knock control provided some protection against engine damage due to the fact that unleaded petrol with 95RON was not widely available. The 911 Carrera 4 was the first car fitted with a metal catalytic converter with lambda control as standard equipment.

ABOVE: The Carrera 4 all-wheel drive system featured a rigid tube encasing the propeller shaft providing drive to the front differential.

BELOW: A sectioned Carrera 4 front differential assembly showing the arrangement of the differential gearing.

The Carrera 3.2 Cabriolet remained unchanged for 1989, the existing Carrera models running in parallel to the new Carrera 4.

Transmission

911 Turbo only: new hydraulic clutch actuation as per the 911 Carrera. New G50/50 five-speed transmission, in principle the same as G50/00, but more robust in certain areas.

911 Carrera 4: hydraulically actuated dry single-plate clutch (F&S GMFZ 240); rubber-damped clutch plate (F&S GUD 240); new G64/00 transmission system. The 911 Carrera 4 transmission consisted of a fully synchronised five-speed manual gearbox with integrated rear-axle differential, as well as a transfer case for permanent all-wheel drive.

The connection to the front-axle differential was produced in the tried and tested transaxle design with a rigid axle tube and a central shaft running on the inside. The transfer case divided the drive torque 31% to the front axle and 69% to the rear. The rear-wheel drive was integrated into the gearbox housing and was fitted with a Porsche friction-disc limited-slip differential or PDAS (Porsche Dynamisches Allrad-System). This axle-differential lock offered yaw stabilisation when cornering.

The Porsche dynamic all-wheel drive system or

PDAS functioned as a planetary transfer case between front and rear axles. When driving normally the drive torque was distributed in such a way that the driver had the impression that his car was rear-wheel drive. When the driveshaft was rotating (as registered by the ABS sensors), the transfer case was blocked partly or completely by the longitudinally arranged multi-plate clutch.

Suspension

The Carrera 4 was fitted with completely new independent suspension that marked the end of the line for torsion bars in the 911. The new system consisted of light-alloy wishbones and MacPherson struts up front, light-alloy semi-trailing arms at the rear and coil springs both front and rear. There was also power-assisted rack-and-pinion steering, dual-circuit braking with a hydraulic brake servo, ventilated disc brakes front and rear with four-piston fixed callipers on all wheels and anti-lock brakes (ABS). The light-alloy wheels were 6Jx16 H2 ET 52.3 front, 8Jx16 H2 ET 52.3 rear, and the tyres 205/55 ZR 16 N1 front, 225/50 ZR 16 N1 rear.

Some changes also arrived for the Turbo chassis: the transverse axle tube was modified in its middle section (because of the new five-speed transmission). Change of the gearing of the rear

ABOVE: The all-new interior of a 1989 911 Carrera 4 3.6 Coupé. The seat design was retained from prevous 911 models.

BELOW: The all-wheel drive system for the Carrera 4 meant that a transmission tunnel now ran through the passenger compartment.

The interior of a right-hand-drive 1989 model 911 Turbo 3.3 Coupé, now fitted with a five-speed gearbox.

axle torsion bars to SAE profile, with a diameter of 27mm instead of 26mm. The anti-roll bar diameter was reduced from 20mm to 18mm (which inhibited the tendency to oversteer). Bilstein gas pressure dampers front and rear with declining damper value (to enhance driving comfort) were standard. Asbestos-free brake pads.

The 911 Turbo featured drilled, ventilated front brake discs with Porsche-designed alloy four-piston callipers.

Body
Even though the body of the Carrera 4 resembled the 911 Carrera, it was entirely new. The structure of the body frame and the floorpan were specially designed for the all-wheel drive system. Although the flat body shape was not universally popular with customers, it slowly found acceptance. The thermoplastic front and rear bumpers looked like they were part of the main bodywork. Partly because of its completely flat undertray, this was a very aerodynamic shape, the absolute coefficient of drag being 0.32 (when multiplied by a frontal area of 1.79m^2 this resulted in an actual drag value of 0.57). It was pleasing to see that the lift coefficient remained near zero in all speed ranges. One very interesting feature was the rear spoiler, which automatically deployed itself via an electric motor at speeds above 80kmh (50mph), retracting back into the rear lid at speeds below 10kmh (6mph).

Equipment and fittings
In the Carrera 4, the rear windscreen wipers operated through a hole in the rear screen.

Interior fittings
The interior trim in the Carrera 4 was a completely new design, but the seats were the same as in Porsche's other production 911s.

Heating and air conditioning
The Carrera 4 was available with two systems: automatically adjustable heating was standard, while automatically adjustable air conditioning was optional (code M 573). Seat heating was adjustable and the side bolsters were also heatable.

Electrical system

The electrics of the Carrera 4 were completely different from those of other Carrera models so far. The central electric unit was fitted in the luggage compartment, and the instruments were illuminated by new back-lit technology. The Carrera 4 was fitted with a central information system for warning signals that was also acoustic, an electrothermal fuel-level sending unit, and completely new cable harnesses. The alarm system of Porsche's 928 was adopted, but activated via the door-locking system: when the alarm was set off, there were flashing light-emitting diodes within the locking knobs.

Additional information

The 911 model range was enhanced by the addition of the new 911 Speedster. Its basis was the 911 Carrera Turbo Look (or Flat-Nose in certain markets) but it had very distinctive features of its own. These included a shortened windscreen with a steeper rake, a manually activated soft top and a cover at the rear made from plastic, under which the folded roof disappeared completely. Its 3.2-litre Carrera engine was available with or without catalytic converter. With the introduction of the fine-weather 911 Speedster for lovers of open-top motoring the dream of many Porsche drivers became a reality. However, unlike the 911 Cabriolet, which had a fully-fledged convertible soft top and was suitable for driving in winter conditions, the 911 Speedster's soft top was really only suitable for 'emergency' use.

Model range	Total production
911 Carrera Coupé	3532 + 1156 USA
911 Carrera Targa	1281 + 1586 USA
911 Carrera Cabriolet	1501 + 2197 USA
911 Carrera Speedster	2102
911 Carrera Club Sport	N/A
911 Turbo Coupé	2068 + 1117 USA
911 Turbo Targa	56
911 Turbo Cabriolet	330
911 Carrera 4 Coupé	2068 + 1117 USA

Model range	911 Carrera	911 Speedster	911 Carrera 4	911 Turbo
Engine				
Engine type, Manual transmission	930/20	=	M64/01	930/66
Bore (mm)	95	=	100	97
Stroke (mm)	74.4	=	76.4	74.4
Displacement (cc)	3164	=	3600	3299
Compression ratio	10.3:1 (9.5:1)*	=	11.3:1	7.0:1
Engine output (kW/hp)	170/231 (160/217)*	=	184/250	221/300
at revolutions per minute (rpm)	5900	=	6100	5500
Torque (Nm)	284 (265)*	=	310	430
at revolutions per minute (rpm)	4800	=	4800	4000
Output per litre (kW/l)	53.7 (50.6)*	=	51.1	67
Max. engine speed (rpm)	6570	=	6720	7200
Engine weight (kg)	219	=	238	269

Carburation, ignition, settings				
Fuel system	DME	=	DME S	K-Jetronic
Type of fuel (RON)	98 (95)*	=	95	98
Ignition system	DME	=	DME	BHKZ breakerless
Ignition	single	=	dual	single
Spark plugs				
Bosch	WR 4 CK	=	FR 5 DTC	W 3 DP 0
Beru	–	–	–	–
Spark plug gap (mm)	0.7	=	0.8	0.7
Anti-knock control	no	no	yes	no
Idle speed (rpm)	880	=	880+-40	900+-50
Exhaust/purification system	L sensor+cat.conv.	L sensor+cat.conv.	L sensor+cat.conv.	SLE+ZLP
CO-content				
without cat. conv. (%)	0.5–1.5	=	0.5–1.0	1.5–2.5
with cat. conv. (%)	0.4–0.8	=	0.4–1.2	–
Fuel consumption acc. to EC Standard, manual transmission (litres/100 km)				
A. at a constant 90kmh	6.8 (7.9)*	=	8.0	10.7
B. at a constant 120kmh	9.0 (9.8)*	=	9.5	13.0
C. EC urban cycle	13.6 (14.9)*	=	17.9	14.3
Euromix	9.8 (10.9)*	=	11.8	12.7

*Cat. conv. figs. in brackets

Model range	911 Carrera	911 Speedster	911 Carrera 4	911 Turbo
Transmission				
Clutch, pressure plate	G MFZ 240	=	=	=
Clutch plate (mm)	GUD 240	=	GUD 240	=
Manual transmission	G50/00	G50/00	G64/00	G50/50
Gear ratios				
1st gear	3.500	=	3.500	3.145
2nd gear	2.059	=	2.118	1.789
3rd gear	1.409	=	1.444	1.269
4th gear	1.074	=	1.086	0.967
5th gear	0.861	=	0.868	0.756
Reverse gear	2.857	=	=	=
Synchromesh system gears 1–5	VK	=	=	=
Synchromesh system reverse gear	VK	=	=	=
Final drive	3.444	=	=	=
Limited-slip differential	Option	Option	Standard	Option
Lock-up factor under load/coasting (%)	40/40	40/40	variable 0–100	40/40
Gearbox weight with oil (kg)	66	=	79.65	70.2
Front differential (kg)	–	–	22.65	–

Key:
VK   Full-cone synchromesh system with molybdenum-coated synchroniser rings
BHKZ Battery, capacitive-discharge ignition system (CDI)
DME   Digital engine electronic system (fuel injection + ignition)
DME S Digital engine electronic system with sequential fuel injection
SLE   Secondary-air injection
ZLP   Auxiliary air pump

Suspension, steering and brakes				
Front axle				
Anti-roll bar dia. (mm)	22	=	20	22
Steering ratio	17.87	=	18.48	17.87
Turning circle dia. (m)	10.95	=	11.95	10.95
Rear axle				
Anti-roll bar dia. (mm)	21	=	20	18
Brake system				
Brake booster dia. (inch)	8	=	hydr.	=
Brake master cylinder dia. (mm)	20.64	=	23.81	=
Pressure reducer				
Cut-in pressure (bar)	33	=	55	–
Reduction factor	0.46	0.46	0.46	–
Brake calliper piston diameter				
front (mm)	48	=	40+36	38+38
rear (mm)	42	=	30+28	30+30
Brake disc diameter				
front (mm)	282.5	=	298	304
rear (mm)	290	=	299	309
Brake disc thickness				
front (mm)	24	=	28	32
rear (mm)	24	=	24	28
Effective brake disc area (cm^2)	258	=	344	344
Handbrake	Operating mechanically on both rear wheels			
Brake drum diameter (mm)	180	=	=	=
Contact area (cm^2)	170	=	=	=

Wheels and tyres				
Standard tyre specification, front	205/55ZR16	=	=	=
wheel	6J x 16 H2	=	=	=
hump depth (mm)	52	=	55	23.3
Standard tyre specification, rear	225/50ZR16	=	215/60VR15	245/45ZR16
wheel	8J x 16 H2	=	=	9J x 16
hump depth (mm)	10.6	=	52	15
Space-saver spare wheel	165-15 89P	=	=	=
Tyre pressure				
front (bar)	2.0	2.0	2.5	2.0
rear (bar)	2.5	2.5	3.0	3.0
Space-saver spare wheel (bar)	2.5	2.5	2.5	2.5

Model range	911 Carrera	911 Speedster	911 Carrera 4	911 Turbo
Body and interior (dimensions at kerb weight)				
Length (mm)	4291	=	4250	4291
Width (mm)	1652	=	1652	1775
Height (mm)	1320	1220	1310	1310
Wheelbase (mm)	2272	=	=	=
Track				
front (mm)	1380	=	=	=
rear (mm)	1372	=	1380	1432
Ground clearance at permissible gross weight (mm)	130	=	120	120
Overhang angle				
front (degree)	12.3	=	12.5	11.7
rear (degree)	13.9	=	12.0	14.0
Electrical system				
Generator output (W/A)	1260/90	=	=	=
Battery (V/Ah)	12/66	=	=	=
Weight according to DIN 70020				
Kerb weight (kg)	1210	1220	1450	1335
Permissible gross weight (kg)	1530	=	1790	1680
Permissible trailer weight				
unbraked (kg)	480	none	500	none
braked (kg)	800	none	1200	none
Performance				
Maximum speed (kmh)				
Manual transmission	245	=	260	260
Acceleration 0–62mph/100kmh (sec)				
Manual transmission	6.1	=	5.7	5.2
Measured kilometre from standing start (sec)				
Manual transmission	26.1	=	25.5	24.0

*Cat. conv. figs. in brackets

Fluid capacities	911 Carrera	911 Speedster	911 Carrera 4	911 Turbo
Engine oil quantity 1* (l)	13	=	11.5	13
Manual transmission 2* (l)	3.4	=	3.6	3.7
Front axle 2* (l)	–	–	1.2	–
Fuel tank (l)	85	=	77	85
Brake fluid reservoir 6* (l)	0.24	=	0.75	0.34
Power steering fluid 3 (l)	–	–	1.0	–
Refrigerant 4* (g)	1350	=	930	1300
Refrigerant oil 5* (ml)	120	=	100	120

* Key to numerals
1* Approved API SE/SF with combinations API SE/CC - SF/CC - SF/CD - SE/CD
   Multigrade engine oil factory recommended
2* Multigrade transmission fluid 75 W 90 acc. MIL-L 2105 B and API-classified GL 5

3* ATF DEXRON II D
4* Refrigerant R 12
5* Commercially available refrigerant oils
6* Use only brake fluid acc. SAE J 1703. DOT 3 or 4

Vehicle Identification Numbers

World manufacturer code	Code body USA (A=Coupé, B=Targa, C=Cabriolet)	Code for engine variants (only USA)	Restraint system (0 = belt, 2 = airbag) only USA	First and second digit for car type	Fill character/ check digit	Model year (K = 1989, L = 1990, etc.)	Manufacturing site (S = Stuttgart)	7th and 8th digit = car type	Code for body + engine	Sequence number	Summary
WPO	Z	Z	Z	91	Z	K	S	1	0	0001–3532	Rest of world, Carrera Coupé
WPO	Z	Z	Z	91	Z	K	S	1	4	0001–1063	Rest of world, Carrera Targa
WPO	Z	Z	Z	91	Z	K	S	1	5	0001–2787	Rest of world, Carrera Cabriolet
WPO	A	B	O	91	C*	K	S	1	2	0001–1156	USA/CDN, Carrera Coupé
WPO	E	B	O	91	C*	K	S	1	6	0001–0860	USA/CDN, Carrera Targa
WPO	C	B	O	91	C*	K	S	1	7	0001–1361	USA/CDN, Carrera Cabriolet
WPO	Z	Z	Z	93	Z	K	S	0	0	0001–0857	Rest of world, 911 Turbo Coupé
WPO	Z	Z	Z	93	Z	K	S	0	1	0001–0115	Rest of world, 911 Turbo Targa
WPO	Z	Z	Z	93	Z	K	S	0	2	0001–0244	Rest of world, 911 Turbo Cabriolet
WPO	J	B	O	93	C*	K	S	0	5	0001–0109	USA/CDN, 911 Turbo Coupé
WPO	E	B	O	93	C*	K	S	0	6	0001–2000	USA/CDN, 911 Turbo Targa
WPO	E	B	O	93	C*	K	S	0	7	0001–0600	USA/CDN, 911 Turbo Cabriolet
WPO	Z	Z	Z	96	Z	K	S	4	0	0001–2068	Rest of world, 911 Carrera 4
WPO	A	B	O	96	C*	K	S	4	5	0001–1117	USA/CDN, 911 Carrera 4

C* = Check digit, can be 0–9 or X (only USA)   Z = Fill character for rest of world cars

Model year 1990
L Programme, Tiptronic

Porsche 911 Carrera 2 Coupé, Targa and
  Cabriolet
Porsche 911 Carrera 4 Coupé, Targa and
  Cabriolet

A revised model range this year saw the Carrera 4
continue as the all-wheel drive 911, and a newly
badged Carrera 2 – with its bodywork effectively
shared with the Carrera 4 – became the rear-wheel
drive model. The 3.6-litre power unit of the 911
Carrera 2 was identical to the 911 Carrera 4's. The
Turbo, Turbo Look and Speedster versions of the
911 were not available in model year 1990. For the
first time Porsche's Tiptronic intelligent transmission
system was offered, which allowed for up- and
down-shifts without traction interruption.

Engine
No important changes to the M64/01 engine. In
Germany, only cars with lambda probe-equipped
catalytic converters were supplied. Unleaded
premium petrol was finally available everywhere
in Germany, but the rest of Europe was still
behind schedule.

Fuel and ignition system
No changes to the digital engine electronics (DME)
system, with the exception of the 911 Carrera 2,

*For 1990, Carrera 2 models adopted the revised styling used on the
Carrera 4 models, as seen on this Carrera 2 Coupé.*

where the DME and the control unit of the
Tiptronic interacted with each other.

Transmission
After several years only being offered with manual
gearboxes, as from January 1990 the 911 was
available with a new Tiptronic transmission. The
four-speed Tiptronic, offered in the Carrera 2,
could be driven like a conventional automatic
transmission. However, by moving the gear lever
from the 'D' position into the gate to the right, the
next gear could be selected manually simply by
moving the gear lever (backwards for downshifts
and forwards for upshifts).

The Tiptronic transmission drew on experience
gained in racing with the Porsche 962, where a
'PDK' power train had been employed for many
years. 'PDK' stood for Porsche *Doppelkupplung*
(Porsche double-clutch), which was the precursor
of a whole generation of automatic racing
transmissions. In the 962 race car, gearchanges
were made via push-buttons on the steering wheel
(as would be the case with the Tiptronic S from
model year 1995), but the 1990 Carrera 2's manual
shift was activated by nudging the gear lever.
Five-speed manual transmission (G50/03) was an
optional extra for the Carrera 2, while the Carrera
4 was only available with a manual five-speed
gearbox (G64/00). In all Carrera 4 and Carrera 2
vehicles with manual transmission, a dual-mass
flywheel was introduced to reduce annoying
transmission rattle at low engine revs.

Suspension
The suspension set-ups of the Carrera 2 and the
Carrera 4 were largely identical. However, while
the rear brake system in the Carrera 2 was still

A sectioned four-speed Tiptronic gearbox, which was introduced on Carrera 2 models for 1990.

fitted with two-piston brake callipers, the 911 Carrera 4 had four-piston callipers at the rear. In addition, the Carrera 4 was equipped with a high-pressure hydraulic brake servo, while the Carrera 2 used the induction manifold vacuum of the engine as a brake servo. The Carrera 2 and 4 were both fitted with light-alloy wheels (design 90). The rim width (*eg* 8) and the wheel hump depth (*eg* 52) were marked on the wheel to the left and right of the filling valve. Forged light-alloy wheels (disc wheel design) were also available as an optional extra (M395).

Body
Cabriolets had fully automatic soft tops as standard. Cars for the USA and Canada were delivered with airbags on both the driver's and passenger's side. The positive experience gained with airbags in the 944 Turbo in the USA had encouraged the decision to fit them in all model year 1990 cars destined for the North American market.

Equipment and fittings
Three-point inertia reel safety belts for the rear seats became standard (with the exception of the Cabriolet).

Electrical system
All vehicles were fitted with headlight-range adjustment. The electronic speedometer no longer received information via the distance pulses from

the transmission but via the wheel pulses of the ABS system. Due to the dual-mass flywheel, a crankshaft-mounted starter motor (1.7kW) had to be fitted. All vehicles were equipped with a knob on the centre console to extend or retract the rear spoiler electrically.

Vehicles with Tiptronic received an on-board computer as standard. This gave information about the remaining range (measuring fuel in the tank), functioned as a trip recorder, calculated the average fuel consumption and average speed, as well as indicating the outside temperature, and was equipped with a digital speed indicator.

Additional information
In addition to the standard production 911 Carrera 2, Carrera Cup cars were built for racing, based on the standard production Carrera 2. Differences to the standard production car: engines were carefully selected at the factory to give equal performance; the air filter and dual-mass flywheel were dispensed with; and the engine control units were checked for consistency and then sealed. The brake system (with large, internally vented brake discs and four-piston aluminium brake callipers) was derived from the 911 Turbo and was fitted with a hydraulic brake servo and ABS. The light-alloy wheels had an

ABOVE: A 1990-model 911 Carrera 4 3.6 Targa equipped with the 'design 90' alloy wheels now fitted as standard to all Carrera models.

BELOW: For 1990, the Carrera 4 3.6 Cabriolet was available with a fully automatic soft top.

asymmetrical safety hump against separation of the tyres from the rims upon loss of air. For safety reasons, there was a steel support bar welded into the body.

At the 1989 IAA international motor show in Frankfurt, Porsche surprised people with its 'Panamericana' design study, an open-roof prototype based on the Porsche 911.

Model range	Total production
911 Carrera 2 Coupé	8328* + 2196* USA
911 Carrera 2 Targa	3410* + 2230* USA
911 Carrera 2 Cabriolet	1298* + 788* USA
911 Carrera 4 Coupé	N/A
911 Carrera 4 Targa	N/A
911 Carrera 4 Cabriolet	N/A

* The vehicle ID numbers no longer allowed for a differentiation between Carrera 2 and Carrera 4. The production numbers mentioned relate to both vehicles and also include vehicles with Tiptronic.

Model range	Carrera 2	Carrera 4	Carrera 2 CUP
Engine			
Engine type			
manual transmission	M64/01	M64/01	M30/
Tiptronic	M64/02	–	–
Bore (mm)	100	100	100
Stroke (mm)	76.4	76.4	76.4
Displacement (cc)	3600	3600	3600
Compression ratio	11.3:1	11.3:1	11.3:1
Engine output (kW/hp)	184/250	184/250	195/265
at revolutions per minute (rpm)	6100	6100	
Torque (Nm)	310	310	
at revolutions per minute (rpm)	4800	4800	
Output per litre (kW/l)	51.1	51.1	
Max. engine speed (rpm)	6720	6720	6800
Engine weight (kg)	238	238	238

Carburation, ignition, settings			
Fuel system	DME S	DME S	DME S
Type of fuel (RON)	95	95	95
Ignition system	DME	=	KFZ
Ignition	dual	dual	dual
Spark plugs			
Bosch	FR 5 DTC	=	=
Beru	–	–	–
Spark plug gap (mm)	0.7	=	0.6
Anti-knock control	yes	yes	yes
Idle speed (rpm)	880+-40	=	
Exhaust/purification system	L sensor +cat.conv.	L sensor +cat.conv.	L sensor +cat.conv.
CO-content			
without cat. conv. (%)	0.5–1.0	=	
with cat. conv. (%)	0.4–1.2	=	
Fuel consumption acc. EC Standard (litres/100km)			
Manual transmission			
A. at a constant 90kmh	7.8	8.0	
B. at a constant 120kmh	9.7	9.5	
C. EC urban cycle	17.1	17.9	
Euromix	11.5	11.8	
Tiptronic			
A. at a constant 90kmh	7.9	–	–
B. at a constant 120kmh	9.6	–	–
C. EC urban cycle	17.1	–	–
Euromix	11.4	–	–

Model range	Carrera 2	Carrera 4	Carrera 2 CUP
Transmission			
Dual-mass flywheel	Syst.F*	Syst.LUK	no
Clutch, pressure plate	G MFZ 240	=	=
Clutch plate (mm)	rigid 240	GUD 240	Sport
Manual transmission	G50/03	G64/00	G50/
Gear ratios			
1st gear	3.500	3.500	
2nd gear	2.059	2.118	
3rd gear	1.407	1.444	
4th gear	1.086	1.086	
5th gear	0.868	0.868	
Reverse gear	2.857	=	=
Synchromesh system gears 1–5	VK	=	POSY
Synchromesh system reverse gear	VK	=	=
Final drive	3.444	3.444	3.444
Limited-slip differential	M	S	S
Lock-up factor under load/coasting (%)	40/40	variable 0–100	40/40
Gearbox weight with oil (kg)	66	79.76	66
Front differential (kg)	–	22.65	–
Tiptronic	A50/02	–	–
Torque converter dia. (mm)	260	–	–
Stall speed (rpm)	2300-400	–	–
Start-off conversion ratio	1.98:1	–	–
Gear ratios			
1st gear	2.479	–	–
2nd gear	1.479	–	–
3rd gear	1.000	–	–
4th gear	0.728	–	–
Reverse gear	2.086	–	–
Intermediate shaft	1.100	–	–
Final drive	3.667	–	–
Limited-slip differential	no	–	–
Gearbox weight with oil and ATF filling (kg)	105	–	–

Key:
DME S   Digital engine electronic system with sequential fuel injection
KFZ   Pressure-controlled mapped ignition
Syst.F*   Dual-mass flywheel System Freudenberg (rubber-damped)
Syst.LUK Dual-mass flywheel System LUK (Steel-spring damped)
POSY   Porsche locking synchromesh system, synchroniser rings, molybdenum-coated
VK   Full-cone synchromesh system with molybdenum-coated synchroniser rings

Suspension, steering and brakes			
Front axle			
Anti-roll bar dia. (mm)	20	=	20
Steering ratio	18.48	=	=
Turning circle dia. (m)	11.95	=	=
Rear axle			
Anti-roll bar dia.			
Manual transmission (mm)	20	=	20
Tiptronic (mm)	19	–	–
Brake system			
Brake booster ratio	3.0:1	hydr.	4.8:1
Brake master cylinder dia. (mm)	20.64	23.81	23.81
Pressure reducer			
Cut-in pressure (bar)	45	55	45
Reduction factor	0.46	0.46	0.46
Brake calliper piston diameter			
front (mm)	40+36	40+36	36+44
rear (mm)	44	30+28	30+34

Model range	Carrera 2	Carrera 4	Carrera 2 CUP
Suspension, steering and brakes (continued)			
Brake disc diameter			
front (mm)	298	298	322
rear (mm)	299	299	299
Brake disc thickness			
front (mm)	28	28	32
rear (mm)	24	24	24
Effective brake disc area (cm²)	284	344	422
Handbrake	Operating mechanically on both rear wheels		
Brake drum diameter (mm)	180	=	=
Contact area (cm²)	170	=	=

Wheels and tyres			
Standard tyre specification, front	205/55ZR16	=	235/45ZR17
wheel	6J x 16 H2	=	8J x 17 H2
hump depth (mm)	52	=	=
Standard tyre specification, rear	225/50ZR16	=	255/40ZR17
wheel	8J x 16 H2	=	9.5J x 17 H2
hump depth (mm)	52	=	55
Space-saver spare wheel	165-15 89P	=	165/70-16 89P
Tyre pressure			
front (bar)	2.5	2.5	2.5
rear (bar)	3.0	3.0	2.5
Space-saver spare wheel (bar)	2.5	3.0	2.5

Body and interior (dimensions at kerb weight)			
Length (mm)	4250	=	=
Width (mm)	1652	=	=
Height (mm)	1310	=	
Wheelbase (mm)	2272	=	=
Track			
front (mm)	1380	=	=
rear (mm)	1374	=	=
Ground clearance at permissible gross weight (mm)	115	120	115
Overhang angle			
front (degree)	11.5	=	
rear (degree)	12.5	=	

Electrical system			
Generator output (W/A)	1610/115	=	=
Battery (V/Ah)	12/75	=	=

Model range	Carrera 2	Carrera 4	Carrera 2 CUP
Weight according to DIN 70020			
Kerb weight (kg)			
Manual transmission	1350	1450	1220
Tiptronic	1380	–	–
Permissible gross weight (kg)			
Manual transmission	1690	1790	1810
Tiptronic	1720	–	–
Permissible trailer weight (kg)			
unbraked	500	500	none
braked	1200	1200	none

Performance			
Maximum speed (kmh)			
Manual transmission	260	260	
Tiptronic	256	–	–
Acceleration 0–62mph/100kmh (sec)			
Manual transmission	5.7	5.7	
Tiptronic	6.6	–	–
Measured kilometre from standing start (sec)			
Manual transmission	25.2	25.5	
Tiptronic	26.2	–	–

Fluid capacities			
Engine oil quantity 1* (l)	11.5	=	=
Manual transmission 2* (l)	3.6	3.8	3.6
Front axle 2* (l)	–	1.2	–
Automatic transm. 3* (l)	9.0	–	–
Final drive, autom.2* (l)	0.9	–	–
Fuel tank (l)	77	=	=
Brake fluid reservoir 6* (l)	0.34	0.75	0.34
Power steering fluid 3 (l)	1.0	1.0	1.0
Refrigerant 4* (g)	930	=	–
Refrigerant oil 5* (ml)	100	=	–

* Key to numerals
1* Approved API SE/SF with combinations API SE/CC - SF/CC - SF/CD - SE/CD
   Multigrade engine oil factory recommended
2* Multigrade gear oil 75 W 90
3* Multigrade transmission fluid 75 W 90 acc. MIL-L 2105 B and API-classified GL 5
   ATF DEXRON II D
4* Refrigerant R 12
5* Commercially available refrigerant oils
6* Use only brake fluid acc. SAE J 1703. DOT 3 or 4

Vehicle Identification Numbers												
World manufacturer code	Code body USA (A=Coupé, B=Targa, C=Cabriolet)	Code for engine variants (only USA)	Restraint system (0 = belt, 2 = airbag) only USA	First and second digit for car type	Fill character/ check digit	Model year (J = 1990, M = 1991, etc.)	Manufacturing site (S = Stuttgart)	7th and 8th digit = car type	Code for body + engine	Sequence number	Summary
WPO	Z	Z	Z	96	Z	L	S	4	0	0001–8328	Rest of world, Coupé
WPO	Z	Z	Z	96	Z	L	S	4	1	0001–1298	Rest of world, Carrera Targa
WPO	Z	Z	Z	96	Z	L	S	4	2	0001–3410	Rest of world, Carrera Cabriolet
WPO	A	B	2	96	C*	L	S	4	5	0001–2116	USA/CDN, Coupé with airbag
WPO	B	B	2	96	C*	L	S	4	6	0001–0727	USA/CDN, Targa with airbag
WPO	C	B	2	916	C*	L	S	4	7	0001–2139	USA/CDN, Cabriolet with airbag

C* = Check digit, can be 0–9 or X (only USA)
Z = Fill character for rest of world cars

Model year 1991

M Programme, relaunch of the Turbo

Porsche 911 Carrera 2 Coupé, Targa and
  Cabriolet
Porsche 911 Carrera 4 Coupé, Targa and
  Cabriolet
Porsche 911 Turbo Coupé, Targa and
  Cabriolet

Porsche continued to build the 911 Carrera 2 and 4 with slight modifications in model year 1991. The 911 Turbo was reintroduced this year, slotting firmly back in as the top model of the range and using the Carrera 4 bodyshell. Its engine (still 3.3 litres) was now fitted with a lambda probe-equipped catalytic converter and offered 235kW (320hp). Despite the bodyshell sharing much of its metalwork with the Carrera, Porsche's trademark Turbo look with its wide wings (fenders) remained intact. An intercooler that was 20% larger than before lay underneath the Turbo's big rear spoiler.

Engine
New pistons were used in the 3.6-litre M64/01 engines for the Carrera. The cylinder head gasket was reworked and the spark plug replacement interval was doubled to 40,000km (24,000 miles).
  A new worldwide 3.3-litre engine (M30/69) was developed for the 911 Turbo. Apart from some

technical specification changes (see table) there were further improvements: new thermally optimised cylinders, cylinder head gaskets made from stainless steel, full-flow oil filter, separate generator belt drives (115amp), and cooling fan. In 1991 European regulations required that the 911 Turbo be fitted with a lambda probe-equipped catalytic converter.

Fuel and ignition system
For the new turbo engine, an enlarged exhaust gas turbocharger was employed as well as the tried and tested K-Jetronic with lambda control. Electronic mapped ignition, a metal catalytic converter and an enlarged intercooler allowed for an increase in performance while reducing the exhaust emissions at the same time.
  As all 911 Carrera engines were now operating with unleaded petrol, combustion chamber deposits were reduced, as was the erosion of the spark plugs, whose service life was therefore doubled.

Transmission
No changes to the Carrera model range. The Turbo used a revised G50/52 five-speed manual transmission, based on the G50/50 transmission of the earlier Turbo but with revised ratios and the shift mechanism of the Carrera 2. New mechanical ZF limited-slip differential was standard, with different lock-up factors under load and coasting (varying from 20% to 100%), unlike earlier systems.

A cutaway illustration of a 1991-model 911 Carrera 2 3.6 Coupé, showing the clever packaging of the suspension and drivetrain.

The 1991-model 911 Turbo 3.3 Coupé was fitted with the new M30/69 engine, producing 235kW (320hp) at 5,750rpm.

The dual-mass flywheel was now also available for the 911 Turbo. This differed significantly from Carrera versions in its configuration: instead of flexible rubber dampers the 911 Turbo used steel springs and the damping action was effected by mechanical friction damping. The manufacturer was LUK.

Suspension

The Carrera model range was fitted with a strengthened anti-roll bar at the rear with a diameter of 20mm. The suspension of the new 911 Turbo was basically identical to that of the Carrera model range, but with enhancements: MacPherson front independent suspension with light-alloy wishbones, rear wheels individually suspended from light-alloy semi-trailing arms, power-assisted

The new oval-shaped aerodynamic mirrors are visible on this 1991-model Turbo, along with the 17in wheels.

rack-and-pinion steering, coil springs on front and rear axles, dual-circuit brake system with hydraulic brake servo, and anti-lock brakes. Turbo anti-roll bars were 21mm diameter at the front, 22mm at the rear. New die-cast light-alloy wheels were in Cup design, 7Jx17 H2 ET 55 at the front, 9Jx17 H2 ET 55 at the rear, tyres 205/50 ZR 17 front and 255/40 ZR 17 rear. This was the first time that Porsche allowed for a wheel diameter of 17in on a production car. The very low 40 profile on the Turbo's rear tyres was also new territory for production cars.

Body

As of 1 February 1991, all left-hand drive Porsches were fitted with airbags for both driver and passenger as standard. The decision to fit two airbags resulted from the view that 'Porsche considers safety not to be for sale, but part of the standard equipment'. The platform and structure of the Turbo bodies were identical to the Carrera. Front wings (fenders), rear sides and removable parts were all modified for the wider bodyshell. The new underbody panelling improved airflow. New oval mirrors also were fitted to the 911 Turbo,

offering improved optics, reduced aerodynamic resistance, lower wind noise and less weight.

Interior fittings

The unlocking of the rear backrest was done via a release push-button. For the 911 Turbo the instrument panel was covered with colour-coded leather as standard (for all other 911 models leather interiors were an optional extra).

Heating and air conditioning

The 911 Turbo was fitted with two heating fans in the rear. The heat exchange apparatus, the warm-air ducting and air conditioning were identical to the Carrera.

Electrical system

Modified alarm control units in all vehicles. The 911 Turbo was fitted with an on-board computer as standard equipment, which also digitally displayed the turbo boost pressure.

Only minor detail modifications were made to the 911 Carrera 4 3.6 Coupé for 1991.

Model range	Total production
911 Carrera 2 Coupé	7840* + 1608* USA
911 Carrera 2 Targa	1196* + 746* USA
911 Carrera 2 Cabriolet	3410* + 2230* USA
911 Carrera 4 Coupé	N/A
911 Carrera 4 Targa	N/A
911 Carrera 4 Cabriolet	N/A
911 Turbo Coupé	2288 + 674 USA

* The vehicle ID numbers no longer allowed for a differentiation between Carrera 2 and Carrera 4. The production numbers mentioned relate to both vehicles and also include vehicles with Tiptronic.

Model range	Carrera 2	Carrera 4	911 Turbo
Engine			
Engine type			
Manual transmission	M64/01	M64/01	M30/69
Tiptronic	M64/02	–	–
Bore (mm)	100	100	97
Stroke (mm)	76.4	76.4	74.4
Displacement (cc)	3600	3600	3299
Compression ratio	11.3:1	11.3:1	7.0:1
Engine output (kW/hp)	184/250	184/250	235/320
at revolutions per minute (rpm)	6100	6100	5750
Torque (Nm)	310	310	450
at revolutions per minute (rpm)	4800	4800	4500
Output per litre (kW/l)	51.1	51.1	71.2
Max. engine speed (rpm)	6720	6720	6900
Engine weight (kg)	238	238	275

Carburation, ignition, settings			
Fuel system	DME S	DME S	K-Jetronic
Type of fuel (RON)	95	95	95
Ignition system	DME	=	KFZ
Ignition	dual	dual	single
Spark plugs			
Bosch	FR 5 DTC	=	WR 4 DPO
Beru			
Spark plug gap (mm)	0.7	=	0.6
Anti-knock control	yes	yes	no
Idle speed (rpm)	880+-40	=	1000+-50
Exhaust/purification system	L sensor+ cat.conv.	L sensor+ cat.conv.	L sensor+ cat.conv.
CO-content			
without cat. conv. (%)	0.5–1.0	=	1+-0.2
with cat. conv. (%)	0.4–1.2	=	1+-0.2
Fuel consumption acc. EC Standard (litres/100km)			
Manual transmission			
A. at a constant 90kmh	7.8	8.0	8.5
B. at a constant 120kmh	9.7	9.5	10.4
C. EC urban cycle	17.1	17.9	21.0
Euromix	11.5	11.8	13.0
Tiptronic			
A. at a constant 90kmh	7.9	–	–
B. at a constant 120kmh	9.6	–	–
C. EC urban cycle	17.1	–	–
Euromix	11.4	–	–

Model range	Carrera 2	Carrera 4	911 Turbo
Transmission			
Dual-mass flywheel	Syst.F*	Syst.F*	Syst.LUK
Clutch, pressure plate	G MFZ 240	=	=
Clutch plate (mm)	rigid 240	rigid 240	rigid 240
Manual transmission	G50/03	G64/00	G50/52
Gear ratios			
1st gear	3.500	3.500	3.154
2nd gear	2.059	2.118	1.789
3rd gear	1.407	1.444	1.269
4th gear	1.086	1.086	0.967
5th gear	0.868	0.868	0.756
Reverse gear	2.857	=	=
Synchromesh system	gears 1–5 VK	=	=
Synchromesh system reverse gear	VK	=	=
Final drive	3.444	3.444	3.444
Limited-slip differential	M	S	S
Lock-up factor under load/coasting (%)	40/40	variable 0–100	20/100
Gearbox weight with oil (kg)	66	79.76	71
Front differential (kg)	–	22.65	–
Tiptronic	A50/02	–	–
Torque converter dia. (mm)	260	–	–
Stall speed (rpm)	2300	–	–
Start-off conversion ratio	1.98:1	–	–
Gear ratios			
1st gear	2.479	–	–
2nd gear	1.479	–	–
3rd gear	1.000	–	–
4th gear	0.728	–	–
Reverse gear	2.086	–	–
Intermediate shaft	1.100	–	–
Final drive	3.667	–	–
Limited-slip differential	no	–	–
Gearbox weight with oil and ATF filling (kg)	105	–	–

Key:
DME S	Digital engine electronic system with sequential fuel injection
KFZ	Pressure-controlled mapped ignition
Syst.F*	Dual-mass flywheel System Freudenberg (rubber -damped)
Syst.LUK	Dual-mass flywheel System LUK (steel-spring damped)
VK	Full-cone synchromesh system with molybdenum-coated synchroniser rings

Suspension, steering and brakes			
Front axle			
Anti-roll bar dia. (mm)	20	=	21
Steering ratio	18.48	=	=
Turning circle dia. (m)	11.95	=	11.45
Rear axle			
Anti-roll bar dia. (mm)			
Manual transmission	20	=	22
Tiptronic	19	–	–
Brake system			
Brake booster ratio	3.0:1	hydr.	4.8:1
Brake master cylinder dia. (mm)	20.64	23.81	23.81
Pressure reducer			
Cut-in pressure (bar)	45	55	45
Reduction factor	0.46	0.46	0.46
Brake calliper piston diameter			
front (mm)	40+36	40+36	36+44
rear (mm)	44	30+28	30+34
Brake disc diameter			
front (mm)	298	298	322
rear (mm)	299	299	299

Model range	Carrera 2	Carrera 4	911 Turbo
Brake disc thickness			
front (mm)	28	28	32
rear (mm)	24	24	24
Effective brake disc area (cm²)	284	344	422
Handbrake	Operating mechanically on both rear wheels		
Brake drum diameter (mm)	180	=	=
Contact area (cm²)	170	=	=

Wheels and tyres

	Carrera 2	Carrera 4	911 Turbo
Standard tyre specification, front	205/55ZR16	=	205/50ZR17
wheel	6J x 16 H2	=	7J x 17
hump depth (mm)	52	=	55
Standard tyre specification, rear	225/50ZR16	=	255/40ZR17
wheel	8J x 16 H2	=	9J x 17
hump depth (mm)	52	=	55
Space-saver spare wheel	165/70-16 92P	=	=
Tyre pressure			
front (bar)	2.5	2.5	2.5
rear (bar)	3.0	3.0	2.5
Space-saver spare wheel (bar)	2.5	3.0	2.5

Body and interior (dimensions at kerb weight)

	Carrera 2	Carrera 4	911 Turbo
Length (mm)	4250	=	=
Width (mm)	1652	=	1775
Height (mm)	1310	=	=
Wheelbase (mm)	2272	=	=
Track			
front (mm)	1380	=	1442
rear (mm)	1374	=	1499
Ground clearance at permissible gross weight (mm)	115	120	115
Overhang angle			
front (degree)	11.5	=	11.5
rear (degree)	12.5	=	12.5

Electrical system

	Carrera 2	Carrera 4	911 Turbo
Generator output (W/A)	1610/115	=	=
Battery (V/Ah)	12/75	=	=

Weight according to DIN 70020

Model range	Carrera 2	Carrera 4	911 Turbo
Kerb weight (kg)			
Manual transmission	1350	1450	1470
Tiptronic	1380	–	–
Permissible gross weight (kg)			
Manual transmission	1690	1790	1810
Tiptronic	1720	–	–
Permissible trailer weight (kg)			
unbraked	500	500	none
braked	1200	1200	none

Performance

	Carrera 2	Carrera 4	911 Turbo
Maximum speed (kmh)			
Manual transmission	260	260	270
Tiptronic	256	–	–
Acceleration 0–62mph/100kmh (sec)			
Manual transmission	5.7	5.7	5.0
Tiptronic	6.6	–	–
Measured kilometre from standing start (sec)			
Manual transmission	25.2	25.5	24.3
Tiptronic	26.2	–	–

Fluid capacities

	Carrera 2	Carrera 4	911 Turbo
Engine oil quantity 1* (l)	11.5	=	13
Manual transmission 2* (l)	3.6	3.8	3.6
Front axle 2* (l)	–	1.2	–
Automatic transm. 3* (l)	9.0	–	–
Final drive, autom.2* (l)	0.9	–	–
Fuel tank (l)	77	=	=
Brake fluid reservoir 6* (l)	0.34	0.75	0.34
Power steering fluid 3 (l)	1.0	1.0	1.0
Refrigerant 4* (g)	930	=	840
Refrigerant oil 5* (ml)	100	=	140

* Key to numerals
1* Approved API SE/SF with combinations API SE/CC - SF/CC - SF/CD - SE/CD Multigrade engine oil factory recommended
2* Multigrade gear oil 75 W 90
3* Multigrade transmission fluid 75 W 90 acc. MIL-L 2105 B and API-classified GL 5 ATF DEXRON II D
4* Refrigerant R 12
5* Commercially available refrigerant oils
6* Use only brake fluid acc. SAE J 1703. DOT 3 or 4

Vehicle Identification Numbers

World manufacturer code	Code body USA (A=Coupé, B=Targa, C=Cabriolet)	Code for engine variants (only USA)	Restraint system (0 = belt, 2 = airbag) only USA	First and second digit for car type	Fill character/ check digit	Model year (M = 1991, N = 1992, etc.)	Manufacturing site (S = Stuttgart)	7th and 8th digit = car type	Code for body + engine	Sequence number	Summary
WPO	Z	Z	Z	96	Z	M	S	4	0	0001–7840	Rest of world, Coupé
WPO	Z	Z	Z	96	Z	M	S	4	3	0001–1196	Rest of world, Carrera Targa
WPO	Z	Z	Z	96	Z	M	S	4	5	0001–3886	Rest of world, Carrera Cabriolet
WPO	Z	Z	Z	96	Z	M	S	4	7	0001–2288	Rest of world, Turbo
WPO	A	B	2	96	C*	M	S	4	1	0001–1608	USA/CDN, Coupé with airbag
WPO	B	B	2	96	C*	M	S	4	4	0001–0746	USA/CDN, Targa with airbag
WPO	C	B	2	96	C*	M	S	4	6	0001–2207	USA/CDN, Cabriolet with airbag
WPO	A	A	2	96	C*	M	S	4	8	0001–0674	USA/CDN, Turbo with airbag

C* = Check digit, can be 0–9 or X (only USA)
Z = Fill character for rest of world cars

Model year 1992

N Programme, Carrera RS

Porsche 911 Carrera 2 Coupé, Targa and
   Cabriolet
Porsche 911 Carrera 4 Coupé, Targa and
   Cabriolet
Porsche 911 Carrera 2 Cabriolet Turbo Look
Porsche 911 Carrera RS Coupé
Porsche 911 RS America Coupé
Porsche 911 Turbo and Turbo S Coupé

In model year 1992 the modifications to the
Carrera 2, Carrera 4 and Turbo were limited to
minor changes that were as much about quality
improvement as technical advancement. Engine
oil and filter changes were done away with for
all 911 vehicles, as well as the tappet clearance
check and transmission oil level check, during the
first service.

One new model was the Carrera 2 Cabriolet
Turbo Look, fitted with the chassis, brake system,

*The 911 Carrera RS was introduced for 1992, with the emphasis on
performance rather than comfort.*

17in wheels and wide wings (fenders) of the 911
Turbo. Its engine, clutch and gearbox were
identical to the 911 Carrera 2.

A very high-performance lightweight Turbo S
was available from Porsche's Exclusive Department
in Zuffenhausen. This car stood out for its higher
turbo boost pressure, modified ignition mapping
and changes to the body and wheels.

Another special new model was the Carrera RS,
designed to be able to race in Group N or Group
GT classes. The RS followed the successful 911 Cup
racing series in 1991, and was introduced as the
'people's version' using the two-wheel drive
Carrera as its basis. Porsche explored new territory
with this car, with less emphasis on comfort and
more on making it a pure driving machine.
Everything that was not absolutely necessary was
dispensed with – Porsche even saved on water for
the windscreen washer, the 7.5-litre container
shrinking to just one litre for the standard 'basic'
version. Three option packages were available over
the basic model:

■ Carrera Cup version (M001): could not be made
   road-legal, designed purely for racing.
■ Touring version (M002): could be made road-
   legal, some driving comfort.
■ Competition or Sport version (M003): could be
   made road-legal, little comfort.

As the 911 Carrera RS could not be homologated for the USA, a special USA edition, the 911 RS America, was built. This was not so much a high-performance model as a stripped-out, sportier version of the 911 Carrera 2, whose standard drive systems and components it shared. However, it boasted sports suspension, 17in Cup Design wheels and a fixed rear spoiler.

Engine
Carrera 2 and 4, Turbo: no notable modifications for the current model year. Carrera RS: M64/03 engine with increased power (191kW/260hp); pistons and cylinders were specially selected; the flywheel was lightweight; the alternator and fan were driven by a single V-belt; and instead of hydraulic engine mountings, stiffer rubber mountings were used. The RS America engine had 184kW (250hp).

Fuel and ignition system
Carrera 2 and 4: no changes. Turbo: modifications to the lambda control unit and new Bosch WR 6 DPO spark plugs at the warm-up control valve. Carrera RS: modified DME control unit and earlier ignition timing, for which 98RON petrol was required. When unleaded 95RON petrol was used, ignition timing adjustment was carried out via the anti-knock control (this also reduced the power output). Even though the RS engine resembled a racing engine, it should be remembered that it was fitted with a lambda probe-equipped catalytic converter.

The modifications to the Tiptronic control unit also had effects on the engine management: improved reactions (trailing throttle on downshifting), downshifts to first gear were possible at speeds under 34mph (55kmh), and there was a special drive-off programme for starting when cold.

Transmission
Carrera 2 and 4: increase of the clutch pressure force. The pedals of the Turbo were fitted with an auxiliary spring to reduce the clutch pedal force, now for naturally aspirated engines too. Transmission G64/00 for the 911 Carrera 4: changeover from the axle-differential lock to improved friction discs.

Tiptronic A50/02 power train system: gearbox mounting in the front gearbox cover; gearchanges were now easier; for the USA (Tiptronic power train system A50/03) there was a changed final-drive ratio of 3.555:1; and modifications to the Tiptronic control unit improved driving comfort.

The 191kW (260hp) 911 Carrera RS featured the oval mirrors first seen on Turbo models.

The selected gear was displayed within the speedometer, and keylock and shiftlock security features were introduced for US and Canadian cars (keylock = gearshift and ignition lock, shiftlock = gearshift lock).

Carrera RS: developed for competitive racing, in its 'basic' version it was equipped with a lightened flywheel and the clutch plate had steel-spring damping. The Touring version was fitted with the dual-mass flywheel of the Carrera 2 and the Sport version was equipped with a rigid sintered clutch plate and lightened flywheel. All RS versions were built with a G50/10 five-speed manual transmission that differed from the Carrera 2's G50/03 through its taller first and second gear ratios.

Further variations to Carrera 2 transmissions: stiffer

A 1992-model 911 Carrera 2 3.6 Cabriolet Turbo Look, featuring the front and rear wheel arches and mirrors from the 911 Turbo.

central mountings made from rubber in the front gearbox cover, limited-slip differential standard (lock-up factor as for the 911 Turbo), steel synchronising ring, changed gearshift sleeves, final drive ratio changed from 4.000:1 to 3.400:1 (sportier).

All RS models sold in Germany were 'basic' versions. Gearbox noise at low speeds was tolerated in order to keep weight and rotating masses as low as possible. Positive experience gained with the 911 Turbo was further utilised: the RS was fitted with the ZF limited-slip differential with differing lock-up values for acceleration and coasting.

Suspension
For the Carrera 2 and 4: modified ZF power steering, whose steering angle was limited because of the big 17in wheels. Identical rear springs for both Carrera models. USA: Carrera 2 with light-alloy four-piston rear brake callipers of the 911 Carrera 4 together with a 55/5 brake pressure limiter. Cup Design 16in light-alloy wheels were standard, 17in ones were an optional extra (7Jx17 AH ET 55 front, 8Jx17 AH ET 52 rear). 'AH' denotes an asymmetrical hump on the outside of a tyre that prevents it from sliding into the centre of the wheel upon loss of air; steering and driving stability as well as the ability to brake were thus maintained to a certain extent. Tyres were 205/50 ZR 17 front and 255/40 ZR 17 rear.

Carrera RS: the suspension was completely reworked and lowered by 40mm. Springs, dampers and anti-roll bars were stiffer for uncompromisingly sporty handling. The rack-and-pinion steering made do without power assistance. The brake system was adopted from the 911 Turbo (front) and the 911 Cup (rear), with a hydraulic brake servo. Wheels were cast magnesium alloy, front 7.5Jx17 AH ET 55, rear 9Jx17 AH ET 55, tyres 205/50 ZR 17 front and 255/40 ZR 17 rear.

The elaborate and expensive manufacture of the wheels for the RS from magnesium led to a 10.6kg reduction in weight. Here is a comparison between kerb weight and power/weight ratio: Carrera 2 Coupé 1,350kg and 5.40kg/hp; Carrera RS 1,220kg and 4.69kg/hp.

Body
Carrera 2 and 4: no changes. Turbo: no changes. Carrera 2 Cabriolet Turbo Look: wings (fenders) as well as front and rear bodywork originated from the 911 Turbo, while the extendable rear spoiler came from the Carrera 2 and 4. Turbo S: one-piece rear spoiler, extra front air intakes, plastic opening panels.

Equipment and fittings
Full leather upholstery for the Carrera 2 Cabriolet Turbo Look. Oval-shaped exterior rear-view mirror as for the Turbo. The basic version of the Carrera RS did not have underbody protection, therefore

A 1992-model 911 Carrera 2 3.6 with a then-cutting-edge-technology telephone fitted next to the centre console.

only had a three-year warranty against rust. The Touring version had the same underbody protection as the Carrera 2 and the usual long-term warranty. No airbags for Carrera RS, and luggage compartment lid made from light alloy. Dropping the airbags to save weight was compensated for by six-point safety belts and the requirement to wear a helmet at events.

Interior fittings
Carrera 2 and 4 and Turbo: no changes. Carrera RS: basic version had bucket seats for driver and passenger, prepared for six-point safety belts; Touring version had electric height-adjustable sports seats. The Turbo S also had a stripped-out cabin.

Heating and air conditioning
All 911s: new heating/air conditioning controller. The Carrera 2 Cabriolet Turbo Look was fitted with air conditioning as standard equipment.

Electrical system
New generation radio, the Symphony RDS (Radio Data System).

Additional information
At the Geneva Motor Show in March 1992 Porsche launched the lightweight 911 Turbo S which was equipped with a 3.3-litre turbo engine with

increased power of 280kW (381hp). The camshafts were altered, the intake system was ported and the injection and ignition systems were optimised. The car's suspension was lowered by 40mm compared with the regular Turbo Coupé and it was fitted with three-piece 18in Cup wheels. The rear wings (fenders) incorporated additional air intake ducts for better cooling of the rear brakes. The bonnet lid and rigid rear wing were made from high-quality plastic. The total weight was reduced by 180kg compared with the standard 3.3-litre Turbo. Only 86 Turbo S cars were made.

Model range	Total production
911 Carrera 2 Coupé	4844* + 1013* USA
911 Carrera 2 Targa	597* + 211* USA
911 Carrera 2 Cabriolet	2885* + 992* USA
911 Carrera 4 Coupé	N/A
911 Carrera 4 Targa	N/A
911 Carrera 4 Cabriolet	N/A
911 Carrera RS Coupé	2282 + 313 USA
911 Turbo Coupé	836 + 309 USA
911 Turbo S lightweight	86

* The vehicle ID numbers no longer allowed for a differentiation between Carrera 2 and Carrera 4. The production numbers mentioned relate to both vehicles and also include vehicles with Tiptronic.

Model range	Carrera 2	Carrera 4	Carrera RS	RS America	911 Turbo	Turbo S	Turbo Look
Engine							
Engine type							
Manual transmission	M64/01	M64/01	M64/03	M64/01	M30/69	M30/69SL	M64/01
Tiptronic	M64/02	–	–	–	–	–	M64/02
Bore (mm)	100	100	100	100	97	97	100
Stroke (mm)	76.4	76.4	76.4	76.4	74.4	74.4	76.4
Displacement (cc)	3600	3600	3600	3600	3299	3299	3600
Compression ratio	11.3:1	11.3:1	11.3:1	11.3:1	7.0:1	7.0:1	11.3:1
Engine output (kW/hp)	184/250	184/250	191/260	184/250	235/320	280/381	184/250
at revolutions per minute (rpm)	6100	6100	6100	6100	5750	6000	6100
Torque (Nm)	310	310	325	310	450	490	310
at revolutions per minute (rpm)	4800	4800	4800	4800	4500	4800	4800
Output per litre (kW/l)	51.1	51.1	53.0	51.1	71.2	84.9	51.1
Max. engine speed (rpm)	6720	6720	6720	6720	6900	6900	6720
Engine weight (kg)	238	238	226	238	275	275	238

Model range	Carrera 2	Carrera 4	Carrera RS	RS America	911 Turbo	Turbo S	Turbo Look
Carburation, ignition, settings							
Fuel system	DME S	DME S	DME S	DME S	K-Jetronic	K-Jetronic	DME S
Type of fuel (RON)	95	95	98	95	95	98	95
Ignition system	DME	=	=	=	KFZ	KFZ	DME
Ignition	dual	dual	dual	dual	single	single	dual
Spark plugs							
Bosch	FR 5 DTC	=	=	=	WR 4 DPO	WR 4 DPO	FR 5 DTC
Beru							
Spark plug gap (mm)	0.7	=	=	=	0.6	0.6	0.7
Anti-knock control	yes	yes	yes	yes	no	no	yes
Idle speed (rpm)	880+-40	=	=	=	1000+-50	=	800+-40
Exhaust/purification system	Lambda sensor/three-way catalytic converter						
CO-content							
without cat. conv. (%)	0.5–1.0	=	=	=	1+-0.2	=	0.5–1.0
with cat. conv. (%)	0.4–1.2	=	=	=	1+-0.2	=	0.4–1.2
Fuel consumption acc. EC Standard, (litres/100km)							
Manual transmission							
A. at a constant 90kmh	7.8	8.0	7.7	7.8	8.5	7.8	
B. at a constant 120kmh	9.7	9.5	9.5	9.7	10.4	9.7	
C. EC urban cycle	17.1	17.9	15.7	17.1	21.0	17.1	
Euromix	11.5	11.8	11.0	11.5	13.3	11.5	
Tiptronic							
A. at a constant 90kmh	7.9	–	–	–	–	–	7.8
B. at a constant 120kmh	9.6	–	–	–	–	–	9.6
C. EC urban cycle	17.1	–	–	–	–	–	17.1
Euromix	11.4	–	–	–	–	–	11.4

Model range	Carrera 2	Carrera 4	Carrera RS	RS America	911 Turbo	Turbo S	Turbo Look
Transmission							
Dual-mass flywheel	Syst.F*	Syst.F*	no	Syst.F*	Syst.LUK	Syst.LUK	Syst.F*
Clutch, pressure plate	G MFZ 240	=	=	=	=	=	=
Clutch plate (mm)	rigid 240	rigid 240	sprung 240	rigid 240	rigid 240	rigid 240	rigid 240
Manual transmission	G50/03	G64/00	G50/10	G50/05	G50/52	G50/52	G50/03
Gear ratios							
1st gear	3.500	3.500	3.154	3.500	3.154	3.154	3.500
2nd gear	2.059	2.118	1.895	2.059	1.789	1.789	2.059
3rd gear	1.407	1.444	1.407	1.407	1.269	1.269	1.407
4th gear	1.086	1.086	1.086	1.086	0.967	0.967	1.086
5th gear	0.868	0.868	0.868	0.868	0.756	0.756	0.868
Reverse gear	2.857	=	=	=	=	=	=
Synchromesh system gears	1–5VK	=	=	=	=	=	=
Synchromesh system r. gear	VK	=	=	=	=	=	=
Final drive	3.444	3.444	3.444	3.333	3.444	3.444	3.444
Limited-slip differential	M	S	S	M	S	S	M
Lock-up factor under load/coasting (%)	40/40	variable 0–100	20/100	40/40	20/100	20/100	40/40
Gearbox weight with oil (kg)	66	79.65	66	66	71	71	66
Front differential (kg)	–	22.65	–	–	–	–	–
Tiptronic	A50/02	–	–	–	–	–	A50/02
Torque converter dia.(mm)	260	–	–	–	–	–	
Stall speed (rpm)	2300-400	–	–	–	–	–	
Start-off conversion ratio	1.98:1	–	–	–	–	–	
Gear ratios							
1st gear	2.479	–	–	–	–	–	
2nd gear	1.479	–	–	–	–	–	
3rd gear	1.000	–	–	–	–	–	
4th gear	0.728	–	–	–	–	–	
Reverse gear	2.086	–	–	–	–	–	

Model range	Carrera 2	Carrera 4	Carrera RS	RS America	911 Turbo	Turbo S	Turbo Look
Transmission (continued)							
Tiptronic (continued)							
Intermediate shaft	1.100	–	–	–	–	–	
Final drive	3.667	–	–	–	–	–	
Limited-slip differential	no	–	–	–	–	–	
Gearbox weight with oil and ATF filling (kg)	105	–	–	–	–	–	

Key:
DME   Digital engine electronic system with sequential fuel injection
KFZ   Pressure-controlled mapped ignition
Syst.F* Dual-mass flywheel System Freudenberg (rubber-damped)

Syst.LUK Dual-mass flywheel System LUK (Steel-spring damped)
VK   Full-cone synchromesh system with molybdenum-coated synchroniser rings

Suspension, steering and brakes	Carrera 2	Carrera 4	Carrera RS	RS America	911 Turbo	Turbo S	Turbo Look
Front axle							
Anti-roll bar dia. (mm)	20	=	24	20	21	21	21
Steering ratio	18.48	=	=	=	=	=	=
Turning circle dia. (m)	11.95	=	=	=	11.45	?	
Rear axle							
Anti-roll bar dia.							
man. trans.(mm)	20	=	18	20	22	22	22
Tiptronic (mm)	19	–	–	–	–	–	21
Brake system							
Brake booster ratio	3.0:1	hydr.	3.6:1	3.0:1	4.8:1	=	4.8:1
Brake master cylinder dia. (mm)	20.64	23.81	25.4	20.64	23.18	=	23.81
Pressure reducer							
Cut-in pressure (bar)	45	55	55	55	60	60	60
Reduction factor	0.46	0.46	0.46	0.46	0.46	0.46	0.46
Brake calliper piston diameter							
front (mm)	40+36	40+36	36+44	40+36	36.44	36.44	44+36
rear (mm)	44	30+28	30+34	44	30+34	30+34	30+34
Brake disc diameter							
front (mm)	298	298	322	298	322	322	322
rear (mm)	299	299	299	299	299	299	299
Brake disc thickness							
front (mm)	28	28	32	28	32	32	32
rear (mm)	24	24	24	24	28	28	28
Effective brake disc area (cm^2)	284	344	284	284	422	422	422
Handbrake	Operating mechanically on both rear wheels						
Brake drum							
diameter (mm)	180	=	=	=	=	=	=
Contact area (cm^2)	170	=	=	=	=	=	=

Wheels and tyres	Carrera 2	Carrera 4	Carrera RS	RS America	911 Turbo	Turbo S	Turbo Look
Standard tyre specification, front	205/55ZR16	=	205/55ZR17	205/50ZR17	205/50ZR17	225/40ZR18	205/50ZR17
wheel	6Jx16H2	=	7.5Jx17H2	7Jx17AH	=	8Jx18H2	J7x17AH
hump depth (mm)	52	=	55	55	55	52	55
Standard tyre specification, rear	225/50ZR16	=	255/40ZR17	255/40ZR17	=	265/35ZR18	255/40ZR17
wheel	8Jx16H2	=	9Jx17H2	8Jx17AH	9Jx17AH	10Jx18H2	9Jx17AH
hump depth (mm)	52	=	55	52	55	55	55
Space-saver spare wheel	165/70-16 92P	=	=	=	=	=	=
Tyre pressure							
front (bar)	2.5	2.5	2.5	2.5	2.5	2.5	2.5
rear (bar)	3.0	3.0	2.5	2.5	2.5	2.5	2.5
Space-saver spare wheel (bar)	2.5	3.0	2.5	2.5	2.5	2.5	2.5

Body and interior (dimensions at kerb weight)	Carrera 2	Carrera 4	Carrera RS	RS America	911 Turbo	Turbo S	Turbo Look
Length (mm)	4250	=	4275	4275	4250	4250	4250
Width (mm)	1652	=	=	=	1775	1775	1775
Height (mm)	1310	=	1270	1310	1310	1270	1310
Wheelbase (mm)	2272	=	=	=	=	=	=
Track							
front (mm)	1380	=	1379	1380	1493	1440	1434
rear (mm)	1374	=	1380	1374	1499	1481	1493
Ground clearance at permissible gross weight (mm)	115	120	92	115	115	115	
Overhang angle							
front (degree)	11.5	=	=	12.5	11.5	11.5	
rear (degree)	12.5	=	=	13.5	13.5	13	

Model range	Carrera 2	Carrera 4	Carrera RS	RS America	911 Turbo	Turbo S	Turbo Look
Electrical system							
Generator output (W/A)	1610/115	=	=	=	=	=	=
Battery (V/Ah)	12/75	=	12/36	12/75	12/75	12/75	

Weight according to DIN 70020							
Kerb weight (kg)							
Manual transmission	1350	1450	1220	1340	1470	1290	1420
Tiptronic	1380	–	–	–	–	–	1450
Permissible gross weight (kg)							
Manual transmission	1690	1790	1420	1520	1810	1510	1760
Tiptronic	1720	–	–	–	–	–	1790
Permissible trailer weight (kg)							
unbraked	500	500	none	none	none	none	none
braked	1200	1200	none	none	none	none	none

Performance							
Maximum speed (kmh)							
Manual transmission	260	260	260	260	270	290	255
Tiptronic	256	–	–	–	–	–	251
Acceleration 0–62mph/100kmh (sec)							
Manual transmission	5.7	5.7	5.3	5.7	5.0	4.66	5.7
Tiptronic	6.6	–	–	–	–	–	6.6
Measured kilometre from standing start (sec)							
Manual transmission	25.2	25.5	25.2	24.3	22.42	25.2	
Tiptronic	26.2	–	–	–	–	–	26.2

Fluid capacities							
Engine oil quantity 1* (l)	11.5	=	=	=	13	13	11.5
Manual transmission 2* (l)	3.6	3.8	3.6	3.6	3.7	3.7	3.6
Front axle 2* (l)	–	1.2	–	–	–	–	–
Automatic transm. 3* (l)	9.0	–	–	–	–	–	9.0
Final drive, autom.2* (l)	0.9	–	–	–	–	–	0.9
Fuel tank (l)	77	=	=	=	=	92	77
Brake fluid reservoir 6* (l)	0.34	0.75	0.34	0.34	0.75	0.75	0.75
Power steering fluid 3 (l)	1.0	1.0	–	–	1.0	1.0	1.0
Refrigerant 4* (g)	930	=	–	930	100	930	
Refrigerant oil 5* (ml)	100	=	–	100	100	100	

* Key to numerals
1* Approved API SE/SF with combinations API SE/CC - SF/CC - SF/CD - SE/CD
    Multigrade engine oil factory recommended
2* Multigrade gear oil 75 W 90
3* Multigrade transmission fluid 75 W 90 acc. MIL-L 2105 B and API-classified GL 5
    ATF DEXRON II D
4* Refrigerant R 12
5* Commercially available refrigerant oils
6* Use only brake fluid acc. SAE J 1703. DOT 3 or 4

Vehicle Identification Numbers											
World manufacturer code	Code body USA (A=Coupé, B=Targa, C=Cabriolet)	Code for engine variants (only USA)	Restraint system (0 = belt, 2 = airbag) only USA	First and second digit for car type	Fill character/ check digit	Model year (N = 1992, P = 1993, etc.)	Manufacturing site (S = Stuttgart)	7th and 8th digit = car type	Code for body + engine	Sequence number	Summary
WPO	Z	Z	Z	96	Z	N	S	4	0	0001–4844	Rest of world, Coupé
WPO	Z	Z	Z	96	Z	N	S	4	3	0001–0597	Rest of world, Carrera Targa
WPO	Z	Z	Z	96	Z	N	S	4	5	0001–2885	Rest of world, Cabriolet (Turbo Look)
WPO	Z	Z	Z	96	Z	N	S	4	7	0001–0336	Rest of world, Turbo Coupé
WPO	Z	Z	Z	96	Z	N	S	4	9	0001–2051	Rest of world, Carrera RS Coupé
WPO	A	A	2	96	C*	N	S	4	8	0001–0309	USA/CDN, Targa with airbag
WPO	A	B	2	96	C*	N	S	4	2	0001–2715	USA/CDN, Coupé with airbag
WPO	B	B	2	96	C*	N	S	4	4	0001–0211	USA/CDN, Targa with airbag
WPO	C	B	2	96	C*	N	S	4	6	0001–0992	USA/CDN, Cabriolet with airbag

C* = Check digit, can be 0–9 or X (only USA)
Z = Fill character for rest of world cars

Model year 1993
P Programme, 3.6-litre Turbo

Porsche 911 Carrera 2 Coupé, Targa and
  Cabriolet
Porsche 911 Carrera 2 Cabriolet Turbo Look
Porsche 911 Carrera 2 Speedster
Porsche 911 Carrera 4 Coupé, Targa and
  Cabriolet
Porsche 911 Carrera 4 Coupé Turbo Look
Porsche 911 Carrera RS
Porsche 911 RS America Coupé
Porsche 911 Carrera RS 3.8
Porsche 911 Turbo 3.6 Coupé

*The 1993 911 Turbo 3.6 Coupé was now fitted with a 3.6-litre
engine developing 265kW (360hp) at 5,500rpm.*

Porsche continued to build the 911 Carrera 2 and
4 with only minor modifications in model year
1993. After the previous year's Turbo S with
280kW (381hp), the new Turbo with its 3.6-litre
engine offered an output of 265kW (360hp) and
was made as from January 1993 in Coupé form
only. The Speedster body variant also made a
brief return for 1993.

Engine
From 1993 onwards Porsche filled all its engines
at the factory with Shell TMO fully synthetic oil
(SAE 5 W-40). The fully synthetic oil was
characterised especially by its broad viscosity
range: in winter it had low viscosity while in
summer it was thicker than previous oils.

Carrera 2 and 4: no significant changes. The
Turbo 3.6 was now fitted with a 3.6-litre six-
cylinder engine where crankshaft drive, cylinders
and other components were identical to those of
the Carrera naturally aspirated engine. Pistons,

ABOVE: The 911 Turbo 3.6 Coupé still featured the unmistakable 'tea-tray' rear spoiler.

BELOW: 1993 proved to be the last year of the 911 Targa for several seasons. A Carrera 2 3.6 model is shown here.

The increasing popularity of the 911 Carrera 2 3.6 Cabriolet led to Porsche ceasing production of Targa models.

camshafts and further optimised K-Jetronic were configured to suit this turbocharged engine. Other details: full-flow oil filter, vibration absorber on the camshaft, cylinder head gasket with stainless steel ring, chain-and-sprocket drive/valve-gear housing (same as Carrera engine), newly tuned camshafts and valve timing, and modified turbo boost pressure valve. The increase in displacement, extra turbo boost pressure and higher compression ratio all helped boost torque to 520Nm, a value that was not even achieved by Porsche's 928 GTS eight-cylinder engine with its 5.4-litre displacement.

Fuel and ignition system

All vehicles: a petrol tank with a capacity of 92 litres was available as an optional extra (M 545). This was a result of requests by customers frustrated by the need for frequent refuelling stops on long-distance

The interior of a 1993-model 911 Turbo 3.6 Coupé. Note the prominence of the rev counter, with the speedometer offset to the right.

The 911 Carrera RS 3.8 Coupé was fitted with a 3.8-litre engine producing 221kW (300hp) at 6,500rpm.

drives. Turbo 3.6: to conform to the enlarged displacement and increased power output, the K-Jetronic and ignition system were modified. The engine had auxiliary air injection, depending on the operating state, to the overrun control valve and thus to the exhaust valve or the catalytic converter.

Transmission
Carrera 2 only: changeover to the LUK dual-mass flywheel system from the 911 Turbo, which compensated for the engine rev variations at low speed via coil springs made from steel. This offered better transmission reliability but could not yet be used in the Carrera 4 as, due to the all-wheel drive power train, there would have been vibration and transmission noise in certain speed ranges.

Keylock (ignition lock) and shiftlock (gearshift lock) – the security system introduced in the USA the previous year – were built into all Tiptronic vehicles worldwide. Carrera 4 only: changeover to more comfortable Valeo clutch plates. Turbo 3.6: the G50/52 five-speed manual transmission from the Turbo 3.3 was adopted unchanged.

Suspension
All vehicles were filled with DOT 4 type 200 brake fluid by the factory. The brake fluid change intervals were extended to three years and the brake system had an increased boiling point with very low intake of moisture. Carrera 2 only: four-piston rear brake callipers were used worldwide.

Turbo 3.6: the suspension was similar to the Turbo 3.3, but lowered by 20mm and retuned. The Turbo featured a crossbar between the suspension struts in the luggage compartment. Front suspension: MacPherson struts with dual-strut gas-pressure dampers, specially adjusted. Rear suspension: light-alloy semi-trailing arms, with spring struts and bars adapted to the car's high performance. The Turbo 3.6 was fitted with three-piece 18in 'Cup' light-alloy wheels.

The newly introduced brake fluid had proved itself over the years in factory race cars such as the Porsche 962, as well as the Carrera Cup cars. This experience also came to bear on the suspension of the 911 Turbo 3.6, the design and calibration of which was entirely adopted from the 911 Cup cars. The three-piece 18in wheels had also made their way from the race car to the production car – the 18in diameter and the ultra-low 35 tyre profile represented new territory for road cars.

Body

All right-hand drive cars were fitted with an airbag on the driver's side. For the first time the complete vehicle identification number (VIN) of the car was also placed on the A-pillar, and was visible from the outside through the windscreen. This VIN had been a standard requirement in the USA for many years, and Porsche decided to provide owners in the rest of the world with the same measure of security against theft.

Heating and air conditioning

All Porsche vehicles with air conditioning were provided with ozone-friendly refrigerant R 134a (tetrafluoroethane) for the first time. Porsche was the first car manufacturer in the world to make use of ozone-friendly refrigerants in all its production cars as early as the summer of 1992.

Electrical system

New radio generation 'London RDM 42' with CD tuner and key card to help prevent theft.

Additional information

A very special version of the RS was the Carrera RS 3.8, built to qualify the car for GT racing. This featured a Turbo Look body with an adjustable

The exclusive Carrera RS 3.8 was unmistakable from the rear, with its distinctive twin-level rear spoiler and 18in wheels.

bi-plane rear wing. The engine was an expanded 3.8-litre M64/04 version with a 102mm bore to make 3,746cc. Its output was 221kW (300hp) at 6,500rpm and torque was 360Nm at 5,250rpm. Less than 100 units were built.

Model range	Total production
911 Carrera 2 Coupé	3249* + 800* USA
Coupé Tiptronic	
Targa	
Targa Tiptronic	
Cabriolet	
Cabriolet Tiptronic	
Speedster	5581 + 469 USA
Speedster Tiptronic	
Cabriolet Turbo Look	
Tiptronic	
911 Carrera 4 Coupé	
Targa	
Cabriolet	
Coupé Turbo Look Anniv.	911
911 Turbo 3.6 Coupé	650 + 288 USA

* The vehicle ID numbers no longer allowed for a differentiation between Carrera 2 and Carrera 4. The production numbers mentioned relate to both vehicles and also include vehicles with Tiptronic.

141

Model range	Carrera 2	Carrera 4	Turbo 3.6
Engine			
Engine type			
Manual transmission	M64/01	M64/01	M64/50
Tiptronic	M64/02	–	
Bore (mm)	100	100	100
Stroke (mm)	76.4	76.4	76.4
Displacement (cc)	3600	3600	3600
Compression ratio	11.3:1	11.3:1	11.3:1
Engine output (kW/hp)	184/250	184/250	265/360
at revolutions per minute (rpm)	6100	6100	5500
Torque (Nm)	310	310	520
at revolutions per minute (rpm)	4800	4800	4200
Output per litre (kW/l)	51.1	51.1	73.6
Max. engine speed (rpm)	6720	6720	6600
Engine weight (kg)	238	238	276

Carburation, ignition, settings			
Fuel system	DME S	DME S	K-Jetronic
Type of fuel (RON)	95	95	95
Ignition system	DME	=	KFZ
Ignition	dual	dual	single
Spark plugs			
Bosch	FR 5 DTC	=	FR 6 LDC
Beru	14Fr-5DTU	=	–
Spark plug gap (mm)	0.7	=	0.8
Anti-knock control	yes	yes	no
Idle speed (rpm)	880+-40	=	950+-50
Exhaust/purification system	Lambda sensor/three-way catalytic converter + SLE + ZLP		
CO-content			
without cat. conv. (%)	0.5–1.0	=	1.0–1.4
with cat. conv. (%)	0.4–1.2	=	0.8–1.2
Fuel consumption acc. EC Standard (litres/100km)			
Manual transmission			
A. at a constant 90 kmh	7.8	8.0	8.3
B. at a constant 120 kmh	9.7	9.5	10.5
C. EC urban cycle	17.1	17.9	21.3
Euromix	11.5	11.8	13.3
Tiptronic			
A. at a constant 90 kmh	7.9	–	–
B. at a constant 120 kmh	9.6	–	–
C. EC urban cycle	17.1	–	–
Euromix	11.4	–	–

Transmission			
Dual-mass flywheel	Syst.LUK	Syst.F*	Syst.LUK
Clutch, pressure plate	G MFZ 240	=	=
Clutch plate (mm)	rigid 240	rigid 240	rigid 240
Manual transmission	G50/03	G64/00	G50/52
Gear ratios			
1st gear	3.500	3.500	3.154
2nd gear	2.059	2.118	1.789
3rd gear	1.407	1.444	1.269
4th gear	1.086	1.086	0.967
5th gear	0.868	0.868	0.756
Reverse gear	2.857	=	=
Synchromesh system gears 1–5	VK	=	=
Synchromesh system reverse gear	VK	=	=
Final drive	3.444	3.444	3.444
Limited-slip differential	Option	Standard	Standard
Lock-up factor under load/coasting (%)	40/40	variable 0–100	20/100
Gearbox weight with oil (kg)	66	79.76	71
Front differential (kg)	–	22.65	–

Model range	Carrera 2	Carrera 4	Turbo 3.6
Tiptronic	A50/02	–	–
Torque converter dia.(mm)	260	–	
Stall speed (rpm)	2300	–	
Gear ratios			
1st gear	2.479	–	
2nd gear	1.479	–	
3rd gear	1.000	–	
4th gear	0.728	–	
Reverse gear	2.086	–	
Intermediate shaft	1.100	–	
Final drive	3.667	–	
Limited-slip differential	no	–	
Gearbox weight with oil and ATF filling (kg)	105	–	

Key:

DME S = Digital engine electronic system with sequential fuel injection

KFZ = Pressure-controlled mapped ignition

Syst.F* = Dual-mass flywheel System Freudenberg (rubber-damped)

Syst.LUK = Dual-mass flywheel System LUK (Steel-spring damped)

VK = Full-cone synchromesh system with molybdenum-coated synchroniser rings

Suspension, steering and brakes			
Front axle			
Anti-roll bar dia. (mm)	20	=	21
Steering ratio	18.48	=	18.48
Turning circle dia. (m)	11.95	=	11.45
Rear axle			
Anti-roll bar dia. (mm)			
Manual transmission	20	=	22
Tiptronic	19	–	–
Brake system			
Brake booster ratio	3.0:1	hydr.	hydr.
Brake master cylinder dia. (mm)	20.64	23.81	23.81
Pressure reducer			
Cut-in pressure (bar)	45	55	60
Reduction factor	0.46	0.46	0.46
Brake calliper piston diameter			
front (mm)	40+36	40+36	36+44
rear (mm)	44	30+28	30+34
Brake disc diameter			
front (mm)	298	298	322
rear (mm)	299	299	299
Brake disc thickness			
front (mm)	28	28	32
rear (mm)	24	24	28
Effective brake disc area (cm²)	284	344	474
Handbrake	Operating mechanically on both rear wheels		
Brake drum diameter (mm)	180	=	=
Contact area (cm²)	170	=	=

Model range	Carrera 2	Carrera 4	Turbo 3.6
Wheels and tyres			
Standard tyre specification, front	205/55ZR16	=	225/40ZR18
wheel	6J x 16 H2	=	8J x 18 H2
hump depth (mm)	52	=	61
Standard tyre specification, rear	225/50ZR16	=	265/35ZR18
wheel	8J x 16 H2	=	10J x 18 H2
hump depth (mm)	52	=	61
Space-saver spare wheel	165/70-16 92P	=	=
Tyre pressure			
front (bar)	2.5	2.5	2.5
rear (bar)	3.0	3.0	2.5
Space-saver spare wheel (bar)	2.5	3.0	2.5

Body and interior (dimensions at kerb weight)			
Length (mm)	4250	=	4275
Width (mm)	1652	=	1775
Height (mm)	1310	=	1290
Wheelbase (mm)	2272	=	=
Track			
front (mm)	1380	=	1442
rear (mm)	1374	=	1506
Ground clearance at permissible gross weight (mm)	115	120	112
Overhang angle			
front (degree)	11.5	=	=
rear (degree)	12.5	=	=

Electrical system			
Generator output (W/A)	1610/115	=	=
Battery (V/Ah)	12/75	=	=

Weight according to DIN 70020			
Kerb weight (kg)			
Manual transmission	1350	1450	1470
Tiptronic	1380	–	–
Permissible gross weight (kg)			
Manual transmission	1690	1790	1810
Tiptronic	1720	–	–
Permissible trailer weight (kg)			
unbraked	500	500	none
braked	1200	1200	none

Model range	Carrera 2	Carrera 4	Turbo 3.6
Performance			
Maximum speed (kmh)			
Manual transmission	260	260	280
Tiptronic	256	–	–
Acceleration 0–62mph/100kmh (sec)			
Manual transmission	5.7	5.7	4.8
Tiptronic	6.6	–	–
Measured kilometre from standing start (sec)			
Manual transmission	25.2	25.5	23.3
Tiptronic	26.2	–	–

Fluid capacities			
Engine oil quantity 1* (l)	11.5	=	12.0
Manual transmission 2* (l)	3.6	3.8	3.6
Front axle 2* (l)	–	1.2	–
Automatic transm. 3* (l)	9.0	–	–
Final drive, autom.2* (l)	0.9	–	–
Fuel tank (l)	77	=	92
Brake fluid reservoir 6* (l)	0.34	0.75	0.34
Power steering fluid 3 (l)	1.0	=	=
Refrigerant 4* (g)	930	=	840
Refrigerant oil 5* (ml)	100	=	140

* Key to numerals
1* Approved API SE/SF with combinations API SE/CC - SF/CC - SF/CD - SE/CD
  Multigrade engine oil factory recommended
2* Multigrade gear oil 75 W 90
3* Multigrade transmission fluid 75 W 90 acc. MIL-L 2105 B and
  API-classified GL 5
  ATF DEXRON II D
4* Only refrigerant R 134 a (Porsche had changed over to CFC-free
  refrigerants in their cooling devices)
5* Commercially available refrigerant oils
6* Use only brake fluid acc. DOT 4. type 200.

Vehicle Identification Numbers												
World manufacturer code	Code body USA (A=Coupé, B=Targa, C=Cabriolet)	Code for engine variants (only USA)	Restraint system (0 = belt, 2 = airbag) only USA	First and second digit for car type	Fill character/ check digit	Model year (P = 1993, R = 1994, etc.)	Manufacturing site (S = Stuttgart)	7th and 8th digit = car type	Code for body + engine	Sequence number	Summary
WPO	Z	Z	Z	96	Z	P	S	4	0	0001–3249	Rest of world, Coupé
WPO	Z	Z	Z	96	Z	P	S	4	3	0001–0419	Rest of world, Targa
WPO	Z	Z	Z	96	Z	P	S	4	5	0001–1414	Rest of world, Cabriolet (Turbo Look)
WPO	Z	Z	Z	96	Z	P	S	4	7	0001–0650	Rest of world, Turbo 3.6 Coupé
WPO	A	B	2	96	C*	P	S	4	2	0001–0520	USA/CDN, Coupé with airbag
WPO	B	B	2	96	C*	P	S	4	4	0001–0317	USA/CDN, Targa with airbag
WPO	C	B	2	96	C*	P	S	4	6	0001–0060	USA/CDN, Cabriolet with airbag
WPO	A	B	2	96	C*	P	S	4	1	9001–9060	USA/CDN, Coupé RS America

C* = Check digit, can be 0–9 or X (only USA)
Z = Fill character for rest of world cars

Model year 1994

R Programme, 993 – the next generation

Porsche 911 Carrera 2 Cabriolet
Porsche 911 Carrera 2 Speedster
Porsche 911 Carrera 4 Turbo Look
Porsche 911 RS America Coupé
Porsche 911 Turbo 3.6 Coupé
Porsche 911 Carrera (993) Coupé, Cabriolet

With the new 993 generation, 1994 marked the first significant changes to the 911 Carrera since its launch in 1989. The bodywork front and rear was completely new, giving it a 'corporate identity' that echoed other Porsche model ranges, including the 968 and 928. The 993 also received a higher performance engine, six-speed manual transmission, completely new rear suspension and a revised interior. Initially the 'new' Carrera was built in rear-wheel drive form only, and available initially as a Coupé only and, shortly after, as a Cabriolet. As of the end of 1993, the previous-generation 964 variants of Coupé, Targa and Cabriolet, as well as the Speedster and the Turbo body, could no longer be built due to the work cycle at the body plant.

964 survivors: Carrera 2 3.6 Speedster (red), Carrera 4 3.6 Anniversary (black), Carrera 2 Convertible (blue), Turbo 3.6 (yellow).

Engine

The output of the M64/05 engine for the new 993 Carrera was increased to 200kW (272hp). This was achieved without modification to the displacement or the compression, helped by the fact that the M64/01 engines manufactured in the previous model year (1993) were all producing significantly above 250hp, and some were dynographed at over 260hp when new. The changes for 1994 included a torsionally stiffer crankshaft, lightened and stronger con rods, lighter and improved pistons, aluminium die-cast cylinders with nickel-silicon surfaces, larger valves and enlarged ports in the cylinder head, rocker arms with hydraulic valve-clearance compensation, tuned camshafts with modified timing, and an additional full-flow oil filter (fine filter 20mu).

Fuel and ignition system

The sequential fuel injection and the ignition system were adopted from the previous engines. The DME system was further improved as version M 2.10.1, which led to a reduction in fuel consumption, fewer pollutants in the exhaust and improved quality and balance in the engine. The intake air was measured via a hot-film mass airflow meter.

Also helping power output was a completely new exhaust system operating with significantly lower exhaust back pressure. This was equipped with an improved exhaust manifold (part of the heat exchanger), and a mixing chamber with lambda probe downstream of the exhaust manifolds merged the exhaust gases from the left and the right and released them via two separate

metal catalytic converters. From there the purified exhaust gases streamed into two final exhaust silencers fitted to the left and right of the engine. These final silencers lowered the drive-by noise level to under 75dBa, which was the threshold required by the EU from 1996.

The 911 Carrera 2 Speedster was built up to the end of 1993, offering extreme open-air thrills..

The flatter line of the folded Cabriolet roof and the flatter-angle headlamps are evident in this view of the 993 generation.

A 1994-model 911 Carrera 3.6 fitted with Tiptronic S transmission. Note the thumb-operated shift buttons (+/−) on the steering wheel.

Transmission

The new G50/20 six-speed manual transmission was well matched to the new engine. Double-cone synchromesh on first and second gears provided for much lower gearchange loads. The driveshaft and ring gear were polished and matched after the hardening process and therefore ran more smoothly. Due to a thin-walled die-cast light-alloy housing, the new six-speed transmission had the same overall weight as the previous five-speed transmission.

The clutch was now much better ventilated, with the cold/hot air exchange being led through openings in the gearbox housing. The cooler temperature of the clutch components, especially the clutch plate, achieved a higher coefficient of friction between the clutch lining and the flywheel/pressure plate, and the clutch was more reliable.

With the Tiptronic A50/04 automatic transmission, Porsche made adjustments to the software of the control unit to bring more comfort and a sportier feel. In manual mode, reverse gear could be pre-selected in the braking phase. Available for both transmissions as an optional extra for the first time was an automatic brake differential lock (ABD). This traction aid

decelerated the spinning driving wheel below 43mph (70kmh). ABD was helpful when accelerating and when moving away on slippery surfaces. Since the Tiptronic power train was not available with a limited-slip differential, ABD was a sensible alternative.

The 993 Carrera had a higher maximum speed of 167mph (270kmh), thanks in part to its taller sixth gear. Porsche realised that its existing five-speed transmission would not work well with the new engine and so it introduced a six-speed transmission for the 993: more gears meant optimal ratios in all driving situations.

Suspension

Reworked front suspension of the Carrera 2 with light-alloy swivel bearings. Negative steering offset of -11.5mm (was previously zero). Improved directional stability and more precise feel were achieved through modified power steering. The multi-wishbone rear axle with subframe allowed for increased lateral acceleration. Significantly less tyre noise was heard inside the car.

Wider wheels were fitted with 20mm wider tyres at the rear. Stronger and improved brake system, drilled brake discs. New ABS 5 anti-lock brake system with shortened braking distances, especially on uneven road surfaces thanks to a rough-road detection unit that continually monitored the state of the road surface during braking.

ABOVE: The front suspension assembly of a 1994-model 911 Carrera 3.6, complete with steering gear, brake servo and anti-roll bar.

BELOW: The rear suspension featured subframe-mounted upper and lower wishbones. This is a Carrera 4 assembly.

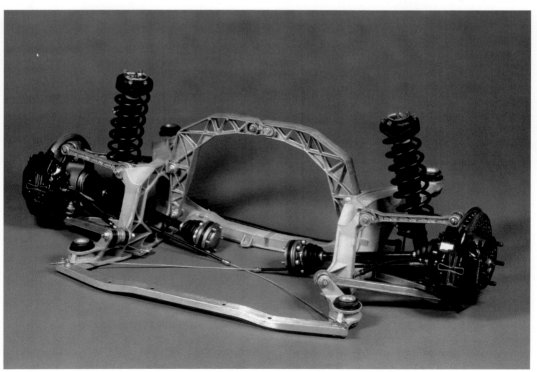

This view of a 1994-model 993 Carrera 3.6 Coupé shows the revised body styling introduced to provide a corporate identity.

Body

This was one area where the 993 evolved very obviously, notably with all-new front and rear ends. New headlights in the front wings (fenders) were mounted at a much flatter angle while the rear end was also wider and flatter. The rear side windows were flush with the body.

The 993 Cabriolet's soft top was totally modified and now boasted a flatter profile towards the rear of the car. The material was in one piece, and the car looked even sportier with the top closed. An optional wind deflector prevented air swirling when driving with the top down. Also, for the first time it was possible to replace the rear screen without any problems in the workshop. There were simpler controls for the Cabriolet top too. Previously it had been necessary to switch the engine off, stop the car completely and move the key into the 'ignition on' position before the soft top could be opened or closed. Now the car only needed to be stationary with the parking brake applied before the electric soft top could be activated.

Equipment and fittings

Modified steering wheel with airbag. The doors

could be opened mechanically from the inside despite being locked. This was another safety feature, since in an emergency situation doors were often locked from the inside by the passenger or driver, and opening them from the inside had only been possible by operating the lock release on the centre console. All cars came with an immobiliser to Allianz Insurance standard.

Interior fittings
Only slight changes to the seats. Completely new door panels with a different speaker layout.

Heating and air conditioning
More user-friendly heating/air conditioning. A new 'maximum cooling' button channelled the full cooling capacity to the interior of the car irrespective of where any of the other controls had been set. When reversing, the heater flaps closed. The heated rear window switched to energy-saving mode after 12 minutes.

Electrical system
Combined central locking/alarm system. New radio generation Blaupunkt Bremen RCM 43. Completely reworked windscreen wiper system, with the pivotal point of the wiper arms in the centre of the windscreen and a greatly enlarged wiping area, which was also more efficient at higher speeds.

Wiring harness in modular design: basic wiring harness and additional car-specific wiring harnesses. Main headlights with completely new light technology and improved light efficiency: in a joint housing, an ellipsoid headlamp with H1 lamp was installed for the dipped headlights and a variable focus reflector system for the full beam.

Additional information
The very last 964 variant of all was the Turbo 3.6 S Flat-Nose. The main headlamps were pop-up lights (similar to Porsche 944) mounted in flattened front wings (fenders). Additional air intakes in the rear wings (fenders) improved rear brake cooling. Front and rear spoilers were also modified. The output of the Turbo engine was boosted to 283kW (385hp). About 85 cars were built in all.

January 1994 saw the start of production of the new 911 Cup race cars with 993 bodywork. The new 993 Cabriolet was launched shortly afterwards at the March 1994 Geneva Motor Show. Tiptronic S, a transmission system that was controlled from the steering wheel, became available in June. The number of services required up to a mileage of 40,000km (24,000 miles) was reduced to two and the service maintenance list was reduced from 16 to seven items.

Model range	Total production
911 Carrera Coupé (993)	505 + 456 USA
911 Carrera Cabriolet (993)	315 + 283 USA
911 Carrera 2 Cabriolet	5581 + 469 USA
911 Carrera 2 Cabriolet Tiptronic	512
911 Carrera 4 Coupé Turbo Look Anniv.	144 USA
911 Turbo 3.6	471 + 466 USA

* The production numbers include vehicles with Tiptronic.

Note: Due to production changes for the 'new' Carrera (internally called type 993) many of the 911 versions produced until then were dropped: as early as July 1993 the Carrera 2 and 4 were no longer built in Coupé or Targa guise. The Carrera 2 Cabriolet and Speedster were produced until January 1994, and there was also a '30 years of 911' Anniversary Carrera 4 Turbo Look in special Viola Metallic (dark purple) paint with a unique interior. The 911 Turbo 3.6 was also no longer built as from January 1994 because from that time onwards only the 'new' 993 body could be built in the body plant.

Model range	Carrera (993)	Carrera 2* Cabriolet	Carrera 2** Speedster	Carrera 4** Turbo Look*	Turbo 3.6**
Engine					
Engine type					
Manual transmission	M64/05	M64/01	M64/01	M64/01	M64/50
Tiptronic	M64/06	M64/02	M64/02	–	–
Bore (mm)	100	100	100	100	100
Stroke (mm)	76.4	76.4	76.4	76.4	76.4
Displacement (cc)	3600	3600	3600	3600	3600
Compression ratio	11.3:1	11.3:1	11.3:1	11.3	7.5:1
Engine output (kW/hp)	200/272	184/250	184/250	184/250	265/360
at revolutions per minute (rpm)	6100	6100	6100	6100	5500
Torque (Nm)	330	310	310	310	520
at revolutions per minute (rpm)	5000	4800	4800	4800	4200
Output per litre (kW/l)	55.6	51.1	51.1	51.1	73.6
Max. engine speed (rpm)	6700	6720	6720	6720	6600
Engine weight (kg)	232	238	238	238	276

* up to 12/93, from 3/94 new generation with data as for 993 Coupé
** up to 12/93, thereafter cancelled

Model range	Carrera (993)	Carrera 2* Cabriolet	Carrera 2** Speedster	Carrera 4** Turbo Look*	Turbo 3.6**
Carburation, ignition, settings					
Fuel system	DME S	DME S	DME S	DME S	K-Jetronic
Type of fuel (RON)	98	95	95	95	95
Ignition system	DME	DME	DME	DME	KFZ
Ignition	dual	dual	dual	dual	single
Spark plugs					
Bosch	FR 6 LDC	FR 5 DTC	=	=	FR 6 LDC
Beru	14Fr-5DTU	14Fr-5DTU	=	=	–
Spark plug gap (mm)	0.7	0.7	=	=	0.8
Anti-knock control	yes	yes	yes	yes	no
Idle speed (rpm)	800+-40	880+-40	=	=	950+50
Exhaust/purification system	Lambda sensor/three-way catalytic converter				=+ SLE + ZLP
CO-content					
without cat. conv. (%)	0.5–1.0	=	=	=	1.0–1.4
with cat. conv. (%)	0.4–1.2	=	=	=	0.8–1.2
Fuel consumption acc. EC Standard (litres/100km)					
Manual transmission					
A. at a constant 90kmh	7.4	7.8	=	8.0	8.3
B. at a constant 120kmh	9.1	9.7	=	9.5	10.3
C. EC urban cycle	17.9	17.1	=	17.9	21.3
Euromix	11.4	11.5	=	11.8	13.3
Tiptronic					
A. at a constant 90kmh	7.9	7.8	7.9	=	–
B. at a constant 120kmh	9.6	9.6	=	–	–
C. EC urban cycle	17.2	17.1	=	–	–
Euromix	11.5	11.4	=	–	–

Key:
Turbo Look*   The technical data refer to the Carrera 4 Turbo Look
DME S   Digital engine electronic system with sequential fuel injection
KFZ   Pressure-controlled mapped ignition
SLE   Secondary-air injection
ZLP   Auxiliary air pump

Transmission					
Dual-mass flywheel	Syst.LUK*	Syst.LUK*	Syst.LUK*	Syst.F*	Syst.LUK*
Clutch, pressure plate	G MFZ 240	=	=	=	=
Clutch plate (mm)	rigid 240	=	=	=	=
Manual transmission	G50/21	G50/03	=	G64/00	G50/52
Gear ratios					
1st gear	3.818	3.500	=	3.500	3.154
2nd gear	2.15	2.059	=	2.118	1.789
3rd gear	1.56	1.407	=	1.444	1.269
4th gear	1.242	1.086	=	1.086	0.967
5th gear	1.027	0.868	=	0.868	0.756
6th gear	0.820	–	–	–	–
Reverse gear	2.857	=	=	=	=
Synchromesh system forward gears	VK	=	=	=	=
Synchromesh system reverse gear	VK	=	=	=	=
Final drive	3.444	=	=	=	=
Limited-slip differential	Option	Option	Option	Standard	Standard
Lock-up factor under load/coasting (%)	25/65	40/40	40/40	variable 0–100	20/100
Gearbox weight with oil (kg)	66	=	=	79.65	71
Front differential (kg)	–	–	–	22.65	–
Tiptronic	A50/04	A50/02	=	–	
Torque converter dia.(mm)	260	=	=	–	
Stall speed (rpm)	2300	=	=	–	
Gear ratios					
1st gear	2.479	=	=	–	
2nd gear	1.479	=	=	–	
3rd gear	1.000	=	=	–	
4th gear	0.728	=	=	–	
Reverse gear	2.086	=	=	–	
Intermediate shaft	1.100	=	=	–	
Final drive	3.667	=	=	–	
Limited-slip differential	no	no	no	–	
Gearbox weight with oil and ATF filling (kg)	105	=	=	–	

Model range	Carrera (993)	Carrera 2* Cabriolet	Carrera 2** Speedster	Carrera 4** Turbo Look*	Turbo 3.6**
Suspension, steering and brakes					
Front axle					
Anti-roll bar dia. (mm)	21	20	=	21*	21
Steering ratio	16.48	18.48	=	=	18.48
Turning circle dia. (m)	11.74	11.95	=	=	11.45
Rear axle					
Anti-roll bar dia. (mm)					
manual transmission	18	20	=	22*	22
Tiptronic	18	19	–	–	–
Brake system					
Brake booster ratio	3.15:1	3.0:1	=	4.8 hydr.	=
Brake master cylinder dia. (mm)	23.81	20.64	=	23.81	23.81
Pressure reducer					
Cut-in pressure (bar)	40	45	=	33*	60
Reduction factor	0.46	0.46	0.46	0.46	0.46
Brake calliper piston diameter					
front (mm)	44+36	40+36	40+36	40+36	36+44
rear (mm)	30+34	44	30+28	30+34	30+34
Brake disc diameter					
front (mm)	304	298	298	298	322
rear (mm)	299	299	299	299	299
Brake disc thickness					
front (mm)	32	28	28	28	32
rear (mm)	24	24	24	28	28
Effective brake disc area (cm²)	422	284	284	344	474
Handbrake	Operating mechanically on both rear wheels				
Brake drum diameter (mm)	180	=	=	=	=
Contact area (cm²)	170	=	=	=	=

Key:
Syst.LUK*   Dual-mass flywheel System LUK (Steel-spring damped)
Syst.F*   Dual-mass flywheel System Freudenberg (rubber-damped)
VK   Full-cone synchromesh system with molybdenum-coated synchroniser rings
Turbo Look* The technical data refer to the Carrera 4 Turbo Look

Wheels and tyres					
Standard tyre specification, front	205/55ZR16	205/55ZR16	205/50ZR17	205/50ZR17	225/40ZR18
wheel	7J x 16	6J x 16 H2	7J x 17 AH	7J x 17 AH	8J x 18 H2
hump depth (mm)	55	52	55	55	52
Standard tyre specification, rear	245/45ZR16	225/50ZR16	255/40ZR17	255/40ZR17	265/35ZR18
wheel	9J x 16	8J x 16 H2	8J x 17 AH	9J x 17 AH	10J x 18 H2
hump depth (mm)	70	52	52	52	61
Space-saver spare wheel	165/70-16 92P	165/70-16 92P	165/70-16 92P	165/70-16 92P	165/70-16 92P
Tyre pressure					
front (bar)	2.5	=	2.5	=	2.5
rear (bar)	3.0	=	3.0	2.5	2.5
Space-saver spare wheel (bar)	2.5	=	3.0	2.5	2.5

Body and interior (dimensions at kerb weight)					
Length (mm)	4245	4250	=	=	4275
Width (mm)	1735	1652	=	1775	1775
Height (mm)	1300	1310	1280	1290	1290
Wheelbase (mm)	2272	2272	=	=	=
Track					
front (mm)	1405	1380	=	1434	1442
rear (mm)	1444	1374	=	1493	1506
Ground clearance at permissible gross weight (mm)	110	115	=	115	112
Overhang angle					
front (degree)	11	11.5	=	=	=
rear (degree)	12.5	=	=	13.5	=

Electrical system					
Generator output (W/A)	1610/115	=	=	=	=
Battery (V/Ah)	12/75	=	=	=	=

* up to 12/93, from 3/94 new generation with data as for 993 Coupé
** up to 12/93, thereafter cancelled

Model range	Carrera (993)	Carrera 2* Cabriolet	Carrera 2** Speedster	Carrera 4** Turbo Look*	Turbo 3.6**
Weight according to DIN 70020					
Kerb weight (kg)					
Manual transmission	1370	1350	1350	1500	1470
Tiptronic	1395	1380	1380	–	
Permissible gross weight (kg)					
Manual transmission	1710	1690	1840	1810	
Tiptronic	1735	1720	–	–	
Permissible trailer weight (kg)					
unbraked	none	500	none	500	none
braked	none	1200	none	1200	none
Performance					
Maximum speed (kmh)					
Manual transmission	270	260	260	255	280
Tiptronic	265	256	256	–	–
Acceleration 0–62mph/100kmh (sec)					
Manual transmission	5.6	5.7	5.7	5.7	4.8
Tiptronic	6.6	6.6	6.6	–	–
Measured kilometre from standing start (sec)					
Manual transmission	25.1	25.2	25.2	25.5	25.3
Tiptronic	25.9	26.2	26.2	–	–
Fluid capacities					
Engine oil quantity 1* (l)	11.5	=	=	=	12.0
Manual transmission 2* (l)	3.6	=	=	3.8	3.9
Front axle 2* (l)	–	–	=	1.2	–
Automatic transm. 3* (l)	9.0	=	=	–	–
Final drive, autom.2* (l)	0.9	0.9	=	–	–
Fuel tank (l)	71.5	77	=	=	92
Brake fluid reservoir 6* (l)	0.34	0.75	=	0.34	=
Power steering fluid 3 (l)	1.0	=	=	=	=
Refrigerant 4* (g)	930	=	=	=	840
Refrigerant oil 5* (ml)	100	=	=	=	140

* Key to numerals
1* Approved API SE/SF with combinations API SE/CC - SF/CC - SF/CD - SE/CD
   Multigrade engine oil factory recommended
2* Multigrade gear oil 75 W 90
3* Multigrade transmission fluid 75 W 90 acc. MIL-L 2105 B and API-classified GL 5
   ATF DEXRON II D

4* Only refrigerant R 134 a (Porsche had changed over to CFC-free refrigerants in its cooling devices)
5* Commercially available refrigerant oils
6* Use only brake fluid acc. DOT 4. type 200.

World manufacturer code	Code body USA (A=Coupé, B=Targa, C=Cabriolet)	Code for engine variants (only USA)	Restraint system (0 = belt, 2 = airbag) only USA	First and second digit for car type	Fill character/ check digit	Model year (R = 1994, S = 1995, etc.)	Manufacturing site (S = Stuttgart)	7th and 8th digit = car type	Code for body + engine	Sequence number	Summary
WP0	Z	Z	Z	96	Z	R	S	4	0	0001–0505	Rest of world, Coupé
WP0	Z	Z	Z	96	Z	R	S	4	5	0001–0315	Rest of world, Cabriolet (Turbo Look)
WP0	Z	Z	Z	96	Z	R	S	4	5	5001–5581	Rest of world, Speedster (964)
WP0	Z	Z	Z	96	Z	R	S	4	7	0001–0471	Rest of world, Turbo 3.6 Coupé
WP0	Z	Z	Z	96	Z	R	S	4	9	6001–	Rest of world, Carrera GT (3.8 l race version)
WP0	Z	Z	Z	96	Z	R	S	4	9	7001–	Rest of world, Carrera GT (3.8 l road version)
WP0	A	B	2	96	C*	R	S	4	1	9001–9144	USA/CDN, Coupé RS America
WP0	B	B	2	96	C*	R	S	4	2	0001–0456	USA/CDN, Coupé
WP0	C	B	2	96	C*	R	S	4	6	0001–0283	USA/CDN, Cabriolet
WP0	C	B	2	96	C*	R	S	4	6	5001–5469	USA/CDN, Speedster (964)
WP0	A	C	2	96	C*	R	S	4	8	0001–0466	USA/CDN, Turbo 3.6
WP0	Z	Z	Z	99	Z	R	S	3	1	0001–6412	Rest of world, Coupé 'New Carrera'
WP0	Z	Z	Z	99	Z	R	S	3	3	0001–5850	Rest of world, Cabriolet 'New Carrera'
WP0	Z	Z	Z	99	Z	R	S	3	9	8001–8060	Rest of world, Cup-car 'New Carrera'

Note: All vehicles built for USA and Canada 'New Carrera' (993) were given vehicle identification numbers for 1995 (WP0 AB2 99 C* S S 3 1 0001–).

Model year 1995

S Programme, new Carrera 4 and RS

Porsche 911 Carrera Coupé and Cabriolet
Porsche 911 Carrera 4 Coupé and Cabriolet
Porsche 911 RS Coupé

The 1995 911 model line-up; 911 Carrera 4 3.6 Coupé (red), 911 Carrera 3.6 Coupé (yellow), 911 Carrera 3.6 Cabriolet (silver).

There were only minor changes to the new-generation 911 Carrera this year but a significant new arrival was the all-wheel drive Carrera 4. This was modified in many areas compared to the earlier all-wheel drive model but basically followed the lead of the new 993 Carrera 2 (with which it shared its engine, manual transmission and suspension layout). In the past, Porsche had used two all-wheel drive systems. The 959 had a continuous electronically controlled front-to-rear lock, while the outgoing Carrera 4 had a planetary transfer case that sent 31% of torque to the front axle and 69% to the rear. The ratio could be changed almost continuously in the earlier Carrera

153

The 3.6-litre engine used in Carrera and Carrera 4 models now featured Varioram variable intake tracts to boost torque and power.

4 through a hydraulically operated trailing clutch. The new 1995 Carrera 4 was fitted with a very light viscous multi-disc trailing clutch.

Arriving in February 1995 was a new RS model, echoing the 964 RS 3.8 of 1993 but in 993 guise. Other newcomers in 1995 were the twin-turbo GT2 and the Turbo, but these were officially 1996 model year cars and are described in the following section.

Engine
Carrera and Carrera 4: modified and lightened pistons. Carrera RS: Porsche used tried and tested components from the M64/05 production engine for the Carrera RS power plant (M64/20). The most important differences: displacement of 3,746cc, fitment of the cylinders into the crankcase, cylinder heads with enlarged ports, intake valve diameter increased to 51.5mm and exhaust valve diameter to 49mm, Grafal-coated pistons, one V-belt for fan and alternator, modified stroke at the camshafts, and Varioram intake

system. The latter variable-intake innovation offered better induction while the Grafal coating of the pistons helped reduce noise.

Fuel and ignition system
Carrera and Carrera 4: no changes. Carrera RS: digital engine electronics 2.10.1 for ignition timing adjustment and fuel injection. A variable-length induction manifold (the Varioram system) allowed for resonance induction and high engine output in the upper speed range, and in addition significantly increased torque in the mid-range. The individual induction pipes consisted of two parts. One part was fixed to the cylinder head while the other was able to slide and thus almost double the length of the pipe. In the lower to middle rev range the induction pipes were long but at 5,160rpm and at wide-open throttle, the length of the pipe was halved.

Transmission
Carrera and Carrera 4: the double-cone synchromesh for first and second gears was further improved. A light-alloy gear selector fork with wear protection was employed for third and fourth gears.

The Tiptronic S transmission for the Carrera was upgraded with the addition of steering wheel-mounted paddles for upshifts and downshifts. Gears could be changed simply be using the thumb when the gearshift lever was in 'manual' position. The control unit prevented erroneous and dangerous gearshifts. Buttons on the steering wheel for Tiptronic were not new at Porsche: during the mid-to-late 1980s a number of 962 race cars had been equipped with Porsche's automatic double-clutch transmission (PDK) with push buttons on the steering wheel. The system allowed the driver to change up and down gears without taking his hands off the wheel, long before this feature appeared in Formula 1.

Carrera 4: the transmission system consisted of a fully synchronised six-speed transmission (G64/21) and a viscous multi-plate clutch in the gearbox housing at the front. The connection to the front axle was effected via a central shaft in the rigid central tube (transaxle design). Drive to the rear wheels was via offset hypoid gears manufactured to the Gleason production method. In addition, after the hardening process, the cogs of the driveshaft and the ring gear were polished for optimum engine smoothness. All cars were equipped with a mechanical ZF limited-slip differential system and all Carrera 4 cars with automatic brake differential (ABD), which offered additional low-speed traction control for the rear wheels in extreme road conditions. The front axle differential was completely reworked and lightened.

The objectives when developing the all-wheel

For 1995, the 911 Carrera 3.6 Cabriolet was now available with an optional lowered suspension package.

1995 saw the arrival of the 911 Carrera 4 3.6 Coupé, fitted with an all-wheel drive system featuring a viscous multi-disc trailing clutch.

drive system for the new Carrera 4 were the following: better performance, optimal handling, high stability, low weight and high efficiency. Improvement of traction in snowy conditions and on difficult terrain was only of secondary importance. While the earlier Carrera 4 was rather lethargic and unwilling during cornering, it could nevertheless develop considerable traction through the front wheels when the rear wheels were off the ground. The new Carrera 4 was considerably better at cornering in both dry and wet conditions in terms of handling and directional stability; however, it was less powerful when extreme traction was required at low speeds, despite ABD. Overall, it was far superior to the rear-wheel drive 911 Carrera.

Carrera RS: the basic version of the Carrera RS was fitted with a dual-mass flywheel while the Club Sport version received a lightweight sports flywheel. There were special gear ratios for the

G50/31 transmission (basic version), the G50/32 (Club Sport version) and the G50/33 (basic version for Switzerland). All transmissions were equipped with a mechanical ZF limited-slip differential (40% lock-up under acceleration and 65% in coasting). Automatic brake differential was standard for all RS cars.

Suspension

Carrera: only slight changes compared to the previous year. Two special suspension set-ups were available from the factory. One was the M030 suspension option (only for the Coupé): lower suspension (10mm at the front, 20mm at the rear), stiffer suspension both front and rear, and special dampers. The other was M033 suspension (also offered for the Cabriolet) with front suspension 10mm and rear 20mm lower.

Carrera and Carrera 4: the standard tyre fitment was front 205/55 ZR 16, rear 245/45 ZR16. As an optional extra (M398) you could order larger wheels: 7Jx17 H2 ET55 front, 9Jx17 H2 ET55 rear, with 205/50 ZR 17 tyres front and 255/40 ZR 17 rear.

Carrera 4: dual-circuit brake system with

hydraulic brake servo. ABS and dynamic automatic brake differential were both standard. The brake discs (internally vented and drilled) were from the Carrera; the four-piston light-alloy brake callipers were titanium-painted.

Carrera RS: compared with the standard Carrera this car was 30mm lower at the front and 40mm lower at the rear. For race applications the RS could be individually prepared for track, tyres and driver. Wheel carriers, tie rods, spring struts and power steering were non-standard for the RS front suspension and were marked with a green dot. There were also changes to the rear suspension: for its intended racing role the RS had elongated suspension adjustment holes, stiffer rubber mountings and a 20mm-diameter anti-roll (stabiliser) bar. The rear spring struts consisted of adjustable single-tube gas pressure dampers. The three-part wheels were made from magnesium.

The Carrera RS used a dual-circuit system with hydraulic brake boost. The brake discs were internally ventilated and drilled, with a diameter of 322mm and thickness of 32mm at the front, and the same diameter but 28mm thickness at the rear.

The Tiptronic S transmission, now available on all Carrera models, allowed gearchanges using push-buttons on the steering wheel.

The four-piston callipers front and rear were painted red.

Body
Carrera and Carrera 4: no changes to the bodywork. Distinctive features were the titanium-coloured 'Carrera 4' script on the lid at the rear and white front indicator lights (the orange light was generated through coloured bulbs.) The indicator unit at the rear was coloured red and the 'orange' effect was achieved through filter technology.

Carrera RS: the bonnet lid was made from light alloy and was fitted with only a lateral support bar in order to reduce weight. The door entry guards were changed for aerodynamic reasons. The RS had unique front spoiler edges that curled up at the sides. There were two types of rear spoiler: for the basic version a fixed rear spoiler with an air intake duct from the production car; and for the RS

Club Sport a fixed rear spoiler with an additional adjustable rear wing and lateral air intake ducts for the engine intake air and the ventilation of the engine compartment. The larger rear wing was optional on the RS and the vast majority of customers, of course, opted for the big 'double-decker' wing. The Club Sport version was equipped with a fixed, welded roll cage. The RS cars had a three-spoke leather-covered steering wheel and were not fitted with airbags (although airbags were available as an option).

Equipment and fittings
The gear lever in the 911 Carrera 4 included a titanium-coloured plate with the gearchange pattern.

Interior fittings
New all-leather sports seats (M383/387), electric height adjustment as standard, foldable and

The 911 Carrera RS featured an uprated 3.8-litre engine, adjustable suspension and distinctive front spoiler with upward-curving sides.

adjustable backrest, manually adjustable lumbar support, seat heating available, seat-belt buckle on the seat frame.

Carrera RS: the bucket seats in the Club Sport model were 30kg lighter than the basic seats and the door trim had a closing pull-handle affixed to it and an opening latch.

Heating and air conditioning
A modified heating/air conditioning controller with additional exterior sensors was used. The recirculation flaps were actuated by means of a vacuum.

Electrical system
The new generation of immobilisers was fitted. Apart from using a handheld transmitter, it was now possible to enter a car-specific code number via the ignition in order to deactivate the immobiliser.

In model year 1995 three different radios were available from Porsche. The new Porsche CR 10 radio could be combined with a CD changer, a co-operation between Porsche and Radio Becker.

The second radio (more reasonably priced) was the Blaupunkt München CR 104 CD player, while the Blaupunkt Düsseldorf RCR 84 served as the basic radio. For many years the installation of the radio had mostly been up to the customer himself, but now Porsche was attempting to improve sound characteristics through tests done in-house, and was keen to offer factory-fitted packages.

In addition Porsche offered a DSP (Digital Sound Processing) sound package, the control unit of which was positioned under the right-hand seat, while the DSP operating control was placed in the compartment inside the door on the driver's side. The cars were made ready for Nokia phones as standard.

Additional information

The new and more powerful 911 Turbo, with twin turbos and four-wheel drive, was rolled out in the spring of 1995. However, as the vehicle identification for the production run showed 'model year 1996' (T programme), this vehicle will be described in detail in the following section.

Model range	Total production
911 Carrera Coupé	7018* + 4139* USA
911 Cabriolet	2878* + 3718* USA
911 Carrera 4 Coupé	N/A
911 Carrera 4 Cabriolet	N/A
911 Carrera 4 RS Coupé	274
911 C. RS Coupé Club Sport	110
911 Turbo 3.6	#
911 GT 2 Coupé	#

* The vehicle ID numbers no longer allowed for a differentiation between Carrera 2 and Carrera 4. The production numbers mentioned relate to both vehicles and also include vehicles with Tiptronic.
# Although production of the Turbo 3.6 and the GT2 started in model year 1995, the vehicles and their ID numbers were allocated to model year 1996.

The Carrera RS also had bucket-style race seats and three-piece magnesium 18in wheels.

Model range	Carrera (993)	Carrera 4	Carrera RS	Turbo 3.6*
Engine				
Engine type				* Although the
Manual transmission	M64/05	M64/05	M64/05	new Turbo 3.6 was
Tiptronic	M64/06	–	–	available from
Bore (mm)	100	100	102	April 1995, it was
Stroke (mm)	76.4	76.4	76.4	introduced as model
Displacement (cc)	3600	3600	3746	year 1996. For data
Compression ratio	11.3:1	11.3:1	11.3:1	see model year 1996.
Engine output (kW/hp)	200/272	200/272	221/300	
at revolutions per minute (rpm)	6100	6100	6500	
Torque (Nm)	330	330	355	
at revolutions per minute (rpm)	5000	5000	5400	
Output per litre (kW/l)	55.6	55.6	59	
Max. engine speed (rpm)	6700	6700	6840	
Engine weight (kg)	232	232	230	

The 911 Carrera RS 3.6 Club Sport (red) was a lightweight version of the Carrera RS (yellow), intended for motorsport use, with a full rollcage, revised front spoiler, adjustable rear spoiler and minimalist, lightweight components throughout.

Model range	Carrera (993)	Carrera 4	Carrera RS	Turbo 3.6*
Carburation, ignition, settings				
Fuel system	DME S	DME S	DME S	* Although the
Type of fuel (RON)	98	98	98	new Turbo 3.6 was
Ignition system	DME	DME	DME	available from
Ignition	dual	dual	dual	April 1995, it was
Spark plugs				introduced as model
Bosch	FR 6 LDC and	FR 5 DTC	=	year 1996. For data
Beru	14 FR -5 DTU	=	=	see model year 1996.
Spark plug gap (mm)	0.7	=	=	
Anti-knock control	yes	yes	yes	
Idle speed (rpm)	800+-40	880+-40	960+-40	
Exhaust/purification system	BLS+DWMK	=	=	
CO-content				
without cat. conv. (%)	0.5–1.0	=	=	
with cat. conv. (%)	0.4–1.2	=	=	
Fuel consumption acc. EC Standard (litres/100km)				
Manual transmission				
A. at a constant 90kmh	7.5	7.5	7.6	
B. at a constant 120kmh	9.2	9.2	9.5	
C. EC urban cycle	17.4	17.6	20.1	
D. Euromix	11.4	11.5	12.4	
Tiptronic				
A. at a constant 90kmh	7.5	–	–	
B. at a constant 120kmh	9.2	–	–	
EC-Urban cycle	16.8	–	–	
Euromix	11.3	–	–	

Key:
BLS   Heated lambda sensor
DME S   Digital engine electronic system with sequential fuel injection
DWMK   Three-way metal-based catalytic converter

KFZ   Pressure-controlled mapped ignition
SLE   Secondary-air injection
ZLP   Auxiliary air pump

Transmission				
Dual-mass flywheel	Syst.LUK*	Syst.LUK*	Syst.LUK*	
Clutch, pressure plate	G MFZ 240	=	=	
Clutch plate (mm)	rigid 240	=	=	
Manual transmission	G50/21	G64/21	G64/31	
Gear ratios				
1st gear	3.818	3.818	3.154	
2nd gear	2.150	2.150	2.000	
3rd gear	1.560	1.560	1.522	
4th gear	1.242	1.242	1.242	
5th gear	1.024	1.024	1.024	
6th gear	0.820	0.820	0.820	
Reverse gear	2.857	2.857	2.857	
Synchromesh system				
Forward gears	VK	VK	VK	
Synchromesh system reverse gear	VK	VK	VK	
Final drive	3.444	3.444	3.444	
Limited-slip differential	Option	S	S	
Lock-up factor under load/coasting (%)	25/65	25/40	40/65	
Gearbox weight with oil (kg)	66	72.5	69.0	
Tiptronic	A50/04	–	–	
Torque converter dia.(mm)	260	–	–	
Stall speed (rpm)	2300	–	–	
Gear ratios				
1st gear	2.479	–	–	
2nd gear	1.479	–	–	
3rd gear	1.000	–	–	
4th gear	0.728	–	–	
Reverse gear	2.086	–	–	
Intermediate shaft, gear ratio	1.100	–	–	
Final drive, gear ratio	3.667	–	–	
Limited-slip differential	no	–	–	
Gearbox weight with oil and ATF filling (kg)	105	–	–	

Key:
S   Standard equipment
Syst.LUK*   Dual-mass flywheel System LUK (steel-spring damped)
VK   Full-cone synchromesh system with molybdenum-coated synchroniser rings

Model range	Carrera (993)	Carrera 4	Carrera RS	Turbo 3.6*
Suspension, steering and brakes				
Front axle				* Although the
Anti-roll bar dia. (mm)	21	21	23	new Turbo 3.6 was
Steering ratio	16.48	16.48	18.25	available from
Turning circle dia. (m)	11.74	11.74	11.76	April 1995, it was
Rear axle				introduced as model
Anti-roll bar dia.				year 1996. For data
Manual transmission (mm)	18	18	20	see model year 1996.
Tiptronic (mm)	18	–	–	
Brake system				
Brake booster ratio	3.15:1	4.8:1	3.6:1	
Brake master cylinder dia. (mm)	23.81	23.81	25.4	
Pressure reducer				
Cut-in pressure (bar)	40	45	40	
Reduction factor	0.46	0.46	0.46	
Brake calliper piston diameter				
front (mm)	44+36	44+36	44+36	
rear (mm)	30+34	28+30	30+36	
Brake disc diameter				
front (mm)	304	304	322	
rear (mm)	299	299	322	
Brake disc thickness				
front (mm)	32	32	32	
rear (mm)	24	24	28	
Effective brake disc area (cm^2)	422	422	522	
Handbrake	Operating mechanically on both rear wheels			
Brake drum diameter (mm)	180	=	=	
Contact area (cm^2)	170	=	=	

Wheels and tyres				
Standard tyre specification, front	205/55ZR16	205/55ZR16	225/40ZR18	
wheel	7J x 16 H2	7J x 16 H2	8J x 18 AH	
hump depth (mm)	55	55	52	
optional	205/50ZR17	205/50ZR17	–	
wheel	7J x 17 H2	7J x 17 H2	–	
hump depth (mm)	55	55	–	
Standard tyre specification, rear	245/45ZR16	245/45ZR16	265/35ZR18	
wheel	9J x 16 H2	9J x 16 H2	10J x 18 AH	
hump depth (mm)	70	70	65	
optional	255/40ZR17	255/40ZR17	–	
wheel	9J x 17 H2	9J x 17 H2	–	
hump depth (mm)	55	55	–	
Space-saver spare wheel	165/70-16 92P	=	=	
Tyre pressure				
front (bar)	2.5	=	=	
rear (bar)	3.0 (2.5)*	3.0 (2.5)*	3.0	
Space-saver spare wheel (bar)	2.5	=	=	

(2.5)* = air pressure for special 17-inch tyres

Body and interior (dimensions at kerb weight)				
Length (mm)	4245	4245	4245	
Width (mm)	1735	1735	1735	
Height (mm)	1300	1300	1270	
Wheelbase (mm)	2272	=	=	
Track				
front (mm)	1405	1405	1413	
rear (mm)	1444	1444	1452	
Ground clearance at permissible gross weight (mm)	110	110	90	
Overhang angle				
front (degree)	11.0	11.0	9.7	
rear (degree)	12.5	12.5	11.0	

Electrical system				
Generator output (W/A)	1610/115	=	=	
Battery (V/Ah)	12/75	12/75	12/36	

Model range	Carrera (993)	Carrera 4	Carrera RS	Turbo 3.6*
Weight according to DIN 70020				
Kerb weight (kg)				* Although the
Manual transmission	1370	1420	1270	new Turbo 3.6 was
Tiptronic	1395	–	–	available from
Permissible gross weight (kg)				April 1995, it was
Manual transmission	1710	1760	1710	introduced as model
Tiptronic	1735	–	–	year 1996. For data
Permissible trailer weight (kg)				see model year 1996.
unbraked	none	none	none	
braked	none	none	none	
Permissible roof load (kg)	35	=	=	
with Porsche System (kg)	75	=	=	

Performance				
Maximum speed (kmh)				
Manual transmission	270	270	277	
Tiptronic	265	–	–	
Acceleration 0–62mph/100kmh (sec)				
Manual transmission	5.6	5.5	5.0	
Tiptronic	6.6	–	–	
Measured kilometre from standing start (sec)				
Manual transmission	25.1	25.3	24.0	
Tiptronic	25.9	–	–	

Fluid capacities				
Engine oil quantity 1* (l)	11.5	11.5	11.5	
Manual transmission 2* (l)	3.6	3.8	3.6	
Front axle 2* (l)	–	0.6	–	
Automatic transm. 3* (l)	9.0	–	–	
Final drive, autom.2* (l)	0.9	–	–	
Fuel tank (l)	73 (92)**	73 (92)**	92	
Brake fluid reservoir 5* (l)	0.34	0.75	0.34	
Power steering fluid 3 (l)	1.0	=	=	
Refrigerant 6* (g)	840	=	=	
Refrigerant oil 7* (ml)	140	=	=	
Washer tank (l)	7.3	7.3	1.2	

*Key and key to numerals
**

1* 92-litres fuel tank available as optional extra
   Approved API SE/SF with combinations API SE/CC - SF/CC - SF/CD - SE/CD
   Multigrade engine oil factory recommended
2* Multigrade gear oil 75 W 90
3* Multigrade transmission fluid 75 W 90 acc. MIL-L 2105 B and API-classified GL 5
   ATF DEXRON II D
4* Only unleaded fuel with minimum standard RON 98/MON 88
5* Use only brake fluid acc. DOT 4. type 200.
6* Only refrigerant R 134 a (Porsche had changed over to CFC-free refrigerants in its cooling devices)
7* Commercially available refrigerant oils

Vehicle Identification Numbers											
World manufacturer code	Code body USA (A=Coupé, B=Targa, C=Cabriolet)	Code for engine variants (only USA)	Restraint system (0 = belt, 2 = airbag) only USA	First and second digit for car type	Fill character/ check digit	Model year (P = 1995, R = 1996, etc.)	Manufacturing site (S = Stuttgart)	7th and 8th digit = car type	Code for body + engine	Sequence number	Summary
WPO	Z	Z	Z	99	Z	S	S	3	1	0001–9000	Rest of world, 911 Carrera or Carrera 4 Coupé
WPO	Z	Z	Z	99	Z	S	S	3	3	0001–9000	Rest of world, 911 Carrera or Carrera 4 Cabriolet
WPO	Z	Z	Z	99	Z	S	S	3	9	0001–0400	Rest of world, 911 Carrera RS
WPO	A	B	2	99	C*	S	S	3	1	0001–5000	USA/CDN, 911 Carrera or Carrera 4 Coupé
WPO	C	B	2	99	C*	S	S	3	6	0001–5000	USA/CDN, 911 Carrera or Carrera 4 Cabriolet

C* = Check digit, can be 0–9 or X (only USA)
Z = Fill character for rest of world cars

Model year 1996

T Programme, new Targa, Carrera 4S, Turbo

Porsche 911 Carrera Coupé, Cabriolet and
    Targa
Porsche 911 Carrera 4 Coupé, Cabriolet and
    Targa
Porsche 911 Carrera 4S Coupé
Porsche 911 Carrera RS Coupé
Porsche 911 Turbo Coupé
Porsche 911 GT2 Coupé

A major item of news for 1996 was the availability
of the Targa body style once more. It was a rather

*The 1996 911 model range. Front row; Turbo 3.6 (red), Carrera 4S 3.6
Coupé (blue), Targa 3.6 (silver). Rear row; Carrera 3.6 Convertible
(yellow), Carrera 3.6 Coupé (blue), Carrera RS 3.8 (yellow).*

different affair to the old style though, using a
fold-away glass roof. The new model was launched
at the 1995 IAA show in Frankfurt, where the
other improved 911s could also be found. The
performance of the naturally aspirated Carrera was
increased to 210kW (285hp) through the use of
the Varioram induction system. Also new this year
was the Carrera 4S with its Turbo-shape body.

Also new in 993 form was the 911 Turbo
(although the new twin-turbo 911 Turbo had been
launched in the spring of 1995, its vehicle ID was
for model year 1996). This sports car stood out
through its significantly improved performance,
high stability and improved traction – mainly
because it now boasted all-wheel drive. The 911
Turbo was the first car on the world market to be
equipped with an OBD II (On-Board Diagnosis II)
emissions monitoring system as standard. Peak
power from the twin-turbo 3.6-litre engine was
now 300kW (408hp). The Turbo was equipped
with hollow-spoke wheels for the first time.

Porsche continued to build the 911 Carrera
RS in basic and Club Sport guises without
any modifications.

Engine

911 Turbo: the M64/60 engine was based on the naturally aspirated M64/05 engine of the Carrera. The crankshaft drive and the crank housing were incorporated from the naturally aspirated engine with only slight modifications. The con rods were strengthened at the crankshaft end, the compressed pistons were Grafal-coated and the light-alloy cylinders had a bore of 100mm and were surface-coated. The inlet duct of 38mm was increased to 43mm in the light-alloy cylinder heads, while the exhaust duct was formed by a cast ceramic port liner that served to lower the temperature in the cylinder heads. The camshafts were modified as well and now had an induction stroke of 11.6mm and an exhaust stroke of 10.5mm. The lubrication of the two turbochargers was offset from the chain tensioner housing. A separate dual-geared pump was used to empty the oil sump, which was positioned underneath the turbochargers. The pump, which consisted of three spur gears, was driven via a Torx gear on the jackshaft from the timing gear.

Fuel and ignition system

911 Carrera and Carrera 4S: performance increase to 210kW (285hp) thanks to the Varioram induction system. Sequential injection and ignition system remained unchanged but the digital engine electronics system was tweaked to match the increased performance of the car.

911 Turbo: a Bosch M 5.2 Motronic system calculated the ignition timing, fuel injection and air mass-dependent turbo boost pressure control. The intake air was divided into two streams

1996 saw the arrival of the 911 GT, with a twin-turbo 3.6-litre engine, producing a remarkable 316kW (430hp) at 5,750rpm.

downstream of the air filter and the hot-film air mass sensor, and was then fed to the two turbochargers. The air compressed by the turbochargers also remained separate and two high-volume intercoolers made sure that its temperature was kept down. The air was only merged again at the throttle valve that served all six cylinders. The two turbochargers were relatively small and driven by the exhaust gas flow from three cylinders each, and the exhaust gas systems on both sides of the boxer engine remained completely independent of each other up to the exhaust pipes. Downstream of the turbochargers two catalytic converters were arranged in the lateral section at the rear. On either side of the catalytic converter was a lambda probe whose readings were sent to the DME controller. The on-board diagnostic system (OBD II) was new in the Turbo and the DME controller was able to follow 83 error paths at the same time, and could save up to 20 exhaust emission errors on the system and then report them via an appropriate diagnostic device. The first detected error would cause a warning light to illuminate ('check engine' light). The move to OBD II was inspired by the 1996 USA exhaust emissions regulations. While all other manufacturers were hesitant and only installed OBD II in cars exported to the USA, Porsche fitted all of its new turbo vehicles with this diagnostic system as from March 1995.

A cutaway view of a 1996-model 911 Turbo, showing the all-wheel drive system and twin-turbo engine installation.

Transmission

911 Turbo: except for a few changes, the transmission system – consisting of a six-speed manual transmission, Visco clutch, transaxle system and front differential – was adopted from the four-wheel drive 911 Carrera 4. The ratios of some gears needed to be matched to the performance, so the G64/51 transmission received taller fourth, fifth and sixth ratios. Oil drip pans situated near the driveshafts provided improved lubrication. The oil that was collected was fed to the hollow shafts, and passed through to idler gears three, four, five and six. Worldwide there was only one transmission for the Turbo, which was equipped with the ZF friction-plate limited-slip differential (lock-up factor under load 25% and under coasting 40%). This system was supported by standard automatic brake differential.

To cope with the new Turbo's enormous torque

of 540Nm, the clutch pressure plate had to manage about 15,000N (1.5 tons). The pedal force needed could only be mustered with hydraulic support. The enhanced hydraulic steering pump was called into service here, its force of up to 70bar being used to help operate the clutch. The clutch release path could be reduced by 15% and the pedal force by 25%.

Suspension

The suspension of the 911 Turbo was further enhanced over the sports suspension (M030) of the Carrera and was made sportier by lowering the body height (1,285mm). Due to the increased weight of the 911 Turbo the coordination between springs and dampers had to be configured differently to the Carrera.

The Turbo was equipped with hollow-spoke wheels, using a new Porsche-developed low-

Another view of a 911 Targa, showing the full-length sliding glass roof panel.

An interior view of a 911 Targa showing the glass roof panel partially retracted.

pressure die-casting method. Friction welding joined the rim and dish together (these had originally been fabricated as two parts). The hollow-spoke light-alloy wheel design produced a weight saving of up to 30% while at the same time achieving higher rigidity. Around 3.2kg in weight was saved per 8x18in wheel. The friction welding was achieved through pressing together the opposing surfaces of rim and dish while at the same time rotating one part. Frictional heat occurred, which led to a gas-tight fusion of the parts.

The dual-circuit brake system operated with a hydraulic brake servo. The internally vented, drilled brake discs were fitted with cooling ducts at the front and the rear.

Body

911 Turbo: the front and rear styling was new, and the door sill area was adapted to match the wider wings (fenders). The one-piece front end now had larger air inlet vents, and the fixed rear spoiler was also a fresh design. The drag coefficient was improved via a front spoiler lip and a more aerodynamic overall front end design (drag coefficient was Cd 0.34, and the frontal area 1.93m^2). The lift coefficient of front and rear axles was almost zero.

Carrera 4S: this was a new model which basically revived the Turbo Look idea: the body of the 911 Turbo was used with a normally aspirated engine. Its extendable rear spoiler was the same as that of the Carrera and Carrera 4.

Targa: a roof module was fitted and bonded to

the body. The top part consisted of tinted safety glass that could slide electrically backwards behind the rear seats.

Interior fittings

In the 911 Turbo, the rear seats were visually coordinated with the front seats. 'Turbo' script was stitched on to the carpet cover of the left rear seat back.

Heating and air conditioning

The 911 Turbo was equipped with an additional rear heater fan in the engine compartment and two extra preheat exchangers for boosted heating power.

Electrical system

A 'check engine' warning light was fitted in the 911 Turbo worldwide, and the calibration on the speedometer was extended to 320kmh. New 'Litronic' light technology improved the dipped beam through a gas-discharge lamp; this was standard for the 911 Turbo and available as an optional extra for all other vehicles. The D2S gas discharge lamp offered multiples of light streams and light densities compared to conventional halogen lamps. The illumination of the road surface as well as the adjoining area was much improved under dipped headlights. The heat inside the headlights was also significantly lower. All cars were now fitted with a mobile phone as standard.

Additional information

On 15 July 1996, the millionth Porsche was built, which was a 911 Coupé for the Autobahn police in Baden-Württemberg, featuring a white body, bright

green doors and bonnet and flashing blue lights. During a special ceremony the head of the company, Prof Dr Ferry Porsche, handed this police car over to the Premier of Baden-Württemberg, who promised always to use this Porsche in convoys for guests of state ahead of Mercedes-Benz limousines.

Porsche also launched the GT2 as a racing version of the 911 Turbo (also sold in roadgoing form). The basic body was identical to the 911 Turbo but received wider plastic wings (fenders) in preparation for 18in racing wheels. Like the 911 Turbo, the engine was 3,600cc and there were two turbochargers but peak power was higher: 330kW (450hp) in race trim or 316kW (430hp) for the road version. Unlike the 911 Turbo, the GT2 was only offered with rear-wheel drive, rather than four-wheel drive. Porsche also continued building the Carrera RS with 3.8-litre displacement.

An interior view of a 1996-model 911 Carrera 3.6 Convertible, fitted with Tiptronic S transmission and in-car phone system.

Model range	Total production
911 Carrera Coupé	6762* + 3671* USA
911 Carrera Targa	1980* + 462* USA
911 Cabriolet	2066* + 2152* USA
911 Carrera 4 Coupé	*
911 Carrera 4 Cabriolet	*
911 Carrera 4S Coupé	*
911 Carrera RS Coupé	849
911 Carrera RS Coupé Club Sport	117
911 Turbo 3.6 Coupé	2484 #
911 GT2 Coupé	202 #

* The vehicle ID numbers no longer allowed for a differentiation between Carrera 2 and Carrera 4. The production numbers mentioned relate to both vehicles and also include vehicles with Tiptronic.
\# Although production of the Turbo 3.6 and the GT2 started in model year 1995, the vehicles and their ID numbers were allocated to model year 1996.

Model range	Carrera	Carrera 4	Carrera 4S	Carrera RS	911 Turbo	911 GT2
Engine						
Engine type						
Manual transmission	M64/05	M64/05	M64/21	M64/20	M64/60	M64/60R
Tiptronic	M64/06	–	–	–	–	–
Bore (mm)	100	100	100	102	100	100
Stroke (mm)	76.4	76.4	76.4	76.4	76.4	76.4
Displacement (cc)	3600	3600	3600	3746	3600	3600
Compression ratio	11.3:1	11.3:1	11.3:1	11.3:1	8.0:1	
Engine output (kW/hp)	210/285	210/285	210/285	221/300	300/408	316/430
at revolutions per minute (rpm)	6100	6100	6100	6500	5750	5750
Torque (Nm)	340	340	340	355	540	
at revolutions per minute (rpm)	5250	5250	5250	5400	4500	
Output per litre (kW/l)	58.3	58.3	58.3	59	83.3	
Max. engine speed (rpm)	6700	6700	6700	6840	6720	
Engine weight (kg)	239*	239*	239*	230	268	

* with underbody panelling, clutch and air-conditioning compressor

Model range	Carrera	Carrera 4	Carrera 4S	Carrera RS	911 Turbo	911 GT2
Carburation, ignition, settings						
Fuel system	DME S + Varioram	=	=	=	DME S	DME S
Type of fuel (RON)	98	98	98	98	98	98
Ignition system	DME	DME	DME	DME	DME	DME
Ignition	dual	dual	dual	dual	dual	dual
Spark plugs						
Bosch	FR 6 LDC and FR5 DTC		=	=	FR 6 LDC	
Beru	14 FR 5 DTU and 14 FR 6 LDU		=	=	=	14 FR 5LDU
Spark plug gap (mm)	0.7	=	=	=	=	
Anti-knock control	yes	yes	yes	yes	yes	
Idle speed (rpm)	800+-40	800+-40	800+-40	960+-40	800+-40	
Exhaust/purification system	BLS+DWMK	=	=	=	4xBLS+ DWML+ZLP	=
CO-content						
without cat. conv. (%)	0.5–1.0	=	=	=	1.0–1.4	
with cat. conv. (%)	0.4–1.2	=	=	=	0.8–1.2	
Fuel consumption acc. C Standard (litres/100km)						
Manual transmission						
A. at a constant 90 kmh	7.6	7.8	8.0	7.6	8.2	
B. at a constant 120 kmh	9.3	9.3	9.6	9.5	10.3	
C. EC urban cycle	16.3	16.9	16.9	20.1	21.0	
D. Euromix	11.2	11.3	11.5	12.4	13.2	
Tiptronic						
A. at a constant 90 kmh	8.2	–	–	–	–	–
B. at a constant 120 kmh	9.8	–	–	–	–	–
C. EC urban cycle	15.8	–	–	–	–	–
D. Euromix	11.3	–	–	–	–	–

Key:
BLS   Heated lambda sensor
DME S   Digital engine electronic system with sequential fuel injection
DWMK   Three-way metal-based catalytic converter

KFZ   Pressure-controlled mapped ignition
SLE   Secondary-air injection
ZLP   Auxiliary air pump

Transmission						
Dual-mass flywheel	Syst.LUK*	Syst.LUK*	Syst.LUK*	Syst.LUK*	Syst.LUK*	
Clutch, pressure plate	G MFZ 240	=	=	=	=	
Clutch plate (mm)	rigid 240	=	=	=	=	
Manual transmission	G50/21	=	=	=	=	
Gear ratios						
1st gear	3.818	3.818	3.818	3.154	3.818	3.818
2nd gear	2.150	2.150	2.150	2.000	2.150	2.150
3rd gear	1.560	1.560	1.560	1.522	1.50	1.560
4th gear	1.242	1.242	1.242	1.242	1.212	1.212
5th gear	1.024	1.024	1.024	1.024	0.937	0.973
6th gear	0.820	0.820	0.820	0.750	0.750	0.750
Reverse gear	2.857	2.857	2.857	2.857	2.857	2.857
Synchromesh system						
Forward gears	VK	VK	VK	VK	VK	VK
Reverse gear	VK	VK	VK	VK	VK	VK
Final drive, ratio	3.444	3.444	3.444	3.444	3.444	3.444
Limited-slip differential	M	S	S	S	S	S
Lock-up factor under load/coasting (%)	25/65	25/40	25/40	40/64	25/40	25/40
Gearbox weight with oil (kg)	66	72.5	72.5	69.0	72.5	
Tiptronic	A50/04	–	–	–	–	–
Torque converter dia.(mm)	260	–	–	–	–	–
Stall speed (rpm)	2300	–	–	–	–	–
Gear ratios						
1st gear	2.479	–	–	–	–	–
2nd gear	1.479	–	–	–	–	–
3rd gear	1.000	–	–	–	–	–
4th gear	0.728	–	–	–	–	–
Reverse gear	2.086	–	–	–	–	–
Intermediate shaft, ratio	1.100	–	–	–	–	–
Final drive, ratio	3.667	–	–	–	–	–
Limited-slip differential	no	–	–	–	–	–
Gearbox weight with oil and ATF filling (kg)	105	–	–	–	–	–

Key:
Syst.LUK*   Dual-mass flywheel system LUK (steel-spring damped)
VK   Full-cone synchromesh system with molybdenum-coated synchroniser rings

Model range	Carrera	Carrera 4	Carrera 4S	Carrera RS	911 Turbo	911 GT2
Suspension, steering and brakes						
Front axle						
Anti-roll bar dia. (mm)	21	21	20	23	22	
Steering ratio	16.48	16.48	16.51	18.25	16.5	
Turning circle dia. (m)	11.74	11.74	11.74	11.76	11.74	
Rear axle						
Anti-roll bar dia.						
Manual transmission (mm)	18	18	18	20	21	
Tiptronic (mm)	18	–	–	–	–	
Brake system						
Brake booster ratio	3.15:1	4.8:1	4.8:1	3.6:1	4.8:1	
Brake master cylinder dia. (mm)	23.81	25.4	25.4	23.81	25.4	25.4
Pressure reducer						
Cut-in pressure (bar)	40	45	40	40	55	
Reduction factor	0.46	0.46	0.46	0.46	0.46	
Brake calliper piston diameter						
front (mm)	44+36	44+36	44+36	44+36	44+36	44+36
rear (mm)	30+34	28+30	28+28	30+36	28+28	30+36
Brake disc diameter						
front (mm)	304	304	322	322	322	322
rear (mm)	299	299	322	322	322	322
Brake disc thickness						
front (mm)	32	32	32	32	32	32
rear (mm)	24	24	28	28	24	24
Effective brake disc area (cm^2)	422	422	522	522	422	
Handbrake	Operating mechanically on both rear wheels					
Brake drum diameter (mm)	180	=	=	=	=	=
Contact area (cm^2)	170	=	=	=	=	=
Wheels and tyres						
Standard tyre specification, front	205/55ZR16	205/55ZR16	205/55ZR16	225/40ZR18	225/40ZR18	225/40ZR18
wheel	7J x 16 H2	7J x 16 H2	8J x 16 H2	8J x 18 AH	8J x 18 H2	8J x 18 H2
hump depth (mm)	55	55	52	52	52	52
optional	205/50ZR17	205/50ZR17	205/50ZR17	235/40ZR18		
wheel	7J x 17 H2	7J x 17 H2	7J x 17 H2	9J x 18 H2		
hump depth (mm)	55	55	55	34		
optional	245/40ZR18					
wheel	9J x 18 H2					
hump depth (mm)	34					
Standard tyre specification, rear	245/45ZR16	245/45ZR16	245/45ZR16	265/35ZR18	285/30ZR18	285/30ZR18
wheel	9J x 16 H2	9J x 16 H2	9J x 16 H2	10J x 18 AH	10J x 18 H2	10J x 18 H2
hump depth (mm)	70	70	40	65	40	40
optional	255/40ZR17	255/40ZR17	255/40ZR17	285/35ZR18		
wheel	9J x 17 H2	9J x 17 H2	9J x 17 H2	11J x 18 H2		
hump depth (mm)	65	65	65	18		
optional	295/35ZR18					
wheel	11J x 18					
H2 hump depth (mm)	18					
Space-saver spare wheel	165/70-16 92P	=	=	=	=	=
Tyre pressure						
front (bar)	2.5	=	=	=	=	=
rear (bar)	2.5	2.5	2.5	3.0	3.0	3.0
Space-saver spare wheel (bar) 2.5	=	=	=	=		
Body and interior (dimensions at kerb weight)						
Length (mm)	4245	4245	4245	4245	4245	4245
Width (mm)	1735	1735	1795	1735	1795	1855
Height (mm)	1300	1300	1300	1270	1285	1270
Wheelbase (mm)	2272	=	=	=	=	=
Track						
front (mm)	1405	1405	1411	1413	1411	1475 (ET 34) 1433 (ET 55)
rear (mm)	1444	1444	1504	1452	1504	1550 (ET 18) 1506 (ET 40)
Ground clearance at permissible gross weight (mm)	110	110	95	90	90	90
Overhang angle						
front (degree)	11.0	10.5	10.0	9.7	9.5	
rear (degree)	12.5	12.5	10.0	12.5	11.0	
Electrical system						
Generator output (W/A)	1610/115	=	=	=	=	
Battery (V/Ah)	12/75	12/75	12/75	12/36	12/75	

171

Model range	Carrera	Carrera 4	Carrera 4S	Carrera RS	911 Turbo	911 GT2
Weight according to DIN 70020						
Kerb weight (kg)						
Manual transmission	1400	1420	1470	1270	1500	1295
Tiptronic	1425	–	–	–	–	–
Permissible gross weight (kg)						
Manual transmission	1740	1760	1790	1710	1840	1575
Tiptronic	1735	–	–	–	–	–
Permissible trailer weight (kg)						
unbraked	none	none	none	none	none	none
braked	none	none	none	none	none	none
Permissible roof load (kg)	35	=	=	=	=	=
with Porsche system (kg)	75	=	=	=	=	=
Performance						
Maximum speed (kmh)						
Manual transmission	275	275	270	277	290	295
Tiptronic	270	–	–	–	–	
Acceleration 0–62mph/100kmh (sec)						
Manual transmission	5.4	5.3	5.3	5.0	4.5	
Tiptronic	6.4	–	–	–	–	
Measured kilometre from standing start (sec)						
Manual transmission	24.6	25.3	24.8	24.0	23.0	
Tiptronic	25.4	–	–	–	–	
Fluid capacities						
Engine oil quantity 1* (l)	11.5	11.5	11.5	11.5	11.5	
Manual transmission 2* (l)	3.6	3.8	3.8	3.6	4.3	
Front axle 2* (l)	..	0.6	0.6	–	0.6	
Automatic transm. 3* (l)	9.0	–	–	–	–	
Final drive, autom. 2* (l)	0.9	–	–	–	–	
Fuel tank 4* (l)	73 (92)**	73 (92)**	73 (92)**	92	92	
Brake fluid reservoir 5* (l)	0.34	0.75	0.75	0.34	0.75	
Power steering fluid 3* (l)	1.0	=	=	=	=	
Refrigerant 6* (g)	840	=	=	=	=	
Refrigerant oil 7* (ml)	140	=	=	=	=	
Washer tank (l)	7.3	7.3	1.2	7.3		

Key and key to numerals
** 92-litres fuel tank available as optional extra
1* Approved API SE/SF with combinations API SE/CC - SF/CC - SF/CD - SE/CD
  Multigrade engine oil factory recommended
2* Multigrade gear oil 75 W 90 acc. MIL-L 2105 B and API-classified GL 5
3* ATF DEXRON II D

4* Only unleaded fuel with minimum standard RON 98/MON 88
5* Use only brake fluid acc. DOT 4. type 200.
6* Only refrigerant R 134 a (Porsche had changed over to CFC-free
  refrigerants in their cooling devices)
7* Commercially available refrigerant oils

Vehicle Identification Numbers												
World manufacturer code	Code body USA (A=Coupé, B=Targa, C=Cabriolet)	Code for engine variants (only USA)	Restraint system (0 = belt, 2 = airbag) only USA	First and second digit for car type	Fill character/ check digit	Model year (P = 1996, R = 1997, etc.)	Manufacturing site (S = Stuttgart)	7th and 8th digit = car type	Code for body + engine	Sequence number	Summary
WPO	Z	Z	Z	99	Z	T	S	3	1	0001–9000	Rest of world, 911 Carrera or Carrera 4 Coupé
WPO	Z	Z	Z	99	Z	T	S	3	8	0001–5000	Rest of world, 911 Carrera or Carrera 4 Targa
WPO	Z	Z	Z	99	Z	T	S	3	3	0001–9000	Rest of world, 911 Carrera or Carrera 4 Cabriolet
WPO	Z	A	Z	99	Z	T	S	3	7	0001–3000	Rest of world, 911 Turbo Coupé
WPO	Z	A	Z	99	Z	T	S	3	9	0001–0400	Rest of world, 911 Carrera RS
WPO	A	B	2	99	C*	T	S	3	2	0001–9000	USA/CDN, 911 Carrera or Carrera 4 Coupé
WPO	D	A	2	99	C*	T	S	3	8	5001–9000	USA/CDN, 911 Carrera or Carrera 4 Targa
WPO	C	B	2	99	C*	T	S	3	4	0001–9000	USA/CDN, 911 Carrera or Carrera 4 Cabriolet
WPO	A	C	2	99	C*	T	S	3	7	5001–6000	USA/CDN, Turbo 3.6

C* = Check digit, can be 0–9 or X (only USA)
Z = Fill character for rest of world cars

Model year 1997

V Programme, Turbo-look Carrera S

Porsche 911 Carrera Coupé, Cabriolet and
  Targa
Porsche 911 Carrera S Coupé
Porsche 911 Carrera 4 Coupé, Cabriolet and
  Targa
Porsche 911 Carrera 4S Coupé
Porsche 911 Turbo Coupé
Porsche 911 GT2

New in model year 1997 was the Carrera S,
essentially a Carrera Coupé with the 911 Turbo's
bodywork and an extendable rear spoiler. All other
changes this year were mere minor modifications.
The 911 RS was no longer available.

Engine

The 3.6-litre engines were adopted unchanged
from the previous year: naturally aspirated engines
M64/21 and M64/22 with 210kW (285hp), or for
the 911 Turbo the M64/60 engine with 300kW
(408hp). The engine sound package (optional extra
M159) that had been available worldwide up until

now was henceforth only available in the USA
because of stricter regulations in Germany and in
the rest of the world.

Fuel and ignition system

No changes.

Transmission

Cars intended for the US export market were only
able to start with the clutch depressed, which
prevented the engine starting up with a gear
engaged. In order to comply with new noise
regulations in Europe and in important export
markets, transmissions with 'tall' gear ratios were
now incorporated into cars worldwide. These had
already been available in the USA for many years.
Transmission type G50/20 for the Carrera and
Carrera S, as well as the G64/20 for the Carrera 4
and Carrera 4S, were adopted worldwide. The
taller ratios of second to sixth gears (up to 10%)
resulted in lower engine revs at any given speed
and thus lower noise levels. At the same time, of
course, less petrol was used and exhaust emissions
were reduced.

*The 1997 Porsche range. Front row, left to right; 911 Targa 3.6, 911
Carrera S 3.6, Boxster 2.5 Roadster. Back row, left to right; 911
Carrera 3.6 Coupé, 911 Carrera 3.6 Cabriolet, 911 Turbo 3.6.*

The 1997-model 911 Targa 3.6 continued with only minor detail changes to interior equipment and trim.

Suspension

No changes to the suspension of the Carrera, Carrera 4 and the Turbo. The suspension of the new Carrera S was lowered by 10mm at the front

Although the 911 Turbo 3.6 remained unchanged, it still bore an obvious resemblance to the first Porsche 911 models.

and 20mm at the rear. To fit the fatter wings (fenders), 31mm wheel spacers were inserted and the 'S' therefore looked very much like the 911 Turbo. The hydraulics of the power steering were changed from ATF (automatic transmission fluid) to Pentosin CHF 11 S. Super DOT 4 was used as brake fluid and had a change interval of every two years.

Body

No significant changes to the 911 Carrera, Carrera 4 and Turbo. The body of the Carrera S was identical to that of the Carrera 4S, except for the

inlet grille in the rear spoiler which was split and painted in body colour. This split gave it the appearance of a double grille. Steel-grey 'Carrera S' script was placed on the engine lid.

Interior fittings

The door panels were now covered in black leather, and the colour of the interior leather was now always black. The armrests were integrated into the door trim panels.

Porsche started to prepare the passenger seat to accommodate a child seat recognition system. The 'BabySafe' child seat from Reboard, available from Porsche dealers, prevented the airbag on the passenger side from deploying in the event of an accident.

As an upgrade of the interior a titanium-coloured switch, a titanium-coloured cover over the handbrake, and script on the door sills were added to the 911 Carrera S. The rev counter dial also featured '911 Carrera S' script.

Heating and air conditioning

No changes.

Electrical system

In the area above the ignition lock a lamp was fitted that made it easier to find the lock in the dark. Since the 911 had a luggage compartment at the front and limited spring travel, headlight

The 1997-model 911 Turbo 3.6 remained unchanged with manual transmission only and 300kW (408hp) 3.6-litre engine.

adjustment could be dispensed with in vehicles with Litronic headlamps.

All radios available from Porsche were fitted with GAL (speed-dependent volume control), dial

This is the competition version of the 911 GT2, intended purely for racing, with stripped-out race interior and huge adjustable rear spoiler.

illumination dimming and volume increase. In cars with hands-free car phone equipment, the sound of the telephone was transmitted via the speakers of the in-car radio system.

Additional information

Autumn 1996 saw the start of production of the Porsche Boxster (Type 986) on the same assembly line as the 911.

Model range	Total production
911 Carrera Coupé	1775*
911 Carrera Targa	1807*
911 Carrera Cabriolet	3098*
911 Carrera S Coupé	3370*
911 Carrera 4 Coupé	379
911 Carrera 4 Cabriolet	650
911 Carrera 4S Coupé	2752
911 Turbo Coupé	1775 + 182 Turbo S
911 GT2 Coupé	35

* The production figures also included vehicles with Tiptronic S.

Model range	Carrera	Carrera S	Carrera 4	Carrera 4S	911 Turbo	911 GT2
Engine						
Engine type						
Manual transmission	M64/21	M64/21	M64/21	M64/21	M64/60	M64/60R
Tiptronic	M64/22	M64/22	–	–	–	–
Bore (mm)	100	100	100	102	100	100
Stroke (mm)	76.4	76.4	76.4	76.4	76.4	76.4
Displacement (cc)	3600	3600	3600	3600	3600	3600
Compression ratio	11.3:1	11.3:1	11.3:1	11.3:1	8.0:1	
Engine output (kW/hp)	210/85	210/85	210/85	210/300	300/408	316/430
at revolutions per minute (rpm)	6100	6100	6100	6100	5750	5750
Torque (Nm)	340	340	340	340	540	
at revolutions per minute (rpm)	5250	5250	5250	5250	4500	
Output per litre (kW/l)	58.3	58.3	58.3	58.3	83.3	
Max. engine speed (rpm)	6700	6700	6700	6700	6720	
Engine weight (kg)	239*	239*	239*	239*	268	

* with underbody panelling, clutch and air-conditioning compressor

Carburation, ignition, settings						
Fuel system	DME S + Varioram	=	=	=	DME S	DME S
Type of fuel (RON)	98	98	98	98	98	98
Ignition system	DME	DME	DME	DME	DME	DME
Ignition	dual	dual	dual	dual	dual	dual
Spark plugs						
Bosch	FR 6 LDC and FR 5 DTC		=	=	FR 6 LDC	
Beru	14 FR 5 DTU and 14 FR 6 LDU		=	=	14 FR 5 LDU	
Spark plug gap (mm)	0.7	=	=	=	=	
Anti-knock control	yes	yes	yes	yes	yes	
Idle speed (rpm)	800+-40	800+-40	800+-40	960+-40	800+-40	
Exhaust/purification system	BLS+DWMK	=	=	=	4xBLS+ DWMK+ZLP	=
CO-content						
without cat. conv. (%)	0.5–1.0	=	=	=	1.0–1.4	
with cat. conv. (%)	0.4–1.2	=	=	=	0.8–1.2	
Fuel consumption acc. 93/116/EC (litres/100km)						
Manual transmission						
A. urban	17.6	17.7	17.9	18.0	23.5	23.3
B. extra-urban	8.6	8.8	8.9	9.1	11.2	10.8
C. combined	11.9	12.0	12.2	12.3	15.7	15.4
D. CO2-emissions (g/km)	295	296	299	301	376	368
Tiptronic						
A. urban	18.2	18.5	–	–	–	–
B. extra-urban	8.7	8.7	–	–	–	–
C. combined	12.2	12.4	–	–	–	–
D. CO2-emissions (g/km)	303	307	–	–	–	–

Key:
BLS   Heated lambda sensor
DME S   Digital engine electronic system with sequential fuel injection
DWMK   Three-way metal-based catalytic converter
KFZ   Pressure-controlled mapped ignition
SLE   Secondary-air injection
ZLP   Auxiliary air pump

Model range	Carrera	Carrera S	Carrera 4	Carrera 4S	911 Turbo	911 GT2
Transmission						
Dual-mass flywheel	Syst.LUK*	Syst.LUK*	Syst.LUK*	Syst.LUK*	Syst.LUK*	
Clutch, pressure plate	G MFZ 240	=	=	=	=	
Clutch plate (mm)	rigid 240	=	=	=	=	
Manual transmission	G50/20	G50/20	G64/20	G64/20	G64/51	
Gear ratios						
1st gear	3.818	3.818	3.818	3.818	3.818	3.818
2nd gear	2.048	2.048	2.048	2.048	2.150	2.150
3rd gear	1.407	1.407	1.407	1.407	1.560	1.560
4th gear	1.118	1.118	1.118	1.118	1.212	1.212
5th gear	0.928	0.928	0.928	0.928	0.937	0.973
6th gear	0.775	0.775	0.775	0.775	0.750	0.750
Reverse gear	2.857	2.857	2.857	2.857	2.857	2.857
Synchromesh system						
Forward gears	VK	VK	VK	VK	VK	VK
Reverse gear	VK	VK	VK	VK	VK	VK
Final drive ratio	3.444	3.444	3.444	3.444	3.444	3.444
Limited-slip differential	M	M	M	M	S	S
Lock-up factor under load/coasting (%)	25/65	25/65	25/65	25/65	25/40	25/40
Gearbox weight with oil (kg)	66	66	72.5	72.5	69	
Tiptronic	A50/04	A50/04	–	–	–	–
Torque converter dia.(mm)	260	260	–	–	–	–
Stall speed (rpm)	2300	2300	–	–	–	–
Gear ratios						
1st gear	2.479	2.479	–	–	–	–
2nd gear	1.479	1.479	–	–	–	–
3rd gear	1.000	1.000	–	–	–	–
4th gear	0.728	0.728	–	–	–	–
Reverse gear	2.086	2.086	–	–	–	–
Intermediate shaft, ratio	1.100	1.100	–	–	–	–
Final drive, ratio	3.667	3.667	–	–	–	–
Limited-slip differential	no	no	–	–	–	–
Gearbox weight with oil and ATF filling (kg)	105	105	–	–	–	–

Key:

Syst.LUK* Dual-mass flywheel system LUK (steel-spring damped)

VK   Full-cone synchromesh system with molybdenum-coated synchroniser rings

Suspension, steering and brakes						
Front axle						
Anti-roll bar dia. (mm)	21	21	21	20	22	
Steering ratio	16.48	16.48	16.48	16.48	16.5	
Turning circle dia. (m)	11.74	11.74	11.74	11.74	11.74	
Rear axle						
Anti-roll bar dia.						
Manual transmission (mm)	18	18	18	18	21	
Tiptronic (mm)	18	18	–	–	–	
Brake system						
Brake booster ratio	3.15:1	3.15:1	4.8:1	4.8:1		
Brake master cylinder dia. (mm)	23.81	25.4	25.4	25.4	25.4	25.4
Pressure reducer						
Cut-in pressure (bar)	40	40	45	40	55	
Reduction factor	0.46	0.46	0.46	0.46	0.46	
Brake calliper piston diameter						
front (mm)	44+36	44+36	44+36	44+36	44+36	
rear (mm)	30+34	30+34	28+30	28+28	28+28	30+36
Brake disc diameter						
front (mm)	304	304	304	322	322	322
rear (mm)	299	299	299	322	322	322
Brake disc thickness						
front (mm)	32	32	32	32	32	
rear (mm)	24	24	24	24	24	
Effective brake disc area (cm^2)	422	422	422	552	422	
Handbrake	Operating mechanically on both rear wheels					
Brake drum diameter (mm)	180	=	=	=	=	=
Contact area (cm^2)	170	=	=	=	=	=

Model range	Carrera	Carrera S	Carrera 4	Carrera 4S	911 Turbo	911 GT2
Wheels and tyres						
Standard tyre specification, front	205/55ZR16	205/55ZR16	205/55ZR16	205/55ZR16	225/40ZR18	225/40ZR18
wheel	7J x 16 H2	7J x 16 H2	7J x 16 H2	7J x 16 AH	8J x 18 H2	8J x 18 H2
hump depth (mm)	55	55	55	55	52	52
optional	205/50ZR17	205/50ZR17	205/50ZR17	205/50ZR17	235/40ZR18	
wheel	7J x 17 H2	7J x 17 H2	7J x 17 H2	7J x 17 H2	9J x 18 H2	
hump depth (mm)	55	55	55	55	34	
optional	225/40ZR18	225/40ZR18	225/40ZR18	225/40ZR18	245/40ZR18	
wheel	8J x 18 H2	8J x 18 H2	8J x 18 H2	8J x 18 H2	9J x 18 H2	
hump depth (mm)	52	52	52	52	34	
Standard tyre specification, rear	245/45ZR16	245/40ZR16	245/45ZR16	245/45ZR16	285/30ZR18	285/30ZR18
wheel	9J x 16 H2	9J x 16 H2	9J x 16 H2	9J x 16 H2	10J x 18 AH	10J x 18 H2
hump depth (mm)	70	70	70	70	40	40
optional	255/40ZR17	255/40ZR17	255/40ZR17	255/40ZR17	285/35ZR18	
wheel	9J x 17 H2	9J x 17 H2	9J x 17 H2	9J x 17 H2	11J x 18 H2	
hump depth (mm)	55	55**	55	55	18	
optional	265/35ZR18	265/35ZR18	285/30ZR18	265/35ZR18	295/35ZR18	
wheel	10J x 18 H2	10J x 18 H2	10J x 18 H2	10J x 18 H2	11J x 18 H2	
hump depth (mm)	65	65	40	40	18	
optional	285/30ZR18					
wheel	8J x 18 H2					
hump depth (mm)	40					
Space-saver spare wheel	165/70-16 92P	=	=	=	=	=
Tyre pressure						
front (bar)	2.5	=	=	=	=	=
rear (bar)	2.5 for 17-inch tyres					
	3.0 for 16 and 18-inch tyres					
Space-saver spare wheel (bar)	2.5	=	=	=	=	=

Body						
Drag coefficient (cd)	0.34	0.34	0.34	0.34	0.34	
Frontal area A (m2)	1.90	1.93	1.93	1.93	1.93	
Aerodynamic drag cd x A (m2)	0.645	0.656	0.656	0.656	0.656	

Dimensions at kerb weight						
Length (mm)	4245	4245	4245	4245	4245	4245
Width (mm)	1735	1795	1735	1795	1795	1855
Height (mm)	1300	1285	1285	1285	1285	1270
Wheelbase (mm)	2272	=	=	=	=	=
Track						
front 16+17 inch (mm)	1405	1405	1405	1405	1411	1475 (ET 34)
front 18 inch (mm)	1411	1411 / 1433 (ET 55**)	1411			
rear 16 inch (mm)	1444	1444	1444	1444	1504	1550 (ET18)
rear 17 inch (mm)	1474	1536	1474	1474		
rear 18 inch (mm)	1454	1454	1454	1454		
Ground clearance at permissible gross weight (mm)	110	95	110	95	90	
Overhang angle						
front (degree)	11.0	10.0	10.0	10	9.5	
rear (degree)	12.5	11.0	12.5	10	11.0	

Key:
55** = for the 911 Carrera S with 31-mm spacers at rear suspension

Electrical system						
Generator output (W/A)	1610/115	=	=	=	=	
Battery (V/Ah)	12/75	12/75	12/75	12/36	12/75	

Model range	Carrera	Carrera S	Carrera 4	Carrera 4S	911 Turbo	911 GT2
Weight according to DIN 70020						
Kerb weight (kg)						
Manual transmission	1370	1400	1420	1450	1500	1295
Tiptronic	1395	1425	–	–	–	–
Permissible gross weight (kg)						
Manual transmission	1710	1740	1760	1790	1840	1575
Tiptronic	1735	1740	–	–	–	–
Permissible trailer weight (kg)						
unbraked	none	none	none	none	none	none
braked	none	none	none	none	none	none
Permissible roof load (kg)	35	=	=	=	=	=
with Porsche System (kg)	75	=	=	=	=	=
Performance						
Maximum speed (kmh)						
Manual transmission	275	270	270	277	290	295
Tiptronic (kmh)	270	265	–	–	–	–
Acceleration 0–62mph/100 kmh (sec)						
Manual transmission	5.4	5.4	5.3	5.3	4.5	
Tiptronic	6.4	6.4	–	–	–	–
Measured kilometre from standing start (sec)						
Manual transmission	24.6	24.8	24.8	25.0	23.0	
Tiptronic	25.4	25.6	–	–	–	–
Fluid capacities						
Engine oil quantity 1* (l)	11.5	11.5	11.5	11.5	11.5	
Manual transmission 2* (l)	3.6	3.8	3.6	3.6	4.3	
Front axle 2* (l)	..	0.6	0.6		0.6	
Automatic transm. 3* (l)	9.0	9.0	–	–	–	
Final drive, autom. 2* (l)	0.9	0.9	–	–	–	
Fuel tank 4* (l)	73 (92)**	73 (92)**	73 (92)**	92	92	
Brake fluid reservoir 5* (l)	0.34	0.34	0.75	0.75	0.75	
Power steering fluid 3* (l)	1.0	=	=	=	=	
Refrigerant 6* (g)	840	=	=	=	=	
Refrigerant oil 7* (ml)	140	=	=	=	=	
Washer tank (l)	7.3	–	–	–	–	

Key and key to numerals:
** 92-litre fuel tank available as optional extra
1* Approved engine oil API SE/SF with combinations API SE/CC - SF/CC - SF/CD - SE/CD
   Multigrade engine oil factory recommended
2* Multigrade gear oil 75 W 90 acc. MIL-L 2105 B and API-classified GL 5
3* ATF DEXRON II D
4* Only unleaded fuel with minimum standard RON 98/MON 88
5* Use only brake fluid acc. DOT 4. type 200.
6* Only refrigerant R 134 a (Porsche had changed over to CFC-free refrigerants in their cooling devices)
7* Commercially available refrigerant oils

World manufacturer code	Code body USA (A=Coupé, B=Targa, C=Cabriolet)	Code for engine variants (only USA)	Restraint system (0 = belt, 2 = airbag) only USA	First and second digit for car type	Fill character/ check digit	Model year (V = 1997, W = 1998, etc.)	Manufacturing site (S = Stuttgart)	7th and 8th digit = car type	Code for body + engine	Sequence number	Summary
WPO	Z	Z	Z	99	Z	V	S	3	1	0001–9000	Rest of world, 911 Carrera or Carrera 4 Coupé
WPO	Z	Z	Z	99	Z	V	S	3	3	0001–9000	Rest of world, 911 Cabriolet
WPO	Z	Z	Z	99	Z	V	S	3	8	0001–5000	Rest of world, 911 Targa
WPO	Z	Z	Z	99	Z	V	S	3	7	0001–3000	Rest of world, 911 Turbo 3.6 Coupé
WPO	A	A	2	99	C*	V	S	3	2	0001–9000	USA/CDN, 911 Carrera or Carrera 4 Coupé
WPO	C	A	2	99	C*	V	S	3	4	0001–9000	USA/CDN, 911 Carrera or Carrera 4 Cabriolet
WPO	D	A	2	99	C*	V	S	3	8	5001–9000	USA/CDN, 911 Targa
WPO	A	C	2	99	C*	V	S	3	7	0001–5000	USA/CDN, 911 Turbo 3.6 Coupé

Vehicle Identification Numbers

C* = Check digit, can be 0–9 or X (only USA)   Z = Fill character for rest of world cars

179

Model year 1998

W Programme, 996 goes water-cooled

Porsche 911 Carrera Coupé (Type 996)
Porsche 911 Carrera Cabriolet (Type 996)
Porsche 911 Carrera S (Type 993)
Porsche 911 Carrera Targa (Type 993)
Porsche 911 Carrera 4S Coupé (Type 993)
Porsche 911 Carrera RS Coupé (Type 993)
Porsche 911 Turbo 3.6 Coupé (Type 993)
Porsche 911 GT2 Coupé (Type 993)

The new Porsche 911, internally codenamed type 996, marked a quantum leap for Porsche: it was the very first time that the company used a water-cooled six-cylinder boxer engine for a road car. Equally significant was the completely new body shape, the first all-new evolution of the 911 in 34 years. The Coupé was the first body style to be

For 1998, the 911 changed dramatically, and featured water-cooled engines and completely new bodywork.

launched, followed closely by the Cabriolet (delivered to dealers from May 1998).

Porsche continued to make the following Type 993 models without modification: Targa, Carrera S, Carrera 4S, Turbo 3.6 and GT2. The Zuffenhausen factory not only had to cope with manufacturing the old 911, Turbo 3.6 and new 996 but also some 80 Boxster cars per day on the same assembly line.

The changeover from air-cooled to water-cooled engines had become inevitable from a technical perspective, as four-valve high-performance technology could only be realised with water-cooled cylinder heads. Porsche had had ample experience with water cooling in its TAG Formula 1 engines for McLaren, which won the world championship three times. It also used water cooling in its GT racing engines from 1977 (water-cooled six-cylinder boxer units), and in the 1998 GT1 engines which brought Porsche a double victory at Le Mans in that year.

The following describes only the new 911 Carrera, known in-house as model range 996.

Engine

The first water-cooled engine for the 911 was 70mm shorter and 120mm lower than its predecessor. The 3,387cc M96/01 engine produced 221kW (300hp) at 6,800rpm and was higher

revving than the previous engines: the rev limit was set at around 7,300rpm. However, there were many key elements that kept Porsche's traditions alive: the six-cylinder boxer design, crankshaft rotating in seven journal bearings, dry sump lubrication, crankcase split lengthways, and dual-mass flywheel.

The split light-alloy die-cast crankcase had been developed using a novel Lokasil surface technology method for the cylinders, developed by Kolbenschmidt and Porsche. The seven-bearing crankshaft was not mounted like the previous engines directly in the cylinder housing/engine block, but had a separate bearing bracket with cast steel seat rings. This bearing bracket, together with the crankshaft, was fastened between the two cylinder blocks. The con rods were forged from one piece. After the large con rod bore had been reworked the con rods were 'broken' at the desired breaking point in the con rod big end. After reassembly there were almost no variations in tolerance due to the crystal structure of the fractured surface.

The pistons were forged by Mahle and machined. They had a diameter of 96mm, the stroke was 78mm and the compression ratio of the oversquare engine was 11.3:1. Super Plus (Premium 98RON) fuel was allowed for.

The two cylinder heads were identical and inlet and exhaust camshafts were seated around them. This was not strictly a quad-camshaft engine but rather a twin-camshaft one. From the crankshaft an intermediate shaft was driven via a double roller chain. This intermediate shaft in turn drove the exhaust camshafts in the two cylinder heads. This arrangement saved a lot of space, and was the main reason why the new engines were 70mm shorter than the previous air-cooled 911 boxer engine.

The exhaust camshafts were connected to the intake camshafts by simplex chains. The Variocam system, which had been introduced in the Porsche 968 engine, influenced the position of the chain between the camshafts, and thus the two intake camshafts could be varied by as much as 25°. This did not result in damaging cam overlap at idle speed, but increased mid-range torque and power, and in connection with the variable induction system and its resonance flap, it was much more efficient at high engine speeds and thus increased performance. There were two inlet and two exhaust valves per cylinder that were actuated through

The completely new 3.4-litre water-cooled six-cylinder boxer engine was more compact than its air-cooled predecessor.

hydraulic tappets. The combustion chamber design allowed for one central spark plug in the top of the combustion chamber, which enabled air and petrol to mix evenly and quickly, also keeping exhaust emissions down. The integrated dry sump lubrication system consisted of an oil tank (approximately 10 litres) under the crankshaft drive, and there was no need for a scavenge pump. The conventional geared pressure supply pump for the whole engine was driven by an intermediate shaft. Return pumps in the cylinder heads arranged for them to be emptied and to channel the excess engine oil back into the oil sump.

Water-cooling circulation was achieved through a single pump. The cooling of the cylinders was by cross-flow, ensuring that the water flowed equally around all the cylinders. The heated water was then passed through to the radiators in the two front wheelarches. In this cooling circuit the water flowed through the two front radiators one after the other. An oil-water heat exchanger served to cool the engine oil (the heated engine oil emitted heat to the cooling water). During cold starts in the winter, this heat exchanger would also heat the oil. The bypass water circuit that would have already been heated after driving even a short distance (with the cooling water thermostat closed) delivered heat to the cold engine oil. Cars with Tiptronic S had an additional water/heat exchanger for the transmission, mounted centrally at the front.

Fuel and ignition system

The induction system was made from fibre-reinforced plastic, which was lightweight as well as having smooth intake manifolds on the inside where the air flowed through at very high speeds.

The variable induction system used a resonance flap which opened at 2,720rpm and closed again at 5,100rpm, and helped very efficient combustion. The aspirated air was controlled by a hot-film air mass sensor and the electronic engine management was done by means of digital engine electronics (DME) with sequential injection valve control.

The fuel tank capacity was significantly reduced (64 litres), and even as an optional extra it was not possible to fit a larger fuel tank. The petrol filler cap was positioned on the right wing (fender) and was centrally locked.

For the first time Porsche used surface-gap spark plugs with an electrode gap of 1.6mm +/- 0.2mm, which showed improved ignition characteristics for the fuel-air mixture. This had a particularly positive effect during cold starts. The four ground electrodes of these spark plugs were positioned laterally to the insulator, enabling the ignition sparks to glide across the surface of the insulator tip and then jump across a little gas to the ground electrode. The spark plugs had single-spark coils

and therefore static distribution of the ignition current. The DME controlled these single-spark coils with 12V low-voltage signals.

The delivery of petrol (98RON unleaded fuel) was effected by means of an electrically driven internal pump. Anti-knock control was provided that set back the ignition timing for each individual combustion chamber, which is why fuel of lesser quality could be used in case of emergency without the engine being damaged. Each cylinder bank had its own exhaust system made from stainless steel, a lambda sensor with one metal catalytic converter each and individual rear silencers. Cars for the US market were fitted with an additional air pump.

Transmission

The new six-speed transmission system (G96/00) developed jointly by Porsche and Getrag was a logical advancement of previous G50 transmission, although only the differential and the gearing of the driveshaft and ring gear were retained. The new transmission consisted of just two housings and a cover on the side for mounting the differential and the ring gear. The gearshift assembly was completely new. The gear selection was made by means of a cable change between the gear lever and the gearbox housing. These complex cables, which had already been tested in the Boxster, were much quieter.

At additional cost a ZF mechanical limited-slip differential was available. The lock-up factor under load was 25% and under coasting 40%. The high coasting value had a stabilising effect when slowing down in corners.

In addition ABD (automatic brake differential) was available with or without mechanical locking. When an individual wheel was spinning, the relevant brake would be activated and the wheel would be slowed briefly. In the case of both wheels spinning, the engine power was cut back through ignition and fuel injection intervention.

For the first time Porsche introduced a five-speed Tiptronic S power train. On the gear lever, the positions P-R-N-D remained unchanged, but the gear lever could then only be pushed to the left into the M (manual) position. If lower gears were to be maintained or the gears changed sequentially, this needed to be carried out via push buttons on the steering wheel spokes while the gear lever was in the M position.

Compared with earlier Tiptronic cars, the controls of the new system in the automatic position D were more sensitive. The system could interpret various driving situations, such as hill climbs, acceleration and cornering, and could respond with upshifts, downshifts or no gearchanges. When automatically changing gears, the engine management system cut back power for a split second, enabling seamless changes.

ABOVE: The all-new front suspension assembly, showing the alloy crossmember, steering rack and ventilated, drilled brake discs.

BELOW: The five-link rear suspension featured an all-new alloy subframe. Note too the ventilated, drilled rear brake discs.

Suspension

The 996's completely new suspension system was much tougher than before, and also allowed for a far tighter turning circle (10.6m compared to the 993's 11.74m). The front suspension was fitted with a crossbar and a semi-trailing arm instead of a lower A-arm. The MacPherson principle was retained and the spring struts were fitted with dual-strut gas pressure dampers. A five-wishbone rear suspension system was used (four wishbones for camber-constant wheel travel and one adjustment rod that altered the toe-in elasto-kinematically in all driving conditions). Coil springs and single-tube gas pressure dampers were used at the rear end. The hydraulically assisted rack-and-pinion steering was located ahead of the front axle and produced slightly understeering handling characteristics.

The new 911 Carrera was fitted with 17in wheels as standard, while 18in wheels were available as an optional extra for the 'Sport' suspension. The Sport package also included ride height reduced by some 10mm, a limited-slip differential with additional ABD and sport seats.

The 996's brake system was reworked as well. Porsche fitted its patented four-piston aluminium brake callipers, which were made from a single piece (monobloc) by Brembo in Italy. This design had proved itself in racing, especially in Formula 1. The monobloc calliper design allowed for a larger brake disc diameter (318mm) at the front. All brake discs were drilled.

The ABS sensor technology was also improved and a modern four-channel 5.3 ABS system was used. The new Carrera was fitted with a ready-to-use emergency spare wheel (rolling circumference as for normal tyres, but narrower), replacing the previous space-saver spare wheel that had to be laboriously pumped up before use.

Body

996 Coupé

Despite its all-new shape, there was no doubting that this was a 911. The roofline (including the windscreen, which sloped an additional 5°) was more flowing, the car body was more streamlined, the panel gaps were minimised and the windows were flush-fitting. The headlamps were also completely smooth with the body, and combined with flat underbody panelling to contribute to a reduced drag coefficient (from 0.34 for the 993 down to 0.30 for the 996). A side effect was significantly less wind noise intrusion.

Completely new supporting structures, which were patented by Porsche, as well as highly rigid steel panels offered significantly higher passive safety levels, and the body stiffness was about 50% higher overall. Porsche was now using galvanised steel panels as general bodywork material. Modern highly rigid steel panels had almost the same strength and rigidity as light-alloy panels. They were easier to repair, too, as almost any garage worldwide could handle steel, while light-alloy panels were really the preserve of specialists.

The two exterior rear-view mirrors were no longer attached to the doors but were mounted in the corners of the front side windows. As the new body no longer had a rain gutter, a fastening system for roof transportation was incorporated, which allowed for a roof load of up to 75kg.

996 Cabriolet

The 996 Cabriolet was fitted with a newly developed electric convertible top which neatly retracted under its own dust-proof metal cover at the back. As additional protection for the occupants, two roll bars were installed behind the rear seats which were only deployed in critical situations. The bars were preloaded with strong springs and a control unit would release the locks as soon as the car was leaning sideways at 90°. These deployed bars would then ensure sufficient head clearance for the passengers with the convertible top either open or closed in the event of the vehicle rolling over.

Each Cabriolet customer received a light-alloy hard top, painted in the colour of the car, at no extra cost. This hard top, which weighed only 33kg (including its heated rear window), could be lifted and fitted easily by two people. It increased driving comfort in winter and protected the folded convertible top lying underneath it against ice and humidity.

Interior fittings

The 996's clutch and brake pedals were arranged in a 'hanging' configuration. The driver and passenger seats were also new, featuring mechanical horizontal and height adjustment and electric seat back adjustment. The headrest was integrated into the seat back as was customary with Porsche. Optional extras included fully electric seats with seat memory, and sports seats. Three-point safety belts for driver and passenger were now height-adjustable and were also fitted to the seats at the rear, worldwide. Additional storage space was created behind the stowable backrests of the rear seats.

The airbags for driver and passenger were newly designed too. The airbag on the passenger's side had a 'hybrid gas generator', which filled the bag with an inert gas (argon) when activated. Damage to the dashboard through activation of the passenger airbag no longer occurred, and expensive

The all-new 1998-model 911 Carrera 3.4 Cabriolet was supplied with a light-alloy body-colour hard top, seen fitted here.

and complex repairs following an accident were therefore dispensed with. The airbag on the driver's side was slightly smaller, and was also filled with acid-free gas when deployed. Side airbags were introduced for the first time, positioned as a module inside the door panel. In the event of a side impact this system, known as POSIP (Porsche Side Impact Protection), protected the head, chest, arms and pelvis, even when driving with the convertible top down or with open side windows. The airbags had a volume of 30 litres when filled.

Heating and air conditioning
Air from outside was largely purified with the aid of a pollen and dust filter. This could be replaced by a carbon filter as an optional extra. The heating system was mostly adopted from the Boxster. Air conditioning was optional and automatic climate control was available in connection with Porsche Communication Management (see below).

Electrical system
The headlamps were almost identical to those of the Boxster: high beam, dipped beam, fog lights and indicator lights were all combined in one unit.

As in all Porsche cars the rev counter was the central gauge, the analogue speedometer was mounted to its left, and even further over sat the voltmeter. In addition the speed was indicated digitally in a display panel situated at the bottom of the rev counter.

The coolant temperature and fuel level were

displayed on the right, and further to the right the oil pressure gauge was mounted. Finally an oil level display showed the level as a picture symbol after a short period.

Switches and controls in the 911 had doubled since the start of production in 1963, when they were accommodated anywhere they could be. Now, however, they were positioned logically and within easy reach. One traditional item was not touched: the ignition key stayed on the left-hand side of the steering wheel. Automatic dimming rear-view mirrors were optional; the degree of tint on the mirrors was controlled via photo cells, which reduced the glare hazard.

Porsche and Siemens jointly developed the Porsche Communication Management (PCM) system, which combined information and navigation. A parking assist system was also available as an optional extra, which measured the distance between the car and obstructions behind by means of ultrasonic sound, giving off a warning signal to prevent a collision.

Additional information
One final development of the air-cooled turbo era came in the Turbo S. This used the high-power 430hp engine from the GT2, strengthened transmission, lower ride height and thicker front crossbrace. Aerodynamic changes included extra air ducts and a huge bi-plane rear wing, while inside were aluminium and carbon-fibre trim accents and Turbo S logos.

Model range	Total production
911 Carrera Coupé (996)	8223+44 MEX+BRA
911 Carrera Cabriolet (996)	937+15 MEX+BRA
911 Carrera Coupé (993)	11
911 Carrera 4 Coupé (993)	37
911 Carrera S Coupé (993)	130+993 USA+CDN
911 Carrera Targa (993)	210+122 USA+CDN
911 Carrera Cabriolet (993)	109+1059 USA+CDN
911 Carrera 4S Coupé (993)	602+298 USA+CDN
911 Turbo 3.6	556
911 Turbo S Coupé	160
911 GT2 Coupé	21
911 Carrera Coupé Cup (996)	29
911 Carrera Coupé Cup (993)	30

Model range	Carrera 996	Carrera 993	Carrera 4S 993	Turbo 3.6 993
Engine				
Engine type				
Manual transmission	M96/01	M64/21	M64/21	M64/60
Tiptronic	M96/01	M64/22	–	–
Bore (mm)	96	100	100	100
Stroke (mm)	78	76.4	76.4	76.4
Displacement (cc)	3387	3600	3600	3600
Compression ratio	11.3:1	11.3:1	11.3:1	8.0:1
Engine output (kW/hp)	221/300	210/285	210/285	300/408
at revolutions per minute (rpm)	6800	6100	6100	5750
Torque (Nm)	350	340	340	540
at revolutions per minute (rpm)	4600	5250	5250	4500
Output per litre (kW/l)	65.2	58.3	58.3	83.3
Max. engine speed (rpm)	7300	6700	6700	6720

Model range	Carrera 996	Carrera 993	Carrera 4S 993	Turbo 3.6 993
Engine (continued)				
Type	six-cylinder aluminium boxer engine			
Engine cooling	water	air	air	air
Crankshaft	forged, rotates in seven journal bearings			
Cylinder surface	Lokasil	Nikasil	=	=
Cylinder head	three-piece	single	=	=
Valve configuration	2 inlet valves	1 inlet valve	=	=
	2 exhaust valves	1 exhaust valve	=	=
Valve control	via bucket tappets			
Timing gear	double chain to the intermediate	double chains to the camshafts		
	double chains to exhaust camshafts			
Variable camshaft settings	Porsche VarioCam 25° setting of intake cams	none	=	=
Valve-clearance compensation	hydraulic	=	=	=
Induction system	two-stage resonance system	Varioram	=	=
Throttle valve	mechanical	=	=	=
Lubrication system	integrated dry sump	dry sump with separate oil tank	=	
Oil supply	one pressure pump, three suction pumps	one pressure pump, one suction pump	=	
Engine Weight according to DIN 70020 A (kg)				
Manual transmission	190*	239*	239*	268*
Tiptronic S	179**			

Key
* with underbody panelling, dual-mass flywheel, clutch and air-conditioning compressor
** with underbody panelling and air-conditioning compressor, without dual-mass flywheel

Carburation, ignition, settings				
Fuel system	DME S	DME S + Varioram	=	DME S
Type of fuel (RON)	98	98	98	98
Ignition system	DME	DME	DME	DME
Ignition	single	dual	dual	dual
Firing order	1-6-2-4-3-5	1-6-2-4-3-5	1-6-2-4-3-5	
Spark plugs				
Bosch	–	FR6 LDC and FR 5 LTC	FR 6 LDC	
Beru	–	14 FR 5 DTU and 14 FR 6 LDU	14 FR 5 LDU	
Spark plug gap (mm)	–	0.7 + 0.1	0.7 + 0.1	0.7 + 0.1
Surface-gap spark plugs				
Bosch	FGR 6 KQC	–	–	–
Beru	14-FGR 6 KQU	–	–	–
Spark plug gap (mm)	1.6+/-0.2	–	–	–
Anti-knock control	yes	yes	yes	yes
Number of turbochargers	–	–	–	2
Idle speed (rpm)	700+-40	800+-40	800+-40	800+-40
Exhaust/purification system	2 BLS+DWMK USA: +ZLP	2 BLS+DWMK	=	4xBLS+DWMK+ZLP
CO-content				
without cat. conv. (%)	0.5–1.0	=	=	1.0–1.4
with cat. conv. (%)	0.4–1.2	=	=	0.8–1.2
Fuel consumption acc. 93/116/EC (litres/100km)				
Manual transmission				
urban	17.2	17.7	17.9	23.5
extra-urban	8.5	8.8	9.6	11.2
combined	11.8	12.0	16.9	15.7
Target value CO2 (g/km)	285	296	299	376
Tiptronic				
urban	18.3	18.5	–	–
extra-urban	8.5	8.7	–	–
combined	12.0	12.4	–	–
Target value CO2 (g/km)	290	307	–	–

Key:
2 BLS Two heated lambda sensors with stereo control
DME S Digital engine electronic system with sequential fuel injection
DWMK Three-way metal-based catalytic converter
KFZ Pressure-controlled mapped ignition
SLE Secondary-air injection
ZLP Auxiliary air pump

Model range	Carrera 996	Carrera 993	Carrera 4S 993	Turbo 3.6 993
Transmission				
Dual-mass flywheel	Syst.LIK*	=	=	=
Clutch, pressure plate	MF 228X MF 240	G MFZ 240	=	=
Clutch plate (mm)	rigid 240	=	=	=
Manual transmission	G96/00	G50/20	G64/20	G64/51
Gear ratios				
1st gear	3.82	3.818	3.818	3.818
2nd gear	2.20	2.048	2.048	2.150
3rd gear	1.52	1.407	1.407	1.560
4th gear	1.22	1.118	1.118	1.212
5th gear	1.02	0.929	0.929	0.937
6th gear	0.84	0.775	0.775	0.750
Reverse gear	3.55	2.857	2.857	2.857
Synchromesh system				
Forward gears	VK	VK	VK	VK
Reverse gear	VK	VK	VK	VK
Final drive, ratio	3.444	3.444	3.444	3.444
Limited-slip differential	M	M	S	S
Lock-up factor under load/coasting (%)	25/40	25/65	25/65	25/40
Gearbox weight with oil (kg)	62.9	66	72.5	72.5
Tiptronic	A96/00	A50/04	–	–
Torque converter dia.(mm)	282	260		
Start-off conversion ratio	1.92	–	–	
Stall speed (rpm)	2450	2300	–	–
Gear ratios				
1st gear	3.66	2.479	–	–
2nd gear	2.00	1.479	–	–
3rd gear	141	1.000	–	–
4th gear	1.00	0.728	–	
5th gear	0.74	–		
Reverse gear	4.10	2.086	–	–
Intermediate shaft, ratio	1.100	–	–	
Final drive, ratio	3.676	3.676	–	–
Limited-slip differential	no	no	–	–
Traction assistance ABD+TC	M	M	–	–
Gearbox weight with oil and ATF filling (kg)	115	105	–	–

Key:
ABD   Automatic brake differential
M   Optional extras
Syst.LUK*   Dual-mass flywheel System LUK (steel-spring damped)
TC   Traction Control
VK   Full-cone synchromesh system with molybdenum-coated synchroniser rings

Suspension, steering and brakes				
Front axle				
Tube anti-roll bar dia. (mm)	23.1 x 3.4	21	20	22
Steering ratio	16.9:1	16.48:1	16.48:1	16.5:1
Turning circle dia. (m)	10.6	11.74	11.74	11.74
Rear axle				
Anti-roll bar dia., manual transmission (mm)	18.5 x 2.5	18	18	21
Brake system				
Brake booster ratio	3.85	3.15:1	4.8:1	4.8:1
Brake master cylinder dia. (mm)	23.8	25.4	25.4	25.4
Pressure reducer				
Cut-in pressure (bar)	55	40	40	55
Reduction factor	0.46	0.46	0.46	0.46
Driving brake	Dual-circuit brake system with four-piston aluminium brake callipers			
Brake calliper piston diameter				
front (mm)	36+40	44+36	44+36	44+36
rear (mm)	28+30	30+34	28+28	28+28
Brake disc diameter				
front (mm)	318	304	322	322
rear (mm)	299	299	322	322
Brake disc thickness				
front (mm)	28	32	32	32
rear (mm)	24	24	28	24
Effective brake disc area (cm^2)	450	422	552	422
Handbrake	Operating mechanically on both rear wheels			
Brake drum diameter (mm)	180	=	=	=
Contact area (cm^2)	170	=	=	=

Model range	Carrera 996	Carrera 993	Carrera 4S 993	Turbo 3.6 993
Wheels and tyres				
Standard tyre specification, front	205/55ZR17	205/55ZR16	205/55ZR16	225/40ZR18
wheel	7J x 17	7J x 16 H2	7J x 16 AH	8J x 18 H2
hump depth (mm)	55	55	55	52
optional	225/40ZR18	205/50ZR17	205/50ZR17	
wheel	7.5J x 18	7J x 17 H2	7J x 17 H2	
hump depth (mm)	50	55	55	
optional	205/50R1789M+S	225/40ZR18	225/40ZR18	
wheel	7J x 17	8J x 18 H2	8J x 18 H2	
hump depth (mm)	55	52	52	
optional	225/40ZR18			
wheel	8J x 18 H2			
hump depth (mm)	52			
Standard tyre specification, rear	255/40ZR17	255/40ZR17	245/45ZR16	285/30ZR18
wheel	9J x 17	9J x 17 x H2	9J x 16 H2	10J x 18 AH
hump depth (mm)	55	70	70	40
optional	265/35ZR18	255/40ZR17	255/40ZR17	
wheel	10J x 18	9J x 17 H2	9J x 17 H2	
hump depth (mm)	65	55**	55	
optional	225/40R1790TM+S	285/30ZR18	285/30ZR18	
wheel	8.5J x 17	10J x 18 H2	10J x 18 H2	
hump depth (mm)	50	65	40	
optional	285/30ZR18			
wheel	8J x 18 H2			
hump depth (mm)	40			
Space saver High-pressure tyre	105/95-R17*			
Space-saver spare wheel	165/70-16 92P	=	=	
Tyre pressure				
front (bar)	2.5	=	=	=
rear (bar)	2.5 for 17-inch tyres	=	=	
	3.0 for 16- and 18 inch tyres	=	=	
Space-saver spare wheel/high-pressure tyre (bar)	4.2*	2.5*	=	=

*The 911 Carrera (996) had an inflated high-pressure tyre, while all other vehicles had the space-saver spare wheel that needed to be inflated by means of an on-board compressor when required

Body				
Drag coefficient (cd)	0.30	0.34	0.34	0.34
Frontal area A (m2)	1.94	1.93	1.93	1.93
Aerodynamic drag cd x A (m2)	0.582	0.656	0.656	0.656
Dimensions at kerb weight				
Length (mm)	4430	4245	4245	4245
Width (mm)	1765	1795	1795	1795
Height (mm)	1305	1285	1285	1285
Wheelbase (mm)	2350	2272	=	=
Track				
front 16+17 inch (mm)	1455	1405	1405	1411
18 inch (mm)	1465	1411		
rear 16 inch (mm)	–	1444	1444	1504
17 inch (mm)	1500	1536	1474	
18 inch (mm)	1480	1454	1454	
Ground clearance at permissible gross weight (mm)	100	95	95	90
Overhang angle				
front (degree)	13	10.0	10	9.5
rear (degree)	14.5	11.0	10	11.0

Electrical system				
Generator output (W/A)	1680	1610/115	=	=
Battery (V/Ah)	12/70	12/75	12/36	12/75

Weight according to DIN 70020				
Kerb weight with (kg)				
Manual transmission	1320	1400	1450	1500
Tiptronic	1365	1425	–	–
Permissible gross weight (kg)				
Manual transmission	1720	1740	1790	1840
Tiptronic	1765	1740	–	–
Permissible trailer weight (kg)				
unbraked	none	none	none	none
braked	none	none	none	none
Permissible roof load (kg)	35	=	=	=
with Porsche System (kg)	75	=	=	=

Model range	Carrera 996	Carrera 993	Carrera 4S 993	Turbo 3.6 993
Performance				
Maximum speed (kmh)				
Manual transmission	280	270	277	290
Tiptronic	275	265	–	–
Acceleration 0–62mph/100kmh (sec)				
Manual transmission	5.2	5.4	5.3	4.5
Tiptronic	6.0	6.4	–	–
Measured kilometre from standing start (sec)				
Manual transmission	24.2	24.8	25.0	23.0
Tiptronic	25.3	25.6	–	–

Fluid capacities				
Engine oil quantity 1* (l)	10.25	11.5	11.5	11.5
Oil change quantity (l)	8.25	10	10	10
Cooling water (l)	22.5	–	–	–
Manual transmission 2* (l)	2.7	3.8	3.6	4.3
Front axle 2* (l)	–	–	0.6	0.6
Automatic transm. 3* (l)	9.5	9.0	–	–
Final drive, autom. 2* (l)	0.8	0.9	–	–
Fuel tank 4* (l)	65	73 (92)**	92	92
Brake fluid reservoir 5* (l)	0.45	0.34	0.75	0.75
Power steering fluid 3* (l)	1.27	1.0	=	=
Refrigerant 6* (g)	900	840	=	=
Refrigerant oil 7* (ml)	195	140	=	=
Washer tank (l)	2.5	7.3	=	=

*Key and key to numerals
** 92-litres fuel tank available as optional extra
1* Approved engine oils according to ACEA A4-96 specification and special Porsche requirements (see technical information for engine oils)
2* Gear oil GL 5 SAE 90
3* ATF ESSO LT 71141
4* Unleaded fuel with minimum standard RON 98/MON 88
5* Use only brake fluid acc. SUPER DOT 4.
6* Only refrigerant R 134 a
7* Commercially available refrigerant oils

	World manufacturer code	Code body USA (A=Coupé, B=Targa, C=Cabriolet)	Code for engine variants (only USA)	Restraint system (0 = belt, 2 = airbag) only USA	First and second digit for car type	Fill character/ check digit	Model year (V = 1997, W = 1998, etc.)	Manufacturing site (S = Stuttgart)	7th and 8th digit = car type	Code for body + engine	Sequence number	Summary
Vehicle Identification Numbers for 911 model range of model year 1998 (W Programme)												
	WPO	Z	Z	Z	99	Z	W	S	6	0	0001–	996 Coupé RoW
	WPO	Z	Z	Z	99	Z	W	S	3	1	0001–	993 Coupé RoW
	WPO	A	A	2	99	C	W	S	3	2	0001–	993 Coupé USA+CDN
	WPO	Z	Z	Z	99	Z	W	S	6	4	0001–	996 Cabriolet RoW
	WPO	Z	Z	Z	99	Z	W	S	3	3	0001–	993 Cabriolet RoW
	WPO	C	A	2	99	C	W	S	3	4	0001–	993 Cabriolet USA+CDN
	WPO	Z	Z	Z	99	Z	W	S	3	8	0001–	993 Targa RoW
	WPO	D	A	2	99	C	W	S	3	8	5001–	993 Targa USA+CDN
	WPO	A	C	2	99	C	W	S	3	7	5001–	993 Turbo 3.6 Coupé USA+CDN
	WPO	Z	Z	Z	99	Z	W	S	3	9	3001–	993 Turbo 3.6 GTR

C* = Check digit, can be 0–9 or X (only USA)
Z = Fill character for rest of world cars

* Note: The vehicle-ID nos. no longer allowed for a differentiation between Carrera 2 and Carrera 4.
    Vehicles type 996 for USA + CDN were not registered in model year 1998 (W programme) but were allocated to model year 1999 (X programme).

Model year 1999

X Programme, the first all-wheel drive automatic

Porsche 911 Carrera 2 Coupé
Porsche 911 Carrera 2 Cabriolet
Porsche 911 Carrera 4 Coupé
Porsche 911 Carrera 4 Cabriolet

In model year 1999 Porsche produced only water-cooled cars and all 911s built this year were Type 996s. In addition to its range of 911s, Porsche also produced around 60 Boxsters per day at Zuffenhausen in two shifts. This led to some bottlenecking in the body shop: even with three shifts it could not complete more than about 110 painted bodies. As the demand for Porsche sports cars continued to rise, approximately 50 further Boxsters per day were assembled by Valmet in Uusikaupunki (Finland). Components for body, engine, transmission, suspension, brakes and steering, as well as much of the interior, were manufactured in Germany and transported to Finland in containers.

The new 996 version of the Carrera 4, with permanent all-wheel drive, arrived in Coupé and Cabriolet from October 1998. The bodywork and water-cooled engine were almost identical to the Carrera 2 that had been manufactured for a year already. External differentiating features were the titanium-coloured 'Carrera 4' script on the engine cover, titanium-coloured brake callipers, white front indicator glass and white-grey rear lamps.

The Carrera 4's permanent all-wheel drive provided for consistent front wheel traction via a viscous clutch. Depending on the driving conditions the torque split to the front axle varied between 5% and 40%. For the first time Porsche made its PSM stability management system standard in the 911 Carrera 4. This stabilised the vehicle in critical driving situations through targeted intervention in the engine management and the brake system. Tiptronic S transmission was also a new option for the Carrera 4.

The following text describes the new 911 Carrera 4.

Engine

The specification of all Carrera engines was virtually identical. Compared to the first water-cooled Carrera engines from 1998, the aluminium-silicon alloy cylinder sleeves were placed in the moulds before the casting process and were finished off afterwards.

Fuel and ignition system

While the throttle valve in the Carrera 2 was still actuated mechanically (via a cable from the accelerator), the Carrera 4 was fitted with an electronic 'drive-by-wire' accelerator (E-gas). This was necessary because the PSM system intervened

A cutaway illustration of a 1999-model 911 Carrera 4 3.4 Coupé showing the layout of the suspension and drive to the front wheels.

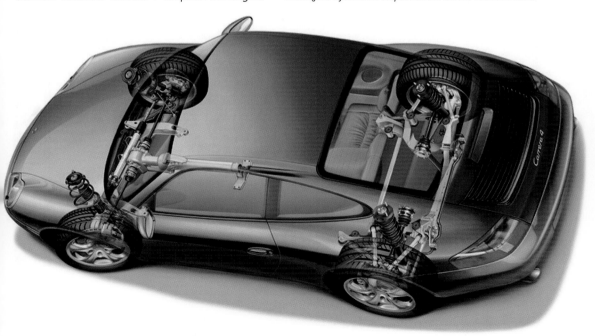

in the engine management in critical driving situations within a split second.

The E-gas accelerator was spring-loaded and you could not tell the difference from a mechanical pedal when you used it. Information about the pedal position was read by a sensor (potentiometer), which transmitted it to the engine management system. The throttle housing had an electric control motor that was able to open and close the throttle smoothly and delicately.

The E-gas system also had a positive effect on fuel consumption and exhaust emissions. As in the 911 Carrera 2, each cylinder bank had its own stainless steel exhaust system, its own lambda probe with one metal catalytic converter and separate rear silencers. The signals of both lambda probes were processed in stereo: each cylinder side was evaluated separately and was also activated separately by the engine management system. Vehicles for the USA were fitted with an additional air pump.

Transmission
The all-wheel drive system of the new Carrera 4 differed from its predecessor in the exposed driveshaft between the transmission at the rear

and the front axle differential. Furthermore, the viscous clutch was moved into the housing of the front differential.

Manual
The ratios of the Carrera 4's six forward gears were identical to those of the 911 Carrera 2. The same 9:31 driveshaft ratio was also retained. The viscous clutch that had already been used in the earlier Carrera 4 was no longer positioned in the hot oil sump of the manual transmission but was moved to a separate housing within the front differential, where it operated at significantly lower temperatures. This also had a positive influence on the car's weight distribution.

The manual transmission and the front differential were permanently connected to each other via a short open driveshaft. Depending on the driving condition the torque split to the front axle varied between 5% and 40%. There was a dry single-plate clutch with a diameter of 240mm which was actuated hydraulically.

Tiptronic S
A96 Tiptronic S automatic transmission was offered for the first time in the Carrera 4. It had five gear ratios and was adopted from the 996 Carrera 2. The free end of the driveshaft from the gearbox was connected to the front differential via a short driveshaft.

The 911 Carrera 4 3.4 Cabriolet, the first 911 Cabriolet model with all-wheel drive, was introduced in October 1998.

Suspension

The front suspension (MacPherson), already well-known from the 996 Carrera 2, with its A-arm, crossbar, semi-trailing arm and dual-strut gas pressure dampers, was further adapted for front-wheel drive. The same type of multi-link rear suspension system (four wishbones for camber-constant wheel travel and one rod that adjusted the toe-in) as the Carrera 2 was adopted.

Special sport suspension was available as an optional extra. This had shorter and stiffer springs front and rear, matching dampers, stronger anti-roll bars, and was lower by 10mm front and rear. The wheels of the Carrera 4 were styled in a new distinctive way, the 'spoke look'. 17in wheels were standard, 18in wheels an optional extra.

The four-piston aluminium brake callipers were also taken from the 996 Carrera 2. They were made from a single piece (monobloc) by Brembo. The brake force was electronically controlled and distributed via the Porsche Stability Management system (PSM), which was standard in the Carrera 4. PSM detected the road condition and distributed the brake force accordingly.

PSM was a driving dynamics control system that improved traction and tracking. It adjusted torque distribution and reined in erratic behaviour, especially on slippery surfaces, but kept the driving feel of a sports car intact. Understeer and oversteer in extreme cornering were improved and braking distances became measurably shorter. As an example, when oversteering through a left turn, the right front wheel would be slowed down; when understeering through a left turn, the left

The running gear of the 911 Carrera 4 3.4, showing the all-wheel drive layout and the compact arrangement of the engine installation.

rear wheel was slowed down. The throttle valve was closed completely or partly at the same time by means of the E-gas. It was possible to turn the PSM system off, but it was reinstated the next time the brakes were used.

Unlike the 996 Carrera 2's ready-inflated spare wheel, the Carrera 4's space-saver spare still needed to be inflated in case of a breakdown and was stowed in the luggage compartment at the front.

Body

The body shapes of the Coupé and the Cabriolet did not change. There were some exterior distinguishing features between the Carrera 4 and Carrera 2: the brake callipers of the Carrera 2 were black while those of the Carrera 4 were titanium-coloured; the 'Carrera 4' script on the engine cover at the rear was also titanium-coloured. The front indicator covers of the Carrera 4 were white, while the rear lamps were white-grey instead of orange-red. Coloured bulbs provided the correct colour in these lamps.

Interior fittings

Porsche's policy of comprehensive standard safety features meant that the new airbag system designed for the 996 model range, as well as the POSIP side airbags, were installed as standard worldwide.

The 911 Carrera 4 3.4 Coupé interior was more refined than ever, and featured an optional satellite navigation system.

Heating and air conditioning

Heating and air conditioning were identical in both 996 models and remained unchanged from the previous year.

Electrical system

The electrics of the Carrera 2 were unchanged from the previous year. The Carrera 4 was fitted with Litronic headlights as standard as well as a dynamic automatic headlight-range adjustment system. A new generation of radios (made by Becker of Pforzheim) was available for the 911 range. The top model of the four Becker units available included a minidisc player for the first time.

Additional information

In addition to the Carrera models, the 911 GT3 was produced in Zuffenhausen as of May 1999. However, it was allocated to model year 2000 and will be described there.

Model range	Total production
911 Carrera 2 Coupé (996)	4349 + 6298 USA+CDN+MEX+BRA
911 Carrera 2 Cabriolet (996)	3784 + 5675 USA+CDN+MEX+BRA
911 Carrera 4 Coupé (996)	3807 + 968 USA+CDN+MEX+BRA
911 Carrera 4 Cabriolet (996)	2272 + 809 USA+CDN+MEX+BRA
911 Carrera Cup (996)	81

Model range	Carrera 2 996	Carrera 4 996
Engine		
Engine type		
Manual transmission	M96/01	M96/02
Tiptronic	M96/01	M96/02
Bore (mm)	96	96
Stroke (mm)	78	78
Displacement (cc)	3387	3387
Compression ratio	11.3:1	11.3:1
Engine output (kW/hp)	221/300	221/300
at revolutions per minute (rpm)	6800	6800
Torque (Nm)	350	350
at revolutions per minute (rpm)	4600	4600
Output per litre (kW/l)	65.2	65.2
Max. engine speed (rpm)	7300	7300
Type	six-cylinder aluminium boxer engine	
Engine cooling	water	water
Crankshaft	forged, rotates in seven journal bearings	
Cylinder surface	Lokasil	Lokasil
Cylinder head	three-piece	three-piece
Valve configuration	2 inlet valves	2 inlet valves
	2 exhaust valves	2 exhaust valves
Valve control	via bucket tappets	via bucket tappets
Timing gear	double chain to intermediate shaft	double chain to intermediate shaft
	Double chains to the exhaust cams	Double chains to the exhaust cams
Variable camshaft settings	Porsche VarioCam 25° setting of intake cams	Porsche VarioCam 25° setting of intake cams
Valve-clearance compensation	hydraulic	hydraulic

Model range	Carrera 2 996	Carrera 4 996
Engine (continued)		
Induction system	Two-stage resonance system	Two-stage resonance system
Throttle valve	mechanical	E-Gas
Lubrication system	integrated dry sump	integrated dry sump
Oil supply	one pressure pump three suction pumps	one pressure pump three suction pumps
Engine Weight according DIN 70020 A (kg)		
Manual transmission	190*	190*
Tiptronic S	179**	179**

Key
* with underbody panelling, dual-mass flywheel, clutch and air-conditioning compressor
** with underbody panelling and air-conditioning compressor, without dual-mass flywheel

Carburation, ignition, settings		
Engine control	Motronic ME 7.2	Motronic ME 7.2
Management throttle valve	E-Gas	E-Gas
Type of fuel (RON)	98	98
Ignition system	Solid-state distributor system, 6 ignition coils	Solid-state distributor system, 6 ignition coils
Ignition	single	single
Surface-gap spark plugs		
Bosch	FGR 6 KQC	FGR 6 KQC
Beru	14 – FGR 6 KQU	14 – FGR 6 KQU
Spark plug gap (mm)	1.6 +/- 0.2	1.6 +/- 0.2
Firing order	1-6-2-4-3-5	1-6-2-4-3-5
Anti-knock control	yes	yes
Idle speed (rpm)	700 +- 40	700 +- 40
Exhaust/purification system	2 BLS+DWMK USA: +ZLP	2 BLS+DWMK USA: +ZLP
CO-content		
without cat. conv. (%)	0.5–1.0	0.5–1.0
with cat. conv. (%)	0.4–1.2	0.4–1.2
Fuel consumption acc. 93/116/EC (litres/100km)		
Manual transmission		
urban	17.2	17.4
extra-urban	8.5	8.8
combined	11.8	12.0
Target value CO2 (g/km)	285	295
Tiptronic S		
urban	18.3	18.6
extra-urban	8.5	8.8
combined	12.0	12.4
Target value CO2 (g/km)	290	304

Key:
2 BLS   Two heated lambda sensors with stereo control
DME S   Digital engine electronic system with sequential fuel injection
DWMK   Three-way metal-based catalytic converter
KFZ   Pressure-controlled mapped ignition
SLE   Secondary-air injection
ZLP   Auxiliary air pump

Transmission		
Dual-mass flywheel	Syst.LUK*	Syst.LUK*
Clutch, pressure plate	MF 228X MF 240	MF 228X MF 240
Clutch plate (mm)	rigid 240	rigid 240
Manual transmission	G96/00	G96/30
Gear ratios		
1st gear	3.82	3.82
2nd gear	2.20	2.20
3rd gear	1.52	1.52
4th gear	1.22	1.22

Model range	Carrera 2 996	Carrera 4 996
Manual transmission gear ratios (continued)		
5th gear	1.02	1.02
6th gear	0.84	0.84
Reverse gear	3.55	3.55
Synchromesh system		
Forward gears	VK	VK
Reverse gear	VK	VK
Final drive	3.444	3.444
Limited-slip differential	M	M
Lock-up factor under load/ coasting (%)	25/40	
Gearbox weight with oil (kg)	62.9	64.5
Tiptronic	A96/00	A96/30
Torque converter dia.(mm)	282	282
Start-off conversion ratio	1.92	1.92
Stall speed (rpm)	2450	2450
Gear ratios		
1st gear	3.66	3.66
2nd gear	2.00	2.00
3rd gear	1.41	1.41
4th gear	1.00	1.00
Reverse gear	4.10	4.10
Intermediate shaft, ratio		
Final drive, ratio	3.676	3.676
Limited-slip differential	no	no
Driving dynamics	M	PSM standard
Gearbox weight with oil and ATF filling (kg)	115	123
All-wheel drive	no	via drive shaft, viscous clutch and front differential

Key:
ABD   Automatic brake differential
M   Optional extras
PSM   Porsche Stability Management
Syst.LUK* Dual-mass flywheel system LUK (steel-spring damped)
TC   Traction control
VK   Full-cone synchromesh system with molybdenum-coated synchroniser rings

Suspension, steering and brakes		
Front axle		
Tube anti-roll bar dia. (mm)	23.1 x 3.4	22.5 x 3.5
Steering ratio	16.9:1	16.9:1
Turning circle dia. (m)	10.6	10.6
Rear axle		
Anti-roll bar dia., manual transmission (mm)	18.5 x 2.5	19.6 x 2.6
Brake system		
Brake booster ratio	3.85	3.85
Brake master cylinder dia. (mm)	23.81	23.81
Pressure reducer		
Cut-in pressure (bar)	55	55
Reduction factor	0.46	0.46
Driving brake	Dual-circuit brake system with four-piston aluminium brake callipers	
Brake calliper piston diameter		
front (mm)	36 + 40	36 + 40
rear (mm)	28 + 30	28 + 30
Brake disc diameter		
front (mm)	318	318
rear (mm)	299	299
Brake disc thickness		
front (mm)	28	28
rear (mm)	24	24
Effective brake disc area (cm²)	450	450
Handbrake	Operating mechanically on both rear wheels	
Brake drum diameter (mm)	180	180
Contact area (cm²)	170	170

Model range	Carrera 2 996	Carrera 4 996
Wheels and tyres		
Standard tyre specification, front	205/50ZR17	205/50ZR17
wheel	7J x 17	7J x 17
hump depth (mm)	55	55
optional	225/40ZR18	225/40ZR18
wheel	7.5J x 18	7.5 x 18
hump depth (mm)	50	50
Winter tyres	205/50R1789M+S	205/50R1789M+S
wheel	7J x 17	7J x 17
hump depth (mm)	55	55
Standard tyre specification, rear	255/40ZR17	255/40ZR17
wheel	9J x 17	9J x 17
hump depth (mm)	55	55
optional	265/35ZR18	265/35ZR18
wheel	10J x 18	10J x 18
hump depth (mm)	65	65
Winter tyres	225/45R1790TM+S	225/45R1790TM+S
wheel	8.5 x 17	8.5 x 17
hump depth (mm)	50	50
optional	–	225/40R17940M+S
wheel	–	9J x 17
hump depth (mm)	–	55
Space saver high-pressure tyre	105/95-R17*	–
Space-saver spare wheel	–	165/70-16 92P
Tyre pressure		
front (bar)	2.5	2.5
rear (bar)	2.5	2.5
with 18" tyre rear (bar)	3.0	3.0
High-pressure tyre/space-saver spare wheel (bar)	4.2*	2.5*

*The 911 Carrera 2 (996) had an inflated high-pressure tyre while the 911 Carrera 4 (996) had a space-saver spare wheel that needed to be inflated by means of an on-board compressor when required.

Body		
Drag coefficient (cd)	0.30	0.30
Frontal area A (m²)	1.94	1.94
Aerodynamic drag cd x A (m²)	0.582	0.582
Dimensions at kerb weight		
Length (mm)	4430	4430
Width (mm)	1765	1765
Height (mm)	1305	1305
Wheelbase (mm)	2350	2350
Track		
front 16+17 inch (mm)	1455	1455
18 inch (mm)	1465	1465
rear 17 inch (mm)	1500	1500
18 inch (mm)	1480	1480
Ground clearance at permissible gross weight (mm)	100	100
Overhang angle		
front (degree)	12	12
rear (degree)	14.5	14.5

Model range	Carrera 2 996	Carrera 4 996
Electrical system		
Generator output (W/A)	1680	1680
Battery (V/Ah)	12/70	12/70

Weight according to DIN 70020		
Kerb weight with (kg)		
manual transmission	1320–1380*	1375–1430*
Tiptronic	1365–1425*	1420–1475*
*depending on options		
Permissible gross weight (kg)		
Man. transm.	1720	1775
Tiptronic	1765	1820
Permissible trailer weight (kg)		
unbraked	none	none
braked	none	none
Permissible roof load (kg)	35	35
with Porsche System (kg)	75	75

Performance		
Maximum speed (kmh)		
Manual transmission	280	280
Tiptronic	275	275
Acceleration 0–62mph/100kmh (sec)		
Manual transmission	5.2	5.2
Tiptronic	6.0	6.0
Measured kilometre from standing start (sec)		
Manual transmission	24.2	24.3
Tiptronic	25.3	25.6

Fluid capacities		
Engine oil quantity 1* (l)	10.25	10.25
Oil change quantity (l)	8.25	8.25
Cooling water (l)	22.5	22.5
Manual transmission 2* (l)	2.7	2.7
Front axle 2* (l)	–	1.5
Automatic transm. 3* (l)	9.5	9.5
Final drive, autom. 2* (l)	0.8	0.8
Fuel tank 4* (l)	64	64
Brake fluid reservoir 5* (l)	0.45	0.63
Power steering fluid 8* (l)	1.27	1.27
Refrigerant 6* (g)	900	900
Refrigerant oil 7* (ml)	195	195
Washer tank (l)	2.5	2.5

*Key and key to numerals
1* Approved engine oils according to ACEA A4-96 specification and special Porsche requirements (see technical information for engine oils)
2* Gear oil GL 5 SAE 90
3* ATF ESSO LT 71141
4* Unleaded fuel with minimum standard RON 98/MON 88
5* Use only brake fluid acc. SUPER DOT 4.
6* Only refrigerant R 134 a
7* Commercially available refrigerant oils
8* Pentosin CHF 11 S

	World manufacturer code	Code body USA (A=Coupé, B=Targa, C=Cabriolet)	Code for engine variants (only USA)	Restraint system (0 = belt, 2 = airbag)	First and second digit for car type	Fill character/ check digit	Model year (W = 1998, X = 1999, Y = 2000)	Manufacturing site (S = Stuttgart)	7th and 8th digit = car type	Code for body + engine	Sequence number	Summary
Vehicle Identification Numbers for 911 model range of model year 1999 (X programme)												
	WPO	Z	Z	Z	99	Z	X	S	6	0	0001–61 8208	996 Coupé RoW
	WPO	A	A	2	99	C	X	S	6	2	0001–62 9802	996 Coupé USA+CDN+MEX
	WPO	Z	Z	Z	99	Z	X	S	6	4	0001–64 6127	996 Cabriolet RoW
	WPO	C	A	2	99	C	X	S	6	5	0001–65 6615	996 Cabriolet USA+CDN+MEX

C* = Check digit, can be 0–9 or X (only USA)
Z = Fill character for rest of world cars
* Note: The vehicle-ID nos. no longer allowed for a differentiation between Carrera 2 and Carrera 4.

Model year 2000

Y Programme, GT3 arrives

Porsche 911 Carrera Coupé
Porsche 911 Carrera Cabriolet
Porsche 911 Carrera 4 Coupé
Porsche 911 Carrera 4 Coupé Millennium
  Special Edition
Porsche 911 Carrera 4 Cabriolet
Porsche 911 GT3

The Carrera cars continued to be produced in model year 2000 without any significant changes. The rear-drive Carrera now received E-gas ('drive-by-wire' throttle valve control via DME) as well, so it could also now be fitted with PSM (Porsche Stability Management). That in turn meant that the Carrera range was no longer available with a limited-slip differential, as the PSM system took over its function.

Before the start of the motorsport season in 1999 for racing purposes, and from May 1999 for the road-going version, the extremely sporty GT3 was manufactured in Zuffenhausen alongside the Carrera. GT stands for 'Gran Turismo', signifying a class of a sports car that is used in motorsport but can also be driven on public roads. Only after a certain number of cars have been manufactured and sold for road use are a number of identical vehicles, modified according to special motorsport regulations, allowed to be built to participate in GT races. The road version of the GT3 could achieve lap times of under eight minutes on the winding 21km North Loop of the Nürburgring. A Clubsport option package made it even more extreme. The following text mostly describes the GT3.

Engine

The engine of the GT3 (M96/76) was based on Porsche's GT1 racing engine. Compared to the engines of the Carrera 996, the output was higher by some 44kW (60hp). The most important differences from the Carrera's M96/02 engine were the following:

- Eight-bearing crankshaft.
- Separate cylinder housing with 'wet' cylinder liners, Nikasil-coated.
- Crankshaft from the GT1, plasma-nitrided, with an extra 2mm stroke.
- Titanium con rods and titanium con rod bolts.
- Pistons similar to GT1, but 2% lighter despite 2mm larger diameter.
- Displacement 3,600cc.
- Modified four-valve technology.
- Modified Variocam settings for the intake camshafts.
- Double valve springs, hydraulic tappet clearance adjustment.
- High 11.7:1 compression ratio.
- Two-step light-alloy resonance intake system.
- Dry sump lubrication system with separate GT1 oil tank (12.5 litres of oil in circulation).
- Dual-branch exhaust system with metal-coated catalytic converters.

The 911 GT3 featured an extensively modified 3.6-litre engine producing 265kW (360hp) at 7,200rpm.

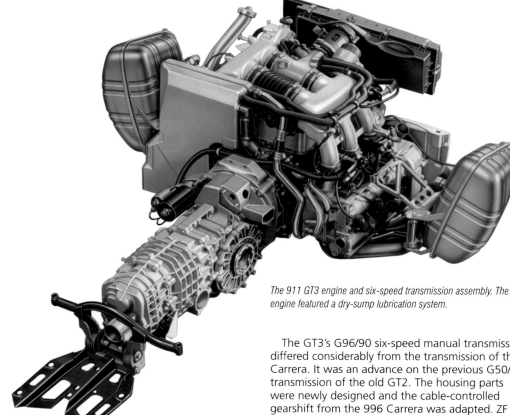

The 911 GT3 engine and six-speed transmission assembly. The engine featured a dry-sump lubrication system.

Fuel and ignition system

Ignition timing and injected fuel quantity were calculated by the Motronic M 5.2.2 system. The following parameters for were taken into account: air mass, engine revs, operating temperature and the signals of the two lambda probes.

Sequential multipoint fuel injection operated via electro-magnetically controlled injection valves. The spark plugs were supplied with static high voltage distribution via the Motronic system. Each spark plug had one single-cylinder ignition coil which formed one unit with the respective spark plug connector.

The engine of the GT3 was fitted with anti-knock control and an additional adaptive lambda control that recognised environment-related changes, making adjustments as needed. The actual exhaust system was almost the same as that of the 911 Carrera but tuning meant the exhaust gas back-pressure could be lowered by 8%.

Transmission

As with the Carrera, the road version of the GT3 was fitted with a dual-mass flywheel for dampening the torsional vibration of the engine. However, the Clubsport version of the GT3 was equipped with a rigid lightened flywheel that promoted high engine revs.

The GT3's G96/90 six-speed manual transmission differed considerably from the transmission of the Carrera. It was an advance on the previous G50/53 transmission of the old GT2. The housing parts were newly designed and the cable-controlled gearshift from the 996 Carrera was adapted. ZF friction-disc limited-slip differential was adapted to the sport suspension: lock-up factor under load 40%, under coasting 60%.

Suspension

The basic concept for the GT3's suspension was taken from the 996 Carrera. Due to the increased performance of the GT3, certain components had to be modified structurally and for use in motorsport.

To lower the centre of gravity, the GT3's ride height was dropped by 30mm. The anti-roll (stabiliser) bars were adjustable depending on requirements. The front damper struts had height-adjustable spring plates and the rebound and compression stages of the single-tube gas pressure dampers had a sportier configuration than the Carrera. The rear suspension was also harder and the spring plates were height-adjustable too.

The steering was identical to the Carrera's while the braking system was near-identical. The diameter of the brake discs was larger (front and rear 330mm) and their thickness was increased to 34mm at the front and 28mm at the rear. The GT3 also had stronger and bigger four-piston brake callipers (painted red).

The GT3 used specially designed 18in light-alloy wheels as standard. These had ten slim dual-spokes and a visible connection between the two wheel parts via 20 titanium bolts. The large gaps between the spokes provided good brake ventilation.

Due to a lack of space in the front because of its 89-litre fuel tank, the GT3 had no spare wheel. And since the front luggage compartment was not large enough to hold a wheel with a puncture, and the sports bucket seats could not be tilted forward to accommodate it, Porsche had to supply a tyre repair kit for the GT3. This consisted of a bottle of repair foam, an on-board compressor and a tyre pressure gauge. The foam would expand and seal the leak.

Body
The GT3 body was essentially a Carrera 4 shell but extensive modifications were made to house, for example, the separate engine oil tank. The mounting points for the engine and transmission were also modified. The luggage compartment lid, doors and rear panelling were identical to the Carrera, but the front end, rear lid and rear spoiler were different and there was 'GT3' script on the rear lid.

Interior fittings
The interior of the GT3 was largely identical to that of the Carrera, although the front seats were different and there were no rear seats. The backrests of the plastic bucket seats could not be tilted forward and fore/aft adjustment was done manually. The light bucket seats and the absence of any rear seats saved 28kg. Two front airbags and the POSIP airbag system on both sides were standard.

Heating and air conditioning
The heating and air conditioning systems were fully adopted from the Carrera.

Electrical system
The on-board electrical system was largely the same as in the Carrera models. However, some individual wiring harnesses were specifically made for the GT3.

Additional information
In addition to the Carrera models and the GT3, the water-cooled 996 Turbo was also manufactured in Zuffenhausen from May 2000. However, Turbo production was assigned to model year 2001 and will be described there.

GT3 Clubsport

Apart from the GT3 road version there was a GT3 Clubsport model for true sports car enthusiasts. The main distinguishing characteristics were: bolt-on roll cage braced on the rear suspension strut support; bucket seats covered with flame-resistant material instead of leather; six-point red safety belt on the driver's seat; fire extinguisher; battery main switch on the centre console; passenger airbag could be disabled; no POSIP side airbags.

Millennium special edition (based on Carrera 4)
Porsche launched a special edition in time for the new millennium, consisting of some 911 identical examples of the all-wheel drive Carrera 4. The Millennium was set apart from other Carrera models by its special colour, Violet Chromaflair, along with elements of the Exclusive and Tequipment programmes and highly polished 18in light-alloy wheels. Just about all the extras available from Porsche were included as standard in this limited edition model. In brief, the features of the Millennium edition were as follows:

Engine
M96/02, identical to Carrera 4 (3,387cc, 221kW/300hp).

Transmission
G 96/30 six-speed manual transmission or Tiptronic S A96/30 five-speed automatic. Four-wheel drive, 5% to 40% tractive force available at the front wheels.

Suspension
Lower sports suspension. Porsche Stability Management (PSM) standard. Front tyres 225/40 ZR 18 on 7.5Jx18 wheels; rear tyres 265/35 ZR 18 on 10Jx18 wheels.

The interior of the 911 Carrera 4 Coupé, with colour-coded leather trim, and optional satellite navigation and in-car phone system.

The 911 GT3 had an imposing presence on the road, with its biplane rear spoiler and 265/35 rear tyres.

Interior fittings

Three-spoke steering wheel, covered with dark burled maple and brown natural leather; fully electric leather-covered seats; sliding sunroof; four airbags (POSIP at sides).

Electrics

Litronic headlamps with headlight-range adjustment, cruise control and automatic air conditioning. PCM (Porsche Communication Management).

Additional information

The Millennium edition's price was DM 185,000 with manual transmission. Optional Tiptronic S cost an extra DM 5,610.

Model range	Total production
911 Carrera 2 Coupé (996)	3544 + 2492
911 Carrera 2 Cabriolet (996)	2804 + 3939
911 Carrera 4 Coupé (996)	3148 + 714 USA+CDN+MEX+BRA
911 Carrera 4 Coupé (996) Millennium	
911 Carrera 4 Cabriolet (996)	1885 + 943 USA+CDN+MEX+BRA
911 GT 3 (996)	1356 + 4 BRAZIL
911 Turbo (996)*	16

* The new water-cooled Turbo was produced from May 2000, but was allocated to model year 2001.

Model range	Carrera	Carrera 4	911 GT3
Engine			
Engine type			
Manual transmission	M96/01	M96/02	M96/76
Tiptronic	M96/01	M96/02	–
Bore (mm)	96	96	100
Stroke (mm)	78	78	76.4
Displacement (cc)	3387	3387	3600
Compression ratio	11.3:1	11.3:1	11.7:1
Engine output (kW/hp)	221/300	221/300	265/360
at revolutions per minute (rpm)	6800	6800	7200
Torque (Nm)	350	350	370
at revolutions per minute (rpm)	4600	4600	5000
Output per litre (kW/l)	65.2	65.2	73.6
Max. engine speed (rpm)	7300	7300	7800

Model range	Carrera	Carrera 4	911 GT3
Type	six-cylinder aluminium boxer engine		
Engine cooling	water	water	water
Crankshaft	forged, rotates in seven journal bearings		
Cylinder surface	Lokasil	Lokasil	Nikasil
Cylinder head	three-piece	three-piece	6 separate cylinder heads
Valve configuration	2 inlet valves	2 inlet valves	2 inlet valves
	2 exhaust valves	2 exhaust valves	2 exhaust valves
Valve control	via bucket tappets		
Timing gear	double chain to intermediate shaft, double chains to the exhaust cams	double chain to intermediate shaft, double chains to the exhaust cams	double chain to intermediate shaft from there via a double chain each to intake and exhaust cams
Variable camshaft settings	Porsche VarioCam 25° setting of intake cams		
Valve-clearance compensation	hydraulic	hydraulic	hydraulic
Induction system	two-stage resonance system	two-stage resonance system	two-stage resonance system
Lubrication system	integrated dry sump	integrated dry sump	dry sump with separate oil tank
Oil supply	1 pressure pump	1 pressure pump	1 pressure pump
	3 suction pumps	3 suction pumps	3 suction pumps
Engine Weight according to DIN 70020 A with			
Manual transmission (kg)	190*	190*	274*
with Tiptronic S (kg)	179**	179**	

Key
* with underbody panelling, dual-mass flywheel, clutch and air-conditioning compressor
** with underbody panelling and air-conditioning compressor, without dual-mass flywheel

Carburation, ignition, settings			
Engine control	Motronic ME 7.2	Motortronic ME 7.2	Bosch M 5.22
Management throttle valve	E-Gas	E-Gas	mechanical
Type of fuel (RON)	98	98	98
Ignition system	Solid-state distributor system	Solid-state distributor system	DME
	6 ignition coils	6 ignition coils	6 ignition coils
Ignition	Single	Single	Single
Anti-knock control	yes	yes	yes
Idle speed (rpm)	700+/-40	800+/-40	900+/-40
Number of turbochargers	–	–	–
Spark plugs			
Bosch	–	–	FR 6 LD
Beru	14 FR 6 LDU		
Spark plug gap (mm)	–	–	0.7 + 0.1
Surface-gap spark plugs			
Bosch	FRG 6 KQC	FRG 6 KQC	–
Beru	14-FRG 6 KQU	14-FRG 6 KQU	–
Spark plug gap (mm)	1.6 +/- 0.2	1.6 +/- 0.2	–
Firing order	1-6-2-4-3-5	1-6-2-4-3-5	1-6-2-4-3-5
Exhaust/purification system	2 BLS+DWMK	2 BLS+DWMK	2 BLS+DWMK
	USA: + ZLP	USA: + ZLP	–
CO-content			
without cat. conv. (%)	0.5–1.0	0.5–1.0	
with cat. conv. (%)	0.4–1.2	0.4–1.2	
Fuel consumption acc. 93/116/EC (litres/100km)			
Manual transmission			
urban	17.2	17.4	20.1
extra-urban	8.5	8.8	8.9
combined	11.8	12.0	12.9
Target value CO2 (g/km)	285	295	320
Tiptronic			
urban	18.3	18.6	20.1
extra-urban	8.5	8.8	8.9
combined	12.0	12.4	12.9
Target value CO2 (g/km)	290	304	320

Key:
2 BLS   Two heated lambda sensors with stereo control
DME S   Digital engine electronic system with sequential fuel injection
DWMK   Three-way metal-based catalytic converter
KFZ   Pressure-controlled mapped ignition
SLE   Secondary-air injection
ZLP   Auxiliary air pump

Porsche 911 Source Book

Model range	Carrera	Carrera 4	911 GT3
Transmission			
Dual-mass flywheel	Syst.LUK	Syst.LUK	Syst.LUK
Clutch, pressure plate	MF 228X MF 240	MF 228X MF 240	MF 228X MF 240
Clutch plate (mm)	rigid 240	rigid 240	rigid 240
Manual transmission	G96/00	G96/30	G96/90
Gear ratios			
1st gear	3.82	3.82	3.82
2nd gear	2.20	2.20	2.15
3rd gear	1.52	1.52	1.56
4th gear	1.22	1.22	1.21
5th gear	1.02	1.02	0.92
6th gear	0.84	0.84	0.82
Reverse gear	3.55	3.55	2.86
Synchromesh system			
Forward gears	VK	VK	VK
Reverse gear	VK	VK	VK
Final drive, ratio	3.44	3.44	3.44
Limited-slip differential	no	no	no
Lock-up factor under load/coasting (%)	25/40	25/40	40/60
Gearbox weight with oil (kg)	62.9	64.5	72.8
Tiptronic	A96/00	A96/30	not available
Torque converter dia.(mm)	282	282	
Start-off conversion ratio	1.92	1.92	
Stall speed (rpm)	2450	2450	
Gear ratios			
1st gear	3.66	3.66	
2nd gear	2.00	2.00	
3rd gear	1.41	1.41	
4th gear	1.00	1.00	
Reverse gear	4.10	4.10	
Intermediate shaft, ratio			
Final drive, ratio	3.676	3.676	
Limited-slip differential	no	no	
Driving dynamics	M	PSM standard	
Gearbox weight with oil and ATF filling (kg)	115	123	
All-wheel drive	no	via driveshaft viscous clutch and front differential	no

Key:
ABD — Automatic brake differential
M — Optional extras
S — Standard equipment
PSM — Porsche Stability Management

Syst.LUK — Dual-mass flywheel system LUK (steel-spring damped)
TC — Traction control
VK — Full-cone synchromesh system with molybdenum-coated synchroniser rings

Suspension, steering and brakes			
Front axle			
Tube anti-roll bar dia. (mm)	23.1	22.5 x 3.5	26.8 x 4
Steering ratio	16.9:1	16.9:1	16.9:1
Turning circle dia. (m)	10.6	10.6	10.6
Rear axle			
Anti-roll bar dia., manual transmission (mm)	18.5 x 2.5	19.6 x 2.6	20.7 x 2.8
Brake system			
Brake booster ratio	3.85	3.85	3.15
Brake master cylinder dia. (mm)	23.81	23.81	25.4
Pressure reducer	no		
Cut-in pressure (bar)	55	55	–
Reduction factor	0.46	0.46	–
Driving brake	Dual-circuit brake system with four-piston aluminium brake callipers		
Brake calliper piston diameter			
front (mm)	36 + 40	36 + 40	44 + 34
rear (mm)	28 + 30	28 + 30	30 + 28
Brake disc diameter			
front (mm)	318	318	330
rear (mm)	299	299	330
Brake disc thickness			
front (mm)	28	28	34
rear (mm)	24	24	28
Effective brake disc area (cm^2)	450	450	568
Handbrake	Operating mechanically on both rear wheels		
Brake drum diameter (mm)	180	180	180
Contact area (cm^2)	170	170	170

202

Model range	Carrera	Carrera 4	911 GT3
Wheels and tyres			
Standard tyre specification, front	205/50ZR17	205/50ZR17	225/40ZR18
wheel	7J x 17	7J x 17	8J x 18
hump depth (mm)	55	55	52**
optional	225/40ZR18	225/40ZR18	
wheel	7.5J x 18	7.5J x 18	
hump depth (mm)	50	50	
Winter tyres	205/50R1789TM+S	205/50R1789TM+S	225/40R1888HM+S*
wheel	7J x 17	7J x 17	8J x 18
hump depth (mm)	55	55	52*
Standard tyre specification, rear	255/40ZR17	255/40ZR17	285/30ZR18
wheel	9J x 17	9J x 17	10J x 18*
hump depth (mm)	55	55	65*
optional	265/35ZR18	265/35ZR18	
wheel	10J x 18	10J x 18	
hump depth (mm)	65	65	
Winter tyres	225/45R1790TM+S	225/45R1790TM+S	265/35R1893H*
wheel	8.5 x 17	8.5 x 17	10J x 18*
hump depth (mm)	50	50	65**#
optional	–	255/40R1794TM+S	
wheel	–	9J x 17	
hump depth (mm)	–	55	
Space saver high-pressure tyre	105/95-R17*	–	
Space-saver spare wheel	–	165/70-16 92P	Tyre Mobility System*
Tyre pressure			
front (bar)	2.5	2.5	2.2
rear (bar)	2.5	2.5	2.7
with 18" tyres rear (bar)	3.0	3.0	2.7
high-pressure tyre/ space-saver spare wheel (bar)	4.2	2.5*	2.2*, and 2.7*

*The 911 Carrera 2 (996) had an inflated high-pressure tyre while the 911 Carrera 4 (996) had a space-saver spare wheel that needed to be inflated by means of an on-board compressor when required. The GT3 had no proper 'spare wheel'.
**Spacer 5mm
with snow chain free travel

Body			
Drag coefficient (cd)	0.30	0.30	0.30
Frontal area A (m²)	1.94	1.94	1.94
Aerodynamic drag cd x A (m2)	0.582	0.582	0.582
Dimensions at kerb weight			
Length (mm)	4430	4430	4430
Width (mm)	1765	1765	1765
Height (mm)	1305	1305	1270
Wheelbase (mm)	2350	2350	2350
Track			
front 16+17 inch (mm)	1455	1455	–
18 inch (mm)	1465	1465	1475
rear 17 inch (mm)	1500	1500	–
18 inch (mm)	1480	1480	1495
Ground clearance at permissible gross weight (mm)	100	100	90
Overhang angle			
front (degree)	12	12	12
rear (degree)	14.5	14.5	14.5

Electrical system			
Generator output (W/A)	1680	1680	1680
Battery (V/Ah)	12/70	12/70	12/36 or 46*

*36AH without air conditioning, 46Ah with air conditioning

Weight according to DIN 70020			
Kerb weight (kg)			
Manual transmission	1320–1380**	1375–1430**	1350–1420**
Tiptronic	1365–1425**	1420–1475**	– –
** depending on options			
Permissible gross weight (kg)			
Manual transmission	1720	1775	1630
Tiptronic	1765	1820	–
Permissible trailer weight (kg)			
unbraked	none	none	none
braked	none	none	none

Model range	Carrera	Carrera 4	911 GT3
Performance			
Maximum speed (kmh)			
Manual transmission	280	280	302
Tiptronic	275	275	–
Acceleration 0–62mph/100kmh (sec)			
Manual transmission	5.2	5.2	4.8
Tiptronic	6.0	–	
Measured kilometre from standing start (sec)			
Manual transmission	24.2	24.3	
Tiptronic	25.3	25.6	

Fluid capacities			
Engine oil quantity 1* (l)	10.25	10.25	12.5
Oil change quantity (l)	8.25	8.25	8.5
Cooling water (l)	22.5	22.5	25
Manual transmission 2* (l)	2.7	2.7	3.8
Front axle 2* (l)	–	1.5	–
Automatic transm. 3* (l)	9.5	9.5	–
Final drive, autom. 2* (l)	0.8	0.8	–
Fuel tank 4* (l)	64	64	90
Brake fluid reservoir 5* (l)	0.45	0.63	0.8
Power steering fluid 8* (l)	1.27	1.27	1.9
Refrigerant 6* (g)	900	900	900
Refrigerant oil 7* (ml)	195	195	195
Washer tank (l)	2.5	2.5	2.5

*Key and key to numerals

1* Approved engine oils according to ACEA A4-96 specification and
   special Porsche requirements (see technical information for engine
   oils)

2* Gear oil GL 5 SAE 90

3* ATF ESSO LT 71141

4* Unleaded fuel with minimum standard RON 98/MON 88

5* Use only brake fluid acc. SUPER DOT 4.

6* Only refrigerant R 134 a

7* Commercially available refrigerant oils

8* Pentosin CHF 11 S

Vehicle Identification Numbers for 911 model range of model year 2000 (Y Programme)											
World manufacturer code	Code body USA (A=Coupé, B=Targa, C=Cabriolet)	Code for engine variants (only USA)	Restraint system (0 = belt, 2 = airbag)	First and second digit for car type	Fill character/ check digit	Model year (X = 1999, Y = 2000, 1 = 2001)	Manufacturing site (S = Stuttgart)	7th and 8th digit = car type	Code for body + engine	Sequence number	Summary
WPO	Z	Z	Z	99	Z	Y	S	6	0	0001–10 0000	996 Coupé RoW
WPO	Z	Z	Z	99	Z	Y	S	6	9	0001–91 900	996 GT3 Coupé RoW
WPO	A	C	S	99	Z	Y	S	6	9	0901–91 904	996 GT3 Coupé Brazil
WPO	A	A	2	99	C	Y	S	6	2	0001–29 000	996 C 2 Coupé USA+CDN+MEX+BRA
WPO	Z	Z	Z	99	Z	Y	S	6	4	0001–49 000	996 Cabriolet RoW
WPO	C	A	2	99	C	Y	S	6	5	0001–59 000	996 Cabriolet USA+CDN+MEX+BRA

C* = Check digit, can be 0–9 or X (only USA)

Z = Fill character for rest of world cars

* Note: The vehicle-ID nos. no longer allowed for a differentiation
between Carrera 2 and Carrera 4.

Model year 2001

1 Programme, Turbo and GT2

Porsche 911 Carrera Coupé and Cabriolet
Porsche 911 Carrera 4 Coupé and Cabriolet
Porsche 911 Turbo
Porsche 911 GT2
Porsche 911 GT3

For easier identification of the cars, as from 2001 each model year was identified by a number. Up until this time, letters appeared in the 17-digit vehicle identification number (for example, W for 1998, X for 1999 and Y for 2000). The letter Z had already been inserted as a fill character a number of times, which is why from model year 2001 numbers were used worldwide. The number for model year 2001 was '1' and model year 2002 was '2', and so on; however as from model year 2010 the alphabet was used again.

The naturally aspirated Carrera models continued almost unchanged. For all Tiptronic cars, there was a new manual temporary override function which made it possible to shift manually even when in automatic mode (gearshift in 'D').

The 911 Turbo (309kW, 420hp) was new this model year. It was available with six-speed manual transmission as well as with automatic Tiptronic S and all-wheel drive.

An even more extreme version of the 911 was the GT2 with no less than 340kW (462hp). This was an ultra-high performance model produced both for the racetrack and for the road and sold solely with six-speed manual transmission and rear-wheel drive (no all-wheel drive was available). The 911 Turbo and GT2 shared many components.

Engine
M96/70 (911 Turbo)
The new engine for the 911 Turbo was directly derived from the engine of the GT1 racer and incorporated many parts from this tried and tested long-distance racing engine that had brought Porsche its double victory at the Le Mans 24-hour race in 1998. The most important features of this power unit were:

- Eight-bearing crankshaft.
- Same crankcase as the GT1, plasma-nitrided, but 2mm longer stroke.
- Displacement 3,600cc.
- New Variocam Plus system provided angular adjustment of the intake cams via a geared transmission at the intake camshafts.
- Valve stroke adjustment of the inlet valves via switchable bucket tappets and special cams.
- Dual valve springs, hydraulic valve clearance compensation.

This cutaway view of a Carrera 3.4 Coupé shows how, by 2001, the 911 was far more complex than the original 1960s model.

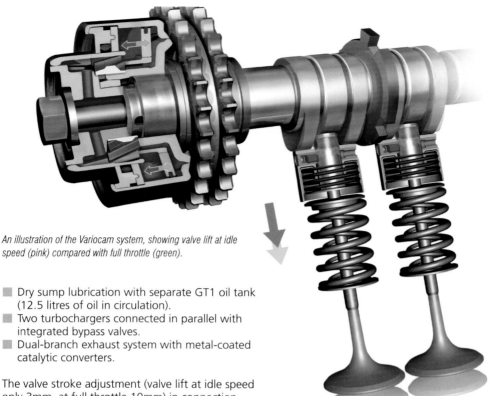

An illustration of the Variocam system, showing valve lift at idle speed (pink) compared with full throttle (green).

■ Dry sump lubrication with separate GT1 oil tank (12.5 litres of oil in circulation).
■ Two turbochargers connected in parallel with integrated bypass valves.
■ Dual-branch exhaust system with metal-coated catalytic converters.

The valve stroke adjustment (valve lift at idle speed only 3mm, at full throttle 10mm) in connection with the Variocam intake camshaft adjustment cut emissions by more than 10% and considerably improved idle speed quality.

The oil supply for the whole engine was configured to suit harsh racetrack applications. The recirculation of the oil back into the separate oil tank (which was rigidly attached to the engine) was effected by a centrally located return pump. Two further return pumps (driven by the exhaust camshafts) were situated in each camshaft housing. They provided fast drainage of the oil from both cylinder heads. There was a further suction pump in each exhaust turbocharger.

A cyclone-type oil strainer was installed in the oil tank in order to skim the oil. A powerful pressure-pump formed the connection between the oil tank and the oil circulation of the engine. Eight oil pumps in all lubricated the 911 Turbo. As in all 996 models, an oil-water heat exchanger cooled the hot engine oil. The hot water was cooled down in three water radiators installed in the front end of the car and was fed back into the engine circulation.

M96/70 S (911 GT2)
As could be seen from the engine designation, the 911 GT2 was equipped with a turbocharged engine with additional power. In fact it boasted around 10% more power than the 911 Turbo, which was achieved by fitting more potent

turbochargers, a modified exhaust system and adapted engine electronics. Nonetheless, the GT2 passed Euro 3 emission tests in Europe as well as the Level 4 (D4) test in Germany without any problems. The oil supply system of the GT2 was designed in the same way as in the 911 Turbo.

Fuel and ignition system
911 Turbo
As with the previous air-cooled Turbo (993), the two turbochargers were connected in parallel. The bypass valves (wastegates) were located within the turbocharger housing. The intercoolers were situated in the two rear wheelarches. Cooling air entered at the openings in the rear wings (fenders), streaming through the air-to-air intercoolers and escaping through the lower air vents behind the rear wheels. The two charge-air lines merged and ended jointly in the E-gas controller.

The 911 Turbo was equipped with an electronic accelerator (E-gas). This became necessary because under critical driving conditions the PSM stability management system was required to change the engine management within a split second. The E-gas system also had a positive influence on fuel consumption and exhaust gas emissions.

The engine management system was now Motronic ME 7.8, which also controlled valve stroke adjustment, turbo boost pressure control and lambda control.

GT2

The charge-air system of the GT2 was similar to that of the 911 Turbo, but it had more powerful turbochargers. The engine management system (Motronic 7.8) was adapted to the increased power of the GT2 engine.

Transmission

Carrera and Carrera 4

All vehicles equipped with Tiptronic S now had a temporary override feature. Using the tip switch on the steering wheel, it was now possible to shift up and down manually even when in automatic mode. However, after approximately eight seconds the automatic programme activated itself again. The advantage of this temporary override was, for example, that you could overtake with a quick downshift without having to 'kick down' on the accelerator to change gear.

911 Turbo

Porsche had been producing the turbocharged 911 for the past 25 years, and for all that time it had only offered it with manual transmissions, initially with just four ratios, then five and finally six gears and all-wheel drive. This non-auto taboo for the Turbo was finally broken with the new water-cooled 996, which combined its powerful turbo engine with a five-speed Tiptronic S gearbox and all-wheel drive for the first time. A six-speed manual transmission was also available, still with all-wheel drive.

Manual transmission Turbo (G96/50)

The Turbo's six-speed manual transmission was similar to that of the 911 Carrera 4 (G96/30). However, the gear ratios were adjusted to match the performance of the turbo engine. The final drive ratio was also retained (3.444:1), and the driveshaft was connected to the front-wheel drive

911 Turbo Coupé featured a new water-cooled 3.6-litre engine, producing 309kW (420hp) at 6,000rpm.

at its free end. The viscous clutch was accommodated in a separate housing in the front differential. A dry single-plate clutch with a diameter of 240mm was hydraulically actuated. The manual transmission and front differential were permanently connected to each other via a short exposed driveshaft, and depending on the driving condition the proportion of the front-wheel drive was between 5% and 40%.

Tiptronic S Turbo (A96/50)
The five gear ratios in the automatic Tiptronic S transmission were newly configured for the 996 Turbo. The driving dynamics and the gearchange pattern were adopted from the Carrera. There were no gearchange programmes as in the earlier Tiptronic cars (economy to sporty). New for all cars with Tiptronic S was a temporary manual override

The 911 GT2 was based on the 911 Turbo, but featured larger turbochargers, reworked exhaust and revised engine management.

via the tip switch on the steering wheel (see above). The free end of the driveshaft exited the gearbox housing to connect to the front differential via a short driveshaft.

Manual transmission GT2
Porsche was able once again to revert to something tried and tested. The transmission of the 993 GT2, which had been successful in many races, was reworked and fitted with the lubrication system of the GT3 RS. In addition, a transmission oil/cooling water heat exchanger was mounted on the side of the gearbox housing to manage the oil temperature even at maximum load. The gear ratios and final drive ratio were identical to those of the 911 Turbo. The familiar cable-controlled gearshift used two precision cables.

Porsche installed a friction-plate limited-slip differential as standard with a lock-up factor under load of 40% and under coasting of 60%. The limited-slip differential was tuned to match the ultra-stiff suspension.

Suspension
911 Turbo

The basic concept for the suspension design was shared with the Carrera but adjusted and strengthened to take into account the significantly higher performance available. The suspension was lowered by 30mm compared to the Carrera, the anti-roll bars were adjustable and even the springs front and rear were interchangeable with racing items. The adjustment range of the suspension (camber and track) allowed for racing tyres to be fitted. Damper struts on the front and rear suspension were fitted with height-adjustable spring plates. The steering was identical to that of the Carrera.

911 GT2

The suspension of the 911 GT3 was adopted for the GT2, with some modifications to suit the higher performance. The GT2 was lowered even further (by another 20mm compared to the Turbo), dropping its centre of gravity. For racing purposes the modifications as described for the Turbo could be implemented as well. The steering was again identical to that of the 911 Carrera.

911 Turbo brakes

The familiar Porsche/Brembo brake system of aluminium monobloc four-piston callipers was reinforced again for the 911 Turbo. Perforated and internally vented discs with a diameter of 330mm (front and rear) were used, the thickness of the front brake discs being increased to 34mm. The brake callipers were painted red.

As an optional extra Porsche Ceramic Composite Brakes (PCCB) could be ordered, the discs of which, as the name implies, were made from ceramic material. Using special brake pads this system was noted for its high stability even under extreme loads, its very long lifespan, its excellent response on wet roads and an unsprung weight saving of approximately 20kg. The callipers of the PCCB brakes were painted yellow. This was a pricey option at DM 15,000.

The 911 Turbo was fitted with PSM (Porsche Stability Management) as standard. This system intervened fully automatically in critical driving situations, such as oversteer or understeer, or when the wheels were spinning or locking up. It restabilised the car not only by controlling the brakes at the wheels but also by closing the throttle (E-gas). PSM could be switched off electrically with the push of a button but was activated again as soon as you next applied the brakes.

911 GT2 brakes

The GT2 was the first Porsche to be equipped with the newly developed Porsche Ceramic Composite Braking system (PCCB) as standard. The diameter of the ceramic brake disc was increased compared with the 911 Turbo to 350mm (front and rear). The monobloc brake callipers had six pistons. Using modified brake pads, the effective pad surface could be increased by 40%. The 911 GT2 was fitted with the ABS system of the 911 GT3 as standard, controlled to match the GT2's high performance. PSM was not available for the GT2.

911 Turbo wheels

18in aluminium wheels with hollow spokes were especially developed for the Turbo. Due to the extensive hollow spoke casting technology, the unsprung mass was reduced by approximately 12kg compared with conventional cast wheels. For tyre and wheel dimensions as well as air pressure, please refer to the technical data on pages 214–215. As space in the front luggage compartment was tight because of the all-wheel drive system, the 911 Turbo was given a space-saver spare wheel with a compressor and accessories.

911 GT2 wheels

Aluminium monobloc wheels in 'turbo design' were fitted (see the technical data on pages 214–215 for full specification details). Because of its large 89-litre fuel tank, the GT2 had no space for a spare wheel, so Porsche included the same tyre repair kit that was already used with the GT3 (repair foam canister, on-board compressor and tyre pressure gauge).

Body
911 Turbo

Starting with the raw shell of the Carrera 4, the outer skin of the 911 Turbo had extensive modifications. The most important visual distinguishing characteristics were different front and rear ends, a rear lid with an extendable wing, underbody panelling and air intake ducts for the intercooler. Further unseen modifications were incorporated in the rear part of the car to accommodate the turbo engine with the separate dry sump oil reservoir and the Tiptronic transmission.

The front wings (fenders) were widened and prepared for the installation of bi-xenon headlights. Completely new was the rear lid with its extendable wing, which had a significant influence on the aerodynamics of the vehicle and its stability at high speed. The two rear wings remained pressed together up to a speed of 75mph (120kmh); thereafter hydraulics would push the top wing up by 65mm and the system became a double-decker. As soon as the speed went below 37mph (60kmh), the wing returned to its normal position.

ABOVE: The automatic hydraulically operated extending rear wing of the Turbo in its rest position...

BELOW: ... and in the fully extended position. The wing lifted by 65mm once the speed of the car reached 120kph (approx 75mph).

911 GT2

The bodyshell of the 911 Turbo formed the basis of the GT2. The GT2's front panelling was completely new and designed to reduce aerodynamic front-end lift at high speeds. This was achieved through a large opening for the centre radiator. Behind the radiator, the air stream was led not downwards but upwards across the luggage compartment lid.

A front spoiler with an additional rubber lip at the same height as the lower edge of the three front air intakes provided additional inflow of air. At the same time it prevented the air going under the car and forming an air cushion that would result in undesirable front-end lift. The luggage compartment at the front was partly used to install a large 89-litre fuel tank in the GT2.

The rear panelling was identical in design to the 911 Turbo but the high-quality plastic rear lid with its rigid wing was new and influenced the aerodynamics of the rear end significantly. Air flowed on the left- and right-hand sides through channels in the wing supports to the airbox in the lid, from which it entered the air filter directly.

Interior fittings
911 Turbo

Initially, the Turbo's interior fittings were identical to the Carrera's. The standardised leather trim (in a choice of five colours) covered the seats and instrument panel as well as door and side panels. Driver and passenger seats were fully electrically adjustable, and the driver's seat had a remotely controlled seat memory that was operated via the ignition key.

911 GT2

The interior corresponded largely to that of the Carrera model range but the seats were very different. Both driver and passenger seats were made from a light plastic shell covered in leather. The backrests of these seats could not be tilted forward and the fore/aft adjustments were done manually. The light bucket seats and the omission of any form of rear seating saved 28kg in weight. The GT2 had two front airbags and the POSIP airbag system on both sides.

Heating and air conditioning
911 Turbo and 911 GT2

Heating, ventilation and the standard automatic air conditioning were identical to the Carrera.

Electrical system
All models

With this new model year a remote control for front and rear lids was introduced. Both lids could be opened electrically by means of a push-button with the ignition key removed from the ignition, replacing the old system of pull levers in the door sill. The buttons could only be activated at speeds under 3mph (5kmh). The lids had to be closed manually for safety reasons.

As an orientation aid the cockpit was dimly illuminated by light-emitting diodes (LEDs) when driving in the dark. One LED was positioned in the handle of the left door and directed a light beam on to the ignition and the headlamp switch. A second was positioned in the roof-mounted interior light cluster and shone down vertically on to the gear lever and centre console. Driver and passenger were screened from both light sources and could not see them, and so were not blinded when driving in darkness. The brightness could be adjusted in two steps via a switch on the light cluster.

911 Turbo and 911 GT2
The electrical system of the two new models was based on that of the Carrera. However, the main headlights differed significantly, both visually and in terms of illumination. The Turbo and GT2 were both fitted with bi-xenon main headlights (dipped and full beam lights were both gas-discharge lamps), with dynamic headlight-range adjustment. Both also came with an integrated headlamp washer system as standard whose extendable spray nozzles emerged through the glass.

Additional information
For the Supercup racing series and the Carrera Cups in Germany and Japan, as well as races in the USA, Porsche produced 113 examples of the 911 GT3 Cup in model year 2001. These were very similar to production vehicles but boasted improved power of 272kW (370hp). Some 50 examples of the 911 GT3 RS were also produced for the GT racing series with peak power of 309kW (420hp).

Apart from the GT2 road version, the GT2 was also offered in Clubsport form to motorsport enthusiasts. Its main distinguishing characteristics were: bolt-on roll cage supported by the rear suspension struts; bucket seats covered with flame-resistant material instead of leather; six-point safety belt for the driver's seat, coloured red; fire extinguisher; battery main switch on the centre console; passenger airbag could be disabled; and no POSIP side airbags.

Model range	Total production
911 Carrera 2 Coupé	6543
911 Carrera 2 Cabriolet	6721
911 Carrera 4 Coupé	4085
911 Carrera 4 Cabriolet	3655
911 GT3	508
911 Turbo	5324
911 GT2	247

The 911 GT2 featured a new front spoiler to provide additional cooling for the radiators, and to reduce front-end lift.

Model range	Carrera	Carrera 4	911 GT3	911 Turbo	911 GT2
Engine					
Engine type					
Manual transmission	M96/04	M96/04	M96/76	M96/70	M96/70 S
Tiptronic	M96/04	M96/04	–	M96/70	–
Bore (mm)	96	96	100	100	100
Stroke (mm)	78	78	76.4	76.4	76.4
Displacement (cc)	3387	3387	3600	3600	3600
Compression ratio	11.3:1	11.3:1	11.7:1	9.4:1	9.4:1
Engine output (kW/hp)	221/300	221/300	265/360	309/420	340/462
at revolutions per minute (rpm)	6800	6800	7200	6000	5700
Torque (Nm)	350	350	370	560	620
at revolutions per minute (rpm)	4600	4600	5000	2700–4600	3500–4500
Output per litre (kW/l)	65.2	65.2	73.6	85.8	94.4
Max. engine speed (rpm)	7300	7300	7800	6750	6750
Engine cooling	water	=	=	=	=
Crankshaft	forged, rotates in seven journal bearings				
Cylinder surface	Lokasil	Lokasil	Nikasil	Nikasil	Nikasil
Cylinder head	three-piece	three-piece	6 separate cyl. heads	three-piece	three-piece
Valve configuration	2 inlet valves, 2 exhaust valves				
Valve control	via bucket tappets				
Timing gear	double chain to intermediate shaft Double chains to the exhaust cams	double chain to intermediate shaft Double chains to the exhaust cams	double chain to intermediate shaft, from there via a double chain each to the intake + exhaust cams	double chain to intermediate shaft, from there via a double chain each to the intake + exhaust cams	double chain to intermediate shaft, from there via a double chain each to the intake + exhaust cams
Variable camshaft settings	Porsche VarioCam 25° setting of intake cams	Porsche VarioCam 25° setting of intake cams	Porsche VarioCam 25° setting of intake cams	Porsche VarioCam Plus 30° setting of intake cams	Porsche VarioCam Plus 30° setting of intake cams
Valve-clearance compensation	hydraulic	=	=	=	=
Induction system	two-stage resonance system	two-stage resonance system	two-stage resonance system	resonance system	resonance system
Lubrication system	integrated dry sump	integrated dry sump	dry sump (separate oil tank)	dry sump (separate oil tank)	dry sump (separate oil tank)
Oil supply	1 pressure pump 3 suction pumps	1 pressure pump 3 suction pumps	1 pressure pump 3 suction pumps	1 pressure pump 7 suction pumps	1 pressure pump 7 suction pumps
Engine Weight according to DIN 70020 A (kg)					
Manual transmission	190*	190*	274***	260*	259***
Tiptronic S	179**	179**	–	253***	–

Key
* with underbody panelling, dual-mass flywheel, clutch and air-conditioning compressor
** with underbody panelling and air-conditioning compressor, without dual-mass flywheel
*** including air-conditioning compressor, fuel cooler, power steering pump, charge-air lines, intercooler, fuel filter, cooling fan, starter and dual-mass flywheel/converter attachment

The 911 Carrera 4 Cabriolet continued almost unchanged for the 2001-model year

Model range	Carrera	Carrera 4	911 GT3	911 Turbo	911 GT2
Carburation, ignition, settings					
Engine control	Motronic ME 7.2	Motronic ME 7.2	Motronic ME 5.22	Motronic ME 7.8	Motronic ME 7.8
Management throttle valve	E-Gas	E-Gas	mechanical	E-Gas	E-Gas
Type of fuel (RON)	98	98	98	98	98
Ignition system	Solid-state distributor system, 6 Ignition coils	Solid-state distributor system, 6 Ignition coils	DME 6 Ignition coils	DME 6 Ignition coils	DME 6 Ignition coils
Ignition	single	single	single	single	single
Anti-knock control	yes	yes	yes	yes	yes
Number of turbochargers	–	–	–	2	2
Spark plugs					
Bosch	–	–	FR 5 LOC	FR 5 LOC	FR 5 LDC
Beru	–	–	14-FR5 LDU	14-FR5 LDU	14-FR5 LDU
Spark plug gap (mm)	–	–	1.6 ± 0.2	1.6 ± 0.2	1.8 ± 0.1
Surface-gap spark plugs					
Bosch	FRG 6 KQC	FRG 6 KQC	–	–	–
Beru	14-FGR 6 KQU	14-FGR 6 KQU	–	–	–
Spark plug gap (mm)	1.6 ± 0.2	1.6 ± 0.2	–	–	–
Firing order	1-6-2-4-3-5	=	=	=	=
Idle speed (rpm)	700 ± 40	800 ± 40	740 ± 40	900 ± 40	740 ± 40
Exhaust/purification system	2 BLS + DWMK	2 BLS + DWMK USA: +ZLP	2 BLS + DWMK	2 BLS + DWMK	2 BLS + DWMK USA: +ZLP
CO-content					
without cat. conv. (%)	0.5–1.0	0.5–1.0	N/A	N/A	N/A
with cat. conv. (%)	0.4–1.2	0.4–1.2	N/A	N/A	N/A
Fuel consumption acc. EC Standard (litres/100km)					
Manual transmission					
urban	17.2	17.2	18.9	20.1	18.9
extra-urban	8.5	8.8	9.2	8.9	9.3
combined	11.8	8.8	9.2	8.9	9.3
Target value CO^2 (g/km)	285	295	309	320	309
Tiptronic					
urban	18.3	18.6	–	21.9	–
extra-urban	8.5	8.8	–	9.6	–
combined	12.0	12.4	–	13.9	–
Target value CO^2 (g/km)	290	304	–	339	–

Key:

2 BLS	Two heated lambda sensors with stereo control	KFZ	Pressure-controlled mapped ignition
DME S	Digital engine electronic system with sequential fuel injection	SLE	Secondary-air injection
DWMK	Three-way metal-based catalytic converter	ZLP	Auxiliary air pump

Transmission

Engine and gearbox are built as one drive unit.
The hydraulically operated dry single-disc clutch is bolted onto the dual-mass flywheel.
Drive train Carrera 2 and 911 GT2: via dual propshafts onto the rear wheels.
Drive configuration Carrera 4, Carrera 4S and 911 Turbo: Connection to gearbox via drive shaft to front differential.
Rear and front wheels are driven via dual propshafts.
Available as optional extras (not GT2) : 5-gear Tiptronic transmission with torque converter.

	Carrera	Carrera 4	911 GT3	911 Turbo	911 GT2
Dual-mass flywheel	Syst.LUK	Syst.LUK	Syst.LUK	Syst.LUK	Syst.LUK
Clutch, pressure plate	MF 228X MF240	MF 228X MF240	MF 228X MF240	MF 228X MF240	MF 228X MF240
Clutch plate (mm)	rigid 240	rigid 240	rigid 240	rigid 240	rigid 240
Transmission type:					
Manual transmission	G96/00	G96/30	G96/901	G96/50	G96/88
Gear ratios					
1st gear	3.82	3.82	3.82	3.82	3.82
2nd gear	2.20	2.20	2.15	2.05	2.05
3rd gear	1.52	1.52	1.56	1.41	1.41
4th gear	1.22	1.22	1.21	1.12	1.12
5th gear	1.02	1.02	0.82	0.75	0.75
6th gear	0.84	0.84	0.82	0.75	0.75
Reverse gear	3.55	3.55	2.86	2.86	2.86
Synchromesh system					
Forward gears	VK	VK	VK	VK	VK
Reverse gear	VK	VK	VK	VK	VK
Final drive, ratio	3.44	3.44	3.44	3.44	3.44
Limited-slip differential	no	no	Standard	no	Standard
Lock-up factor under load/coasting (%)	–	–	40/60	–	40/60
Gearbox weight with oil (kg)	63	64.5	72.8	72	74
All-wheel drive	no	yes	no	yes	no
Front-wheel drive transmission	no	Z96/30	no	Z96/00	no
Front axle ratio	–	3.44	3.44	3.44	–
FA transmission weight (kg)	–	23	–	23	–

213

Model range	Carrera	Carrera 4	911 GT3	911 Turbo	911 GT2
Transmission					
Tiptronic S	A96/00	A96/35	no	A96/50	not available
Torque converter dia.(mm)	282	282	–	282	–
Start-off conversion ratio	1.92	1.92	–	1.92	–
Stall speed (rpm)	2450	2450	–	2600	–
Gear ratios					
1st gear	3.66	3.66	3.59	N/A	-
2nd gear	2.00	2.00	2.19	N/A	-
3rd gear	1.41	1.41	1.41	N/A	-
4th gear	1.00	1.00	1.00	N/A	-
5th gear	–	–	–	-	-
Reverse gear	4.10	4.10	3.44	N/A	-
Final drive, ratio	3.676	3.676	2.889	N/A	-
Limited-slip differential	no	no	no	no	-
Stability Management PSM	Option	Standard	no	Standard	-
Gearbox weight with oil and ATF filling (kg)	115	123	125.2		-
All-wheel drive	no	Z 96/35	no	Z96/00	no
Front axle ratio	–	3.676	–	3.44	–
FA transmission weight (kg)	–	23	–	23	–

Key:
ABD   Automatic brake differential
PSM   Porsche Stability Management
Syst. LUK   Dual-mass flywheel system LUK (steel-spring damped)
TC   Traction control
VK   Full-cone synchromesh system with molybdenum-coated synchroniser rings

Suspension, steering and brakes					
Front suspension	Individually suspended on wishbones, semi-trailing arms and spring struts (MacPherson design, optimised by Porsche); one conical spring per wheel with internal shock absorber;				
Shock absorbers	dual function hydraulic dual-struts gas-pressure shock absorber				
Anti-roll bar dia. (mm)	23.1 x 3.4	22.5 x 3.5	26.8 x 4	23. 6 x 3.5	26.8 x 4
Steering ratio	16.9:	=	=	=	=
Turning circle dia. (m)	10.6	=	=	=	=
Rear axle					
Anti-roll bar dia. (mm)	18.5 x 2.5	19.6 x 2.6	20.7 x 2.8	21.7 x 3.0	20.7 x 2.8
Brake system					
Brake booster ratio	3.85	3.85	3.15	3.85	3.15
Brake master cylinder dia. (mm)	23.81	23.81	25.4	25.4	=
Pressure reducer	yes	yes	no	no	no
Cut-in pressure (bar)	55	55	–	–	–
Reduction factor	0.46	0.46	–	–	–
Driving brake	Dual-circuit brake system with four-piston aluminium brake callipers				= 6 pistons
Brake calliper piston diameter					
front (mm)	36 + 40	36 + 40	44 + 34	36 + 44	38 + 32 + 28
rear (mm)	28 + 30	28 + 30	30 + 28	28 + 30	30 + 28
Brake disc diameter					
front (mm)	318	318	330	330	350 (PCCB)
rear (mm)	299	299	330	330	350 (PCCB)
Brake disc thickness					
front (mm)	28	28	34	34	34
rear (mm)	24	24	28	28	28
Effective brake disc area (cm^2)	450	450	568	568	696
Handbrake	Operating mechanically on both rear wheels				
Brake drum diameter (mm)	180	=	=	=	=
Contact area (cm^2)	170	=	=	=	=

Wheels and tyres					
Standard tyre specification, front	205/50ZR17	205/50ZR17	225/40ZR18	225/40ZR18	235/40ZR18
wheel	7J x 17	7J x 17	8J x 18	8J x 18	8.5J x 18
hump depth (mm)	55	55	52**	50	40
optional	225/40ZR18	225/40ZR18	–	–	–
wheel	7.5J x 18	7.5J x 18	–	–	–
hump depth (mm)	50	50	–	–	–
Winter tyres	205/50R1789TM+S	205/50R1789TM+S	–	–	–
wheel	7J x 17	7J x 17	8J x 18	8J x 18	8J x 18
hump depth (mm)	55	55	52**	50	50

Model range	Carrera	Carrera 4	911 GT3	911 Turbo	911 GT2
Wheels and tyres (continued)					
Standard tyre specification, rear	255/40ZR17	255/40ZR17	285/30ZR18	295/30ZR18	315/30ZR18
wheel	9J x 17	9J x 17	10J x 18*	11J x 18	12J x 18
hump depth (mm)	55	55	65**	45	45
optional	265/35ZR18	265/35ZR18	–	–	–
wheel	10J x 18	10J x 18	–	–	–
hump depth (mm)	65	65	–	–	–
Winter tyres	225/45R1790TM+S	225/45R1790TM+S	265/35R1893H	265/35R1893H	265/35R1893H
wheel	8.5J x 17	8.5J x 17	10J x 18	10J x 18	10J x 18
hump depth (mm)	50	50	65**#	47#	47#
optional	–	255/40R1794TM+S	–	–	–
wheel	–	9J x 17	–	–	–
hump depth (mm)	–	55	–	–	–
Space saver high-pressure tyre	105/95R17*	–	–	–	–
Space-saver spare wheel	–	165/70-1692P	Tyre Mobility System*	Tyre Mobility System*	165/70-1692P
Tyre pressure					
front (bar)	2.5	2.5	2.2	2.5	2.2
rear (bar)	2.5	2.5	2.7	–	2.7
with 18" tyres rear (bar)	3.0	3.0	2.7	3.0	2.7
High-pressure tyres/ space-saver System*spare wheel (bar)	4.2*	2.5*	2.2* or 2.7*	2.5	2.2 or 2.7*

* The 911 Carrera 2 (996) had an inflated high-pressure tyre while the 911 Carrera 4 (996) had a space-saver spare wheel that needed to be inflated by means of an on-board compressor when required. The GT3 had no proper 'spare wheel'.
** Spacer 5mm
\# with snow chain free travel
PCCB   Drilled, internally vented ceramic brake discs

Body					
Monocoque structure, hot-dip galvanised lightweight steel body, partial use of HSLA* steel; airbags and side airbags for driver and passenger; number of seats: 2 + 2					
Drag coefficient (cd)	0.30	0.30	0.30	0.31	0.34
Frontal area A (m²)	1.94	1.94	1.94	2.00	1.96
Aerodynamic drag cd x A (m²)	0.582	0.582	0.582	0.62	0.67
Dimensions at kerb weight					
Length (mm)	4430	4430	4430	4435	4450
Width (mm)	1765	1765	1765	1830	1830
Height (mm)	1305	1305	1270	1295	1275
Wheelbase (mm)	2350	2350	2350	2350	2355
Track					
front 16+17 inch (mm)	1455	1455	–	–	–
18 inch (mm)	1465	1465	1475	1465	1495
rear 17 inch (mm)	1500	1500	–	–	–
18 inch (mm)	1480	1480	1495	1522	1520
Ground clearance at permissible gross weight (mm)	100	100	90	90	70
Overhang angle					
front (degree)	12	12	12	10	6.0
rear (degree)	14.5	14.5	14.5	13	13.0

Electrical system					
Generator output (W/A)	1680	1680	1680	1680	1680
Battery (V/Ah)	12/70	12/70	12/36 or 46**	12/80	12/60

Weight according to DIN 70020					
Kerb weight (kg)					
Manual transmission	1320–1380***	1375–1430***	1350–1420***	1540	1440
Tiptronic	1365–1425***	1420–1475***	–	1585	–
Permissible gross weight (kg)					
Manual transmission	1720	1775	1630	1885	1730
Tiptronic	1765	1820	–	1930	–
Permissible trailer weight (kg)					
unbraked	none	=	=	=	=
braked	none	=	=	=	=
Permissible roof load (kg)	35	35	none	none	none
with Porsche-System (kg)	75	75	50	75	50

Model range	Carrera	Carrera 4	911 GT3	911 Turbo	911 GT2
Performance					
Maximum speed (kmh)					
Manual transmission	280	280	302	305	315
Tiptronic	275	275	–	298	–
Acceleration 0–62mph/100 kmh (sec)					
Manual transmission	5.2	5.2	4.8	4.2	4.1
Tiptronic	6.0	6.0	–	4.9	–
Measured kilometre from standing start (sec)					
Manual transmission	24.2	24.3	22.4	21.9	
Tiptronic	25.3	25.6	–	23.9	–

Fluid capacities					
Engine oil quantity 1* (l)	10.25	10.25	12.5	11.0	11.0
Oil change quantity (l)	8.25	8.25	8.5	8.0	7.8
Cooling water (l)	22.5	22.5	25	28	28
Manual transmission 2* (l)	2.7	2.7	3.8	3.8	3.8
Front axle 2* (l)	–	1.5	–	1.5	–
Automatic transm. 3* (l)	9.5	9.5	–	9.0 3**	–
Final drive, autom. 2* (l)	0.8	0.8	–	1.2	–
Fuel tank 4* (l)	64	64	89	64	89
Brake fluid reservoir 5* (l)	0.45	0.63	0.8	0.63	0.63
Power steering fluid 8* (l)	1.27	1.27	1.9	2.14	2.14
Refrigerant 6* (g)	900	=	=	=	=
Refrigerant oil 7* (ml)	195	=	=	=	=
Washer tank (l)	2.5	=	=	=	=

Key and key to numerals
*   HSLA steel = description used internationally for high-strength, low-alloy steel
** 36Ah without, 46Ah with air conditioning depending on options
*** Depending on equipment
1* Approved engine oils according to ACEA A4-96 specification and special Porsche requirements
2* Gear oil GL 5 SAE 90 MOBILUBE PTX
3* ATF ESSO LT 71141
3**ATF SHELL3403-M115
4* Unleaded fuel with minimum standard RON 98/MON 88
5* Use only brake fluid acc. SUPER DOT 4.
6* Only refrigerant R 134 a
7* Commercially available refrigerant oils
8* Pentosin CHF 11 S

Vehicle Identification Numbers for 911 model range of model year 2001 (1* Programme)											
World manufacturer code	Code body USA (A=Coupé, B=Targa, C=Cabriolet)	Code for engine variants (only USA)	Restraint system (0 = belt, 2 = airbag)	First and second digit for car type	Fill character/ check digit	Model year (Y = 2000, 1 = 2001, 2 = 2002)	Manufacturing site (S = Stuttgart)	7th and 8th digit = car type	Code for body + engine	Sequence number	Summary
WPO	Z	Z	Z	99	Z	1	S	6	0	0001–	996 Coupé RoW
WPO	Z	Z	Z	99	Z	1	S	6	9	0001–	996 GT3 Coupé RoW
WPO	Z	Z	Z	99	Z	1	S	6	9	2001–	996 GT3 Coupé (M005) RoW
WPO	Z	Z	Z	99	Z	1	S	6	9	8001–	996 Cup Coupé RoW
WPO	Z	Z	Z	99	Z	1	S	6	4	0001–	996 Cabriolet RoW
WPO	Z	Z	Z	99	Z	1	S	6	8	0001–	996 Turbo RoW
WPO	A	B	2	99	C	1	S	6	8	5001–	996 Turbo USA+CDN+MEX+BRA
WPO	A	C	2	99	C	1	S	6	9	1901–	996 GT3 Coupé MEX+BRA
WPO	A	A	2	99	C	1	S	6	2	0001–	996 Coupé USA+CDN+MEX+BRA
WPO	C	A	2	99	C	1	S	6	5	0001–	996 Cabriolet USA+CDN+MEX+BRA

C* = Check digit, can be 0–9 or X (only USA)
Z = Fill character for rest of world cars
*Note: The vehicle-ID nos. no longer allowed for a differentiation between Carrera 2 and Carrera 4.
1* = model years up to 2010 were no longer assigned letters but numbers. 1 = model year 2001. The letter 'Z' was not assigned.

Model year 2002

2 Programme, bigger engines, new Targa, Carrera 4S with turbo body

Porsche 911 Carrera Coupé, Cabriolet and Targa
Porsche 911 Carrera 4 Coupé and Cabriolet
Porsche 911 Carrera 4S Coupé
Porsche 911 Turbo
Porsche 911 GT2

The main news for 2002 was the introduction of a larger 3.6-litre engine for the Carrera and Carrera 4, which not only boosted power and torque but also offered better fuel consumption and emissions. Most enthusiasts agreed that the engine sounded better too.

A newcomer for 2002 was the 911 Targa with its interesting glass roof design, echoing that of the 993 Targa produced in 1996. The Targa was only built with rear-wheel drive. In the all-wheel drive line-up, the 911 Carrera 4S was another new model this year, fitted with the body of the 911 Turbo as well as Turbo suspension and Turbo brakes. However, it used the same naturally aspirated engine as the Carrera. The GT3 was axed at this point, after some 1,932 examples had been produced.

Engine
The displacement for naturally aspirated engines in the Carrera model range was raised to 3,596cc by increasing the stroke to 82.8mm. The basics of the old water-cooled four-valve M96/04 engine were kept, and as well as the longer stroke, the pistons and con rods were modified, which helped boost power by 14kW (20hp) and torque by 20Nm. The new 3.6-litre engine achieved an output of 235kW (320hp).

Variocam Plus variable valve control (adjustment of the intake camshaft by 40°) and the valve stroke adjustment that had already been introduced in the 2001 Turbo was now also implemented in the naturally aspirated engines. The camshaft chain system was also modified, with the roller chain between crankshaft and intermediate shaft being replaced by a quieter tooth-type chain.

Despite the raised power, a reduction in fuel consumption was also achieved and the exhaust emissions were improved again. A revised exhaust system made the sporty sound of the 911 even

A new 911 Targa was introduced for 2002, with a similar sliding-glass roof to the previous Targa model.

more appealing. The oil pressure pump was reworked in order to achieve safer delivery of oil to all lubrication points.

Comparison of engine data:

Engine	Maximum output (kW/hp)	At rpm	Maximum torque (Nm)	At rpm
M 96/03	235/320	6800	370	4250
M 96/04	221/300	6800	350	4600

Fuel and ignition system
911 Carrera
All Porsche vehicles were equipped with a modified fuel supply system as from model year 2002. The fuel was now delivered through a filter to the injection nozzles with the aid of an electric pump in the tank. A pressure controller mounted near the engine provided the necessary operating pressure. Unused fuel flowed back to the tank through a return pipe, during which process the fuel was warmed by heat from the engine.

For 2002, the capacity of the 911 non-turbo engine was increased to 3.6 litres, producing 235kW (320hp) in manual-gearbox models.

Especially at high temperatures in the summer and when there was little fuel in the tank, the fuel heated up to such an extent that fuel vapour formed in the tank needed to be neutralised in the activated carbon canister in the fuel tank ventilation system. Vapour bubbles in tubes and pipes could lead to hot start problems. The new 'returnless fuel system' was the most effective way of preventing the fuel from heating up. In the new system a pressure controller and a lifetime fuel filter was situated next to the fuel pump in the tank. A single fuel supply pipe led to the engine. The tank capacity was unaffected, remaining at 64 litres.

Engine management was taken over by Bosch Motronic ME 7.8. This was configured similarly to the set-up in the 911 Turbo from model year 2001, but was adapted to the naturally aspirated engine. New were the valve-lift changeover function and the stageless control of the inlet valve timings.

Compared with the model year 2001 vehicles (Euro 3), the new 3.6-litre naturally aspirated engines passed the more stringent Euro 3/D4 exhaust emission standard. In Germany this resulted in an annual tax advantage of 300 Euros.

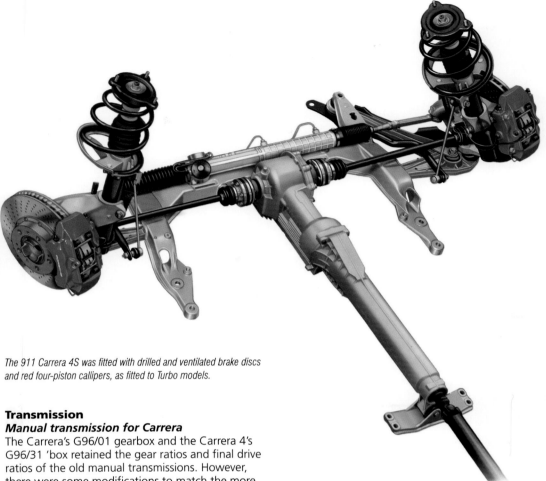

The 911 Carrera 4S was fitted with drilled and ventilated brake discs and red four-piston callipers, as fitted to Turbo models.

Transmission
Manual transmission for Carrera
The Carrera's G96/01 gearbox and the Carrera 4's G96/31 'box retained the gear ratios and final drive ratios of the old manual transmissions. However, there were some modifications to match the more powerful engine:

- The driveshafts in the transmissions now ran in three bearings.
- The gears were made from heavy-duty compounds.
- The gearing of the driveshafts was shot-blasted.
- The differentials now had four differential bevel gears.
- The gearbox was filled with lifetime oil ex-works.

The vibration-damping dual-mass flywheel and the dry single-plate clutch were adopted from the previous year without any modifications, except that the contact pressure of the diaphragm spring was adjusted to cope with the higher torque.

Tiptronic S for Carrera
The more robust transmission of the 911 Turbo was used as the new Tiptronic S transmission for naturally aspirated engines. All vehicles with Tiptronic S were fitted with 'centrifugal protection' to protect the converter components and the ATF (automatic transmission fluid) pump. The engine could only accelerate up to 4,000rpm with the gearshift in the 'P' or 'N' position. The Tiptronic system was filled with lifetime oil ex-works. The temporary manual override function remained (see model year 2001).

Manual transmission for 911 Turbo
There were no significant changes to the G96/50 manual transmission for the 911 Turbo. Here too the gearbox was filled with lifetime oil ex-works.

Tiptronic S for 911 Turbo
There were no significant changes to the A96/50 Tiptronic S automatic transmission at the time of the model change (nor to the G96/88 manual transmission for the 911 GT2). The system was filled with lifetime transmission fluids.

Suspension
The suspension of the Carrera and Carrera 4 was carried over from model year 2001 with only minor

ABOVE: The 911 Carrera 4S Coupé used the 911 Turbo body, suspension and brakes, but with normally aspirated Carrera engine.

BELOW: The 911 Turbo model was fitted with bi-xenon headlights and a headlight cleaning system.

changes. Porsche made modifications so that its new 18in wheels and bigger tyres would fit.

Carrera 4S

The new Carrera 4S mostly used the tried and tested components of the 911 Turbo, including its brakes with red-painted four-piston monobloc brake callipers, perforated and internally vented brake discs with a diameter of 330mm, and 10mm lower suspension. Turbo Look 18in wheels were fitted as standard.

Porsche's PSM stability management system was also standard in the all-wheel drive versions of the 911 model range, and was available as an optional extra for the 911 Carrera and the 911 Targa. The advantages of the PSM system were:

- Excellent traction and directional stability even in varying road surface conditions.
- Lateral acceleration was monitored and controlled.
- Dynamic oversteer could be avoided.
- Shortening of the braking distance, especially in corners and on changing road surfaces.
- The system could be turned off in order to give experienced drivers full control over the car's behaviour at sporting events.

Body

The new nose, front wings (fenders) and headlamps were the principal visual changes for the new model year. The nose had different air intake ducts which, along with modifications to the underbody panelling, achieved improved cooling air circulation. In addition, the aerodynamics in this area were also greatly enhanced.

In order to increase static resistance to bending and torsional rigidity, modifications were also made to the structure of the cars, for example around the seat pan, the door sill and the roof frame. Porsche achieved body rigidity of about 25% higher in the Coupé and the Targa and about 10% higher in the Cabriolet.

All Carrera models, including the Carrera 4S and the 911 Targa, were equipped with an automatic rear spoiler that extended at about 75mph (120kmh) and returned to its closed position when the speed dropped under 37mph (60kmh). The Cabriolets were fitted with a solid glass heated rear window that could be easily replaced.

Targa

Underneath the window line, the 911 Targa was identical to the Carrera. As with the earlier 993, the Targa had a module consisting of a mounting frame and roof. Compared with the earlier version,

The 911 Targa rear glass window could be lifted, like a hatchback tailgate, for access to the luggage space behind the seats.

the roof pillars were further strengthened and joined by transverse members. Another important improvement was the rear glass window, which could be lifted up, making it easier to reach the luggage space behind the driver and passenger seats through the open window.

The operation of the actual glass roof, which could be moved regardless of the car's speed, was effected via a push button on the centre console. The sun blind positioned underneath the glass window could also be used as a protection from the cold in winter.

Carrera 4S

The wider front wings (fenders) of the bodyshell were identical to those of the 911 Turbo apart from the absence of side air intake ducts, which were not needed in the Carrera 4S as it was not fitted with intercoolers. The 4S was some 65mm wider than the standard 911. The rear panelling was also almost identical to the Turbo's but additional measures were taken at the rear to protect from the heat of the 3.6-litre naturally aspirated engine.

The 911 Carrera 4S featured a similar interior to the Carrera models, with extensive use of leather trim.

Interior fittings
Carrera 4S
Interior fittings were initially identical to those of the Carrera model range. The standard leather interior (in a choice of five colours) comprised the seats, the instrument panel, the doors and the side panels. Driver and passenger seats were fully electrically adjustable, and the driver's seat had remote-controlled memory by means of the ignition key as standard.

Targa
The 911 Targa came with newly designed seats, incorporating a headrest whose upholstery was 20mm thicker, while the backrest side bolsters and seat upholstery matched the seating position, which was 8mm lower.

Heating and air conditioning
Heating, ventilation and standard automatic air conditioning were carried over from the previous model year unchanged.

Electrical system
All models
The Carrera as well as the Carrera 4 and 4S were

all fitted with completely new main headlights with halogen technology. The outer shape of the headlights matched those of the 911 Turbo. A major improvement was the H7 light bulbs (12V/55W), which illuminated the road through a 70mm glass lens. The H7 bulbs offered great advantages, especially when driving with dipped headlights: high light volume, more light in the border area between light and dark, and no blinding of pedestrians thanks to a clear-cut upper beam border, achieved by an additional light cone. The full-beam H9 bulbs provided excellent illumination of the road up to a distance of more than 150m.

As an optional extra, all vehicles were available with bi-xenon headlights, in which both the dipped beam and full beam lights used gas-discharge lamps. Dynamic headlight range adjustment also formed part of this system, which represented a significant contribution to road safety.

While glare-free interior lighting had only been offered with the 911 Turbo in the previous model year, it now came as standard in the 911 Targa and 911 Carrera 4S too, and could be ordered as an optional extra on all other 911 models. This provided LEDs to illuminate the ignition lock, light switch, centre console and door handles.

A further optional extra was a parking assist system, with sensors in the rear end of the car. The ugly 'warts' that had been used in previous years were now replaced by much smaller sensors that were fitted flush with the rear panelling.

The following radio equipment was available: Porsche cassette radio CDR 22 as standard for all vehicles with four-band speakers; Porsche cassette radio CDR 32; and Porsche cassette radio MDR 32. In addition, a Bose Sound System with up to 12 speakers could be fitted on request.

Model range	Total production
911 Carrera Coupé	6249
911 Carrera Cabriolet	6978
911 Carrera Targa	2630
911 Carrera 4 Coupé	1722
911 Carrera 4S Coupé	4802
911 Carrera 4 Cabriolet	3870
911 Turbo	5908
911 GT2	716
911 Cup	138

Model range	Carrera	Carrera 4	Carrera 4S	911 Turbo	911 GT2
Engine					
Water-cooled six-cylinder boxer engine, engine casing made from light alloy					
Engine type					
Manual transmission	M96/03	M96/03	M96/03	M96/70	M96/70 S
Tiptronic	M96/04	M96/04	M96/04	M96/70	–
Bore (mm)	96	96	96	100	100
Stroke (mm)	82.8	82.8	82.8	76.4	76.4
Displacement (cc)	3596	3596	3596	3600	3600
Compression ratio	11.3:1	11.3:1	11.3:1	9.4:1	11.7:1
Engine output (kW/hp)	235/320	235/320	235/320	309/420	340/462
at revolutions per minute (rpm)	6800	6800	6800	6000	5700
Torque (Nm)	370	370	370	560	620
at revolutions per minute (rpm)	4250	4250	4250	2700–4600	3500–4500
Output per litre (kW/l)	65.3	65.3	65.3	85.8	94.4
Max. engine speed (rpm)	7300	7300	7300	6750	6750
Type	six-cylinder aluminium boxer engine				
Engine cooling	water	=	=	=	=
Crankshaft	forged, rotates in seven journal bearings				
Cylinder surface	Lokasil	Lokasil	Nikasil	Nikasil	Nikasil
Cylinder head	three-piece	=	=	=	=
Valve configuration	2 inlet valves, 2 exhaust valves				
Inlet valve dia. (mm)	40.2	40.2	40.2		
Exhaust valve dia. (mm)	34.5	34.5	34.5		
Valve control inlet	via adjustable bucket tappets				
Valve stroke inlet (mm)	11.0 or 3.6	11.0 or 3.6	11.0 or 3.6	11.0 or 3.0	11.0 or 3.0
Exhaust	11	11	11	10	10
Timing gear	double chain to intermediate shaft Double chains to the exhaust cams	double chain to intermediate shaft Double chains to the exhaust cams	double chain to intermediate shaft Double chains to the exhaust cams	double chain to intermediate shaft from there via a one double chain to intake and exhaust cams	double chain to intermediate shaft from there via a one double chain to intake and exhaust cams
Variable camshaft settings	Porsche VarioCam 42° setting of intake cams	Porsche VarioCam 42° setting of intake cams	Porsche VarioCam 42° setting of intake cams	Porsche VarioCam Plus 30° setting of intake cams	Porsche VarioCam Plus 30° setting of intake cams
Valve-clearance compensation	hydraulic	=	=	=	=
Induction system	two-stage	two-stage	two-stage	two-stage	resonance system
Resonance system	resonance system	resonance system	resonance system		
Throttle valve	mechanical	=	=	=	
Lubrication system	integrated dry sump	integrated dry sump	integrated dry sump	dry sump (separate oil tank)	dry sump (separate oil tank)
Oil supply	1 pressure pump 3 suction pumps	1 pressure pump 3 suction pumps	1 pressure pump 3 suction pumps	1 pressure pump 7 suction pumps	1 pressure pump 7 suction pumps
Engine Weight according to DIN 70020 A (kg)					
Manual transmission	203.7*	203.7*	203.7***	260*	259***
Tiptronic S	194**	194**	194***	253**	–

Key
* with underbody panelling, dual-mass flywheel, clutch and air-conditioning compressor
** with underbody panelling and air-conditioning compressor, without dual-mass flywheel
*** including air-conditioning compressor, fuel cooler, power steering pump, charge-air lines, intercooler, fuel filter, cooling fan, starter and dual-mass flywheel/converter attachment

Model range	Carrera	Carrera 4	Carrera 4S	911 Turbo	911 GT2
Carburation, ignition, settings					
For USA: On-board Diagnostic System II, for Europe: Euro III On-board Diagnostic System					
Engine control	Motronic ME 7.8	=	=	=	=
Management Throttle valve	E-Gas	=	=	=	=
Type of fuel (RON)	98	=	=	=	=
Ignition system	DME, 6 Ignition coils	=	=	=	=
Ignition	Single	=	=	=	=
Anti-knock control	yes	=	=	=	=
Number of turbochargers	–	–	–	2	2
Idle speed (rpm)	700 ± 40	700 ± 40	700 ± 40	900 ± 40	700 ± 40
Spark plugs					
Bosch	FGR 6 KQC	=	=	FR 5 LCD1.6	FR 5 LDC
Beru	14-FGR 6 KQU	=	=	14-FR 5 LDU	14-FR 5 LDU
Spark plug gap (mm)	1.6 ± 0.2	=	=	0.8 ± 0.1	0.7 ± 0.1
Firing order	1-6-2-4-3-5	=	=	=	=
Idle speed (rpm)	720 ± 40	720 ± 40	720 ± 40	740 ± 40	740 ± 40
Exhaust/purification system	2 BLS+DWMK	=	=	=	=
CO-content					
with cat. conv. (%)	0.4–1.2	0.4–1.2	0.4–1.2	N/A	N/A
Fuel consumption acc. 93/116/EC (litres/100km)					
Manual transmission					
urban	16.1	16.3	16.3	18.9	18.9
extra-urban	8.1	8.3	8.5	9.2	9.3
combined	11.1	11.3	11.4	12.9	12.9
Target value CO_2 (g/km)	269	274	277	309	309
Emission standard	Euro3/D4	Euro3/D4	Euro3/D4	Euro3/D4	Euro3/D4
Tiptronic					
urban	16.9	18.1	21.9	21.9	–
extra-urban	8.1	8.7	8.9	9.6	–
combined	11.3	11.9	12.1	13.9	–
Target value CO_2 (g/km)	274	289	294	339	–
Emission standard	Euro3/D4	Euro3/D4	Euro3/D4	Euro3/D4	–

Key:

2 BLS	Two heated lambda sensors with stereo control
DME S	Digital engine electronic system with sequential fuel injection
DWMK	Three-way metal-based catalytic converter
KFZ	Pressure-controlled mapped ignition
SLE	Secondary-air injection
ZLP	Auxiliary air pump

Transmission

Engine and gearbox are built as one drive unit.
The hydraulically operated dry single-disc clutch is bolted onto the dual-mass flywheel.
Drive train Carrera 2 and 911 GT2: via dual propshafts onto the rear wheels.
Drive configuration Carrera 4, Carrera 4S and 911 Turbo: Connection to gearbox via drive shaft to front differential.
Rear and front wheels are driven via dual propshafts.
Available as optional extra (not GT2) : 5-gear Tiptronic transmission with torque converter.

Dual-mass flywheel	Syst.LUK	=	=	=	=
Clutch, pressure plate	MF 228X MF 240	=	=	=	=
Clutch plate (mm) dia. (mm)	rigid 240	=	=	=	=
Manual transmission	G96/01	G96/31	G96/31	G96/50	G96/88
Gear ratios					
1st gear	3.82	3.82	3.82	3.82	3.82
2nd gear	2.2	2.2	2.2	2.05	2.05
3rd gear	1.52	1.52	1.52	1.41	1.41
4th gear	1.22	1.22	1.22	1.12	1.12
5th gear	1.02	1.02	1.02	0.92	0.92
6th gear	0.84	0.84	0.84	0.75	0.75
Reverse gear	3.55	3.55	3.55	2.86	2.86
Synchromesh system					
Forward gears	VK	=	=	=	=
Reverse gear	VK	=	=	=	=
Final drive, ratio	3.44	3.44	3.44	3.44	3.44
Limited-slip differential	no	no	no	no	no
Gearbox weight with oil (kg)	65	66	66	72	74
All-wheel drive	no	From the transmission at the rear via driveshaft to the viscous clutch and to the front differential			
Front-wheel drive transmission	no	Z96/35	X96/35	Z96/00	no
Front axle ratio	–	3.44	3.44	3.44	
FA transmission weight (kg)	–	23	23	23	–

Model range	Carrera	Carrera 4	Carrera 4S	911 Turbo	911 GT2
Tiptronic S	A96/10	A96/35	A96/35	A96/50	not available
Torque converter dia.(mm)	282	282	282	282	–
Start-off conversion ratio	1.92	1.85	1.85	1.92	–
Stall speed (rpm)	2450	2450	2450	2600	–
Gear ratios					
1st gear	3.6	3.6	3.6	3.59	–
2nd gear	2.19	2.19	2.19	2.19	–
3rd gear	1.41	1.41	1.41	1.41	–
4th gear	1	1	1	1	–
5th gear	0.83	0.83	0.83	0.83	–
Reverse gear	3.17	3.17	3.17	3.16	–
Final drive, ratio	3.37	3.37	3.37	2.89	–
Limited-slip differential	no	no	no	no	–
Stability Management PSM	Option	Standard	Standard	Standard	–
Gearbox weight with oil and ATF filling (kg)	122.6	112.6	112.6	116.5	–
All-wheel drive	no	From the transmission at the rear via driveshaft to the viscous clutch and to the front differential			no
Front-wheel drive transmission	no	Z96/35	Z96/35	Z96/00	no
Front axle ratio	–	3.37	3.37	2.88	–
FA transmission weight (kg)	–	23	23	23	–

Key:
ABD   Automatic brake differential
PSM   Porsche Stability Management
Syst.LUK   Dual-mass flywheel system LUK (steel-spring damped)
TC   Traction control
VK   Full-cone synchromesh system with molybdenum-coated synchroniser rings

Suspension, steering and brakes					
Front suspension	Individually suspended on wishbones, semi-trailing arms and spring struts (MacPherson design, optimised by Porsche); one conical spring per wheel with internal shock absorber				
Shock absorbers	dual function hydraulic dual-struts gas-pressure shock absorber				
Anti-roll bar dia. (mm)	23.1 x 3.4	22.5 x 3.5	22.5 x 3.5	23.6 x 3.5	26.8 x 4
Steering ratio	16.9:1	=	=	=	=
Turning circle dia. (m)	10.6	=	=	=	=
Rear suspension	Multi-wishbone rear suspension, individually suspended on five wishbones, one cylinder coil spring per wheel				
Shock absorbers	dual function hydraulic single-strut gas-pressure shock absorber				
Anti-roll bar dia. (mm)	18.5 x 2.5	19.6 x 2.6	20.7 x 2.8	21.7 x 3.0	20.7 x 2.8
Brake system	Hydraulic dual-circuit brake system with aluminium monobloc brake callipers on all wheels, internally vented brake discs on all wheels, ABS standard				
PSM	M	S	S	S	S
Brake booster ratio	3.85	3.85	3.15	3.15	3.15
Brake master cylinder dia. (mm)	23.81	23.81	25.4	25.4	25.4
Pressure reducer	yes	yes	no	no	no
Cut-in pressure (bar)	55	55	–	–	–
Reduction factor	0.46	0.46	–	–	–
Brake calliper piston diameter					
front (mm)	36 + 40	36 + 40	44 + 34	36 + 44	38 + 32 + 28
rear (mm)	28 + 30	28 + 30	30 + 28	28 + 30	30 + 28
Brake disc diameter					
front (mm)	318	318	330	330	350 PCCB
rear (mm)	299	299	330	330	350 PCCB
Brake disc thickness					
front (mm)	28	28	34	34	34
rear (mm)	24	24	28	28	28
Effective brake disc area	450	450	568	568	696
Handbrake	Operating mechanically on both rear wheels				
Brake drum diameter (mm)	180	=	=	=	=
Contact area (cm^2)	170	=	=	=	=

Model range	Carrera	Carrera 4	Carrera 4S	911 Turbo	911 GT2
Wheels and tyres					
Standard tyre specification, front	205/50ZR17	205/50ZR17	225/40ZR18	225/40ZR18	235/40ZR18
wheel	7J x 17	7J x 17	8J x 18	8J x 18	8.5J x 18
hump depth (mm)	50	55	50	50	40
optional	225/40ZR18	225/40ZR18	–	–	–
wheel	8J x 18	8J x 18	–	–	–
hump depth (mm)	50	50	–	–	–
Winter tyres	205/50R1789T	205/50R1789T	225/40R1888H	225/40R1888H	225/40R1888H
wheel	7J x 17	7J x 17	8J x 18	8J x 18	8J x 18
hump depth (mm)	55	55	50	50	50
Standard tyre specification, rear	255/40ZR17	225/40ZR17	295/30ZR18	295/30ZR18	315/30ZR18
wheel	9J x 17	9J x 17	11J x 18	11J x 18	12J x 18
hump depth (mm)	55	55	65**	45	45
optional	265/35ZR18	265/35ZR18	–	–	–
wheel	10J x 18	10J x 18	–	–	–
hump depth (mm)	65	65	–	–	–
Winter tyres	225/45R1790TM+S	225/45R1790TM+S	265/35R1893HM+S	265/35R1893HM+S	265/35R1893HM+S
wheel	8.5J x 17	8.5J x 17	10J x 18	10J x 18	10J x 18
hump depth (mm)	50	50	65**#	47#	47#
optional	–	255/40R1794TM+S	–	–	–
wheel	–	9J x 17	–	–	–
hump depth (mm)	–	55	–	–	–
Space saver High-pressure tyre	105/95-R17*	–			
Space-saver spare wheel	–	165/70-1692P	Tyre Mobility System*	Tyre Mobility System*	165/70-1692P
Tyre pressure					
front (bar)	2.5	2.5	2.2	2.5	2.2
rear (bar)	2.5	2.5	2.7	–	–
with 18" tyres rear (bar)	3	3	2.7	3	2.7
High-pressure tyres/Space-saver spare wheel (bar)	4.2*	2.5*	2.2* or 2.7*	2.5	2.2 or 2.7*

*   The 911 Carrera 2 (996) had an inflated high-pressure tyre while the 911 Carrera 4 (996) had a space-saver spare wheel that needed to be inflated by means of an on-board compressor when required. The GT3 had no proper 'spare wheel'.

**   Spacer 5mm

\#   with snow chain free travel

PCCB   drilled, internally vented ceramic brake discs

PSM   Porsche Stability Management

Body					
Monocoque structure, hot-dip galvanised lightweight steel body, partial use of HSLA* steel; airbags and side airbags for driver and passenger; number of seats: 2 + 2					
Drag coefficient (cd)	0.3	0.3	0.3	0.31	0.34
Frontal area A (m²)	1.94	1.94	1.94	2	1.96
Aerodynamic drag cd x A (m2)	0.58	0.58	0.58	0.62	0.67
Dimensions at kerb weight					
Length (mm)	4430	4430	4435	4435	4450
Width (mm)	1770	1765	1765	1830	1830
Height (mm)	1305	1305	1305	1295	1275
Wheelbase (mm)	2350	2350	2350	2350	2355
Track					
front 16+17 inch (mm)	1465	1455	–	–	–
18 inch (mm)	1465	1465	1475	1465	1495
rear 17 inch (mm)	1500	1500	–	–	–
18 inch (mm)	1480	1480	1495	1522	1520
Ground clearance at permissible gross weight (mm)	100	100	100	90	70
Overhang angle					
front (degree)	13	13	13	10	6
rear (degree)	14.5	14.5	14.5	13	13

Model range	Carrera	Carrera 4	Carrera 4S	911 Turbo	911 GT2
Electrical system					
Generator output (W/A)	1680	1680	1680	1680	1680
Battery (V/Ah)	25903	25903	12/36 or 46**	29556	22251
Weight according to DIN 70020					
Kerb weight (kg)					
manual transmission	1345–1480***	1375–1430***	1470–1565***	1540	1440
with Tiptronic	1400–1535***	1420–1475***	1525–1620***	1585	–
Permissible gross weight (kg)					
Man. transm.	1790	1775	1870	1885	1730
Tiptronic					
Permissible trailer weight (kg)					
unbraked	none	=	=	=	=
braked	none	=	=	=	=
Permissible roof load (kg)	35	35	none	none	none
with Porsche System (kg)	75	75	75	75	50
Performance					
Maximum speed (kmh)					
Manual transmission	>280	>280	280	305	315
Tiptronic	>275	>275	275	298	–
Acceleration 0–62mph/100kmh (sec)					
Manual transmission	5	5.2	5.1	4.2	4.1
Tiptronic	5.5	6	5.6	4.9	–
Measured kilometre from standing start (sec)					
Manual transmission	23.8	24.3	24.1	22.4	21.9
Tiptronic	24.6	25.6	25.2	23.9	–
Fluid capacities					
Engine oil quantity 1* (l)	10.25	10.25	10.25	11	11
Oil change quantity (l)	8.75	8.75	8.75	8	7.8
Cooling water (l)	22.5	22.5	22.5	28	28
Manual transmission 2* (l)	2.7	2.7	2.7	3.8	3.8
Front axle 2* (l)	–	1.5	1.5	1.5	–
Automatic transm. 3* (l)	9	9	9	9	–
Final drive, autom. 2* (l)	1.2	1.2	1.2	1.2	–
Fuel tank 4* (l)	64	64	64	64	89
Brake fluid reservoir 5* (l)	0.45	0.63	0.63	0.63	0.64
Power steering fluid 8* (l)	1.27	1.27	1.27	2.14	2.14
Refrigerant 6* (g)	900	900	900	900	900
Refrigerant oil 7* (ml)	195	195	195	195	195
Washer tank (l)	3	3	3	2.5	2.5

Key and key to numerals
* HSLA steel = description used internationally for high-strength, low-alloy steel
** 36Ah without, 46Ah with air conditioning depending on options
*** Depending on equipment
1* Approved engine oils according to ACEA A4-96 specification and special Porsche requirements
2* Life-time filling with BP Olex GO 4927; Life-time filling with MOBILUBE PTX SAE 75 W90
3* Life time filling with ATF SHELL3403-M115
4* Unleaded fuel with minimum standard RON 98/MON 88
5* Use only brake fluid acc. SUPER DOT 4.
6* Only refrigerant R 134 a
7* Commercially available refrigerant oils
8* Pentosin CHF 11 S

Model year 2002

227

Model year 2003
3 Programme, GT3 returns

Porsche 911 Carrera Coupé, Cabriolet and
    Targa
Porsche 911 Carrera 4 Coupé and Cabriolet
Porsche 911 Carrera 4S Coupé
Porsche 911 Turbo
Porsche 911 GT2
Porsche 911 GT3

All 911s produced in model year 2003 were almost identical to those from model year 2002. Such small changes as there were mostly served to make the manufacturing process easier. However, the GT3 made a welcome return this year with a phenomenal power output of 280kW (381hp), and the GT2 received a power boost of 15kW (21hp).

911 GT3

After a break, the focused GT3 returned during the course of the year, both for racing applications and

The new 911 GT3 featured a completely new front end and distinctive 18in alloy wheels.

as a roadgoing version. The naturally aspirated 3,600cc engine now boasted peak output of 280kW (381hp), which made it the most powerful naturally aspirated engine in its class worldwide.

Visually it featured a new front end, which was tested in the wind tunnel, as well as a completely new rear spoiler that distinguished it from its predecessor. The drag coefficient was an impressive 0.30 and its maximum speed was around 190mph (306kmh).

Engine
The M96/79 engine originated from a famous predecessor – the long-distance racing engine of the GT1. Many parts were identical to those used in the 1998 Le Mans 24-hour race-winning engine. A forged eight-bearing steel crankshaft was used that was plasma-nitrided for durability under race conditions.

The con rods were made from forged titanium alloy, and to further increase their durability they were also steel shot-blasted. The surfaces of these compacted con rods were less prone to hairline cracks that could lead to engine damage, especially at very high revs. The engine's limit was set at 8,200rpm. The GT3 easily complied with emission standard Euro 4.

Transmission
The G96/96 six-speed manual transmission was fitted with an oil cooler that used internal oil-spray

cooling. For racing, the ratios of gears two to six could be changed depending on the characteristics of the race circuit.

Suspension
The suspension settings of the GT3 were very sporty. PCCB ceramic brakes were available as an optional extra. The lifespan of the brake pads was significantly longer with PCCB than the standard system with steel disc/friction pads, while the ceramic discs could be expected to last almost as long as the whole car.

Body
The GT3's front and rear ends were clearly different from the Carrera. The front was aerodynamically advanced, the air intakes for the engine cooling and the front brakes being adapted to the GT3's huge potential performance. The rear end with its distinctive fixed rear wing had a big influence on cornering speeds without any negative effect on the drag coefficient (Cd = 0.30).

Clubsport version

Even though special motorsport equipment was permitted on public roads to a certain extent, the Clubsport programme was mostly intended for use on the racetrack. These were some of the optional extras available ex-works:

- Bolt-on half-cage that could be upgraded to a full roll cage for racing applications.
- Flame-resistant racing bucket seats.
- Fire extinguisher.
- Battery main switch (for safety shutdown in an accident).
- Full harness.

911 GT2

During model year 2003, the new-generation 911 GT2 was rolled out. The starting point for the GT2 was as ever, the then-current 911 Turbo. The tweaked twin-turbo engine (M96/70 SL) achieved a peak figure of 355kW (483hp). The suspension was lowered and a new fixed rear wing was installed on the engine lid, while Porsche's PCCB ceramic braking system was now standard.

Engine
Increased power of 355kW (483hp) at 5,700rpm with an engine compression ratio of 9.4:1. Maximum torque of 640Nm was available between 3,500rpm and 4,500rpm. The new GT2 complied with stringent USA exhaust emission regulations by employing four lambda sensors and two cascade catalytic converters, and an OBD II on-board-monitoring system was used.

The rear end of the roadgoing 911 GT3 featured a distinctive fixed rear wing.

The 911 GT3 used a 3.6-litre normally aspirated engine, producing an impressive 280kW (381hp).

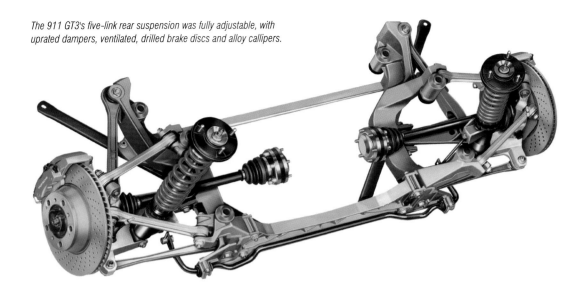

The 911 GT3's five-link rear suspension was fully adjustable, with uprated dampers, ventilated, drilled brake discs and alloy callipers.

Suspension and brakes

Suspension height as well as track and camber were all adjustable. The anti-roll (stabiliser) bars could be exchanged for either stronger or weaker items for special applications.

Unlike many other car manufacturers, Porsche always developed its own brake systems for its

The 911 GT3 could be fitted with the Porsche Ceramic Composite Brake (PCCB) system, with six-piston alloy callipers at the front.

racing and production cars. At the time of changing over from drum brakes to disc brakes at the beginning of the 1960s, Porsche tested inner-action brake discs and fitted them in its type 804 Formula 1 race cars as well as the 356 range. Internally vented and perforated brake discs were developed for the 917 long-distance race car, which reached speeds of 223mph (360kmh) in the turbo version. The brake callipers were made from high-quality light-alloy and had four pistons per calliper. This system was used in

the 911 Turbo and later in other Porsche production cars.

However, another brake system was developed at Weissach as an alternative to grey cast iron discs: brakes made from ceramic composites. One of the advantages of the PCCB (Porsche Composite Ceramic Brake) discs was definitely their lower weight, less than half that of conventional metal discs. As the discs and callipers were part of the unsprung mass of the suspension, driving dynamics were significantly improved. A further advantage was the brakes' resistance to wear and consistent braking efficiency, even at the high operating temperatures that would typically occur in racing applications.

These ceramic discs were furnished with internal cooling ducts that drew in cool air when they were rotating and discharged warm air away from the discs. In addition, bores were drilled in the direction of the internal cooling ducts, which allowed grit and hot gasses to escape during braking. In wet conditions these also allowed the steam that developed while braking to dissipate. The monobloc callipers in the PCCB system were fitted with six pistons at the front, four at the rear. The PCCB system had first seen production in the Porsche Carrera GT roadster, and became standard on the 911 GT2 from 2003. The system was available for all 911 models as an optional extra.

Body

The GT2 made do without rear seats, but air conditioning was still fitted as standard. Various visible parts, such as the exterior rear-view mirror and the rear wing, came unpainted if so desired, so that the carbon surface remained visible. A Clubsport package with a bolt-on roll cage, flame-resistant upholstery, battery main switch and fire extinguisher was available for the motorsport enthusiast.

Additional information

Note that from the start of production in the spring of 2003, the GT3 was listed in the statistics of model year 2004; the GT3 RS is also described in next year's entry.

Model range	Total production
911 Carrera (997)	2
911 Carrera S (997)	9
911 Carrera 2 Coupé (996)	4978
911 Carrera 4 Cabriolet (996)	4973
911 Targa (996)	1812
911 Carrera 4 Coupé (996)	1147
911 Carrera 4 Cabriolet (996)	2930
911 Carrera 4S Coupé (996)	7388
911 Carrera 4S Cabriolet (996)	415
911 Turbo Coupé (996)	5908
911 Turbo Cabriolet (996)	308
911 "40 years 911"	9
911 GT2 (996)	233
911 GT3 (996)	781
911 GT3 RS (996)	4
911 Cup (996)	200

The roadgoing 911 GT3 was designed to be the perfect car for track-day enthusiasts.

Model range	911 Carrera	911 Carrera 4	911 Carrera 4S	911 Turbo	911 GT2	911 GT3
Engine						
Water-cooled six-cylinder boxer engine, engine casing made from light alloy						
Engine type						
Manual transmission	M96/03	M96/03	M96/03	M96/70	M96/70S	M96/79
Tiptronic	M96/04	M96/04	M96/04	M96/70	–	–
Bore (mm)	96	96	96	100	100	100
Stroke (mm)	82.8	82.8	82.8	76.4	76.4	76.4
Displacement (cc)	3596	3596	3596	3600	3600	3600
Compression ratio	11.3:1	11.3:1	11.3:1	9.4:1	9.4:1	11.7:1
Engine output (kW/hp)	235/320	235/320	235/320	309/420	355/483	280/381
at revolutions per minute (rpm)	6800	6800	6800	6000	5700	7400
Torque (Nm)	370	370	370	560	640	385
at revolutions per minute (rpm)	4250	4250	4250	2700–4600	3500–4500	5000
Output per litre (kW/l)	65.3	65.3	65.3	85.8	98.61	77.8
Max. engine speed (rpm)	7300	7300	7300	6750	6800	8200
Type	six-cylinder aluminium boxer engine					
Engine cooling	water	=	=	=	=	=
Crankshaft	forged rotates in 7 journal bearings	=	=	= x 8	= x 8	= x 7
Con rods	steel, forged Length 142 mm			Steel forged	=	Titanium, forged
Cylinder surface	Lokasil	Lokasil	Lokasil	Nikasil	Nikasil	Nikasil
Cylinder head	three-piece	=	=	=	=	=
Valve configuration	2 inlet valves 2 exhaust valves	=	=	=	=	=
inlet valves dia. (mm)	40.2	40.2	40.2	41		
exhaust valves dia. (mm)	34.5	34.5	34.5	35.5		
Valve control, inlet	via adjustable bucket tappets	=	=	=	=	=
Exhaust	directly via bucket tappets	=	=	=	=	=

By 2003, the 911 Carrera Cabriolet was more refined than ever before, and featured a solid-glass heated rear window.

Model range	911 Carrera	911 Carrera 4	911 Carrera 4S	911 Turbo	911 GT2	911 GT3
Engine (continued)						
Valve stroke inlet (mm)	11.0 or 3.6	11.0 or 3.6	11.0 or 3.6	10.0 or 3.6	10.0 or 3.0	12.3
Exhaust (mm)	11	11	11	10	10	11.1
Timing gear	double chain to intermediate shaft Double chains to exhaust camshafts	=	=	double chain to interm. shaft from there via a double chain each to I and E camshafts	gears to Intermediate shaft from there via a double chain each to I and E camshafts	gears to Intermediate shaft from there via a double chain each to I and E camshafts
Variable camshaft settings	VarioCam 42° setting of Intake cams	VarioCam 42° setting of Intake cams	VarioCam 42° setting of Intake cams	VarioCam 30° setting of Intake cams	VarioCam 30° setting of Intake cams	VarioCam Plus 45° setting of Intake cams
Valve-clearance compensation	hydraulic	=	=	=	=	=
Induction system	two-stage resonance system	two-stage resonance system	two-stage resonance system	two-stage resonance system	reson. system	two-stage resonance system
Lubrication system	integrated dry sump	=	=	dry sump (sep. oil tank)	=	=
Oil supply	1 pressure pump 3 suction pumps	1 pressure pump 3 suction pumps	1 pressure pump 3 suction pumps	1 pressure pump 3 suction pumps	1 pressure pump 7 suction pumps	1 pressure pump 3 suction pumps
Engine Weight according to DIN 70020 A (kg)						
Manual transmission (kg)	203.7*	203.7*	203.7***	260*	260***	205***
Tiptronic S (kg)	194**	194**	194***	253**	–	–

Key
*   with underbody panelling, dual-mass flywheel, clutch and air-conditioning compressor
**   with underbody panelling and air-conditioning compressor, without dual-mass flywheel
***   including air-conditioning compressor, fuel cooler, power steering pump, charge-air lines, intercooler, fuel filter, cooling fan, starter and dual-mass flywheel/converter attachment

Carburation, ignition, settings						
For USA: On-board Diagnostic System II, for Europe: Euro III On-board Diagnostic System						
Engine control	Motronic ME 7.8	=	=	=	=	=
Throttle valve management	E-Gas	=	=	=	=	=
Type of fuel (RON)	98	=	=	=	=	=
Ignition system	DME 6 Ignition coils	=	=	=	=	=
Ignition	Single	=	=	=	=	=
Anti-knock control	yes	yes	yes	yes	yes	yes
Number of turbochargers	–	–	–	2	2	–
Spark plugs						
Bosch	FGR 6 KQC	=	=	FR 5 LCD	=	FR 6 LDC
Beru	14-FGR 6 KQU	=	=	14-FR 5 LDU	=	–
Spark plug gap (mm)	1.6+0.2	=	=	0.8 ± 0.1	=	=
Firing order	1-6-2-4-3-5	=	=	=	=	=
Idle speed (rpm)	720 ± 40	720 ± 40	720 ± 40	740 ± 40	740 ± 40	800 ± 40
Exhaust/purification system	2 BLS + DWMK USA: + ZLP	= USA: + ZLP	2 BLS + DWMK	2 BLS + DWMK	=	=
CO-content						
without cat. conv. (%)	0.5–1.0	0.5–1.0	0.5–1.0			
with cat. conv. (%)	0.4–1.2	0.4–1.2	0.4–1.2			
Fuel consumption acc. 93/116/EC (litres/100km)						
Manual transmission						
urban	16.1	16.3	16.3	18.9	18.9	18.9
extra-urban	8.1	8.3	8.5	9.2	9.3	9.0
combined	11.1	11.3	11.4	12.9	12.9	12.9
Target value CO_2 (g/km)	269	274	277	309	309	315
Emission standard	Euro3/D4	Euro3/D4	Euro3/D4	Euro3/D4	Euro3/D4	Euro3/D4
Tiptronic						
urban	16.9	18.1	21.9	21.9	–	–
extra-urban	8.1	8.7	8.9	9.6	–	–
combined	11.3	11.9	12.1	13.9	–	–
Target value CO_2 (g/km)	274	289	294	339	–	–
Emission standard	Euro3/D4	Euro3/D4	Euro3/D4	Euro3/D4	–	–

Key:
2 BLS   Two heated lambda sensors with stereo control
DME S   Digital engine electronic system with sequential fuel injection
DWMK   Three-way metal-based catalytic converter
KFZ   Pressure-controlled mapped ignition
SLE   Secondary-air injection
ZLP   Auxiliary air pump

Model range	911 Carrera	911 Carrera 4	911 Carrera 4S	911 Turbo	911 GT2	911 GT3
Transmission						

Engine and gearbox are built as one drive unit.
The hydraulically operated dry single-disc clutch is bolted onto the dual-mass flywheel.
Drive configuration Carrera 2, 911 GT2 and 911 GT3: via dual propshafts to the rear wheels.
Drive configuration Carrera 4, Carrera 4S and 911 Turbo: Connection to gearbox via driveshaft to front differential.
Rear and front wheels are driven via dual propshafts.
Available as optional extra (not 911 GT2 and GT3) : 5-gear Tiptronic transmission with torque converter.

Model range	911 Carrera	911 Carrera 4	911 Carrera 4S	911 Turbo	911 GT2	911 GT3
Dual-mass flywheel	Syst LUK	=	=	=	=	=
Clutch, pressure plate	MF 228X MF 240	=	=	=	=	=
Clutch plate (mm)	rigid	=	=	=	=	=
dia. (mm)	240	=	=	=	=	=
Manual transmission	G 96/01	G 96/31	G 96/31	G 96/50	G 96/88	G 96/96
Gear ratios						
1st gear	3.82	3.82	3.82	3.82	3.82	3.82
2nd gear	2.20	2.20	2.20	2.05	2.05	2.15
3rd gear	1.52	1.52	1.52	1.41	1.41	1.56
4th gear	1.22	1.22	1.22	1.12	1.12	1.00
5th gear	1.02	1.02	1.02	0.92	0.92	1.00
6th gear	0.84	0.84	0.84	0.75	0.75	0.85
Reverse gear	3.55	3.55	3.55	2.86	2.86	2.86
Synchromesh system						
Forward gears	VK	VK	VK	VK	VK	VK
Reverse gear	VK	VK	VK	VK	VK	VK
Final drive, ratio	3.44	3.44	3.44	3.44	3.44	3.44
Limited-slip differential	–	no	no	no	no	standard
Lock-up factor under load/ coasting (%)	–	–	–	–	–	–
Gearbox weight with oil (kg)	65	66	66	72	74	73.5
All-wheel drive	no	From the transmission at the rear via driveshaft to the viscous clutch and to the front differential			no	no
Front-wheel drive transmission	no	Z96/35	Z96/35	Z96/00	no	no
Front axle ratio	–	3.44	3.44	3.44	–	–
FA transmission weight (kg)	–	23	23	23	–	–
Tiptronic S	A96/10	A96/35	A96/35	A96/50	not available	=
Torque converter dia.(mm)	282	282	282	282	–	–
Start-off conversion ratio	1.92	1.85	1.85	1.92	–	–
Stall speed (rpm)	2450	2450	2450	2600	–	–
Gear ratios						
1st gear	3.60	3.60	3.60	3.59	–	–
2nd gear	2.19	2.19	2.19	2.19	–	–
3rd gear	1.41	1.41	1.41	1.41	–	–
4th gear	1.00	1.00	1.00	1.00	–	–
5th gear	0.83	0.83	0.83	0.83	–	–
Reverse gear	3.17	3.17	3.17	3.16	–	–
Final drive, ratio	3.37	3.37	3.37	2.889	–	–
Limited-slip differential	no	no	no	no	–	–
Stability Management PSM	Option	Standard	Standard	Standard	–	–
Gearbox weight with oil and ATF filling (kg)	122.6	112.6	112.6	116.5	–	–
All-wheel drive	no	From the transmission at the rear via driveshaft to the viscous clutch and to the front differential			–	–
Front-wheel drive transmission	no	Z 96/35	Z 96/35	Z 96/00	–	–
Front axle ratio	–	3.37	3.37	2.883	–	–
FA transmission weight (kg)	–	23	23	23	–	–

Key:
ABD   Automatic brake differential
PSM   Porsche Stability Management
Syst.LUK   Dual-mass flywheel system LUK (steel-spring damped)
TC   Traction control
VK   Full-cone synchromesh system with molybdenum-coated synchroniser rings

Model range	911 Carrera	911 Carrera 4	911 Carrera 4S	911 Turbo	911 GT2	911 GT3
Suspension, steering and brakes						
Front suspension	Individually suspended on wishbones, semi-trailing arms and spring struts (MacPherson design, optimised by Porsche); one conical spring per wheel with internal shock absorber;					
Shock absorbers	dual function hydraulic dual-struts gas-pressure shock absorber					
Anti-roll bar dia. (mm)	23.1 x 3.4	22.5 x 3.5	22.5 x 3.5	23.6 x 3.6	26.8 x 4	26.8 x 4
Steering ratio	16.9 : 1	=	=	=	=	=
Turning circle dia. (m)	10.6	=	=	=	=	=
Rear suspension	Multi-wishbone rear suspension, individually suspended on five wishbones, one cylinder coil spring per wheel					
Shock absorbers	dual function hydraulic single-strut gas-pressure shock absorber					
Anti-roll bar dia. (mm)	18.5 x 2.5	19.6 x 2.6	20.7 x 2.8	21.7 x 3.0	20.7 x 2.8	20.7 x 2.8
Brake system	Hydraulic dual-circuit brake system with aluminium monobloc brake callipers on all wheels, internally vented brake discs on all wheels, ABS standard					
PSM	M	S	S	S	only ABS	only ABS
Brake booster ratio	3.85	3.85	3.85	3.85	3.15	3.15
Brake master cylinder dia. (mm)	23.81	23.81	25.4	25.4	25.4	25.4
Pressure reducer	yes	yes	no	no	no	no
Cut-in pressure (bar)	55	55	–	–	–	–
Reduction factor	0.46	0.46	–	–	–	–
Brake calliper piston diameter						
front (mm)	36 + 40	36 + 40	44 + 34	36 + 44	38+32+28	38+32+28
rear (mm)	28 + 30	28 + 30	30 + 28	28 + 30	30 + 28	
Brake disc diameter						
front (mm)	318	318	330	330	350 PCCB	350
rear (mm)	299	299	330	330	350 PCCB	350
Brake disc thickness						
front (mm)	28	28	34	34	34	34
rear (mm)	24	24	28	28	28	28
Effective brake disc area (cm^2)	450	450	568	568	696	696
Handbrake	Operating mechanically on both rear wheels					
Brake drum diameter (mm)	180	=	=	=	=	=
Contact area (cm^2)	170	=	=	=	=	=

Wheels and tyres	911 Carrera	911 Carrera 4	911 Carrera 4S	911 Turbo	911 GT2	911 GT3
Standard tyre specification, front	205/50ZR17	205/50ZR17	225/40ZR18	225/40ZR18	235/40ZR18	235/40ZR18
wheel	7J x 17	7J x 17	8J x 18	8J x 18	8.5J x 18	8.5J x 18
hump depth (mm)	50	55	50	50	40	40
optional	225/40ZR18	225/40ZR18	–	–	–	–
wheel	8J x 18	8J x 18				
hump depth (mm)	50	50				
Winter tyres	205/50R1789T	205/50R1789T	225/40R1888H	225/40R1888H	225/40R1888H	225/40R1888H
wheel	7J x 17	7J x 17	8J x 18	8J x 18	8J x 18	8J x 18
hump depth (mm)	55	55	50	50	50	50
Standard tyre specification, rear	255/40ZR17	255/40ZR17	295/30ZR18	295/30ZR18	315/30ZR18	295/30ZR18
wheel	9J x 17	9J x 17	11J x 18	11J x 18	12J x 18	11J x 18
hump depth (mm)	55	55	45	45	45	63
optional	285/30ZR18	285/30ZR18	–	–	–	–
wheel	10J x 18	10J x 18	–	–	–	–
hump depth (mm)	65	65				
Winter tyres	225/45R1790T	255/40R1794H	265/35R1893H	265/35R1893H	265/35R1893H	265/35R1893H
wheel	8.5J x 17	9J x 17	10J x 18	10J x 18	10J x 18	10J x 18
hump depth (mm)	50	50	47#	47#	47#	65
Space saver high-pressure tyre	105/95-R17*	–	–	–	–	–
Space-saver spare wheel	–	165/70-1692P	Tyre Mobility System*	165/70-1692P	Tyre Mobility System*	=
Tyre pressure						
front (bar)	2.5	2.5	2.2	2.5	2.2	N/A
rear (bar)	2.5	2.5	2.7	–	–	-
with 18" tyres rear (bar)	3.0	3.0	2.7	3.0	2.7	N/A
High-pressure tyre/space-saver spare wheel (bar)	4.2*	2.5*	2.2 or 2.7*	2.5	2.2 or 2.7*	=

Key:
* The 911 Carrera 2 (996) had an inflated high-pressure tyre while the 911 Carrera 4 (996) had a space-saver spare wheel that needed to be inflated by means of an on-board compressor when required. The GT3 had no proper 'spare wheel'.
** Spacer 5mm
# with snow chain free travel
PCCB drilled, internally vented ceramic brake discs
PSM Porsche Stability Management

Model range	911 Carrera	911 Carrera 4	911 Carrera 4S	911 Turbo	911 GT2	911 GT3
Body						
Monocoque structure, hot-dip galvanised lightweight steel body, partial use of HSLA* steel; airbags and side airbags for driver and passenger; number of seats: 2 + 2						
Drag coefficient (cd)	0.30	0.30	0.30	0.31	0.34	0.30
Frontal area A (m²)	1.94	1.94	1.94	2.00	1.96	1.95
Aerodynamic drag cd x A (m²)	0.582	0.582	0.582	0.62	0.67	0.585
Dimensions at kerb weight						
Length (mm)	4430	4430	4435	4435	4450	4435
Width (mm)	1770	1765	1765	1830	1830	1770
Height (mm)	1305	1305	1305	1295	1275	1275
Wheelbase (mm)	2350	2350	2350	2350	2355	2355
Track						
front 16 + 17 inch (mm)	1465	1455	–	–	–	–
18 inch (mm)	1465	1465	1475	1465	1495	1488
rear 17 inch (mm)	1500	1500	–	–	–	–
18 inch (mm)	1480	1480	1495	1522	1520	
Ground clearance at permissible gross weight (mm)	100	100	100	90	70	75
Overhang angle						
front (degree)	13	13	13	10	6.0	7.0
rear (degree)	14.5	14.5	14.5	13	13.0	13.0
Electrical system						
Generator output (W/A)	1680	1680	1680	1680	1680	1680
Battery (V/Ah)	12/70	12/70	12/36 or 46**	12/80	12/60	12/60
Weight according to DIN 70020						
Kerb weight (kg)						
Manual transmission	1345–1480***	1375–1430***	1470–1565***	1540	1440	1360
Tiptronic	1400–1535***	1420–1475***	1535–1620***	1585	–	–
Permissible gross weight with (kg)						
Manual transmission	1790	1775	1870	1885	1730	1660
Tiptronic	1765	1910	1925	1930	–	–
Permissible trailer weight (kg)						
unbraked	none	=	=	=	=	=
braked	none	=	=	=	=	=
Permissible roof load (kg)	35	35	none	none	none	35
with Porsche System (kg)	75	75	75	75	50	75
Performance						
Maximum speed (kmh)						
Manual transmission	>280	>280	280	305	315	306
Tiptronic	>275	>275	275	298	–	–
Acceleration 0–62mph/100 kmh (sec)						
Manual transmission	5.0	5.2	5.1	4.2	4.1	4.5
Tiptronic	5.5	6.0	5.6	4.9	–	–
Measured kilometre from standing start (sec)						
Manual transmission	23.8	24.3	24.1	22.4	21.9	22.8
Tiptronic	24.6	35.6	25.2	23.9	–	–
Fluid capacities						
Engine oil quantity 1* (l)	10.25	10.25	10.25	11.0	11.0	12
Oil change quantity (l)	8.75	8.75	8.75	8.0	7.8	9
Cooling water (l)	22.5	22.5	22.5	28	28	28
Manual transmission 2* (l)	2.7	2.7	2.7	3.8	3.8	3.3
Front axle 2* (l)	..	1.5	1.5	1.5	–	–
Automatic transm. 3* (l)	9.0	9.0	9.0	9.0	–	–
Final drive, autom. 2* (l)	1.2	1.2	1.2	1.2	–	–
Fuel tank 4* (l)	64	64	64	64	89	89
Brake fluid reservoir 5* (l)	0.45	0.63	0.63	0.63	0.63	0.63
Power steering fluid 8* (l)	1.27	1.27	1.27	2.14	2.14	1.27
Refrigerant 6* (g)	900	900	900	900	900	900
Refrigerant oil 7* (ml)	195	195	195	195	195	195
Washer tank (l)	3.0	3.0	3.0	2.5	2.5	3.0

Key and key to numerals
* HSLA steel = description used internationally for high-strength, low-alloy steel
** 36Ah without, 46Ah with air conditioning
***Depending on options
1* Approved engine oils according to ACEA A4-96 specification and special Porsche requirements (see technical information for engine oils)
2* Life-time filling with BP Olex GO 4927;
3* Life-time filling with SHELL ATF 3403-M115
4* Unleaded fuel with at least RON 98/MON 88
5* Use only brake fluid acc. SUPER DOT 4.
6* Only refrigerant R 134 a
7* Commercially available refrigerant oils
8* Pentosin CHF 11 S

Model year 2004

4 Programme, Turbo Cabriolet, '40 years of 911' special edition

Porsche 911 Carrera Coupé, Cabriolet and Targa

Porsche 911 Carrera Coupé '40 years of 911' special edition

Porsche 911 Carrera 4 Coupé and Cabriolet

Porsche 911 Carrera 4S Coupé

Porsche 911 Turbo Coupé and Cabriolet

Porsche 911 Turbo S Coupé and Cabriolet

Porsche 911 GT2 Coupé

Porsche 911 GT3 Coupé

Porsche 911 GT3 RS Coupé

In model year 2004 many new 911 versions were reintroduced or became available in a higher performance variant. The two stars of the new model range were undoubtedly the 911 Turbo Cabriolet and the 911 GT3 RS, the latter being an even more focused version of the GT3 and, despite being developed for motorsport applications, remaining perfectly legal on public roads.

Once again there was an anniversary model: the '40 years of 911' edition. This special car had many comfort-enhancing features but also more power to brag about: an engine with 254kW (345hp).

Engine

Since the last air-cooled 911s left the factory at the end of model year 1998, Porsche had successfully concentrated its efforts on increasing the performance of its water-cooled engines. The powerplant of the 40th anniversary 911 model produced 19kW (25hp) more than the regular Carrera – up to 254kW (345hp). As for the 911 Turbo S M96/70 E engine, that increased by 30hp to 331kW (450hp) and its torque rose from 560 to 620Nm.

Fuel, ignition and exhaust systems

During the process of increasing engine performance, the fuel and ignition systems also required certain modifications. Exhaust emission limits became even more stringent in model year 2004, which necessitated detailed improvements in the lambda control system and the catalytic converters.

Transmission

No noteworthy modifications to the six-speed manual transmission or the automatic five-speed Tiptronic S for production vehicles.

The 911 Turbo Cabriolet was a particularly striking looking car, with 331kW (450hp) available in Turbo S form.

ABOVE: The 911 Turbo Cabriolet was equipped with driver's, passenger's and side airbags as standard.

BELOW: The Turbo Cabriolet featured an electrically operated roof comprising cloth-covered steel sections.

911 Turbo Cabriolet

The 911 Turbo Cabriolet was produced for the first time between 1987 and 1989, when its turbo engine achieved 221kW (300hp) with a maximum speed of 161mph (260kmh). Whether as a result of low demand or a change in company philosophy is not clear, but either way it took Porsche 15 years to produce a 911 with both a turbocharger and convertible roof again.

If you so wished, the new version allowed you to enjoy driving with the top down at more than 186mph (300kmh), with 105kW (150hp) more than the first Turbo Cabriolet. The wide body of the 911 Turbo was the basis of the bodyshell, with a significantly reinforced undercarriage to compensate for the loss of rigidity from having no roof structure. Even without the steel roof, the Turbo Cabriolet was some 70kg heavier than the fixed-head car.

Engine
The same engines were used as for the standard Turbo Coupé: the M96/70 unit with 309kW (420hp) and, in Turbo S form, the more powerful M96/70 E engine with 331kW (450hp).

Transmission
The G96/50 six-speed manual transmission and the A96/50 five-speed Tiptronic transmission were adopted unchanged from the Turbo Coupé. Of course, the Turbo Cabriolet was also fitted with all-wheel drive.

Body
While the convertible roof of the Cabriolet looked s if it was all cloth, 50% of it consisted of shaped steel sheet sections (tap the roof with your knuckles and you could instantly feel this). Passengers sitting in the rear were protected from the car overturning by automatically extending roll bars in the bulkhead area between the passenger cell and engine, which could deploy whether the roof was up or down. All Cabriolets had been equipped with these roll bars as standard from model year 1998 (the start of production of the 996 model). In addition, Porsche POSIP side airbags were installed as standard.

911 GT3 RS

The basis of the GT3 RS was, of course, the standard GT3. In order for a class of vehicle to be granted homologation for racing, a certain number of vehicles had to be produced within the space of one year, and for the GT (Gran Turismo) class the required number was 200 (this figure has since been reduced to 25). For racing applications these cars had to be fitted with a roll cage, safety tanks and fire extinguishers to homologate them: for example, deviations from the production vehicle were not permitted in racing classes GT2 and GT3.

The GT3 RS was a competition vehicle that was also road-legal. It conformed to the various regulations of the FIA-N/GT for Europe and the ACO for North America. The suspension was lowered by 30mm compared to the Carrera and was extremely sporty in its specification. The more powerful M96/79 sports engine with precisely 3,600cc corresponded exactly to the sports regulations and achieved 280kW (381hp) at 7,400rpm. The top speed was 190mph (306kmh), with acceleration from 0–62mph (0–100kmh) in 4.4 seconds. The 911 GT3 RS was equipped with a dual-mass flywheel and six-speed manual transmission.

Engine
The increase in output from the earlier 911 GT3's 265kW (360hp) to 280kW (381hp) from the same engine size (3,600cc) was achieved firstly through a higher engine rev redline, and also through an improved Variocam system that allowed for an intake camshaft setting of 45°. Bosch Motronic 7.8 engine management calculated the optimal intake camshaft settings depending on the loading and made changes hydraulically. Since the opening angle of the throttle valve was now controlled by the E-gas system, Motronic calculated the position of the throttle valve, the injected fuel quantity and the ignition timing. Because the metal catalytic converters, which were significantly more effective, treated the exhaust gases and the four lambda sensors were continuously reporting the residual oxygen content in the exhaust gas flow to the Motronic, the GT3 was a vehicle that complied with the stringent Euro 4 exhaust emission regulations and was even classed as an LEV (low emission vehicle) in the USA.

Transmission
Despite its extremely focused character, the GT3 RS had a dual-mass flywheel that dampened vibrations at low engine revs. The transmission itself was identical to that of the other naturally aspirated 911 cars: a cable-operated six-speed manual transmission with limited-slip differential (type G96/96). However, in accordance with the performance of the car, the gear ratios were adapted to racing applications.

Suspension, steering and brakes
The internally vented brake discs were perforated and had a diameter of 350mm at the front and 330mm at the rear. The monobloc brake callipers at the front were fitted with six pistons and those at the rear with four. The ceramic brake disc PCCB braking system was available as an optional extra, and for visual differentiation the brake callipers were painted yellow.

The 911 GT3 RS was a lightweight road-legal competition car, available only in white, with red or blue 'GT3 RS' script.

Wheels and tyres

On the 911 GT3 RS, 18in aluminium wheels with ten spokes were fitted as standard. At the front 8.5Jx18 wheels with a hump depth of 40mm and

The 911 Turbo Cabriolet featured a discreet 'turbo' logo on the speedometer dial face.

235/40 ZR 18 tyres were used, at the rear 11Jx18 wheels with hump depth of 63mm and 295/30 ZR 18 tyres.

Body

The body of the GT3 RS was markedly different from that of the standard Carrera. The nose and rear end were modified in that, as with the GT2, the cooling air streaming in after flowing past the radiator was no longer guided underneath the car, where it would heat up the floorpan, the gearbox and the engine, but instead streamed out above

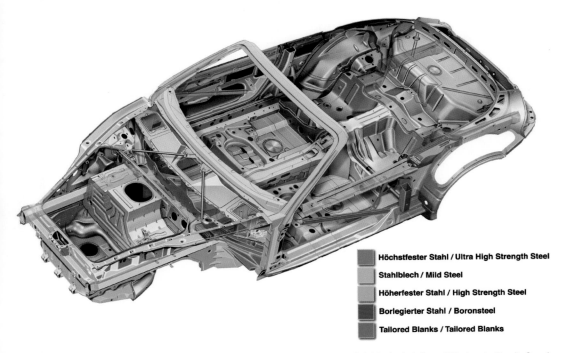

	Höchstfester Stahl / Ultra High Strength Steel
	Stahlblech / Mild Steel
	Höherfester Stahl / High Strength Steel
	Borlegierter Stahl / Boronsteel
	Tailored Blanks / Tailored Blanks

the luggage compartment at the front and over the windscreen.

The GT3's new fixed rear wing not only reduced the drag coefficient Cd to 0.30 but also put a higher load on the driven rear wheels through aerodynamic downforce. For weight-saving reasons any form of rear seating was omitted. All GT3 RS cars were painted in Carrera White, but there was a choice of 'GT3 RS' script in either blue or red.

'40 years of 911' special edition

Although Porsche rolled out its first 911 cars to customers in 1964, the 911 had first been presented to a rapt audience at the IAA show in Frankfurt in the autumn of 1963. A limited number of more powerful 40th anniversary Coupés was therefore produced from 2003 as model year 2004 cars. The bodyshell of the standard Carrera formed the basis, but the special edition had a nose with larger air intakes for cooling the more powerful engine, and the side inlet grilles were painted in the uniform body colour, GT Silver Metallic. All vehicles were fitted with an electrically operating sliding roof that could be lifted at the back for improved ventilation.

Engine

The anniversary model was equipped with a more powerful engine (M96/03 S) with an additional 25hp (254kW, 345hp).

The 911 Turbo Cabriolet bodyshell was 70kg heavier than its Coupé counterpart due to the need for a stiffer structure.

Transmission

The anniversary model was fitted exclusively with a six-speed transmission, and a friction-plate limited-slip differential was standard. PSM stability management was also part of the standard equipment.

Additional information

The new-generation 997 model made its first appearance in July 2004 but is covered in the 2005 model-year section.

Model range	Total production
911 Carrera (997)	1464
911 Carrera S (997)	1917
911 Carrera Coupé (996)	1866
911 Carrera Cabriolet (996)	2809
911 Targa (996)	508
911 "40 years 911"	1527
911 Carrera 4 Coupé (996)	362
911 Carrera 4 Cabriolet (996)	355
911 Carrera 4S Coupé (996)	4365
911 Carrera 4S Cabriolet (996)	4543
911 Turbo Coupé (996)	1273
911 Turbo Cabriolet (996)	3099
911 Turbo S Coupé	2
911 Turbo S Cabriolet	3
911 GT3 (996)	1532
911 GT3 RS (996)	678
911 GT2 (996)	73
911 Cup (996)	150

Engine

Water-cooled six-cylinder boxer engine, engine casing made from light alloy

Model range	911 Carrera 911 Targa **	911 Carrera "40 years 911"	911 Carrera 4S	911 Turbo	911 Turbo S	911 GT2	911 GT3	911 GT3 RS
Engine type	M96/03 for man. transm. M96/04* for Tiptronic	M96/03 S man. transm. M96/04 S*	M96/03 man. transm. M96/04*	M96/70	M96/70E	M96/70SL	M96/79	M96/79
Displacement (cc)	3596	=	=	3600	=	=	=	=
Bore (mm)	96	=	=	100	=	=	=	=
Stroke (mm)	82.5	=	=	76.4	=	=	=	=
Compression ratio	11.3:1	11.3:1	11.3:1	9.4:1	=	=	11.7:1	=
Engine output (kW/hp)	235 (320)	254 (345)	235 (320)	309 (420)	331 (450)	355 (483)	280 (381)	=
at revolutions per min. (rpm)	6800	6800	6800	6000	5700	5700	7400	
Torque (Nm)	370	370	370	560	620	640	385	=
at revolutions per min. (rpm)	4250	4800	4250	2700–4600	3500–4500	3500–4500	5000	=
Output per litre (kW/l)	65.35	70.63	65.35	85.8	91.4	98.6	77.8	=
Max. engine speed (rpm)	7300	=		6750	=	=	7800	=
Type	six-cylinder four-stroke boxer engine							
Engine cooling	water	=	=	=	=	=	=	=
Crankshaft	steel, forged	=	=	=	=	=	=	=
Crankshaft bearings	x 7	=	=	x 8	=	=	=	=
Con rods	steel, forged	=	=	=	=	=	=	=
Cylinder surface	NIKASIL	=	=	=	=	=	=	=
Cylinder head type	2 OHC + 4 OHV	=	=	=	=	=	=	=
Config. of inlet valves	2 overhead	=	=	=	=	=	=	=
Config. of exhaust valves	2 overhead	=	=	=	=	=	=	=
Camshaft drive	Spur gears + chain	=	=	=	=	=	=	=
Variable camshaft settings	VarioCam Plus	=	=	=	=	=	=	=
Induction system	Var.induct. syst.	=	=	rigid	=	=	Var.induct. syst.	=
Turbocharging	–	–	–	2 ATL+2LLK	=	=	–	–
Exhaust system	stand. exhaust silencer	=	=	=	=	=	Sports exh. silencer	=
Exhaust gas control EURO II	Lambda control 3-way catalytic conv	=	=	2 DWK 4LS	=	=	4LS+ 2 DWK	=
Exhaust gas control EURO III	Second. air + readjustm.with 4 Lambda sensors	=	=	=	=	=	=	=
Exhaust gas control USA	plus cascade type cat. conv. +OBD II	=	=	=	=	=	=	=
Lubrication system	dry sump with integrated oil tank	=	=	dry sump with separate oil tank	=	=	=	=
Oil cooling	Oil-water heat exchanger	=	=	=	=	=	=	=
Engine weight dry (kg)	204 with ZMS	=	=	259 with aggregates	=	=	205	=

The silver '40 years of 911' model was produced in 2004 to celebrate the 40th anniversary of the car.

Model range	911 Carrera 911 Targa **	911 Carrera "40 years 911"	911 Carrera 4S	911 Turbo	911 Turbo S	911 GT2	911 GT3	911 GT3 RS
Carburation, ignition, settings								
Engine Managem. System	DME (Digital engine electronic system) ME 7.8; ignition, fuel injection, camshaft control							
Fuel injection	sequential, multi-point	=	=	=	=	=	=	=
Fuel quality	Super Plus	=	=	=	=	=	=	=
Octane rating RON	98 unleaded	=	=	=	=	=	=	=
Throttle adjustment	electronic E-gas	=	=	=	=	=	=	=
Ignition	electronic	=	=	=	=	=	=	=
Distributor	solid-state distr. syst.	=	=	=	=	=	=	=
Spark plugs manufacturer	Beru	=	=	=	=	=	Bosch	=
Type	14-FGR 6 KQU	=	=	14-FR 6 LDU	=	=	FT6LCD	=
Spark plug gap	1.6±0.2	=	=	0.8	=	=	0.8	=
Firing order	1-6-2-4-3-5	=	=	=	=	=	=	=

Key and abbreviations:

M96/04*   Engine number with * = engine specifically for Tiptronic S.

911 Targa ** 911 Targa and 911 Targa 4 are independent vehicle types that differ from 911 Carrera 4 and Carrera 4S with respect to body as well as other technical details.

ATL   Exhaust turbocharger.

DWK   Three-way catalytic converter. The DWK can burn hydro-carbon, carbon monoxide and nitrogen oxide in the exhaust utilising the lambda sensor.

EURO II   European emission standard from 1996 (HC + NOx max. 0.50g/km, CO max. 2.20g/km).

EURO III   European emission standard from 2000 (HC max. 0.20g/km, NOx max. 0.15g/km, CO max. 2.3g/km).

LOKASIL   Running surface technology for cylinder walls. Silicon is enriched in the running surface area when the engine block is cast.

LS   Lambda sensor, measures the remaining oxygen content in hot exhaust gases.

NIKASIL   Light-alloy cylinder with piston surface coated with nickel-silicon-carbide.

OBD II   Regulation with respect to electronic data storage of malfunctioning of the monitored emission system according to the State of California, USA. If an error is detected, a malfunction indicator light (MIL) flashes in order to alert the driver to the identified malfunction and to save the respective error code in the system.

RoW   Abbreviation for "Vehicle for rest of world", including Germany.

RON   Octane number (anti-knock properties of the fuel) R = Research method, the acceleration pinging is measured.

USA   Vehicles for the North American market, including Canada.

W   Heat rating (of the spark plug).

ZMS   Dual mass flywheel for the avoidance of torsional vibration in the drive train at low engine revolutions.

2 OHC   OHC = overhead camshaft. 2 OHC = twin overhead camshafts in the cylinder head.

4 OHV   OHV = overhead valves, 4 OHV 4 valves per combustion chamber (2 inlet and 2 exhaust valves).

Model range	911 Carrera 911 Targa **	911 Carrera "40 years 911"	911 Carrera 4S	911 Turbo	911 Turbo S	911 GT2	911 GT3	911 GT3 RS
Transmission								
Engine and gearbox are built as one drive unit.								
The hydraulically operated dry single-plate clutch is bolted on to the dual-mass flywheel.								
Drive configuration Carrera 2, 911 GT2 and 911 GT3: via dual propshafts to the rear wheels.								
Drive configuration Carrera 4, Carrera 4S and 911 Turbo: connection to the front differential via driveshaft.								
Rear and front wheels are driven via dual propshafts.								
Available as optional extra (not 911 GT2 and GT3) : 5-gear Tiptronic transmission with torque converter.								
Clutch dual-mass flywheel	yes, system LUK	=	=	=	=	=	=	=
Clutch, pressure plate	MF 228X MF 240	=	=	=	=	=	=	=
Clutch plate (mm)	rigid	=	=	=	=	=	=	=
dia. (mm)	240	=	=	=	=	=	=	=
Manual transmission	G96/01	=	G96/31	G96/50	=	G96/88	G96/96	=
Gearbox design	fully synchronised 6-speed manual transmission							
Number of gears forward/reverse	6/1	=	=	=	=	=	=	=
Gear ratios								
1st gear	3.91	=	3.82	3.82	=	=	=	=
2nd gear	2.32	=	2.20	2.05	=	=	2.15	=
3rd gear	1.61	=	1.52	1.41	=	=	1.56	=
4th gear	1.28	=	1.22	1.12	=	=	1.21	=
5th gear	1.08	=	1.02	0.92	=	=	1.00	=
6th gear	0.88	=	0.84	0.75	=	=	0.85	=
Synchromesh system	VK	=	=	=	=	=	=	=
Reverse gear	-3.59	=	-3.55	-2.86	=	=	=	=
Final drive ratio, rear axle	3.44	=	=	=	=	=	=	=
Final drive ratio, front axle	–	–	3.44	=	=	–	–	–
Limited-slip differential Acceleration/coasting	Option 40/40	Option	Option	Option	Option	Standard	Standard	=
Oil cooler	no	=	=	S	=	=	=	=
Gearbox weight with oil (kg)	54	=	=	56	=	=	54	=
Tiptronic S type	A96/10	=	A96/35	A96/50	=	–	–	–
Gearbox design	Md-Converter + 5-speed planetary gear	=	=	=	=			
Torque converter dia. (mm)	270	=	=	=	=			
Stall speed (rpm)	2650	=	=	2600	=			
Number of gears forward/reverse	5/2	=	=	=	=			
1st gear	3.60	=	=	3.59	=			
2nd gear	2.19	=	=	2.19	=			
3rd gear	1.41	=	=	1.41	=			
4th gear	1.00	=	=	1.00	=			
5th gear	0.83	=	=	0.83	=			
Reverse gear	1.93/3.16	=	1.93/3.16	=	N/A	N/A	N/A	N/A
Final drive ratio, rear axle	3.37	=	2.88	=	N/A	N/A	N/A	N/A
Weight with converter + cooling (kg)	115.3	=	=	125.3	=			

Model range	911 Carrera 911 Targa **	911 Carrera "40 years 911"	911 Carrera 4S	911 Turbo	911 Turbo S	911 GT2	911 GT3	911 GT3 RS
Suspension, steering and brakes								
Front suspension: Individually suspended on wishbones with semi-trailing arms and MacPherson spring struts; one conical spring per wheel with internal shock absorber; dual-function hydraulic gas-pressure shock absorbers; Rear suspension: Multi-wishbone rear suspension with five wishbones per wheel, cylindrical coil springs with internal shock absorbers, dual-function hydraulic gas pressure shock absorbers. Steering: Hydraulic rack-and-pinion steering. Brakes: power-assisted hydraulic-mechanical dual-circuit brake system with monobloc brake callipers. Internally ventilated brake discs. ABS standard and PSM optional.								
Anti-roll bar dia. front (mm)	23.1 x 3.4 tube	= tube	22.5 x 3.5 tube	23.6 x 3.5 tube	26.8 x 4 or stronger	=	26.8 x 4.0	N/A
Anti-roll bar dia. rear (mm)	18.5 x 2.5 tube	= tube	19.6 x 2.6 tube	21.7 x 3.0 tube	20.7 x 2.8 or stronger	=	20.7 x 2.8	N/A
Steering ratio	16.9:1	=	=	=	=	=	=	=
Turning circle dia. (mm)	10.6	=	=	=	=	=	=	=
Brake system								
Brake circuit configuration	per axle	=	=	=	=	=	=	=
Brake master cylinder dia. (mm)	23.81	=	23.81	25.4	=	=	=	=
Brake calliper piston diameter								
front (mm)	36+40	=	=	=	38 + 32 + 28	38 + 32 + 28	38 + 32 + 28	N/A
rear (mm)	28+30	=	=	=	=	=	=	=
Brake disc dia.								
front (mm)	318	=	=	330	=	350	350	=
rear (mm)	299	=	=	330	=	350	350	=
Brake disc thickness								
front (mm)	28	=	=	34	=	34	34	=
rear (mm)	24	=	=	28	=	28	28	=
Effective brake area (cm²)	450	=	=	568	=	698	698	=
PCCB	–	–	–	Option	Option	Standard	Option	Option
Wheels and tyres								
Standard tyre specification, front	205/50ZR17	225/40ZR18	225/40ZR18	225/40ZR18	=	235/40ZR18	=	
wheel (rim)/ hump depth	7J x 17/50	8J x 18/50	8J x 18/50	=	=	8.5J x 18/40 =	=	
Standard tyre specification, rear	255/40ZR17	285/30ZR18	295/30ZR18	295/30ZR18	=	315/30ZR18	=	N/A
wheel (rim)/ hump depth	9J x 17/55	10J x 18/65	11J x 18/45	=	=	12J x 18/45	11J x 18/63	=
Option tyres front	225/40ZR18	–	–	–	–	–	N/A	N/A
wheel (rim)/ hump depth	8J x 18/50	–	–	–	–	–	N/A	N/A
Option tyres rear	285/30ZR18	–	–	–	–	–	N/A	N/A
wheel (rim)/ hump depth	10J x 18/65	–	–	–	–	–	N/A	N/A

Key:
PCCB   Porsche Composite Ceramic Brake

	911 Carrera 911 Targa **	911 Carrera "40 years 911"	911 Carrera 4S	911 Turbo	911 Turbo S	911 GT2	911 GT3	911 GT3 RS
Body								
Monocoque structure, hot-dip galvanised lightweight steel body, partial use of HSLA* steel; airbags and side airbags for driver and passenger; number of seats: 2 + 2								
Drag coefficient (cd)	0.30	=	=	0.31	=	0.34	0.30	0.30
Frontal area A (m²)	1.94	=	=	2.00	=	1.96	1.95	1.94
Aerodynamic drag cd x A (m²)	0.58	=	=	0.62	=	0.66	0.585	0.68
Dimensions at kerb weight								
Length (mm)	4430	=	=	4435	=	4450	4436	4430
Width (mm)	1770	=	=	1830	=	=	1770	1770
Height (mm)	1305	=	=	1295	=	1275	=	=
Wheelbase (mm)	2350	=	=	=	=	2355	=	=
Track								
front (mm)	1465	=	1472	1472	=	1495	1488	1485
rear (mm)	1500	=	1528	1528	=	1520	1488	1495
Ground clearance at permissible gross weight (mm)	65	=	55	=	=	=	=	=

Model range	911 Carrera 911 Targa **	911 Carrera "40 years 911"	911 Carrera 4S	911 Turbo	911 Turbo S	911 GT2	911 GT3	911 GT3 RS
Electrical system								
Generator output (V/W)	12/1680	=	=	=	=	=	=	=
Battery (Ah/A)	80/380	=	=	=	=	=	60/270	=
Weight according to DIN 70020								
Kerb weight (kg)								
Manual transmission	1370 1440**	1430	1495	1590	=	1420	1380	=
Tiptronic	1425 1595**	1485	1550	1630	=	–	–	–
Permissible gross weight (kg)								
Manual transmission	1790 1845**	1850	1870	1935	1730	1660	=	
Tiptronic	1845 1900**	1905	1925	1975	–	–		
Permissible trailer weight (kg)	none	=	=	=	=	=	=	
Permissible roof load (kg)	35	none**	35	=	none	none	35	=
with Porsche roof system (kg)	75	none**	75	50	75	=	75	=
Performance								
Maximum speed (kmh)								
Manual transmission	285 285**	290	280	305	307	319	302	306
Automatic transmission	280 280**	–	275	298	300	–	–	–
Acceleration 0–62mph/100kmh (sec)								
Manual transmission	5.0 5.2**	4.9	5.1	4.2	4.2	4.1	4.8	4.5
Automatic transmission	5.5 5.7**	–	5.6	4.9	4.5	–	–	–
Power/weight ratio (kg/kW)	5.83 6.13**	5.39	6.36	4.98	4.80	4.0	4.93	4.90
Fluid capacities								
Engine oil, change with filter (l)	8.25	=	=	8.0	=	=	8.75	=
Manual transmission (l)	2.7	2.9	2.7	3.8	=	=	3.3	=
Automatic transmission with converter (l)	9.0	=	=	9.0	=	–	–	–
Differential automatic (l)	1.2	=	=	=	=	–	–	–
All-wheel drive front differential (l)	–	–	1.5	=	=	–	–	–
Fuel tank/reserve tank (l)	64/10	=	=	=	=	=	89	=
Cooling water (l)	22.5	=	=	28	=	=	25	=
Brake fluid reservoir (l)	0.45	=	0.63	=	=	=	0.8	=
Headlamp cleaning reservoir (l) 3.0	=	=	=	=	=	=	=	
Washer tank (l)	5.7	=	=	6.5	=	=	–	–
Power steering fluid	1.27	=	=	2.14	=	=	1.9	=
Fluid specifications								
Engine oil	ACEA A4-96 and special Porsche requirements							
Gearbox	GL5 SAE75W-90							
Automatic transmission	SHELL ATF 3403-M115							
Differential	SAE 85 W 90							
Front differential	GL5 SAE 75W-90							
Brake fluid	SUPER DOT 4							
Air conditioning	exclusively R134 a							
Power steering	Pentosin CHF 11 S							
Fuel	Branded fuel with minimum standard RON 98/MON 88 unleaded							

911 Targa** 911 Targa and 911 Targa 4 are independent vehicle types that differ from 911 Carrera 4 and Carrera 4S with respect to body as well as other technical details. Differing data are marked by **.

Model year 2005

5 Programme, the new 911 generation – 997

Porsche 911 Carrera and Carrera S Coupé and Cabriolet (997)

Porsche 911 Carrera 4S Coupé and Cabriolet (996)

Porsche 911 Turbo and Turbo S Coupé (996)

Porsche 911 GT2 Coupé (996)

Porsche 911 GT3 Coupé (996)

The 997 marked another new chapter for Porsche, although to look at, the new generation seemed to hark back to former glories, particularly in the design of its oval headlamps. The 997 was initially available from July 2004 in two guises: Carrera and Carrera S. These were rear-wheel drive only and had identical bodywork. The base Carrera stuck with the 3.6-litre engine that had been well-known for years, producing 239kW (325hp). The Carrera S had useful extra power – some 261kW (355hp) – thanks to a larger displacement engine (3.8 litres).

Other 997 enhancements included better suspension, reduced drag coefficient, a more appealing interior and extra room for passengers. Both new Carreras were produced in Coupé and Cabriolet form.

Alongside these new 997 models, the 996 carried on going almost unchanged this year in the following forms: Carrera 4 and Carrera 4S, Turbo, Turbo S, GT2 and GT3.

Engine

The water-cooled 3.6-litre engine that had been produced almost unchanged for many years received a big make-over in Carrera S form. The new M97/01 engine was fitted with larger pistons with a diameter of 99mm, which resulted in a displacement of 3,824.2cc. The compression ratio could be increased to 11.8:1 through use of fuel with at least 98RON available in Europe, and the respective knock sensors. This led to an increase in power of some 22kW (30hp) to 261kW (355hp) and increased torque of 400Nm at 4,600rpm.

For 2005, the 997-series 911 was introduced, featuring an all-new body, as seen on this 911 Carrera Coupé.

Transmission

Due to the increased engine output, the Carrera S G97/01 six-speed manual transmission and A97/01 five-speed automatic transmission had to be adapted and reinforced. However, the gear ratios remained the same.

Suspension, steering and brakes

The track both front and rear was increased for the 997 and the MacPherson strut front and multi-link rear suspension were both upgraded. A new variable-ratio steering system meant that the steering ratio became more direct the more the wheel was turned.

The braking system was adapted to the increased performance of the Carrera S: the main brake cylinder now had a diameter of 25.4mm (1in) and the brake discs front and rear were both thicker (front 34mm, rear 28mm) and larger (330mm diameter front and rear). The brake callipers for the 997 model range were modified and reinforced as well.

ABOVE: The 997-series featured oval-shaped headlights, and the 911 Carrera S Cabriolet, seen here, featured bi-xenon headlights.

BELOW: This 911 Carrera 4S Cabriolet is fitted with the Sport Chrono package, including dashboard-mounted analogue/digital stopwatch.

Wheels and tyres

The new Carrera S was exclusively fitted with 19in wheels and tyres from the start of production: 8Jx19 aluminium front wheels with 235/35 ZR 19 tyres, and 11Jx19 rear wheels with 295/30 ZR 19 tyres. The regular Carrera 997 had 18in wheels and

tyres as standard, but could be equipped with 19in Carrera S wheels as an optional extra.

Body

Visually, the oval-shaped headlights of the 997 model range were eye-catching and appeared from a distance to be almost circular. Porsche was responding to customers who had not liked the fact that the 996's front end resembled the early Boxster too closely; and many commentators thought the 996's headlights looked like runny fried eggs.

The new-shape oval lights may have looked more '911' than the Boxster-style headlights but they suffered in one respect. The 996 had combined the side light, fog light, low-beam headlight and indicator into one unit covered with a clear, impact-resistant plastic surface. This protected them from parking damage and enabled the owner to change the bulbs himself. By contrast, the separate bumper-mounted light units of the 997 were almost unprotected and could be damaged more easily.

In order to keep the weight of the 997 as low as possible, the doors were made almost completely from light alloy. However, care was taken to ensure that the safety of the occupants in side impacts was nevertheless improved. The front lid of the 997 was made from aluminium with the result that

the new model was only marginally heavier than the previous 911.

The new 997 was honed in the modern wind tunnel at Porsche's Weissach development centre. Porsche reduced the drag coefficient substantially. Even though the frontal area was larger (due to a 38mm increase in overall width) and the greater cooling air requirement did not help aerodynamics, the drag coefficient Cd of 0.28 was the lowest value ever achieved for any Porsche production car. A CdA value of 0.56 for the 997 Coupé was exceptional, achieved through an almost completely smooth floorpan and carefully engineered cool air ducting.

Interior fittings

The 997 boasted a new cockpit with five round, easily read gauges, of which the rev counter was as always positioned in the middle. The speed was again displayed twice: in the analogue dial to the left of the rev counter, and digitally in the lower part of the rev counter (useful when judging speed more accurately, especially in low speed limit areas).

A completely new seating generation was also introduced with the 997. The backrests were

Although the suspension layout of the 997-series remained largely unchanged, the front and rear track were increased.

heightened and boasted a more anatomical form with even better lateral support. Overall the seats sat 10mm lower, which afforded more headroom for the passengers. Sports seats were available as an optional extra.

Porsche also improved safety for passengers inside the car. In addition to the airbags in the steering wheel and the instrument panel, both doors contained head airbags for protection against side impacts, and the backrests close to the doors were fitted with airbags to protect the chest area in side impacts.

Model range	Total production
911 Carrera Coupé (997)	6239
911 Carrera Cabriolet (997)	3019
911 Carrera S Coupé (997)	10501
911 Carrera S Cabriolet (997)	4058
911 Carrera 4 Coupé (996)	215
911 Carrera 4 Cabriolet (996)	87
911 Carrera 4S Coupé (996)	314
911 Carrera 4S Cabriolet (996)	112
911 Turbo (996)	13
911 GT3 (996)	1
911 GT3 RS (996)	2
911 Cup (996)	35

Model range	911 Carrera (997)	911 Carrera 2 (997)	911 Carrera 4S (996)	911 Turbo (996)	911 Turbo S (996)	911 GT2 (996)	911 GT3 (996)
Engine	Water-cooled six-cylinder boxer engine, engine casing made from light alloy						
Engine type	M96/05	M97/01	M96/05	M96/70	M96/70E	M96/70SL	M96/79
Displacement (cc)	3596	3824	3596	3600	=	=	=
Bore (mm)	96	99	96	100	=	=	=
Stroke (mm)	82.8	=	=	76.4	=	=	=
Compression ratio	11.3:1	11.8:1	11.3:1	9.4:1	=	=	12.0:1
Engine output EC kW (hp)	239 (325)	261 (355)	239 (325)	309 (420)	331 (450)	355 (483)	280 (381)
Engine output SAE (HP)	320	355	320	415	415	N/A	380
at revolutions per minute (rpm)	6800	6600	6800	6000	5700	5700	7400
Torque (Nm)	370	400	370	560	620	640	385
at revolutions per minute (rpm)	4250	4600	4250	2700–4600	3500–4500	3500–4500	5000
Output per litre (kW/l)	66.46	68.25	66.46	85.83	91.94	98.6	77.8
Max. engine speed (rpm)	7300	=	=	6750	=	=	8200
Engine cooling	water	=	=	=	=	=	=
Crankshaft	steel, forged	=	=	=	=	=	=
Crankshaft bearings	x 7	=	=	x 8	=	=	=
Con rods	steel, forged	=	=	=	=	=	=
Cylinder surface	LOKASIL	=	=	NIKASIL	=	=	=
Cylinder head, type	2 OHC + 4 OHV	=	=	=	=	=	=
Configuration of inlet valves	2. overhead	=	=	=	=	=	=
Configuration of exhaust valves	2. overhead	=	=	=	=	=	=
Camshaft drive	Spur gears + chain	=	=	=	=	=	=
Variable camshaft settings	VarioCam Plus 42°	=	=	=	=	=	=
Induction system	Var. induct. syst.	=	=	rigid	=	=	Var. induct. syst.
Turbocharging	–	–	–	2 ATL, 2LLK in rear	=	=	–
Exhaust system	Stand. exh. sil.	=	=	=	=	=	Sports exh. sil.
Exhaust gas control EURO II	Lambda control+ 2 DWK	=	=	Stereo-Lambda control	=	=	three-way cat. conv.
Exhaust gas control EURO III	second.air and readjustment with 4 Lambda sensors	=	=	=	=	=	plus second.air and readjustment with 4 Lambda sensors
Exhaust gas control USA	additionally cascade-type cat. conv. + OBD II + ORVR	=	=	=	=	=	as for EURO IV
Lubrication system	dry sump with integrated oil tank	=	=	dry sump with separate oil tank	=	=	=
Oil cooling	Oil-water heat exchanger	=	=	=	=	=	=
Engine weight dry (kg)	202	=	=	230	206	=	206

Model range	911 Carrera (997)	911 Carrera 2 (997)	911 Carrera 4S (996)	911 Turbo (996)	911 Turbo S (996)	911 GT2 (996)	911 GT3 (996)
Carburation, ignition, settings							
Engine control	DME (Digital engine electronic system), ME 7.8; ignition, fuel injection, camshaft control						
Fuel injection	sequential, multi-point	=	=	=	=	=	=
Fuel quality	Super Plus	=	=	=	=	=	=
Octane rating RON	98 unleaded	=	=	=	=	=	=
Throttle adjustment	electronic	=	=	=	=	=	=
Ignition	electronic	=	=	=	=	=	=
Distributor	Solid-state dist.	=	=	=	=	=	=
Spark plugs manufacturer	Bosch	=	=	Beru	=	=	Bosch
Type	FRG 5KQEO	=	=	14-FR 6LDU	=	=	FR6 LDC
Spark plug gap	1.6 ± 0.5	=	=	0.8 ± 0.1	=	=	=
Firing order	1-6-2-4-3-5	=	=	=	=	=	=

Model range	911 Carrera (997)	911 Carrera 2 (997)	911 Carrera 4S (996)	911 Turbo (996)	911 Turbo S (996)	911 GT2 (996)	911 GT3 (996)
Transmission							
Engine and gearbox are built as one drive unit.							
The hydraulically operated dry single-plate clutch is bolted onto the dual-mass flywheel.							
Drive configuration Carrera 2, 911 GT2 and 911 GT3: via dual propshafts to the rear wheels.							
Drive configuration Carrera 4, Carrera 4S and 911 Turbo: connection to the front differential via driveshaft.							
Rear and front wheels are driven via dual propshafts.							
Available as optional extra (not 911 GT2 and GT3) : 5-gear Tiptronic transmission with torque converter.							
Clutch dual-mass flywheel	yes, system LUK	=	=	=	=	=	=
Clutch, pressure plate	MF 228X, MF 240	=	=	=	=	=	
Clutch plate (mm) dia. (mm)	240	=	=	=	=	=	=
Manual transmission	G97/01	=	G96/31	G96/50	=	G96/88	G96/96
Gearbox design	fully synchronised 6-speed manual transmission						
Number of gears forward/reverse	6/1	=	=	=	=	=	=
Gear ratios							
1st gear	3.91	=	=	3.82	=	=	=
2nd gear	2.32	=	=	2.05	=	=	=
3rd gear	1.61	=	=	1.41	=	=	=
4th gear	1.28	=	=	1.12	=	=	=
5th gear	1.08	=	=	0.92	=	=	=
6th gear	0.88	=	=	0.75	=	=	=
Synchromesh system	VK	=	=	=	=	=	=
Reverse gear	3.59	=	=	2.86	=	=	=
Final drive ratio, rear	3.44	=	=	=	=	=	=
Final drive ratio, front	–	–	3.44	3.44	=	–	–
Oil cooler	no	=	=	standard	=	=	=
Gearbox weight with oil (kg)	65	=	66	76.3	=	74	76.2

Key and abbreviations:

ATL — Exhaust turbocharger.

DWK — Three-way catalytic converter. The DWK can burn hydro-carbon, carbon monoxide and nitrogen oxide in the exhaust utilising EURO II European emission standard from 1996 (HC + NOx max. 0.50g/km, CO max. 2.20g/km).

EURO III — European emission standard from 2000 (HC max. 0.20g/km, NOx max. 0.15g/km, CO max. 2.3g/km).

LLK — Intercooler.

EURO IV — European emission standard from 2005 (HC max. 0.10g/km, NOx max. 0.08g/km, CO max. 1.0g/km).

LOKASIL — Running surface technology for cylinder walls. Silicon is enriched in the running surface area when the engine block is cast.

LS — Lambda sensor, measures the remaining oxygen content in hot exhaust gases.

NIKASIL — Light-alloy cylinder with piston surface coated with nickel-silicon-carbide.

OBD II — Regulation with respect to electronic data storage of malfunctioning of the monitored emission system according to the State of California, USA. If an error is detected, a malfunction indicator light (MIL) flashes in order to alert the driver to the identified malfunction and to save the respective error code in the system.

ORVR — On-board refuelling vapour recovery = system that accumulates fuel vapour which is formed when refuelling. It is collected in an activated carbon canister and returned to the running engine once certain operating conditions have been achieved.

RoW — Abbreviation for "Vehicle for rest of world", including Germany.

RON — Octane number (anti-knock properties of the fuel) R = Research method, the acceleration pinging is measured.

USA — Vehicles for the North American market, including Canada.

W — Heat rating (of the spark plug).

ZMS — Dual-mass flywheel for the avoidance of torsional vibration in the drive train at low engine revolutions.

2 OHC — OHC = overhead camshaft. 2 OHC = twin overhead camshafts in the cylinder head.

4 OHV — OHV = overhead valves, 4 OHV = 4 valves per combustion chamber (2 inlet and 2 exhaust valves).

Model range	911 Carrera (997)	911 Carrera S (997)	911 Carrera 4S (996)	911 Turbo (996)	911 Turbo S (996)	911 GT2 (996)	911 GT3 (996)
Transmission (continued)							
Tiptronic S	A97/01	=	A96/35	A96/50	=	–	–
Gearbox design	Md-converter + 5-speed planetary gear					–	–
Torque converter dia. (mm)	270	=	=	=		–	–
Stall speed (rpm)	2660	2750	2650	2600	2600	–	–
Number of gears forward/reverse	5/2	=	=	=	=	–	–
1st gear	3.60	=	=	3.59	=	–	–
2nd gear	2.19	=	=	2.19	=	–	–
3rd gear	1.41	=	=	1.41	=	–	–
4th gear	1.00	=	=	1.00	=	–	–
5th gear	0.83	=	=	0.83	=	–	–
Reverse gear	-3.17/-1.93	=	=	-1.93/-3.16	=	–	–
Final drive ratio, rear axle	3.56	=	3.37	2.88	=	–	–
Dry gearbox weight with converter and oil (kg)	114.8	=	=	125.2	=	–	–

Suspension, steering and brakes

	911 Carrera (997)	911 Carrera S (997)	911 Carrera 4S (996)	911 Turbo (996)	911 Turbo S (996)	911 GT2 (996)	911 GT3 (996)
Front suspension	Individually suspended on wishbones with semi-trailing arms and MacPherson spring struts; one conical spring per wheel with internal shock absorber; dual-function hydraulic gas-pressure shock absorbers						
Rear suspension	Multi-wishbone rear suspension with five wishbones per wheel, cylindrical coil springs with internal shock absorbers, dual-function hydraulic gas pressure shock absorbers						
Brake system	Power-assisted hydraulic-mechanical dual-circuit brake system with monobloc brake callipers. Internally ventilated brake discs. ABS and PSM standard.						
Steering	Hydraulic rack-and-pinion steering						
Anti-roll bar dia. front (mm)	23.6 x 3.5 tube	24.0 x 3.8 tube	23.6 x 3.5 tube	26.8 x 4 tube	=	=	26.8 x 4.0 tube
Anti-roll bar dia. rear (mm)	18.5 x 2.5 tube	19.6 x 2.6 tube	21.7 x 3.0 tube	20.7 x 2.8 tube	=	=	20.7 x 2.8 tube
Steering ratio	17.11:1	=	=	=	=	16.9	17.11
Turning circle dia. (m)	10.9	=	=	=	=	10.6	10.9
Brake system							
Brake-circuit configuration	per axle	=	=	=	=	=	=
Brake master cylinder dia.(mm)	23.81	25.4	=	=	=	=	=
Stability Management PSM 8.0	S	S	S	S	S	S	S
Brake calliper piston diameter							
front (mm)	36 + 40	36 + 44	=	38+32+28	=	=	=
rear (mm)	28 + 30	=	=	=	=	=	=
Brake disc diameter							
front (mm)	318	330	330	=	350	=	=
rear (mm)	299	330	330	=	350	=	=
Brake disc thickness							
front (mm)	28	34	34	=	34	=	=
rear (mm)	24	28	28	=	28	=	=
Effective brake area (cm²)	450	568	568	=	698	=	=
PCCB	–	–	Option	Option	Standard	Standard	Option

Wheels and tyres

	911 Carrera (997)	911 Carrera S (997)	911 Carrera 4S (996)	911 Turbo (996)	911 Turbo S (996)	911 GT2 (996)	911 GT3 (996)
Standard tyre specification, front	235/40ZR18	235/35ZR19	225/40ZR18	225/40ZR18	=	235/40ZR18	=
wheel (rim) / hump depth	8Jx18/57	8Jx19/57	8Jx18/50	=	8.5Jx18/40	=	
Standard tyre specification, rear	265/40ZR18	295/30ZR19	295/30ZR18	295/30ZR18	=	315/30ZR18	295/30ZR18
wheel (rim) / hump depth	10Jx18/58	11Jx19/67	11Jx18/45	=	=	12Jx18/45	11Jx18
Optional tyres front	235/35ZR19	–	–	–	–	–	–
wheel (rim) / hump depth	8Jx19/57	–	–	–	–	–	–
Optional tyres rear	295/30ZR19	–	–	–	–	–	–
wheel (rim) / hump depth	11Jx19/67	–	–	–	–	–	–

Key:
PCCB   Porsche Composite Ceramic Brake

Model range	911 Carrera (997)	911 Carrera S (997)	911 Carrera 4S (996)	911 Turbo (996)	911 Turbo S (996)	911 GT2 (996)	911 GT3 (996)
Body							
Monocoque structure, hot-dip galvanised lightweight steel body, partial use of HSLA* steel; airbags and side airbags for driver and passenger; number of seats: 2 + 2							
Drag coefficient (cd)	0.28	0.29	0.30	0.31	=	0.34	0.30
Frontal area A (m²)	2.00	2.00	2.00	2.00	=	1.96	1.95
Aerodynamic drag cd x A (m²)	0.56	0.58	0.60	0.62	=	0.66	0.585
Dimensions at kerb weight							
Length (mm)	4427	=	4430	4435	=	4450	4436
Width (mm)	1808	=	1770	1830	=	=	1770
Height (mm)	1310	=	1305	1295	=	1275	=
Wheelbase (mm)	2350	=	=	=	=	2355	=
Track, front (mm)	1486	=	1472	1472	=	1495	1488
Track, rear (mm)	1534 with 18in tyres	1516 with 19in tyres	1528	1528	=	1520	1488
Ground clearance at permissible gross weight (mm)	76	=	=	=	=	70	75
Electrical system							
Generator output (V/W)	12/2100	=	12/1680	=	=	=	=
Battery (Ah/A)	70/340	=	80/380	=	=	=	60/270
Weight according to DIN 70020							
Kerb weight							
Manual transmission (kg)	1395	1420	1600	1590	=	1420	1380
Tiptronic (kg)	1435	1510	1655	1630	=	–	–
Permissible gross weight							
Manual transmission (kg)	1875	1885	1925	1935	=	1730	1660
Tiptronic (kg)	1920	1930	1982	1975	=	–	–
Permissible trailer weight (kg)	none	=	=	=	=	=	=
Permissible roof load (kg)	35	=	=	none	=	=	35
with Porsche roof system (kg)	75	=	=	=	=	50	75
Performance							
Maximum speed (kmh)							
Manual transmission	285	293	280	305	307	319	306
Automatic transmission	280	285	275	298	300	–	–
Acceleration 0–62mph/100 kmh (sec)							
Manual transmission	4.8	4.6	5.1	4.2	4.2	4.1	4.5
Automatic transmission	5.2	5.0	5.6	4.9	4.5	–	–
Power/weight ratio (kg/kW)	5.83	5.39	6.36	6.14	4.80	4.0	4.90
Fluid capacities							
Engine oil, change with filter (l)	8.25	=	=	8.0	8.0	=	8.75
Manual transmission (l)	2.7	2.9	2.7	3.8	3.8	=	3.3
Automatic transmission with converter (l)	9.0	=	=	9.0	9.0	–	–
Differential automatic (l)	1.2	=	=	=	=	–	–
All-wheel drive front differential (l)	–	–	1.5	=	=	–	–
Fuel tank/reserve tank (l)	64/10	=	=	=	=	=	89
Cooling water (l)	22.5	=	=	28	28	=	25
Brake fluid reservoir (l)	0.45	=	0.63	=	=	=	0.8
Headlamp cleaning reservoir (l)	3.0	=	=	=	=	=	=
Washer tank (l)	5.7	=	=	6.5	6.5	6.5	–
Power steering fluid	1.27	=	=	2.14	2.14	=	1.9
Fluid specifications							
Engine oil	ACEA A4-96 and special Porsche requirements						
Gearbox	GL5 SAE75W-90						
Automatic transmission	SHELL ATF 3403-M115						
Differential	SAE 85 W 90						
Front differential	GL5 SAE 75W-90						
Brake fluid	SUPER DOT 4						
Air conditioning	exclusively R134 a						
Power steering	Pentosin CHF 11 S						
Fuel	Branded fuel with minimum standard RON 98/MON 88 unleaded						

Key:
* HSLA steel = description used internationally for high-strength, low-alloy steel

Model year 2006

6 Programme, new 911 Turbo and two GT3s

Porsche 911 Carrera and Carrera S Coupé and Cabriolet (997)
Porsche 911 Carrera 4 and Carrera 4S Coupé and Cabriolet (997)
Porsche 911 Turbo Coupé (997)
Porsche 911 GT3 and GT3 RS Coupé (997)

In March 2006, at the Geneva Motor Show, Porsche launched the new 997 version of the 911 Turbo as well as two roadgoing GT3s, the regular GT3 and the GT3 RS. The 911 Turbo was fitted with an improved all-wheel drive system and a significantly modified twin-turbo engine. The GT3 model range was also substantially new and the engines were significantly more powerful. The 997 Carrera, first seen in model year 2005, continued almost unchanged. Two new four-wheel drive 997 additions were the new Carrera 4 and 4S models. Both the Carrera S and Carrera 4S could be ordered with an optional power upgrade this year.

Carrera S and Carrera 4S

Optional power upgrade engine
The Carrera S and Carrera 4S were offered with an

The latest 997-series Turbo saw the sixth generation of 911 Turbo since the first 911 Turbo was introduced in 1975.

ex-factory optional power upgrade (M97/01 S) offering 280kW (381bhp). The technical details were as follows:

Engine type	M97/01 S	
Displacement	3824cc	
Bore	99mm	
Stroke	82.8mm	
Compression ratio	12:1	
Output	280kW (381bhp)	
At revolutions	7200rpm	
Torque	415Nm	
At revolutions	5500rpm	
Maximum power output per litre displacement	73.22kW	
Maximum revolutions	7500rpm	
With this engine the vehicles performed as follows:		
	911 Carrera S	911 Carrera 4S
Maximum speed	186mph (300kmh)	183mph (295kmh)
0–62mph (0–100kmh) acceleration (manual)	4.6 seconds	4.7 seconds
0–62mph (0–100kmh) acceleration (automatic)	5.1 seconds	5.6 seconds

911 Turbo

M97/70 engine
The 997-generation 911 Turbo now had a significantly modified twin-turbo engine to match its improved all-wheel drive system. While the mechanical side of this new engine varied only slightly from the preceding model, major modifications were done to the Variocam Plus system for the intake camshafts and turbochargers.

The inlet timing adjustment of the camshafts was no longer affected by a hydraulically operated piston but by a rotary vane adjuster. This adjuster allowed the camshaft to vary by up to 30 degrees with respect to the position of the crankshaft. In

The striking lines of the 997-series 911 Turbo, with three large air intakes at the front to cool the engine's radiators.

Electronically controlled Variable Turbine Geometry (VTG) turbochargers were fitted to Turbo models for the first time.

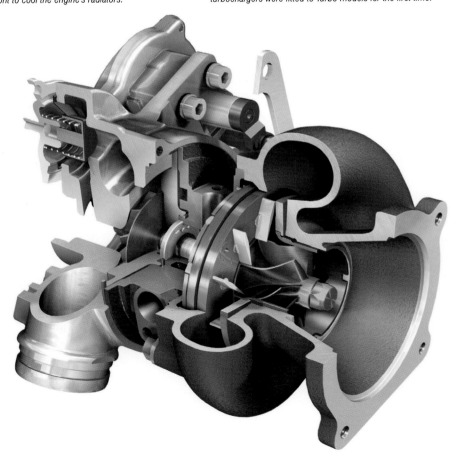

addition, the camshafts and tappets were configured in such a way that the valve stroke was reduced from 11mm to 3.6mm at low engine revs and loads. At the same time a second cam profile became operative, which had no overlap on the outlet side. This noticeably reduced fuel consumption and emissions.

If more performance was required the bucket tappets were changed over to bring the two outer cams into operation, whose profiles boosted performance. The camshafts were rotated infinitely variably, changing the timing in order to achieve optimum performance for the driving conditions. At full load, the two lateral cams of the Variocam Plus system increased the valve lift of the 'big' bucket tappet to 11mm.

The new Turbo's increase in power output of 44kW (60hp) from an unchanged 3.6-litre displacement was mostly due to the new turbochargers with variable turbine geometry (VTG) that had been developed in co-operation with BorgWarner. Despite an exhaust gas temperature of approximately 700°C in these turbochargers, it was possible to adapt the turbo boost pressure to suit all driving conditions via electric servo-motors.

The extremely heat-resistant compounds used in

the housing as well as the adjustable guide vanes originated in aerospace technology. The VTG system avoided the plague of turbos everywhere: so-called 'turbo lag' which meant that large turbos were slow to respond when the accelerator was pressed down.

It was possible to maintain a high engine torque of 620Nm between 2,100 and 4,000rpm. If that wasn't enough, you could opt for the 'Sport Chrono' package, which brought you a sport button that would activate an 'overboost' function. This meant that the turbo boost pressure could be increased by an extra 0.2bar for a maximum of ten seconds, providing short-term torque of an extra 60Nm (up to 680Nm). This force was comparable with that of a fighter jet with its afterburners ignited.

Fuel, ignition and exhaust systems

No important changes to the model from the previous year. The Bosch ME 7.8.1 Digital Motor Electronics system was tuned to the two new turbochargers and the 'overboost' function. Like all 911s, the Turbo complied with international emission standards EURO 4/EOBD for Europe and TIER2/LEV II as well as OBDII/ORVR for the USA and Canada.

Transmission

There were two types of transmission available for the model year 2006 Turbo: a stronger six-speed

The 911 Turbo also featured an electromagnetic multiplate clutch to vary the torque split between the front and rear wheels.

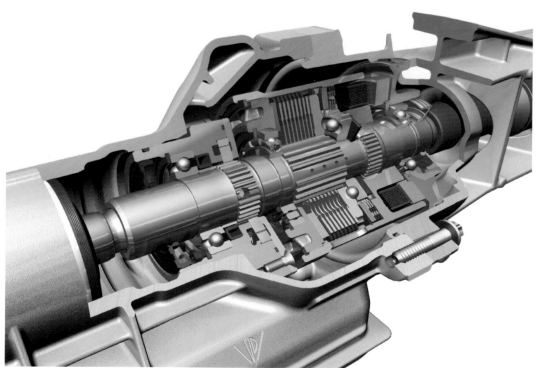

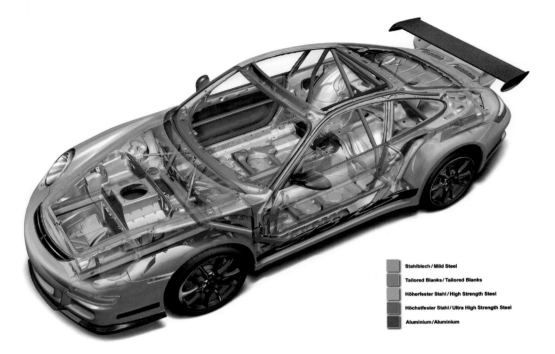

▦	Stahlblech / Mild Steel
▦	Tailored Blanks / Tailored Blanks
▦	Höherfester Stahl / High Strength Steel
▦	Höchstfester Stahl / Ultra High Strength Steel
▦	Aluminium / Aluminium

The lightweight 911 GT3 RS Coupé with Clubsport package included an integral rollcage.

manual gearbox with improved gearshift operation that allowed for even shorter gearshift travel; and the Tiptronic S automatic five-speed with a torque converter connected upstream including lock-up clutch. A bevel gear differential was installed in both transmissions as standard. The function of the limited-slip differential was taken over by the Porsche Traction Management (PTM) system, which detected spinning wheels as well as the initial locking of the brakes. Through quick braking of the spinning wheel, constant velocity was achieved. For real limited-slip differential fans, a friction-plate limited-slip differential was available as an optional extra with varying lock-up values under load and coasting.

Full acceleration from 0–62mph (0–100kmh) in high-performance cars makes high demands on both the driver and the function of the clutch. With a manual gearbox it is unavoidable that the tractive force to the driven wheels is temporarily interrupted, even if that's less than half a second in motorsport. Such interruptions were dispensed with in the Tiptronic S. Indeed, the 911 Turbo Tiptronic S was able to outperform the regular manual version of the Turbo, both off the line and through the gears, thanks to its electronically monitored accelerator.

Acceleration	Five-speed Tiptronic S	Six-speed manual transmission
0–62mph (0–100kmh)	3.7 seconds	3.9 seconds
0–100mph (0–160kmh)	7.8 seconds	8.4 seconds
0–124mph (0–200kmh)	12.2 seconds	12.8 seconds
Maximum speed	192mph (310kmh)	192mph (310kmh)

In previous generations of the 911 Turbo with identical engines, the acceleration with automatic transmission had always been slower and the top speed about 4mph (7kmh) lower than that of a 911 Turbo with manual transmission.

Another curious characteristic of the Turbo's Tiptronic S transmission was that it had two reverse gears. The reason for this was that, after a cold start, the catalytic converters needed to be brought up to operating temperature as soon as possible. In gear selector position 'R' the reverse gear had a very short ratio. Once the operating temperature of the catalytic converters had been reached, the longer gear ratio of the reverse gear was automatically adopted again, which was able to achieve significantly higher speeds. The same applied to a cold start with the gear lever in the 'D' position, when a shorter first gear ratio would be selected.

The new 911 Turbo was fitted with a dual-mass flywheel in order to dampen the torsional vibrations of the engine. The dry single-plate clutch had a diameter of 240mm. The downforce of the clutch spring was increased to match the engine torque and the 'overboost' function.

All-wheel drive

In all previous all-wheel drive systems that Porsche had used for the 911, a viscous clutch had been

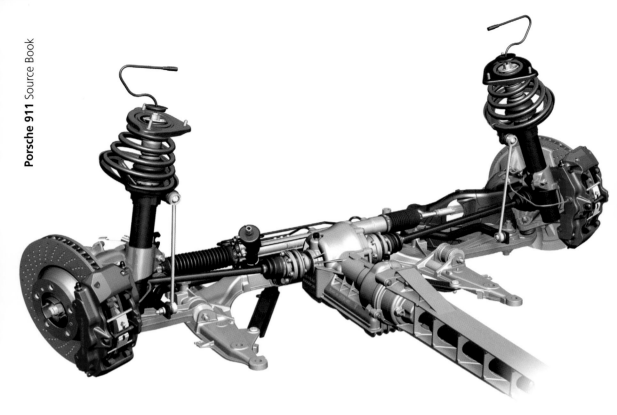

The front suspension of the 911 Turbo Coupé, with Porsche's Active Suspension Management (PASM) shock absorber system.

installed between the front-wheel drive and the differential of the rear-wheel drive, permanently connecting the two axles. Depending on the driving condition, between 5% and 40% of the drive was directed to the front wheels.

The front-wheel drive of the new 911 Turbo was different in that it was fitted with an electronically controlled and electro-magnetically actuated multi-plate clutch which could activate or deactivate front-wheel drive. During the start-up process, full traction of all four wheels could be engaged straightaway.

Suspension and steering
The new 911 Turbo was equipped with Porsche's own air suspension and PASM (Porsche Active Suspension Management) damper system as standard, which was able to adjust the characteristics of the dampers depending on the changing road conditions while driving. Through further development of the stability management and variable-ratio steering, driving safety as well as driving comfort were improved.

Brake system
Two brake systems were available for the 911

Turbo from the factory. The conventional braking system with brake discs made from special cast-iron alloys had a diameter of 350mm and front monobloc callipers with six pistons. The second brake system was the PCCB ceramic set-up. These discs were 50% lighter than metal brake discs of the same size. Used in combination with special brake pads they had a much higher resistance to wear, were also more corrosion-resistant and were not susceptible to road salt and liquid salt used on icy roads.

Wheels and tyres
A new generation of light-alloy wheels was developed for the 911 Turbo. The forged wheels were produced in a 19in wheel size for the first time. Wheels at the front were 8.5Jx19 ET 56, at the rear 11Jx19 ET 51. They were fitted with 235/35 ZR 19 tyres at the front, 305/30 ZR 19 at the rear. Worldwide all 911 Turbo vehicles were equipped with a tyre pressure control system (RDK) on all four wheels.

Body
Hot-dip galvanised steel continued to be used by Porsche, enabling it to extend the warranty period against rust continually. Despite increased body stiffness the new Turbo bodies were lighter than their predecessors. This was achieved by using light-alloy for the bonnet lid and the doors. The

door frames of the 911 Turbo (as well as for the GT3) were made from vacuum-cast light alloy. The cast unit measured approximately 1.28m in width and 580mm in height, while the thickness of the wall was only 2mm. The complete door without glass, window lift and door closing mechanism weighed just 10.3kg, which was 7.2kg less than a comparable door made from steel.

Up front there were three large air intakes for the cooling of the three heat exchangers located immediately behind. The airflow rate was 4,000 litres per second at maximum speed.

Electrical system
The new 911 Turbo was fitted with oval main

headlamps with bi-xenon light technology, and the front indicators were positioned in the lateral cooling air inlets and consisted of light-emitting diodes.

911 GT3 and GT3 RS

Porsche pushed the 911 GT3 model range into its new 997 generation this year. Here again, 3.6-litre naturally aspirated engines with significantly more power were developed, and the new GT3 generation was easily recognisable by its oval-shaped main headlights.

In order to bring a certain order to the huge variety of GT3 cars produced, please find hereunder the full line-up:

Type	Model year	Output kW (hp)	Weight (kg)	Max. speed (kmh)	Notes
911 GT3 (Standard)	1999	265 (360)	1350	302	Official approval and homologation for road service
911 GT3 (Standard)	2003	280 (381)	1380	306	Official approval and homologation for road service
911 GT3 (Standard)	2004	280 (381)	1380	306	Official approval and homologation for road service
911 GT3 RS	2004	280 (381)	1360	306	Official approval and homologation for road service still possible
911 GT3 Rallye	2004	280 (381)	1370	250	Official approval and homologation for road service still possible
911 GT3 Cup	2004	287 (390)	1160	n/s	Racing
911 GT3 RSR	2004	327 (445)	1100	n/s	Racing
911 GT3 (Standard)	2005	280 (381)	1360	306	Official approval and homologation for road service
911 GT3 Rallye	2005	280 (381)	1370	250	Official approval and homologation for road service still possible
911 GT3 Cup	2005	287 (381)	1160	n/s	Racing
911 GT3 Supercup	2005	294 (400)	1140	n/s	Racing
911 GT3 RSR	2005	327 (445)	1100	n/s	Racing
911 GT3 (Standard)	2006	305 (415)	1350	310	Official approval and homologation for road service
911 GT3 RS	2006	305 (415)	1395	310	Official approval and homologation for road service still possible
911 GT3 Cup	2006	294 (400)	1150	n/s	Racing
911 GT3 Supercup	2006	294 (400)	1120	n/s	Racing
911 GT3 (Standard)	2007	305 (415)	1395	310	Official approval and homologation for road service
911 GT3 RS	2007	305 (415)	1375	310	Official approval and homologation for road service
911 GT3 RSR	2007	357 (485)	n/s	n/s	Racing
911 GT3 (Standard)	2008	305 (415)	1395	310	Official approval and homologation for road service
911 GT3 RS	2008	305 (415)	1375	310	Official approval and homologation for road service still possible
911 GT3 Cup	2008	309 (420)	1150	n/s	Racing
911 GT3 Cup S	2008	324 (440)	1170	n/s	Racing

n/s: not supplied by the manufacturer

Engine
The reworked engine for the new GT3 and GT3 RS had familiar ancestors. The basic concept originated in the GT1 racing engine with its water-cooled six-cylinder boxer layout, dry sump lubrication system with separate oil tank, titanium con rods, forged light-alloy pistons, light bucket tappets and 'simple' Variocam camshaft settings. The cam lifting adjustment for this engine was dropped, creating a limited-rev sports engine with up to 8,400rpm.

It can be seen from the table above that the GT3's power output increased from 265kW (360hp) to 308kW (420hp) within nine development years while its displacement of 3.6 litres did not change. The comparison of specific power output (kW or hp per litre displacement) is

equally astonishing: in model year 1999 the power output of the GT3 was 73.65kW (100.05hp) per litre, a seemingly impossibly high figure; but by 2008, 324kW (440hp) would be achieved with the same displacement – an incredible specific output of 90.05kW (122.29hp) per litre.

As turbochargers were not allowed in GT3 racing, it was the induction system that saw most attention in obtaining higher and higher power outputs. The 997 GT3's induction system had two resonance flaps to supply an optimal amount of air to the cylinders depending on the engine revolutions. It was this intake system, together with exhaust gas routing that created very little exhaust gas back pressure, and the Variocam camshaft setting, that was responsible for such a high power output from a naturally aspirated engine.

The 911 GT3 range. Front row: 911 GT3 Cup (white) and 911 GT3 RS (orange). Rear row: 911 GT3 (silver) and 911 GT3 RSR (white).

Transmission

The GT3 was equipped with G97/90 six-speed transmission and limited-slip differential with varying lock-up values. Compared to the earlier transmissions, the new gearbox had shorter ratios from second gear up and the gearshift travel became shorter. An upshift indicator would flash when the engine reached a certain rev point and an upshift was required, enabling the driver to concentrate on other things than watching the rev counter while accelerating. The RS version had a non-dual-mass flywheel and bigger clutch.

Suspension

Even though the basic version of the GT3 fulfilled all the requirements for homologation for road service, it was nonetheless a vehicle configured for racing applications. Actively adjustable dampers were standard and Porsche Active Suspension Management (PASM) facilitated an extremely high level of performance, especially on the race track. The following automatic control systems fitted as standard in the GT3 were combined under the heading of 'traction control' (TC):

ABS   anti-lock braking.
ABD   automatic brake differential.
ASR   anti-slip regulation.
MSR   engine drag torque control.

Brakes

When buying a GT3 you could choose from two brake systems: the conventional brake system with special cast-iron discs, where the front discs had a diameter of 350mm; and the PCCB brake system with ceramic brake discs that were made from carbon-fibre reinforced ceramic material, plus special brake pads.

Wheels and tyres

Both the 911 Turbo and the 911 GT3 were fitted with 19in wheels. Porsche used monobloc cast light-alloy wheels with a width of 8.5in at the front and 12in at the rear. Tyre pressure control was available as an optional extra.

Body

The model year 2006 GT3 was extensively tested in the wind tunnel at Weissach, and it proved possible to lower the drag coefficient Cd further to 0.29. The three intakes for cooling air on the newly designed front end stood out distinctly, each feeding three water radiators. The heated exhaust air from the middle radiator was no longer led downwards into the space between the road and the floorpan, but upwards to an opening in front of the bonnet, then across the bonnet, the windscreen and the roof. This also helped aerodynamic downforce on the front axle. A rigid rear wing was attached to the newly designed rear end of the car, and at top speed this produced an aerodynamic downforce of around 25kg. The engine lid at the rear contained openings for ventilation to the engine bay and for intake air. Slits were positioned underneath the rear lights to cool the catalytic converters.

The RS version was 44mm wider at the rear (a legacy from the Carrera 4 with which it shared its shell) to conceal a wider track. The RS was 20kg lighter than the GT3, thanks to its adjustable carbon-fibre rear spoiler, plastic rear lid and lightweight plastic rear window.

Clubsport package

In order to take part in official motorsport competitions, cars needed to comply with certain rules and regulations, which concerned the safety

The 2006-model 911 GT3 RS was available in this distinctive orange colour scheme.

of the driver. In this respect a Clubsport package was available ex-factory, consisting of the following:

- Lightweight bucket seats made from carbon-fibre and covered with a flame-resistant material.
- Bolt-on roll cage.
- Six-point safety belt for the driver.
- Fire extinguisher with bracket.
- Preparation for battery main switch.

For racing to FIA 5 GT regulations the following were also required:

- Battery main switch.
- Full roll cage using lateral bracket for roof and A-column.

Model range	Total production
911 Carrera Coupé	3559
911 Carrera Cabriolet	3083
911 Carrera S Coupé	6935
911 Carrera S Cabriolet	5714
911 Carrera 4 Coupé	1766
911 Carrera 4 Cabriolet	1706
911 Carrera 4S Coupé	6057
911 Carrera 4S Cabriolet	5059
911 Targa 4	86
911 Targa 4S	141
911 Turbo	2150
911 GT3	44
911 GT3 RS	9
911 Cup	195

Model range	911 Carrera 2	911 Carrera 2S	911 Carrera 4	911 Carrera 4S	911 Turbo	911 GT3	911 GT3 RS
Engine	Water-cooled six-cylinder boxer engine, engine casing made from light alloy						
Engine Type	M96/05	M97/01	M96/5	M97/01	M97/70	M97/76	=
Displacement (cm²)	3596	3824	3596	3824	3600	=	=
Bore (mm)	96	99	96	99	100	=	=
Stroke (mm)	82.8	=	=	=	76.4	=	=
Compression ratio	11.3:1	11.8:1	11.3:1	11.8:1	9.01:1	12.0:1	=
Engine output EC kW (hp)	239 (325)	261 (355)	239 (325)	261 (355)	353 (480)	305 (415)	=
Engine output SAE (HP)	325	355	325	355	480	415	=
at revolutions per minute (rpm)	6800	6600	6800	6600	6000	7600	=
Torque (Nm)	370	400	370	400	620(680 w. overboost)	405	=
at revolutions per minute (rpm)	4250	4600	4250	4600	2100–4000	5500	=
max. output per litre (kW/l)	66.5	73.22	66.5	73.22	98.0	84.7	=
Max. engine speed (rpm)	7300	=	=	=	6750	8400	=
Engine type	6-cylinder 4-stroke boxer engine						
Engine cooling	water	=	=	=	=	=	=
Crankshaft	steel, forged	=	=	=	=	=	=
Crankshaft bearings	x 7	=	=	=	x 8	=	=
Con rods	steel, forged	=	=	=	=	=	=
Cylinder surface	LOKASIL	=	=	=	NIKASIL	=	=
Cylinder head, type	2 OHC + 4 OHV	=	=	=	=	=	=
Configuration of inlet valves	2 overhead	=	=	=	=	=	=
Configuration of exhaust valves	2 overhead	=	=	=	=	=	=
Camshaft drive	Spur gears + chain	=	=	=	=	=	=
Variable camshaft settings	VarioCam Plus	=	=	=	=	=	=
Induction system	Var.induct.syst.	=	=	=	rigid	2 reson. flaps	=
Turbocharging	–	–	–	–	2 ATL with VTG + 2 LLK	–	–
Exhaust system	Standard exh. silencer	=	=	=	2G-Kat + 2LS Sport Exhaust syst.	=	=
Exhaust gas control EURO II	Lambda control + 2 DWK	=	=	=	=	=	=
Exhaust gas control EURO III	second.air and readjustm. with 4 Lambda sensors	=	=	=	=	–	–
Exhaust gas control USA	plus cascade-type cat. conv. + OBD II	=	=	=	=	=	=
Lubrication system	dry sump with integrated oil tank	=	=	=	dry sump with separate oil tank	=	=
Oil cooling	Oil-water heat exchanger	=	=	=	=	=	=
Engine weight dry (kg)	204	=	=	=	230	206	206

Carburation, ignition, settings

	911 Carrera 2	911 Carrera 2S	911 Carrera 4	911 Carrera 4S	911 Turbo	911 GT3	911 GT3 RS
Engine control	DME (Digital engine electronic system), ME 7.8; ignition, fuel injection, camshaft control						
Fuel injection	sequential, multi-point	=	=	=	=	=	=
Fuel quality	Super Plus unleaded	=	=	=	=	=	=
Octane rating (RON)	98	=	=	=	=	=	=
Throttle adjustment	electronic	=	=	=	=	=	=
Ignition	electronic	=	=	=	=	=	=
Distributor	solid-state distr. syst.	=	=	=	=	=	=
Spark plugs manufacturer	Bosch	=	Beru	=	=	Bosch	Bosch
Type	FRG 5KQEO	=	14-FRG 6 KQU	=	14-FR 6 LDU	FR6 LDC	FR6 LDC
Spark plug gap	1.6 ± 0.5	=	=	=	0.8 ± 0.1	=	=
Firing order	1–6–2–4–3–5	=	=	=	=	=	=

Model range	911 Carrera 2	911 Carrera 2S	911 Carrera 4	911 Carrera 4S	911 Turbo	911 GT3	911 GT3 RS
Transmission							
Engine and gearbox are built as one drive unit.							
The hydraulically operated dry single-plate clutch is bolted onto the dual-mass flywheel.							
Drive configuration Carrera 2, 911 GT2 and 911 GT3: via dual propshafts to the rear wheels.							
Drive configuration Carrera 4, Carrera 4S and 911 Turbo: connection to the front differential via driveshaft.							
Rear and front wheels are driven via dual propshafts.							
Available as optional extra (not 911 GT2 and GT3) : 5-gear Tiptronic transmission with torque converter.							
Clutch, dual-mass flywheel	yes, System LUK	=	=	=	=	=	no, rigid flywheel
Clutch, pressure plate	MF 228X	=	=	=	=	=	MF240
Clutch plate (mm) dia. (mm)	240	=	=	=	=	=	=
Manual transmission	G97/01	=	=	=	G97/50	G97/90	G97/90
Gearbox design	fully synchronised 6-speed manual transmission						
Number of gears forward/rev.	6/1	=	=	=	=	=	=
Gear ratios							
1st gear	3.91	=	=	=	3.82	=	=
2nd gear	2.32	=	=	=	2.14	2.26	=
3rd gear	1.61	=	=	=	1.48	1.64	=
4th gear	1.28	=	=	=	1.18	1.29	=
5th gear	1.08	=	=	=	0.97	1.06	=
6th gear	0.88	=	=	=	0.79	0.92	=
Synchromesh system							
Forward gears	VK	=	=	=	=	=	=
Reverse gear ratio	-3.59	=	=	=	=	=	=
Final drive ratio	3.44	=	=	=	=	=	=
Limited-slip differential	M	M	M	M	M	S	S
Lock-up factor under load/ coasting (%)						recomm. 40/60	recomm. 40/60
Oil cooler	no	=	=	=	yes	=	
Gearbox weight with oil (kg)	65	72.5	=	=	76.2	=	

Key and abbreviations:

ATL   Exhaust turbocharger.

BHKZ   Battery, capacitive-discharge ignition system (CDI).

DWK   Three-way catalytic converter. The DWK can burn hydro-carbon, carbon monoxide and nitrogen oxide in the exhaust utilising the lambda sensor.

EURO II   European emission standard from 1996 (HC + NOx max. 0.50g/km, CO max. 2.20g/km).

EURO III   European emission standard from 2000 (HC max. 0.20g/km, NOx max. 0.15g/km, CO max. 2.3g/km).

EURO IV   European emission standard from 2005 (HC max. 0.10g/km, NOx max. 0.08g/km, CO max. 1.0g/km).

EURO V   European emission standard, planned from 2010: It is intended to tighten the limit values of NOx still further.

LOKASIL   Running surface technology for cylinder walls. Silicon is enriched in the running surface area when the engine block is cast.

LS   Lambda sensor, measures the remaining oxygen content in hot exhaust gases.

NIKASIL   Light-alloy cylinder with piston surface coated with nickel-silicon-carbide.

OBD II   Regulation with respect to electronic data storage of malfunctioning of the monitored emission system according to the State of California, USA. If an error is detected, a malfunction indicator light (MIL) flashes in order to alert the driver to the identified malfunction and to save the respective error code in the system.

ORVR   On-board refuelling vapour recovery = system that accumulates fuel vapour which is formed when refuelling. It is collected in an activated carbon canister and returned to the running engine once certain operating conditions have been achieved.

RoW   Abbreviation for "Vehicle for rest of world", including Germany.

RON   Octane number (anti-knock properties of the fuel) R = Research method, the acceleration pinging is measured.

USA   Vehicles for the North American market, including Canada.

VTG   Variable turbine geometry.

W   Heat rating (of the spark plug).

ZMS   Dual-mass flywheel for the avoidance of torsional vibration in the drive train at low engine revolutions.

2 OHC   OHC = overhead camshaft. 2 OHC = twin overhead camshafts in the cylinder head.

4 OHV   OHV = overhead valves, 4 OHV 4 valves per combustion chamber (2 inlet and 2 exhaust valves).

Model range	911 Carrera 2	911 Carrera 2S	911 Carrera 4	911 Carrera 4S	911 Turbo	911 GT3	911 GT3 RS
Transmission (continued)							
Tiptronic S	A97/01	A96/50	A96/35	A96/35	A97/50	–	–
Gearbox design	fully automatic 5-speed transmission						
Torque converter 0 (mm)	270	=	=	=	=	–	–
Stall speed (rpm)	2660	2650	=	=	2700	–	–
Number of gears forward/ reverse	5/2	=	=	=	=	–	–
Gear ratios							
1st gear	3.60	=	=	=	=	–	–
2nd gear	2.19	=	=	=	=	–	–
3rd gear	1.41	=	=	=	=	–	–
4th gear	1.00	=	=	=	=	–	–
5th gear	0.83	=	=	=	=	–	–
Reverse gear 1 / 2	3.16 / 1.93	=	=	=	=	–	–
Final drive ratio	3.56	=	=	=	=	–	–
Limited-slip differential	no	=	=	=	=	–	–
Stability Management	PSM standard	=	=	=	=	–	–

Suspension, steering and brakes

Front suspension	Individually suspended on wishbones with semi-trailing arms and MacPherson spring struts; one conical spring per wheel with internal shock absorber; dual-function hydraulic gas-pressure shock absorbers						
Rear suspension	Multi-wishbone rear suspension with five wishbones per wheel, cylindrical coil springs with internal shock absorbers, shock absorbers: dual-function hydraulic gas pressure shock absorbers						
Steering	Hydraulic rack-and-pinion steering						
Brake system	Power-assisted hydraulic-mechanical dual-circuit brake system with monobloc brake callipers. Internally ventilated brake discs. ABS and PSM standard.						
Anti-roll bar dia. front (mm)	24.0 x 3.8 tube	=	26.8 x 4 tube	=	23.6 x 3.5 tube	26.8 x 4 tube	= =
Anti-roll bar dia. rear (mm)	–		–	20.7 x 2.8 tube	=	21.7 x 3.0 tube	20.7 x 2.8
Steering ratio	17.11:1	=	=	=	=	=	=
Turning circle dia. (m)	10.9	=	=	=	=	10.6	10.9
Brake system							
Brake circuit configuration	per axle	=	=	=	=	=	=
Brake master cylinder dia.(mm)	25.4	=	=	=	=	=	=
Stability Management							
PSM 8.0	S	S	S	S	S	S	S
Brake calliper piston diameter							
front (mm)	36+44	=	38+32+28	=	=	=	=
rear (mm)	28+30	=	=	=	=	=	=
Brake discs dia.							
front (mm)	330	=	=	=	350	=	=
rear (mm)	330	=	=	=	350	=	=
Brake disc thickness							
front (mm)	34	=	=	=	34	=	=
rear (mm)	28	=	=	=	28	=	=
Effective brake area (cm²)	568	=	=	=	698	=	=
PCCB	–		Option	Option	Option	Standard	Option

Wheels and tyres

Standard tyre specification, front	235/40ZR18	235/35ZR19	235/35ZR19	235/35ZR19	235/35ZR19	=	=
wheel (rim) / hump depth	8JX18/57	8JX19/57	8JX19/57	8JX19/57	8.5JX19/56	8.5JX19/53	=
Standard tyre specification, rear	265/40ZR18	295/30ZR19	295/30ZR19	305/30ZR19	305/30ZR19	=	=
wheel (rim) / hump depth	10JX18/58	11JX19/67	11JX19/67	11JX19/67	11JX19/51	12JX19/68	12JX19/51
Optional tyres front	235/35ZR19	–	–	–	–	–	
wheel (rim) / hump depth	8JX19/57	–	–	–	–	–	
Optional tyres rear	295/30ZR19	–	–	–	–	–	
wheel (rim) / hump depth	11Jx19/67	–	–	–	–	–	

Key:
PCCB   Porsche Composite Ceramic Brake

Model range	911 Carrera 2	911 Carrera 2S	911 Carrera 4	911 Carrera 4S	911 Turbo	911 GT3	911 GT3 RS
Body							
Monocoque structure, hot-dip galvanised lightweight steel body, partial use of HSLA* steel; airbags and side airbags for driver and passenger; number of seats: 2 + 2							
Drag coefficient (cd)	0.28	0.29	0.30	=	0.31	0.29	0.30
Frontal area A (m²)	2.00	2.00	2.00	=	2.04	2.00	2.04
Aerodynamic drag cd x A (m2)	0.56	0.58	0.60	=	0.63	0	0.611
Dimensions at kerb weight							
Length (mm)	4427	4427	4427	=	4450	4445	4460
Width (mm)	1808	1808	1852	=	1852	1808	1852
Height (mm)	1310	=	=	1300	1300	1280	=
Wheelbase (mm)	2360	=	=	=	=	=	=
Track, front (mm)	1486	1486	1488	=	1490	1497	=
Track, rear (mm)	1534	1516	1548	=	1548	1558	=
Ground clearance at permissible gross weight (mm)	65	=	=	=	55	=	=
Electrical system							
Generator output (V/W)	12/2100	=	=	=	=	=	=
Battery (Ah/A)	70/340	=	80/380	=	=	60/270	=
Weight according to DIN 70020							
Kerb weight (kg)							
Manual transmission	1395	1420	1450	1475	1585	1395	1375
Tiptronic	1435	1460	1490	1515	1620	–	–
Permissible gross weight (kg)							
Manual transmission	1810	1820	1925	1845	1950	1680	1680
Tiptronic	1855	1865	1982	1900	1980	–	–
Permissible trailer weight (kg)	none	=	=	=	=	=	=
Permissible roof load (kg)	35	=	=	=	none	=	=
with Porsche roof system (kg)	75	=	=	=	=	none	=
Performance							
Maximum speed (kmh)							
Manual transmission	285	293	280	288	310	310	=
Automatic transmission	280	285	275	280	310	–	–
Acceleration 0–62mph/100kmh (sec)							
Manual transmission	5.0	4.8	5.1	4.8	3.9	4.3	4.3
Automatic transmission	5.5	5.3	5.8	5.4	3.7	–	–
Power/weight ratio (kg/kW)	5.34	5.07	6.06	5.34	4.49	4.57	4.50
Fluid capacities							
Engine oil, change with filter (l)	8.25	=	=	=	7.8	8.75	8.75
Manual transmission (l)	2.7	2.9	2.7	=	3.8	3.3	3.3
Automatic transmission with converter (l)	9.0	=	=	=	9.0	–	–
Differential automatic (l)	1.2	=	=	=	=	–	–
All-wheel drive front differential (l)	–	–	1.5	=	=	–	–
Fuel tank/reserve tank (l)	64/10	=	=	=	=	89	89
Cooling water (l)	22.5	=	=	=	28	23	=
Brake fluid reservoir (l)	0.45	=	0.63	=	=	0.8	0.8
Headlamp cleaning reservoir (l)	3.0	=	=	=	3.0	=	=
Washer tank (l)	5.7	=	=	=	6.5	–	–
Power steering fluid	1.27	=	=	=	2.14	1.9	1.9
Fluid specifications							
Engine oil	ACEA A4-96 and special Porsche requirements						
Gearbox	GL5 SAE75W-90						
Automatic transmission	SHELL ATF 3403-M115						
Differential	SAE 85 W 90						
Front differential	GL5 SAE 75W-90						
Brake fluid	SUPER DOT 4						
Air conditioning	exclusively R134 a						
Power steering	Pentosin CHF 11 S						
Fuel	Branded fuel with minimum standard RON 98/MON 88 unleaded						

Key:
* HSLA steel = description used internationally for high-strength, low-alloy steel

Model year 2007

7 Programme, Targa 4, Turbo Cabriolet

Porsche 911 Carrera and Carrera S Coupé and
  Cabriolet
Porsche 911 Carrera 4 and Carrera 4S Coupé
  and Cabriolet
Porsche 911 Targa 4 and Targa 4S
Porsche 911 Turbo and Turbo Cabriolet
Porsche 911 GT3 and GT3 RS Coupé

After extensive modifications to the 911 Turbo and
the two 911 GT3 versions of model year 2006, the
fourth 911 Targa generation was introduced and
distributed worldwide for 2007. This marked the
first time that a Targa had been equipped with the
all-wheel drive system of the Carrera 4.

Also new for model year 2007 was the 911
Turbo in Cabriolet form, which for the first time
was fitted with the electronically controlled high-
tech all-wheel drive of the then-current Turbo.

*The fourth-generation 911 Targa was introduced in 2007 – the 911
Targa 4 was the first all-wheel drive Targa model.*

The other 911 cars (Carrera, Carrera 4 and Turbo
Coupé) continued to be produced almost
unaltered. However, there were changes to the
service intervals for the whole 911 range (except
the GT3). Previous vehicles had to be booked into a
Porsche Centre for a service every 20,000km
(12,000 miles) but from model year 2007 these
intervals were lengthened to 30,000km (18,000
miles) across the board, which significantly reduced
maintenance costs. Further measures were taken
to reduce the cost of repair for minor damage to
the bodywork. Modified impact absorbers in the
bumpers, for example, helped to protect the
supporting frame of the body.

Targa 4 and Targa 4S

There were two new Targa 4 models, the main
difference between them being their engines. The
Targa 4 used the familiar 3.6-litre M96/05 engine
with 239kW (325hp), while the Targa 4S was
equipped with the larger-capacity 3,824cc M97/01
unit, which achieved an output of 261kW (355hp).

For the first time the power train of the Carrera 4
with all-wheel drive was the basis for the two Targa
models. Between 5% and 40% of the drive could
be transmitted via the front wheels. Not only the
transmissions of the then-current Carrera 4 and
Carrera 4S were used, but also the suspension and

The 911 Targa 4 roof was improved over the previous model, running the full length of the roof, and retaining the glazed tailgate.

The new 911 Turbo Cabriolet was fitted with the M97/70 bi-turbo engine, producing 353kW (480hp) at 6,000rpm.

The 911 Turbo Cabriolet was fitted with airbags in the doors and front seat backrests, as well as driver and passenger airbags.

brakes (there was no difference between the Coupé and Cabriolet body variants). Two types of suspension were available: firstly, conventional steel-spring suspension, and secondly, Porsche Active Suspension Management (PASM) with variable

The discreet split rear wing of the 911 Turbo Cabriolet remained closed at speeds below 120kmh (72mph),...

damper adjustment, offered as an optional extra. The latter provided a choice between firm sporty tuning and a more comfortable touring setting.

Body

Since its launch in model year 1967, the Porsche 911 Targa not only represented a 911 with a detachable roof but was always a unique model: the word 'Targa' is a registered trademark belonging to Porsche AG.

The new 2007 Targa stood out visually through its improved glass roof, which extended from the windscreen frame to the middle of the roof; the

generously glazed tailgate opened up to reveal the rear luggage space, as in the previous model. The front area of the glazed roof was designed as an electric sliding module that could glide smoothly beneath the tailgate at the push of a button. The glass roof itself was made from safety glass, which was able to absorb UV rays. An electric cover was installed directly underneath the sliding roof to provide additional protection from the direct rays of the sun, as well as frost. The tailgate could be opened remotely from the outside, providing access to the 230-litre luggage space behind the seats. High-gloss polished aluminium trim bars stretched along the roofline from the A-pillars all the way to the tail.

Due to the fact that the car had no hard top, the body, especially the floorpan, needed to be significantly strengthened compared to the Coupé. This was not only noticeable in the Targa's greater kerb weight (an extra 115kg) but also its slower acceleration times.

... but opened automatically by 65mm at speeds above 120kmh (72mph) to increase downforce and improve high-speed stability.

911 Turbo Cabriolet

Driving dynamics and performance, as well as the joy of open-top driving, were at the top of the agenda when the new 911 Turbo Cabriolet was designed in the styling studio in Weissach. The following were adopted from the 997 Turbo Coupé:

- The M97/70 twin-turbo engine with variable turbine geometry, with an output of 353kW (480hp).
- The G97/50 six-speed manual transmission with limited-slip differential, or A97/50 five-speed automatic transmission.
- The complete suspension, all-wheel drive, wheels, tyres and brake system (PCCB carbon-fibre-reinforced ceramic brakes were available as an optional extra).

Body and convertible top

In the development of the Cabriolet body, particular attention was paid to the torsional stiffness of the body. In order to keep the extra weight required to strengthen the body as low as possible, high-strength sheet metal was used. So-called tailored blanks were used in the production of the bodyshell; these were fine plates of high-strength steel, varying in thickness, and alloy, welded to one another by means of laser technology, followed by a pressing process. The Cabriolet also featured a bonnet and doors made from aluminium and overall the Turbo Cabriolet weighed only 70kg more than the Coupé.

The frame around the windscreen (A-pillar) was reinforced with high-strength steel pipes and was considered a safe roll-over bar. Two further roll-over bars were installed in the partition between the rear

seats and the engine compartment, which were deployed automatically within a split second as soon as the sensor recognised that there was impending danger of the car rolling over. At the same time the driver and passengers were strapped tightly to their seats through the seatbelt tensioners.

Six airbags provided additional protection for passenger and driver. POSIP (Porsche Side Impact Protection) was another safety feature, where airbags were installed on the outside of the seat backrests as well as in the doors as protection against possible injuries.

The Turbo Cabriolet featured a remarkably low drag coefficient of 0.31. The split rear wing moved automatically upwards by 65mm to increase downforce over the rear axle, with the result that stability at high speeds was exemplary.

Model range (all 997)	Total production
911 Carrera Coupé	3168
911 Carrera Cabriolet	1684
911 Carrera S Coupé	4797
911 Carrera S Cabriolet	3141
911 Carrera 4 Coupé	1068
911 Carrera 4 Cabriolet	783
911 Carrera 4S Coupé	5084
911 Carrera 4S Cabriolet	4372
911 Targa 4	894
911 Targa 4S	1761
911 Turbo Coupé	7885
911 GT3	2333
911 GT3 RS	1095
911 Cup	233

Model range	911 Carrera	911 Carrera S	911 Carrera 4 911 Targa 4**	911 Carrera 4S 911 Targa 4S**	911 Turbo 911 Turbo Cabriolet***	911 GT3 911 GT3 RS****
Engine						
Water-cooled six-cylinder boxer engine, engine casing made from light alloy						
Engine Type	M96/05	M97/01	M96/05	M97/01	M97/70	M97/76
Displacement (cm^2)	3596	3824	3596	3824	3600	=
Bore (mm)	96	99	96	99	100	=
Stroke (mm)	82.5	=	=	=	76.4	=
Compression ratio	11.3:1	11.8:1	11.3:1	11.8:1	9.01:1	12.0:1
Engine output EC kW (hp)	239 (325)	261 (355)	239 (325)	261 (355)	353 (480)	305 (415)
Engine output SAE (HP)	325	355	325	355	480	415w
at revolutions per min. (rpm)	6800	6600	6800	6600	6000	7600
Torque (Nm)	370	400	370	400	620(680 w. overboost)	405
at revolutions per min. (rpm)	4250	4600	4250	4600	1950–5000	5500
Output per litre (kW/I)	66.5	68.3	66.5	68.3	98.1	84.7
Max. engine speed (rpm)	7300	=	=	=	6750	8400
Engine-Type	6-cylinder 4-stroke boxer engine					
Engine cooling	water	=	=	=	=	=
Crankshaft	steel, forged	=	=	=	=	=
Crankshaft bearings	x 7	=	=	=	x 8	=
Con rods	steel, forged	=	=	=	Titanium forged	=
Cylinder surface	NIKASIL	=	=	=	=	=
Cylinder head, type	2 OHC + 4 OHV	=	=	=	=	=
Configuration of inlet valves	2 overhead	=	=	=	=	=
Configuration of exh. valves	2 overhead	=	=	=	=	=
Camshaft drive	Spur gears + chain	=	=	=	=	=
Variable camshaft settings	VarioCam Plus 42°	=	=	=	VarioCam Plus 40°	VarioCam Plus 52°
Induction system	Var.induct.syst.	=	=	=	rigid	Var.induct.syst.
Turbocharging	–	–	–	–	2 ATL with VTG + 2 LLK	–
Exhaust system	Standard exhaust silencer	=	=	=	=	Sports exhaust silencer
Exhaust gas control EURO II	Lambda control + 2 DWK	=	4LS	=	4LS +2DWK	2LS +2DWK
Exhaust gas control EURO III	second.air + readjustm.with 4 Lambda sensors	=	=	=	=	=
Exhaust gas control USA	plus cascade-type cat.conv. + OBD II	=	=	=	=	=
Lubrication system	dry sump with integrated oil tank	=	=	=	dry sump with separate oil tank	=
Oil cooling	Oil-water heat exchanger	=	=	=	=	=
Engine weight dry (kg)	204	=	=	=	230	

Carburation, ignition, settings						
Engine control	DME (Digital engine electronic system), ignition, fuel injection, camshaft control					
Fuel injection	sequential, multi-point	=	=	=	=	=
Fuel quality	Super Plus unleaded	=	=	=	=	=
Octane rating RON	RON98. MON88	=	=	=	=	=
Throttle adjustment	electronic	=	=	=	=	=
Ignition	electronic	=	=	=	=	=
Distributor	solid-state distr. syst.	=	=	=	=	=
Spark plugs' manufacturer	Bosch	=	=	=	=	=
Type	FRG 5KQEO	=	=	=	FR6 DPP 332 S	FR6 LDC
Spark plug gap	1.6 ± 0.5	=	=	=	0.8 ± 0.1	=
Firing order	1–6–2–4–3–5	=	=	=	=	=

911 Targa 4**   911 Targa 4 and 911 Targa 4S are independent vehicle types that differ from the 911 Carrera 4 and Carrera 4S with respect to body as well as other technical details. Differing data are marked by **.

911 Turbo Cabriolet***   The 911 Turbo Cabriolet differs from the 911 Turbo Coupé with respect to body as well as other technical details. Differing data are marked by ***.

911 GT3 RS****   The 911 GT3 RS was designed as a competition car but could also be licensed for public road use. Technical data that differ from the 911 GT3 are marked by ****.

Key and abbreviations:

ATL   Exhaust turbocharger

BHKZ   Battery, capacitive-discharge ignition system (CDI)

DWK   Three-way catalytic converter. The DWK can burn hydro-carbon, carbon monoxide and nitrogen oxide in the exhaust utilising the lambda sensor.

EGR   Exhaust Gas Recirculation

EURO-OBD European Regulation regarding electronic data storage of engine malfunction. Data can be read retrospectively.

EURO I   European emission standard from 1992 (HC + NOx max. 0.97g/km, CO max. 2.72g/km)

EURO II European emission standard from 1996 (HC + NOx max. 0.50g/km, CO max. 2.20g/km)

EURO III European emission standard from 2000 (HC max. 0.20g/km, NOx max. 0.15g/km, CO max. 2.3g/km)

EURO IV European emission standard from 2005 (HC max. 0.10g/km, NOx max. 0.08g/km, CO max. 1.0g/km)

EURO V European emission standard, planned from 2010: It is intended to tighten the limit values of NOx still further.

LOKASIL Running surface technology for cylinder walls. Silicon is enriched in the running surface area when the engine block is cast.

LS   Lambda sensor, measures the remaining oxygen content in hot exhaust gases.

NIKASIL Light-alloy cylinder with piston surface coated with nickel-silicon-carbide

OBD II Regulation with respect to electronic data storage of malfunctioning of the monitored emission system according to the State of California, USA. If an error is detected, a malfunction indicator light (MIL) flashes in order to alert the driver to the identified malfunction and to save the respective error code in the system.

ORVR   On-board refuelling vapour recovery = system that accumulates fuel vapour which is formed when refuelling. It is collected in an activated carbon canister and returned to the running engine once certain operating conditions have been achieved.

RoW   Abbreviation for "Vehicle for rest of world", including Germany

RON   Octane number (anti-knock properties of the fuel) R = Research method, the acceleration pinging is measured

USA   Vehicles for the North American market, including Canada

VTG   Variable turbine geometry

W   Heat rating (of the spark plug)

ZMS   Dual-mass flywheel for the avoidance of torsional vibration in the drive train at low engine revolutions

2 OHC OHC = overhead camshaft. 2 OHC = twin overhead camshafts in the cylinder head

4 OHV OHV = overhead valves, 4 OHV 4 valves per combustion chamber (2 inlet and 2 exhaust valves)

Model range	911 Carrera	911 Carrera S	911 Carrera 4 911 Targa 4**	911 Carrera 4S 911 Targa 4S**	911 Turbo 911 Turbo Cabriolet***	911 GT3 911 GT3 RS****
Transmission						
Engine and gearbox are built as one drive unit.						
The hydraulically operated dry single-disc clutch is bolted onto the dual-mass flywheel.						
Drive configuration Carrera 2, 911 GT2 and 911 GT3: via dual propshafts to the rear wheels.						
Drive configuration Carrera 4, Carrera 4S and 911 Turbo: Connection transmission with the front differential via driveshaft.						
Rear and front wheels are driven via dual propshafts.						
Available as optional extra (not 911 GT2 and GT3) : 5-gear Tiptronic transmission with torque converter.						
Clutch dual-mass flywheel	yes, system LUK	=	=	=	=	=
Clutch, pressure plate	MF 228X	=	=	=	=	G MFZ 240
Clutch plate (mm) dia. (mm)	240	=	=	=	=	=
Manual transmission	G97/01	G97/01	G97/01	G97/01	G97/50	G97/90
Gearbox design	fully synchronised 6-speed manual transmission					
Number of gears forward/rev	6 + 1	=	=	=	=	=
Gear ratios						
1st gear	3.91	=	=	=	3.82	=
2nd gear	2.32	=	=	=	2.14	2.26
3rd gear	1.61	=	=	=	1.48	1.64
4th gear	1.28	=	=	=	1.18	1.29
5th gear	1.08	=	=	=	0.97	1.06
6th gear	0.88	=	=	=	0.79	0.92
Synchromesh system						
Forward gears	VK	=	=	=	=	=
Reverse gear ratio	-3.59	=	=	=	-2.67	-2.67
Final drive ratio	3.44	=	=	=	=	=
Limited-slip differential	Option	Option	Option	Option	Option	Option
Active susp. man. PASM	Standard	Standard	Standard	Standard	Standard	Option
Oil cooler	no	=	Standard	Standard	Standard	Standard
Gearbox weight with oil (kg)	65	=	72.5	=	76.2	=
All-wheel drive	–	–	Z 96/35	Z 96/35	Z 96/35	–
Front drive ratio	–	–	3.44	=	=	–
Front axle transmission weight (kg)	–	–	23	=	=	–

Model range	911 Carrera	911 Carrera S	911 Carrera 4 911 Targa 4**	911 Carrera 4S 911 Targa 4S**	911 Turbo 911 Turbo Cabriolet***	911 GT3 911 GT3 RS****
Transmission (continued)						
Tiptronic S	A97/01	A97/01	A97/01	A97/01	A97/50	–
Gearbox design	fully automatic 5-speed transmission					
Torque converter dia. (mm)	270	=	=	=	=	–
Stall speed (rpm)	2660	=	2650	=	2700	–
Number of gears forward/rev	5/2	=	=	=	=	–
1st gear	3.60	=	=	=	=	–
2nd gear	2.19	=	=	=	=	–
3rd gear	1.41	=	=	=	=	–
4th gear	1.00	=	=	=	=	–
5th gear	0.83	=	=	=	=	–
Reverse gear 1 / 2	3.17 / 1.93	=	=	=	=	–
Final drive ratio	3.56	=	=	=	=	–
Limited-slip differential	no	=	=	=	=	–
Active susp. man. PASM	Standard	Standard	Standard	Standard	Standard	–
Weight incl. converter + cooler (kg)	115.3	=	=	=	=	–

Key:
ABD   Automatic brake differential
PASM   Porsche Active Suspension Management
Syst.LUK Dual-mass flywheel system LUK (steel-spring damped)
TC   Traction control
VK   Full-cone synchromesh system with molybdenum-coated synchroniser rings

The 911 Targa 4S featured the 3.8-litre M97/01 engine, producing 261kW (355hp).

Model range	911 Carrera	911 Carrera S	911 Carrera 4 911 Targa 4**	911 Carrera 4S 911 Targa 4S**	911 Turbo 911 Turbo Cabriolet***	911 GT3 911 GT3 RS****
Suspension, steering and brakes						
Front suspension	Individually suspended on wishbones with semi-trailing arms and MacPherson spring struts; one conical spring per wheel with internal shock absorber; dual-function hydraulic gas-pressure shock absorbers					
Rear suspension	Multi-wishbone rear suspension with five wishbones per wheel, cylindrical coil springs with internal shock absorbers, dual-function hydraulic gas pressure shock absorbers					
Steering	Hydraulic rack-and-pinion steering					
Braking system	Power-assisted hydraulic-mechanical dual-circuit brake system with monobloc brake callipers. Internally ventilated brake discs. ABS and PSM standard					
Anti-roll bar dia. front (mm)	24.0 x 3.8 tube	=	26.8 x 4 tube	=	23.6 x 3.5 tube	26.8 x 4 tube
Anti-roll bar dia. rear (mm)	– –	– –	20.7 x 2.8 tube	=	21.7 x 3.0 tube	20.7 x 2.8 tube
Steering ratio	17.11:1	=	=	=	=	=
Turning circle dia. (m)	10.9	=	=	=	10.6	=
Braking system						
Brake circuit configuration	per axle	=	=	=	=	=
Brake master cylinder dia.(mm)	25.4	=	=	=	=	=
Stability Management PSM 8.0	S	S	S	S	S	S
Brake calliper piston diameter						
front (mm)	36+44	=	38+32+28	=	=	=
rear (mm)	28+30	=	=	=	=	=
Brake discs dia.						
front (mm)	330	=	=	=	350	350
rear (mm)	330	=	=	=	350	=
Brake disc thickness						
front (mm)	34	=	=	=	=	=
rear (mm)	28	=	=	=	=	34
Effective brake area (cm²)	568	=	=	=	698	=
PCCB	–	Option	Option	Option	Option	Option

Wheels and tyres						
Standard tyre specification, front	235/40ZR18	235/35ZR19	235/40ZR18	235/35ZR19	235/35ZR19	=
wheel (rim) / hump depth	8Jx18/57	8Jx19/57	8Jx18/57	8Jx19/57	8.5Jx19/56	8.5Jx19/53
Standard tyre specification, rear	265/40ZR18	295/30ZR19	295/35ZR18	305/30ZR19	305/30ZR19	305/30ZR19
wheel (rim) / hump depth	10Jx18/58	11Jx19/67	11Jx18/67	11Jx19/67	11Jx19/51	12Jx19/68
Optional tyres front	235/35ZR19	–	–	–	–	–
wheel (rim) / hump depth	8Jx19/57	–	–	–	–	–
Optional tyres rear	295/30ZR19	–	–	–	–	–
wheel (rim) / hump depth	11Jx19/67	–	–	–	–	–

Key:
PCCB   Porsche Composite Ceramic Brake

Body						
Monocoque structure, hot-dip galvanised lightweight steel body, partial use of HSLA* steel; airbags and side airbags for driver and passenger; number of seats: 2 + 2						
Drag coefficient (cd)	0.28	0.29	0.30	0.29	0.31	0.29 0.30****
Frontal area A (m²)	2.00	2.00	2.04	=	2.04	2.00 2.04****
Aerodynamic drag cd x A (m²)	0.56	0.58	0.61	0.59	0.63	0.58 0.61****
Dimensions at kerb weight						
Length (mm)	4427	=	=	=	4450	4445 4460****
Width (mm)	1808	=	1852	=	1852	1808 1852****
Height (mm)	1310	1300	1310	1300	1300	1280 1280****
Wheelbase (mm)	2350	=	=	=	=	2355 2360****
Track						
front (mm)	1486	1486	1488	=	1490	1497 1497****
rear (mm)	1529	1511	1548	=	1548	1524 1558****
Ground clearance at permissible gross weight (mm)	65	=	=	=	55	=

Model range	911 Carrera	911 Carrera S	911 Carrera 4 911 Targa 4**	911 Carrera 4S 911 Targa 4S**	911 Turbo 911 Turbo Cabriolet***	911 GT3 911 GT3 RS****
Electrical system						
Generator output (V/W)	12/2100	=	=	=	=	=
Battery (Ah/A)	70/340	=	=	=	=	60/270
Weight according to DIN 70020						
Kerb weight (kg)						
Manual transmission	1395	1429	1450 1510**	1475 1535**	1585 1655***	1395 1375****
Tiptronic	1425	1460	1490 1550**	1515 1575**	1620 1690***	–
Permissible gross weight (kg)						
Manual transmission	1810	1820	1865 1900**	1875 1916**	1950 2000***	1680 1680****
Tiptronic	1855	1865	1910 1945**	1920 1960**	1980 2035***	–
Permissible trailer weight (kg)	none	=	=	=	=	=
Permissible roof load (kg)	35	=	=	=	none	=
with Porsche roof system (kg)	75	=	=	=	=	=
Performance						
Maximum speed (kmh)						
manual transmission	285	293	280 280**	288 288**	310 310***	310 310****
automatic transmission (kmh)	280	285	275 275**	280 280**	310 310***	–
Acceleration 0–100kmh						
Manual transmission	5.0	4.8	5.1 5.3**	4.8 4.9**	3.9 4.0	4.3 4.2****
automatic transmission	5.5	5.3	5.6 5.8**	5.3 5.4**	3.7 3.8***	–
Power/weight ratio (kg/kW)	5.84	5.44	6.06 6.32**	5.65 6.32**	4.49 4.69***	4.51****
Fluid capacities						
Engine oil, change with filter (l)	8.25	=	=	=	7.8	8.75
Manual transmission (l)	2.7	2.9	2.7	=	3.8	3.3
Automatic transmission with converter (l)	9.0	=	=	=	9.0	–
Differential automatic (l)	1.2	=	=	=	=	–
All-wheel drive front differential (l)	–	–	1.5	=	=	–
Fuel tank/reserve tank (l)	64/10	=	=	=	=	=
Cooling water (l)	22.5	=	=	=	28	25
Brake fluid reservoir (l)	0.45	=	0.63	=	=	0.8
Headlamp cleaning reservoir (l)	3.0	=	=	=	=	–
Washer tank (l)	5.7	=	=	=	6.5	–
Power steering fluid	1.27	=	=	=	2.14	1.9
Fluid specifications						
Engine oil	ACEA A4-96 and special Porsche requirements					
Gearbox	GL5 SAE75W-90					
Automatic transmission	SHELL ATF 3403-M115					
Differential	SAE 85 W 90					
Front differential	GL5 SAE 75W-90					
Brake fluid	SUPER DOT 4					
Air conditioning	exclusively R134 a					
Power steering	Pentosin CHF 11 S					
Fuel	Branded fuel with minimum standard RON 98/MON 88 unleaded					

Notes:

911 Targa 4**   911 Targa 4 and 911 Targa 4S are independent vehicle types that differ from the 911 Carrera 4 and Carrera 4S with respect to body as well as other technical details.
Differing data are marked by **.

911 Turbo Cabriolet***   The 911 Turbo Cabriolet differs from the 911 Turbo Coupé with respect to body as well as other technical details. Differing data are marked by ***.

911 GT3 RS****   The 911 GT3 RS has been designed as a competition car but can also be licensed for public road use. Technical data that differ from the 911 GT3 are marked by ****.

Key:
* HSLA steel = description used internationally for high-strength, low-alloy steel

Model year 2008

8 Programme, GT2 with all-wheel drive, GT3 RSR

Porsche 911 Carrera Coupé and Cabriolet
Porsche 911 Carrera 4 and Carrera 4S Coupé and Cabriolet
Porsche 911 Targa 4 and Targa 4S
Porsche 911 Turbo Coupé and Turbo Cabriolet
Porsche 911 GT2 Coupé
Porsche 911 GT3, GT3 RS and GT3 RSR Coupé

After renewing the model range so significantly in model year 2007, there were no major modifications to existing 911s in model year 2008. The changes that were made were upgrades which had no influence on driving performance. For this reason this chapter will cover the new GT2 model and the racing cars that were derived from the 911 production road cars. For the two manufacturer cup series – Porsche Carrera Cup and Porsche Mobil 1 Supercup – a total of 265 GT3 race cars were produced in Zuffenhausen for the 2008 season on the same production line as the roadgoing versions. These Cup cars had six-cylinder 3.6-litre naturally aspirated engines, derived from the M97/76 engine of the 911 GT3 but with their power increased to 420hp.

911 GT3 Cup and GT3 Supercup

These were pure race cars that took part in the Porsche Carrera Cup classes of the DTM (German Touring Car Championship) on national and international racetracks. The Porsche Mobil 1 Supercup class was an international supporting race that preceded Formula 1 races on 12 weekends in Bahrain and Europe. The cars for both Porsche events were technically identical except for some minor regulation-related changes regarding safety and power limitation.

The engine output was up by about 15kW (20hp) in 2008 compared to the previous year, at 309kW (420hp). The Cup racers were also fitted with fully controlled catalytic converters. The transmission was a sequential six-speed gearbox with uninterrupted traction during upshifts so no gears could be jumped, intentionally or unintentionally. Instead of a single-plate clutch the cars were fitted with a triple-plate sintered clutch with a diameter of only 140mm, which produced important advantages in pure race applications.

In basic layout the suspension remained the same as in the GT3 production car, but it was tuned for racetrack applications, and could be tweaked depending on the racetrack and the driver's wishes. The brake system was equipped

During the course of 2008, 35 examples of the 911 GT3 RSR were built for racing teams around the world.

ABOVE: The 911 GT3 RSR was fitted with a full-race 3,795cc engine, developing 342kW (465hp) at 8,000rpm.

BELOW: The various cooling vents, the huge adjustable rear wing, and the large-bore exhausts are evident in this view of a 911 GT3 RSR.

The stripped-out race interior of the 911 GT3 RSR was devoid of all road-car comforts.

with a balance bar system that could be individually adjusted to the two brake circuits (front and rear axle).

Three-piece BBS light-alloy 18in wheels with central bolts were specified. The following were required: 9in front wheels with 24/64-18 Michelin racing tyres, and 11in rear wheels with 27/68-18 Michelin racing tyres.

The bodywork was essentially the same hot-dip galvanised steel shell as the roadgoing GT3, but with aerodynamically altered front and rear ends. The doors, window frames, engine lid and adjustable rear wing were all made from carbon-fibre reinforced plastic. The roll cage was welded to the body. To facilitate quick wheel changes a compressed-air lifter was installed, which lifted the entire car up so that all four wheels could be changed at the same time. Total weight was 1,150kg including oil and cooling water.

911 GT3 RSR

Whilst in the two GT3 Cup classes Porsches always competed against each other, guaranteeing a Porsche victory every time (!), the 911 GT3 RSR version faced strong competition from other marques in international long-distance events, such as the 24-hour races at Le Mans, Spa and the Nordschleife at the Nürburgring. The RSR had already achieved international class victories at 24-hour races the previous year, and the racing

department in Weissach delivered a series of 35 new race cars during the course of the 2008 model year to race teams all over the world.

The RSR's water-cooled six-cylinder boxer engine had a displacement of 3,795cc, achieved through using the crankshaft of the 911 Turbo/GT2 which had a stroke of 76.4mm, and pistons with a diameter of 102.7mm. This engine produced 342kW (465hp) at 8,000rpm despite being fitted with two air restrictors (each 29.5mm diameter), which were required by the racing regulations. The racing engine reached its maximum torque of 430Nm at 7,200rpm.

The transmission for the RSR was completely new and considerably lighter, comprising a sequential six-speed transmission with friction-plate limited-slip differential (45% lock-up factor under load and 65% under coasting). This transmission was developed at Weissach using experience gathered from the RS Spyder at races in the USA over the last few years, as well as races in Europe. Friction and power losses in the transmission were significantly less than before. Attention was also paid to the driveshafts to create diffraction angles as low as possible for racing applications.

Three-piece BBS light-alloy wheels were fitted all

ABOVE: The 911 GT3 Cup was a racing model built to compete in the Porsche Carrera Cup championship.

BELOW: The 2008-model 911 GT2 was fitted with a reworked twin-turbo engine, developing 390kw (530hp) at 6,500rpm.

round, 11Jx18 ET 34 at the front and 13Jx18 ET 12.5 at the rear. The RSR had to conform to different regulations in the USA to when taking part in long-distance races such as Le Mans. According to ACO regulations in the USA, the RSR was required to have a weight of at least 1,225kg, while European FIA regulations stipulated only 1,200kg.

911 GT2

The new 911 GT2 arrived as the fastest-ever 911 for the 2008 model year. Available exclusively with rear-wheel drive and a manual six-speed gearbox, its 3.6-litre twin-turbo power unit with variable turbine geometry (VTG) achieved 390kW (530hp) at 6,500rpm, with maximum torque of 680Nm between 2,200 and 4,500rpm. The increase in power over the 'regular' 911 Turbo came courtesy of larger compressor wheels for the turbos and a better turbine housing. For the first time, Porsche combined the turbocharged engine with an expansion-type intake manifold, which kept the temperature of the fuel/air mixture lower than the 911 Turbo's. This also lowered fuel consumption:

the GT2 returned a remarkable average fuel consumption of 22.6mpg (12.5 litres/100km). Emissions and weight were kept low by a titanium rear silencer and tailpipes.

The new GT2 featured standard Porsche Ceramic Composite Brakes (PCCB) and Porsche Active Suspension Management (PASM). It rode on 19in wheels and 235/35 ZR 19 front/ 325/30 ZR 19 rear tyres.

Model range	Total production
911 Carrera Coupé	Exact numbers for model
911 Carrera Cabriolet	year 2008 were not
911 Carrera S Coupé	available at time of going
911 Carrera S Cabriolet	to print
911 Carrera 4 Coupé	
911 Carrera 4 Cabriolet	
911 Carrera 4S Coupé	
911 Carrera 4S Cabriolet	
911 Targa 4	
911 Targa 4 S	
911 Turbo	
911 Turbo Cabriolet	
911 GT2	
911 GT3	
911 GT3 RS	

Model range	911 Carrera	911 Carrera S	911 Carrera 4 911 Targa 4**	911 Carrera 4S 911 Targa 4S**	911 Turbo 911 Turbo Cabriolet***	911 GT2	911 GT3 911 GT3 RS****
Engine	Water-cooled six-cylinder boxer engine, engine casing made from light alloy						
Engine Type	M96/05	M97/01	M96/05	M97/01	M97/70	M97/70S	M97/76
Displacement (cc)	3596	3824	3596	3824	3600	=	=
Bore (mm)	96	99	96	99	100	=	=
Stroke (mm)	82.5	=	=	=	76.4	=	=
Compression ratio	11.3:1	11.8:1	11.3:1	11.8:1	9.01:1	=	12.0:1
Engine output EC kW (hp)	239 (325)	261 (355)	239 (325)	261 (355)	353 (480)	390 (530)	305 (415)
Engine output SAE (HP)	325	355	325	355	480	530	415
at revolutions per minute (rpm) 6800	6600	6800	6600	6000	6500	7600	
Torque (Nm)	370	400	370	400	620(680 w. overboost)	680	405
at revolutions per min. (rpm)	4250	4600	4250	4600	1950–5000	2200–4500	5500
Output per litre (kW/l)	66.5	68.3	66.5	68.3	98.1	108.3	84.7
Max. engine speed (rpm)	7300	=	=	=	6750	6750	8400
Engine-Type	6-cylinder 4-stroke boxer engine						
Engine cooling	water	=	=	=	=	=	=
Crankshaft	steel, forged	=	=	=	=	=	=
Crankshaft bearings	x 7	=	=	=	x 8	=	=
Con rods	steel, forged	=	=	=	Titanium forged	=	=
Cylinder surface	NIKASIL	=	=	=	=	=	=
Cylinder head, type	2 OHC + 4 OHV	=	=	=	=	=	=
Configuration of inlet valves	2 overhead	=	=	=	=	=	=
Configuration of exhaust valves	2 overhead	=	=	=	=	=	=
Camshaft drive	Spur gears + chain	=	=	=	=	=	=
Variable camshaft settings	VarioCam Plus 42°	=	=	=	VarioCam Plus 40°	=	VarioCam Plus 52°
Induction system	Var.induct.syst.	=	=	=	rigid	rigid	Var.induct. syst.
Turbocharging	–	–	–	–	2 ATL with VTG + 2 LLK	=	–

Model range	911 Carrera	911 Carrera S	911 Carrera 4 911 Targa 4**	911 Carrera 4S 911 Targa 4S**	911 Turbo 911 Turbo Cabriolet***	911 GT2	911 GT3 911 GT3 RS****
Exhaust system	Standard exhaust silencer	=	=	=	=	=	Sports exhaust silencer
Exhaust gas control EURO II	Lambda control + 2 DWK	=	4LS	=	4LS+2DWK	=	2LS+2DWK
Exhaust gas control EURO III	second.air and readjustm. with 4 LS	=	=	=	=	=	=
Exhaust gas control USA	plus cascade-like cat.conv. + OBD II	=	=	=	=	=	=
Lubrication system	dry sump with integrated oil tank	=	=	=	dry sump with separate oil tank	=	=
Oil cooling	Oil-water heat exchanger	=	=	=	=		
Engine weight dry (kg)	204	=	=	=	230		

Carburation, ignition, settings							
Engine control	DME (Digital engine electronic system), ignition, fuel injection, camshaft control						
Fuel injection	sequential, multi-point	=	=	=	=	=	=
Fuel quality	Super Plus unleaded	=	=	=	=	=	=
Octane rating RON	RON98. MON88	=	=	=	=	=	=
Throttle adjustment	electronic	=	=	=	=	=	=
Ignition	electronic	=	=	=	=	=	=
Distributor	solid-state distr. syst.	=	=	=	=	=	=
Spark plugs manufacturer	Bosch	=	=	=	=	=	=
Type	FRG 5KQEO	=	=	=	FR6 DPP 332 S	FR6 DPP 332	SFR6 LDC
Spark plug gap	1.6 ± 0.5	=	=	=	0.8 ± 0.1		
Firing order	1–6–2–4–3–5	=	=	=	=	=	=

Abbreviations and notes:

911 Targa 4** — 911 Targa 4 and 911 Targa 4S are independent vehicle types that differ from the 911 Carrera 4 and Carrera 4S with respect to body as well as other technical details. Differing data are marked by **.

911 Turbo Cabriolet*** — The 911 Turbo Cabriolet differs from the 911 Turbo Coupé with respect to body as well as other technical details. Differing data are marked by ***.

911 GT3 RS**** — The 911 GT3 RS has been designed as a competition car but can also be licensed for public road use. Technical data that differ from the 911 GT3 are marked by ****.

Key:

ATL — Exhaust turbocharger.

BHKZ — Battery, capacitive-discharge ignition system (CDI).

DWK — Three-way catalytic converter. The DWK can burn hydro-carbon, carbon monoxide and nitrogen oxide in the exhaust utilising the lambda sensor.

EGR — Exhaust Gas Recirculation.

EURO-OBD — European Regulation regarding electronic data storage of engine malfunction. Data can be read retrospectively.

EURO I — European emission standard from 1992 (HC + NOx max. 0.97g/km, CO max. 2.72g/km).

EURO II — European emission standard from 1996 (HC + NOx max. 0.50g/km, CO max. 2.20g/km).

EURO III — European emission standard from 2000 (HC max. 0.20g/km, NOx max. 0.15g/km, CO max. 2.3g/km).

EURO IV — European emission standard from 2005 (HC max. 0.10g/km, NOx max. 0.08g/km, CO max. 1.0g/km).

EURO V — European emission standard, planned from 2010: It is intended to tighten the limit values of NOx still further.

LOKASIL — Running surface technology for cylinder walls. Silicon is enriched in the running surface area when the engine block is cast.

LS — Lambda sensor, measures the remaining oxygen content in hot exhaust gases.

NIKASIL — Light-alloy cylinder with piston surface coated with nickel-silicon-carbide.

OBD II — Regulation with respect to electronic data storage of malfunctioning of the monitored emission system according to the State of California, USA. If an error is detected, a malfunction indicator light (MIL) flashes in order to alert the driver to the identified malfunction and to save the respective error code in the system.

ORVR — On-board refuelling vapour recovery = system that accumulates fuel vapour which is formed when refuelling. It is collected in an activated carbon canister and returned to the running engine once certain operating conditions have been achieved.

RoW — Abbreviation for "Vehicle for rest of world", including Germany.

RON — Octane number (anti-knock properties of the fuel) R = Research method, the acceleration pinging is measured.

USA — Vehicles for the North American market, including Canada.

VTG — Variable turbine geometry.

W — Heat rating (of the spark plug)

ZMS — Dual-mass flywheel for the avoidance of torsional vibration in the drive train on low engine revolutions.

2 OHC — OHC = overhead camshaft. 2 OHC = twin overhead camshafts in the cylinder head.

4 OHV — OHV = overhead valves, 4 OHV 4 valves per combustion chamber (2 inlet and 2 exhaust valves).

Model range	911 Carrera	911 Carrera S	911 Carrera 4 911 Targa 4**	911 Carrera 4S 911 Targa 4S**	911 Turbo 911 Turbo Cabriolet***	911 GT2	911 GT3 911 GT3 RS****

Transmission

Engine and gearbox are built as one drive unit.
The hydraulically operated dry single-plate clutch is bolted onto the dual-mass flywheel.
Drive configuration Carrera 2, 911 GT2 and 911 GT3: via dual propshafts to the rear wheels.
Drive configuration Carrera 4, Carrera 4S and 911 Turbo: connection to the front differential via driveshaft.
Rear and front wheels are driven via dual propshafts.
Available as optional extra (not 911 GT2 and GT3) : 5-gear Tiptronic transmission with torque converter.

	911 Carrera	911 Carrera S	911 Carrera 4 911 Targa 4**	911 Carrera 4S 911 Targa 4S**	911 Turbo 911 Turbo Cabriolet***	911 GT2	911 GT3 911 GT3 RS****
Clutch dual-mass flywheel	yes, System LUK	=	=	=	=	=	=
Clutch, pressure plate	MF 228X	=	=	=	=	=	G MFZ 240
Clutch plate (mm) dia. (mm)	240	=	=	=	=	=	=
Manual transmission	G97/01	G97/01	G97/01	G97/01	G97/50	G97/88	G97/90
Gearbox design	fully synchronised 6-speed manual transmission						
Number of gears forward/rev	6 + 1	=	=	=	=	=	=
Gear ratios							
1st gear	3.91	=	=	=	3.82	3.15	=
2nd gear	2.32	=	=	=	2.14	1.89	2.26
3rd gear	1.61	=	=	=	1.48	1.40	1.64
4th gear	1.28	=	=	=	1.18	1.09	1.29
5th gear	1.08	=	=	=	0.97	0.89	1.06
6th gear	0.88	=	=	=	0.79	0.73	0.92
Synchromesh system							
Forward gears	VK	=	=	=	=	=	=
Reverse gear ratio	-3.59	=	=	=	-2.67	-2.86	=
Final drive ratio	3.44	=	=	=	=	=	=
Limited-slip differential	Option	Option	Option	Option	Option	Standard	Option
Active susp. man. PASM	Standard	Standard	Standard	Standard	Standard	Standard	Standard
Oil cooler	no	=	Standard	Standard	Standard	Standard	Standard
Gearbox weight with oil (kg)	65	=	72.5	=	76.2	=	=
All-wheel drive	–	–	Z 96/35	Z 96/35	Z 96/35	–	–
Front drive ratio	–	–	3.44	=	=	–	–
Front axle transmission weight (kg)	–	–	23	=	=	–	–
Tiptronic S	A97/01	A97/01	A97/01	A97/01	A97/50	–	–
Gearbox design	fully automatic 5-speed transmission						
Torque converter dia. (mm)	270	=	=	=	=		
Stall speed (rpm)	2660	=	2650	=	2700		
Number of gears forward/rev	5+2	=	=	=	=		
Gear ratios							
1st gear	3.60	=	=	=	=		
2nd gear	2.19	=	=	=	=		
3rd gear	1.41	=	=	=	=		
4th gear	1.00	=	=	=	=		
5th gear	0.83	=	=	=	=		
Reverse gear 1 / 2	3.16 / 1.93	=	=	=	=		
Final drive ratio	3.56	=	=	=	=		
Limited-slip differential	no	=	=	=	=		
Active susp.man. PASM	S	S	S	S	S		
Weight incl. converter and cooler (kg)	115.3	=	=	=	=		

Key:
ABD   Automatic brake differential.
PASM   Porsche Active Suspension Management.
Syst.LUK Dual-mass flywheel system LUK (steel-spring damped).
TC   Traction contro.l
VK   Full-cone synchromesh system with molybdenum-coated synchroniser rings.

Suspension, steering and brakes

Model range	911 Carrera	911 Carrera S	911 Carrera 4 / 911 Targa 4**	911 Carrera 4S / 911 Targa 4S**	911 Turbo / 911 Turbo Cabriolet***	911 GT2	911 GT3 / 911 GT3 RS****
Front suspension	Individually suspended on wishbones with semi-trailing arms and MacPherson spring struts; one conical spring per wheel with internal shock absorber; dual-function hydraulic gas-pressure shock absorbers						
Rear suspension	Multi-wishbone rear suspension with five wishbones per wheel, cylindrical coil springs with internal shock absorbers, dual-function hydraulic gas pressure shock absorbers						
Steering	Hydraulic rack-and-pinion steering						
Brake system	Power-assisted hydraulic-mechanical dual-circuit brake system with monobloc brake callipers. Internally ventilated brake discs. ABS and PSM standard						
Anti-roll bar dia. front (mm)	24.0 x 3.8 tube	=	26.8 x 4 tube	=	23.6 x 3.5 tube	=	26.8 x 4 tube
Anti-roll bar dia. rear (mm)	–	–	20.7 x 2.8 tube	=	21.7 x 3.0 tube	=	20.7 x 2.8 tube
Steering ratio	17.11:1–13.8	=	=	=	=	=	=
Turning circle dia. (m)	10.9	=	=	=		=	10.6
Braking system							
Brake circuit configuration	per axle	=	=	=	=	=	=
Brake master cylinder dia.(mm)	25.4	=	=	=	=	=	=
Stability Management PSM 8.0	Standard	Standard	Standard	Standard	Standard	Standard	Standard
Brake calliper piston diameter							
front (mm)	36+44	=	38+32+28	=	=	=	=
rear (mm)	28+30	=	=	=	=	=	=
Brake discs dia.							
front (mm)	330	330	=	=	350	380	350
rear (mm)	330	330	=	=	350	350	=
Brake disc thickness							
front (mm)	34	34	=	=	34	34	=
rear (mm)	28	28	=	=	28	28	=
Effective brake area (cm²)	568	568	=	=	698	=	=
PCCB	–	Option	Option	Option	Option	Standard	Option

Wheels and tyres

	911 Carrera	911 Carrera S	911 Carrera 4 / 911 Targa 4**	911 Carrera 4S / 911 Targa 4S**	911 Turbo / 911 Turbo Cabriolet***	911 GT2	911 GT3 / 911 GT3 RS****
Standard tyre specification, front	235/40ZR18	235/35ZR19	235/40ZR18	235/35ZR19	235/35ZR19	=	=
wheel (rim) / hump depth	8Jx18/57	8Jx19/57	8Jx18/57	8Jx19/57	8.5Jx19/56	8.5Jx19/53	8.5Jx19/53
Standard tyre specification, rear	265/40ZR18	295/30ZR19	295/30ZR19	305/30ZR19	305/30ZR19	325/30ZR19	305/30ZR19
wheel (rim) / hump depth	10Jx18/58	11Jx19/67	11Jx18/67	11Jx19/67	11Jx19/51	12Jx19/68	12Jx19/68
Optional tyres front	235/35ZR19	–	–	–	–	–	–
wheel (rim) / hump depth	8Jx19/57	–	–	–	–	–	–
Optional tyres rear	295/30ZR19	–	–	–	–	–	–
wheel (rim) / hump depth	11Jx19/67	–	–	–	–	–	–

Key:
PCCB   Porsche Composite Ceramic Brake

Body

	911 Carrera	911 Carrera S	911 Carrera 4 / 911 Targa 4**	911 Carrera 4S / 911 Targa 4S**	911 Turbo / 911 Turbo Cabriolet***	911 GT2	911 GT3 / 911 GT3 RS****
Monocoque structure, hot-dip galvanised lightweight steel body, partial use of HSLA* steel; airbags and side airbags for driver and passenger; number of seats: 2 + 2							
Drag coefficient (cd)	0.28	0.29	0.30	0.29	0.31 0.31***	0.32	0.29 0.30****
Frontal area A (m²)	2.00	2.00	2.04	=	2.04 2.04***	2.05	2.00 2.04****
Aerodynamic drag cd x A (m²)	0.56	0.58	0.61	0.59	0.63 0.63***	0.66	0.58 0.61****
Dimensions at kerb weight							
Length (mm)	4427	=	=	=	4450	4469	4445 4460****
Width (mm)	1808	=	1852	=			1808 1852****
Height (mm)	1310	1300	1310	1300		1285	1280 1280****
Wheelbase (mm)	2350	=	=	=	=	=	2355 2360****
Track							
front (mm)	1486	=	1488	=	1490	1515	1497 1497****
rear (mm)	1529	1511	1548	=		1550	1524 1558****
Ground clearance at permissible gross weight (mm)	65	=	=	=	55	=	=

Model range	911 Carrera	911 Carrera S	911 Carrera 4 911 Targa 4**	911 Carrera 4S 911 Targa 4S**	911 Turbo 911 Turbo Cabriolet***	911 GT2	911 GT3 911 GT3 RS****
Electrical system							
Generator output (V/W)	12/2100	=	=	=	=	=	=
Battery (Ah/A)	70/340	=	=	=	=	=	60/270
Weight according to DIN 70020							
Kerb weight (kg)							
Manual transmission	1395	1420	1450 1510**	1475 1535**	1585 1655***	1440	1395 1375****
Tiptronic	1435	1460	1490 1560**	1515 1575**	1620 1690***	–	–
Permissible gross weight (kg)							
Manual transmission	1810	1820	1865 1900**	1875 1915**	1950 2000***	1750	1680 1680****
Tiptronic	1855	1865	1910 1945**	1920 1960**	1980 2035***	–	–
Permissible trailer weight (kg)	none	=	=	=	=	=	=
Permissible roof load (kg)	35	35	= none**	= none**	none none**	=	=
with Porsche roof system (kg)	75	75	= none**	= none**	75 none**	none	none
Performance							
Maximum speed (kmh)							
Manual transmission	285	293	280	288	310	329	310
Automatic transmission	280	285	275	280	310	–	–
Acceleration 0–62mph/100kmh (sec)							
Manual transmission	5.0	4.8	5.1 5.3**	4.8 4.9**	3.9 4.0***	3.7	4.3 4.2****
Automatic transmission	5.5	5.3	5.6 5.8**	5.3 5.4**	3.7 3.8***	–	–
Power/weight ratio (kg/kW)	5.84	5.44	6.06 6.32**	5.65 6.32**	4.49 4.69***	3.69	4.51****
Fluid capacities							
Engine oil, change with filter (l)	8.25	=	=	=	7.8	=	8.75
Manual transmission (l)	2.7	2.9	2.7	=	3.8	=	3.3
Automatic transmission with converter (l)	9.0	=	=	=	9.0	–	–
Differential automatic (l)	1.2	=	=	=	=	–	–
All-wheel drive front differential (l)	–	–	1.5	=	=	–	–
Fuel tank/reserve tank (l)	64/10	=	=	=	67	90	89
Cooling water (l)	22.5	=	=	=	28	28	23
Brake fluid reservoir (l)	0.45	=	0.63	=	=	0.8	0.8
Headlamp cleaning reservoir (l)	3.0	=	=	=	=	=	=
Washer tank (l)	5.7	=	=	=	6.5	–	–
Power steering fluid	1.27	=	=	=	2.14	2.14	1.9
Fluid specifications							
Engine oil	ACEA A4-96 and special Porsche requirements						
Gearbox	GL5 SAE75W-90						
Automatic transmission	SHELL ATF 3403-M115						
Differential	SAE 85 W 90						
Front differential	GL5 SAE 75W-90						
Brake fluid	SUPER DOT 4						
Air conditioning	exclusively R134 a						
Power steering	Pentosin CHF 11 S						
Fuel	Branded fuel with minimum standard RON 98/MON 88 unleaded						

Notes:

911 Targa 4** — 911 Targa 4 and 911 Targa 4S are independent vehicle types that differ from the 911 Carrera 4 and Carrera 4S with respect to body as well as other technical details. Differing data are marked by **.

911 Turbo Cabriolet*** — The 911 Turbo Cabriolet differs from the 911 Turbo Coupé with respect to body as well as other technical details. Differing data are marked by ***.

911 GT3 RS**** — The 911 GT3 RS has been designed as a competition car but can also be licensed for public road use. Technical data that differ from the 911 GT3 are marked by ****.

Key:
* HSLA steel = description used internationally for high-strength, low-alloy steel.

Model year 2009

9 Programme, direct injection and PDK double-clutch transmission

Porsche 911 Carrera and Carrera S Coupé and Cabriolet

Porsche 911 Carrera 4 and 4S Coupé and Cabriolet

Porsche 911 Targa 4 and Targa 4S

Porsche 911 Turbo Coupé and Cabriolet

Porsche 911 GT2 Coupé

Porsche 911 GT3, GT3 RS and GT3 RSR Coupé

The 2009 model year range started to roll off the production line at Zuffenhausen on 5 July 2008.

The 2009 911 model line-up. Anti-clockwise from bottom left: 911 Carrera S Coupé (blue) and Carrera S Cabriolet (green) with 3.8-litre, 283kW (385hp) engine and Porsche double-clutch transmission, providing a top speed of just over 300kmh (186mph) and acceleration from 0 to 100kmh (0 to 62mph) in 4.3 seconds; Carrera Cabriolet (yellow) and Carrera Coupé (white) with 3.6-litre, 254kW (345hp) engine.

The rear-wheel drive Carrera and Carrera S were fitted with a completely new six-cylinder boxer engine with direct fuel injection into the combustion chambers, and were (finally!) available with Porsche double-clutch transmission (PDK) as an optional extra. The new 911 was more powerful, more economical and faster in terms of both top speed and acceleration.

Engine

The totally new water-cooled six-cylinder boxer engine initially powered only two 911s: the rear-wheel drive Carrera and Carrera S. While the displacement remained at 3.6 litres for the Carrera and 3.8 litres for the Carrera S, their exact sizes showed that they were a new generation. Power was also up: 254kW (345hp) for the regular 911 and 283kW (385hp) for the 'S' version.

The main difference in the new engines was the direct fuel injection system, which pumped fuel directly into the combustion chambers and made it possible for an air-fuel mixture to form directly in the chamber. Because the fuel was injected fractions of a second prior to combustion, the engines responded more directly and spontaneously to the slightest movement of the driver's right foot. Fuel consumption was significantly reduced using this method, as well as emissions.

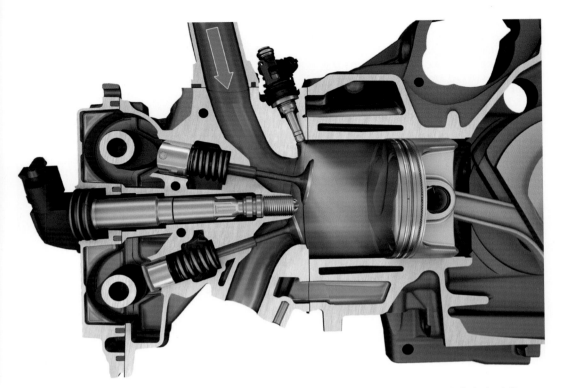

Cross-section through a cylinder block and cylinder head. The injector nozzles in the cylinder head injected directly into the combustion chamber at a high pressure of 120bar. Combined with the aspirated fresh air, this resulted in a particularly homogeneous air-fuel mixture. Up to 50% higher torque was consequently achieved in the partial-load operational range, plus lower emissions in all load ranges.

The new DFI (Direct Fuel Injection) system consisted of the following components:

■ High-pressure fuel-injection pump (120bar), driven by the engine.
■ Fuel feed through high-pressure pipes.
■ Six electrically controlled fuel injection valves.
■ Digital Engine Electronics system that took over the activation of the ignition and the management of the six injector nozzles depending on the position of the crankshaft and the load.

On a continuous basis, the Digital Engine Electronics system processed a wide variety of information received from the sensors on the car:

■ Position of the crankshaft.
■ Engine revolutions.
■ Position of the throttle valve.
■ Data from the lambda probes.
■ Operating temperature of the engine.
■ Temperature of the intake air and many other parameters.
■ Exchange of data with the PDK transmission control.

While all self-igniting diesel engines have been operating with direct injection into their combustion chambers since their invention by Rudolf Diesel in 1895, petrol-fuelled engines were initially equipped with carburettors in which aspirated fresh air was mixed with the fuel, after which this mixture was transported into the cylinder. One disadvantage of this has always been the sensitivity required in positioning the carburettors and controlling the amount of fuel in all load ranges.

Such disadvantages became especially noticeable in aeroplane engines, as with increasing altitude less and less oxygen was available for optimum combustion, and looping the loop when descending, and flying upside down, were hardly possible with carburettors, or only possible at huge expense. That is why the first suitable direct fuel injectors were those in the DB 605 DC aeroplane engine from Mercedes-Benz (12-cylinder V-engine, 36-litre displacement, 1,475hp at 2,800rpm), which was used especially in Messerschmitt Me 109 G fighter planes from 1940.

One name was inseparably connected with the development of direct fuel injection technology for four-stroke petrol engines: Dr Ing Hans

Scherenberg. He was responsible for the fuel injection of the DB 605 engines, and after the war he initially developed a small sports car, the Gutbrod Superior, in Plochingen, Germany, whose two-cylinder two-stroke engine was productionised with direct fuel injection. It was also Scherenberg who developed the direct fuel injection for the Daimler-Benz 300 SL engine in 1952.

Thereafter, direct fuel injection was forgotten about within the automobile industry for about 40 years, as improved carburettors and induction-manifold fuel injection were less costly, less complex and less prone to failure, as well as more resistant to the sulphur particles present in petrol. It was also technically very difficult to control the high injection pressure of 120bar.

However, once lead- and sulphur-free fuels became available worldwide, direct fuel injection systems slowly found their way back on to the road:

The new engine type, with direct fuel injection into the combustion chambers. Technical data of the engine for the 911 S: displacement 3.8 litres, output 283kW (385hp), maximum torque 420Nm.

1997   Mitsubishi with GDI (Gasoline Direct Injection).
1999   Renault, Peugeot and Citroën with IDE (Injection Direct Essence).
2000   VW with FSI (Fuel Stratified Injection).
2000   Alfa Romeo with JTS (Jet Thrust Stoichiometric).
2003   Porsche with DFI (Direct Fuel Injection) in the Cayenne.

Compared to pre-DFI engines, power increased by 14.7kw (20hp) for the Carrera, and by 22kW (30hp) for the Carrera S. The torque of the new engines also increased: for instance the Carrera's torque rose from 370Nm at 4,250rpm to 390Nm at 4,400rpm.

The fuel consumption for the new models, according to EU standards, now stood at 10.3 litres per 100km (27.4mpg) for the Carrera (previously 11.0/25.6) and at 10.6 litres (26.6mpg) for the Carrera S (previously 11.5/24.5).

Transmission
Both new Carreras were equipped with a fully synchronised manual six-speed gearbox as standard. For the previous two years a dual-mass

Porsche PDK double-clutch transmission for the 911 Carrera and 911 Carrera S model ranges. The transmission had seven forward gears and one reverse gear. The double clutch was positioned inside the two-piece transmission housing as well as the seven-speed transmission, a third gearbox shaft with a geared driveshaft and the differential.

flywheel had been mounted at the end of the crankshaft, which significantly damped the torsional vibrations of the six-cylinder engine. A mechanical dry single-plate clutch worked well with the manual transmission.

The earlier Tiptronic S automatic transmission with five forward gears and two reverse gears was replaced by a new seven-speed Porsche Doppelkupplungsgetriebe (PDK) double-clutch transmission. The double-clutch gearbox had certain advantages over both manual and conventional automatic (torque converter) transmissions. The benefits compared with automatic transmission were:

- No loss of power through the use of a hydraulic torque converter.
- No costly oil hydraulics and no lining wear of multi-plate clutches in the hydraulic automatic transmission fluid.
- Freely selectable gear ratios for all gears.
- No torque-converter slip when accelerating.

Advantages compared with manual transmission were:

- Uninterrupted traction upon acceleration, gearchange uninterrupted through the changeover from one dry clutch to another, even under full load.
- Two driving states available for the driver: in the automatic position the car's gearchanges would depend on the accelerator pedal position in mid-range torque, while at full throttle it would

utilise the full range of torque. In the 'manual' position the driver decided via a tip switch on the steering wheel when to change gear.
- Gear ratios could be freely selected for each gear (normal synchronised helical spur gears formed a gear ratio) – something impossible with automatic transmission with planetary gear sets.
- Seventh gear was designed as an overdrive gear so that engine revs would be lower at cruising speeds. At such speeds fuel consumption decreased considerably, and as with conventional automatic transmissions, it could be automatically down-shifted via 'kickdown'.

The first basic trials with double-clutch transmissions were carried out at Porsche's test facility in Zuffenhausen in the early 1970s (the development centre at Weissach was then still under construction.)

It was not until the next decade that Porsche first raced with double-clutch PDK transmissions in the 962 C race car. PDK gearchanges were no longer achieved via a gear lever but through an electrically operated tip switch on the steering wheel (it would be years before this gearchange method was

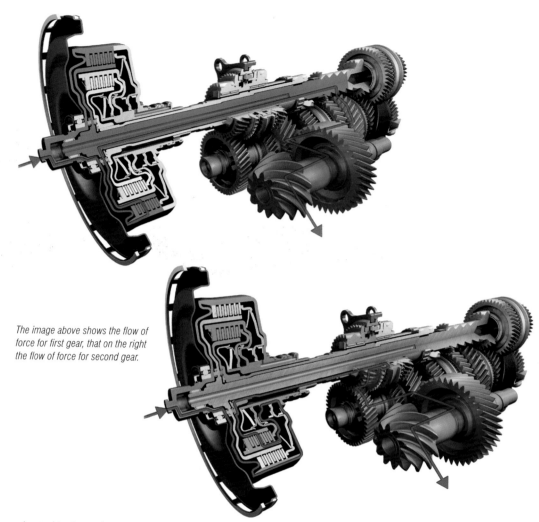

The image above shows the flow of force for first gear, that on the right the flow of force for second gear.

adopted in Formula 1 racing). The most important advantage of this system was that the driver could keep both hands on the steering wheel and concentrate on steering rather than gearchanging.

At the same time as the factory 962 C was competing in races, a PDK transmission was developed for Audi for rally applications, which former Audi works pilot Walter Röhrl did not like at all during his first test drives. He criticised the fact that all of a sudden an electronic 'manager' was shifting gears for him without being asked. Only the excellent lap times convinced him!

Volkswagen and Audi offered double-clutch systems in road cars from 2003 under the name 'direct-shift gearbox' (DSG). Porsche had more challenges to overcome. It first had to find a manufacturer, as the company was too small to consider in-house manufacture, even though it had big factories at Zuffenhausen and Leipzig.

Although the PDK transmissions were developed and tested in Weissach, production and assembly was actually carried out by ZF.

Another feature of the PDK transmission in the 911 was that it incorporated 'launch control' in racing mode (brake fully depressed, accelerator on full throttle), which enabled the car to launch itself from a standing start at some 6,000rpm and accelerate away dramatically. Thus the new Carrera S reached the 62mph (100kmh) mark from rest in just 4.3 seconds. With a standard manual six-speed gearbox, even the best drivers would take 0.2 seconds longer.

Brief description of PDK transmission

Both of the accompanying pictures depict the double-clutch unit on the left. The outer housing was rigidly connected to the dual-mass flywheel and rotates with the engine. The outer clutch K1 (left image, in blue) was connected with the inner shaft (blue). Odd-numbered gears (first, third, fifth, seventh and reverse) were located on this shaft.

The inner clutch K2 (right image, depicted in green) was connected to a hollow shaft (green) on which the shiftable gears for second, fourth and sixth gear were located. In the picture on the left, the flow of force is depicted with first gear (blue) engaged; in the picture on the right, with second gear (green) engaged.

While driving, sensors monitored whether acceleration or deceleration was taking place and the next gear was automatically pre-selected. When in automatic mode, the gears changed automatically when the programmed gearchange speed was reached. In manual mode, the driver could shift gears either by tipping toggles on the steering wheel or by moving the gear lever, but only if the programme determined that the shift was sensible: for instance it would not complete downshifts at speeds that could lead to over-revving and thus damage the engine/gearbox unit.

A further advantage of PDK was the noticeably lower fuel consumption when driving in automatic mode. The transmission shifted into higher gears from low engine revs with uninterrupted traction, and quickly reached seventh gear, which worked as an 'overdrive' with a tall ratio and low engine revs. PDK-equipped cars boasted better fuel consumption by 1.4 litres (Carrera) and 1.5 litres (Carrera S) per 100km compared to the model year 2008 range with Tiptronic S transmission (see table at the end of the chapter).

Suspension
Even though information regarding the modifications to the suspension of model year 2009 cars was not available at the time of writing, a new generation of wheels in a new design arrived for 2009: the Carrera was fitted with 18in light-alloy wheels and the Carrera S with 19in wheels as standard.

Porsche's PCCB ceramic brake system was available as an optional upgrade for all Carrera models, offering lighter weight, less unsprung mass for better driving dynamics on bumpy surfaces, low disc wear and much extended service life for the special brake pads.

Body
The visible changes were only apparent if you looked closely: a new front spoiler with larger air intakes for engine cooling and front brake cooling. One small difference between the two new Carrera models was their exhaust tailpipes: the Carrera had two oval tailpipes while the Carrera S received four round ones.

Interior fittings
The cockpit was newly designed, as was the steering wheel, which received further function

The new operating lever for the PDK transmission. The automatic programme could be found on the right gate. If the gear selector was moved to the left, manual operation (M) was engaged. If the selector was pushed forwards (+), an upshift with uninterrupted traction was carried out, while a downshift was effected by tipping the selector backwards (-).

buttons in addition to the new gear selector toggles for the PDK transmission.

Electrical system
All model year 2009 Carrera models received LED daytime driving lights as standard, integrated into the front indicator light unit, as well as bi-xenon main headlights. Dynamic cornering lights were available as an option. LED light technology was also used in the freshly designed rear lamps.

Standard light-alloy 18in wheel for the 911 Carrera; behind it the brake system with internally-vented and drilled steel brake disc. Brake calliper colour: black.

The 911 Carrera S was fitted with 19in light alloy wheels. In this picture the PCCB brakes with yellow brake callipers are visible. The ceramic brake discs were internally-vented and drilled.

Comparison of most important technical data:	911 Carrera Model year 2008	911 Carrera Model year 2009	911 Carrera S Model year 2008	911 Carrera S Model year 2009
Drive train				
Water-cooled, six-cylinder boxer engine, engine casing made from light-alloy forged, 7-bearing steel crankshaft; four-valve technology with adjustable valve timing of intake camshafts (VarioCam)				
Displacement (cc)	3596	3614	3824	3800
Engine output EC kW (hp)	239 (325)	254 (345)	261 (355)	283 (385)
at revolutions per minute (rpm)	6800	6500	6600	6700
Max. engine speed (Nm)	370	390	400	420
at revolutions per minute (rpm)	4250	4400	4600	4700

Carburation				
Fuel injection	before inlet valves sequential, multi-point	directly into combustion chamber	before inlet valves sequential, multi-point	directly into combustion chamber

Transmission				
Engine and gearbox are built as one drive unit.				
The hydraulically operated dry single-disc clutch is bolted onto the dual-mass flywheel; fully synchronised 6-speed manual transmission with integrated differential; dual propshafts drive the rear wheels				
Optional extras	Tiptronic S	PDK transmission	Tiptronic S	PDK transmission
Gears, forward/reverse	5/2	7/1	5/2	7/1

Performance				
Maximum speed (kmh)				
Manual transmission	285	289	293	302
Automatic transmission/PDK	280	289	285	302
Acceleration from 0–100kmh (sec)				
Manual transmission	5.0	4.7	4.8	4.5
Automatic transmission/PDK	5.5	4.5	5.3	4.3
Fuel consumption acc. ECE standards (litres/100km)				
Manual transmission	11.0	10.3	11.5	10.6
Automatic transm./PDK	11.2	9.8	11.7	10.2

ABOVE: Model year 2009 Porsche 911 Carrera S with bi-xenon main headlights and daytime driving lights located in the indicator light unit. The new front end with enlarged air intakes for cooling the engine and front brakes is clearly visible.

BELOW: The 911 Carrera Cabriolet's striking rear end with newly designed rear lamps, now with LED light technology. The 911 Carrera cars were fitted with two oval-shaped tailpipes, while the Carrera S had four round ones.

Carrera 4 and Carrera 4S

At the end of June 2008 the first technical details were published for the Carrera 4 and Carrera 4S for model year 2009, with all-wheel drive 911s arriving at Porsche Centres from 25 October 2008. These vehicles were equipped with the same direct fuel injection engines as their two-wheel drive counterparts: 3.6-litre displacement in the Carrera 4 and 3.8 litres in the Carrera 4S. PDK double-clutch transmission was also available for all four-wheel drive models, and of course had a driveshaft running to the front end to make the cars all-wheel drive. The new Carrera 4 models were faster and more economical than before, and the Carrera 4 with PDK transmission had similar fuel consumption of 10.1 litres per 100km (27.9mpg) to the Carrera 2. Visual identifying features of the Carrera 4 model range compared with the Carrera 2 were a 44mm wider rear end and a red reflector trim bar between the rear lights.

Drivetrain

Electronically controlled Porsche Traction

The all-wheel-drive 911 cars were also equipped with the new direct fuel injection engines. A six-speed transmission driving all four wheels was standard. The Porsche double-clutch transmission with seven forward gears was also offered as an optional extra for the Carrera 4 Coupé and Cabriolet.

Management (PTM) replaced the previous all-wheel drive with its viscous multiple-plate clutch. The transmissions were equipped with a mechanical transverse lock on the rear axle (limited-slip differential) as standard.

Model range	Total production
911 Carrera Coupé	Production numbers were not yet available at time of going to print.
911 Carrera Cabriolet	
911 Carrera S	
911 Carrera S Cabriolet	
911 Carrera 4 Coupé	
911 Carrera 4 Cabriolet	
911 Carrera 4S Coupé	
911 Carrera 4S Cabriolet	
911 Turbo	
911 GT3	

'Engine of the year 2008' award for Porsche

When the British specialist magazine *Engine Technology International* announced its awards for outstanding engines in 2008, Porsche emerged pre-eminent. The 'Engine of the Year 2008' contest was judged by 65 renowned specialist journalists from over 30 different countries. As well as engine performance and fuel consumption, the running characteristics of the engine and use of pioneering technology were also evaluated. The prize was finally awarded to Porsche's 911 Turbo M97/70 engine, a 3.6-litre boxer engine with two turbochargers with variable turbine geometry and a healthy output of 480hp (and an even healthier 530hp in the 911 GT2). The prize-giving ceremony was held at the Automotive Testing Expo Europe 2008 international trade fair in Stuttgart on 7 May 2008. Porsche won the 'Best Performance Engine' award with 137 points, against such strong competitors as BMW's 5.0-litre V10 engine for the M5 and M6 (134 points); BMW's 4.0-litre V8 engine for the M3 (133 points); Ferrari's 6.0-litre V12 engine for the 599 GTB (125 points); Nissan's 3.8-litre twin-turbo engine for the GT-R (124 points); and Audi's 5.0-litre V10 engine for the RS6 (108 points).

The engine of the 911 Turbo – the increased-power rated version of which was also installed in the 911 GT2 – won the 'Best Performance Engine' award in May 2008. The important characteristics of the engine in the S-version for the 911 GT2 were: it was a six-cylinder boxer engine with two exhaust-gas turbochargers with variable turbine geometry; it complied with all known emission threshold values worldwide; displacement was 3,600cc, output 390kW (530hp) at 6,500rpm, torque 680Nm at 1,950–5,000rpm.

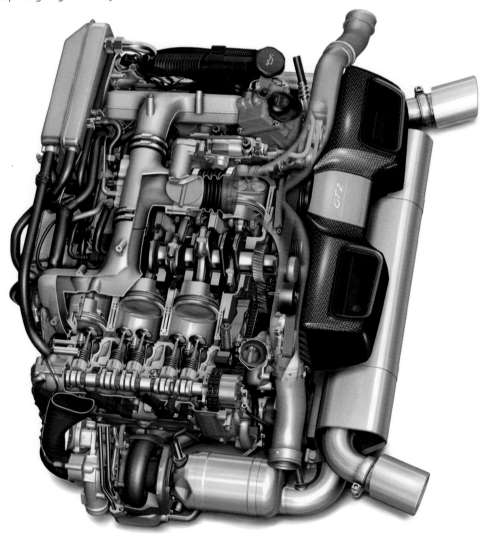

Epilogue

A novel for children and young adults by Michael Ende has the title *The Neverending Story*, subsequently made into a film by Wolfgang Petersen. When the movie appeared in the summer of 2008, the Porsche 911 model range was also becoming a never-ending story.

The first edition of *Porsche 911: The Technical Documentation* was published in Germany in 1996. Back then, the engines of the 911 model range did not need cooling water. As Porsche continued with the development of its 911 range, in 1998 another edition was published which included the first water-cooled 911s.

But that was still not the end. In 1999 the first all-wheel drive 911 with automatic transmission entered the market. This led in turn to another new edition of the book including cars up to model year 2001. That edition fascinated Italian sports car lovers too, and so was consequently also printed in Italian.

At the time of writing, the 911 has been produced at Zuffenhausen uninterruptedly for 45 years, and still there is no end in sight. This latest edition describes the technology of all new vehicles up to and including model year 2009.

Even though 911 rally and race cars are only mentioned in passing in this book, the triple victory of the Porsche 911 GT3 RSR in the hardest long-distance race in the world, the 24-hours on the Nordschleife of the Nürburgring, on 24 and 25 May 2008 should nonetheless be mentioned here.

Thanks

I have received assistance from many quarters in bringing this book up to date, for which I would like to thank everyone, but especially:
Dr Ing h.c. F. Porsche AG in Stuttgart
Dieter Landenberger, Dieter Gross and Jens Torner from the Historisches Archiv Porsche
Dr Heinz Rabe for data and facts regarding the early history of Porsche

Picture credits

Historisches Archiv und Presse-Datenbank of Dr Ing h.c. F. Porsche AG
Bernd Austen, Leonberg
Jörg Austen, Weissach

At home on the Nordschleife of the Nürburgring: a 911 GT3 during the 24-hour race in May 2008. The event attracted 220,000 spectators. Apart from the Nordschleife the Grand Prix circuit also had to be driven, which made each lap a length of more than 25km. This photo shows the GT3 of the Manthey Team, which came second. Eight Porsche 911 GT3s were amongst the first ten cars to cross the finish line.

Power/weight ratios of Porsche 911 and Porsche 959

Car type	Model year	Displacement (l)	Engine output		Kerb weight (kg)	Power/weight ratio	
			kW	hp		kg/kW	kg/hp
911 GT1 racing version	1997	3.2	441	600	1050	2.38	1.75
911 GT1 road-going version	1997	3.2	400	544	1150	2.87	2.11
Carrera GT, series production	2003	5.73	450	612	1380	3.06	2.25
911 GT2 racing version	1995	3.6	330	450	1150	3.48	2.55
911 GT2	2003	3.6	355	483	1420	4.00	2.94
959 Sportversion A*	1987	2.85	331	450	1350	4.07	3.00
911 GT2 road-going version	1995	3.6	318	430	1290	4.06	3.00
911 GT2 (996)	2001/03	3.6	340	462	1440	4.23	3.11
959 luxury version	1987	2.85	331	450	1450	4.38	3.22
911 Turbo	2006	3.6	353	480	1585	4.49	3.30
911 GT3 RS	2007	3.6	305	415	1375	4.51	3.31
911 GT3	2006	3.6	305	415	1395	4.57	3.36
911 Turbo	2004	3.6	331	450	1540	4.65	3.42
911 Turbo S	2005	3.6	331	450	1590	4.80	3.53
911 GT3	2003	3.6	280	381	1360	4.86	3.57
911 Turbo	2001/03	3.6	309	420	1540	4.98	3.67
911 Turbo 3.6 all-wheel	1996	3.6	300	408	1500	5.00	3.68
911 GT3	2001	3.6	265	360	1350	5.09	3.75
911 Carrera SC RS	1984	3.0	188	255	960	5.10	3.76
911 Turbo 3.3 power version	1982/89	3.3	243	330	1300	5.35	3.94
911 Carrera anniversary car	2004	3.6	254	343	1370	5.39	3.99
911 Carrera S	2004	3.8	261	355	1420	5.44	4.00
911 Turbo 3.6	1993	3.6	265	360	1470	5.55	4.08
911 Turbo S power version	1991/92	3.3	261	355	1470	5.63	4.14
911 Carrera 4S	2006	3.8	261	355	1475	5.65	4.15
911 Carrera 4S lightweight design	1974	3.0	169	230	960	5.68	4.17
911 Carrera	2002/03	3.6	235	320	1345	5.72	4.20
911 Carrera 2 Cup	1990/91	3.6	195	265	1120	5.74	4.23
911 Carrera RS	1995	3.8	221	300	1270	5.74	4.23
911 Carrera	2004	3.6	239	325	1395	5.84	4.29
911 Carrera 4	2002/03	3.6	235	320	1375	5.85	4.30
911 Coupé (996)	1998	3.4	221	300	1320	5.97	4.40
911 Targa 4S	2007	3.8	261	355	1575	6.03	4.44
911 Turbo 3.3	1985/89	3.3	221	300	1335	6.04	4.45
911 Carrera 4	2006	3.6	239	325	1450	6.06	4.46
911 Carrera 4	2001/03	3.4	221	300	1375	6.22	4.58
911 Carrera RS 2.7	1979	2.7	154	210	960	6.23	4.57
911 Turbo 3.3 with cat. converter	1991/92	3.3	235	320	1470	6.23	4.59
911 Carrera 4 S	2002/03	3.6	235	320	1470	6.25	4.59
911 Turbo 3.0	1975/76	3.0	191	260	1195	6.25	4.60
911 Targa 4	2007	3.6	239	325	1510	6.32	4.65
911 Carrera 2 RS	1992	3.6	191	260	1220	6.39	4.69
911 Carrera	1996/97	3.6	210	285	1370	6.52	4.80
911 Carrera Cabriolet	1996/97	3.6	210	285	1400	6.66	3.67
911 Turbo 3.6	2001/03	3.6	309	420	1540	4.98	3.67
911 Carrera 3.2 without cat. conv.	1984/86	3.2	170	231	1160	6.82	5.02
911 Carrera 4	1996/97	3.6	210	285	1440	6.86	5.05
911 Carrera 4S	1996/97	3.6	210	285	1450	6.90	5.08
911 Carrera	1974/75	2.7	154	210	1075	6.98	5.12
911 Carrera 3.2 without cat. conv.	1987/89	3.2	170	231	1210	7.12	5.24
911 Speedster without cat. conv.	1989	3.2	170	231	1220	7.18	5.28
911 Carrera 3.2 power version	1987/89	3.2	160	217	1160	7.25	5.35
911 Carrera 2 Speedster	1993	3.6	184	250	1350	7.34	5.40
911 Carrera 2 5G*	1990	3.6	184	250	1350	7.34	5.40
911 Carrera 3.2 TL*	1985/89	3.2	170	231	1260	7.41	5.45
911 Carrera 2 Tiptronic	1990	3.6	184	250	1380	7.50	5.52
911 S	1972/73	2.4	140	190	1050	7.50	5.53
911 SC power version	1981/82	3.2	154	210	1160	7.53	5.52
911 Carrera 3.2 with cat. converter	1987/89	3.2	160	217	1210	7.56	5.58
911 Carrera 3.0	1976/77	3.0	147	200	1120	7.60	5.60
911 Speedster TL with cat. conv.	1989	3.2	160	217	1220	7.63	5.62
911 S	1970	2.2	132	180	1020	7.72	5.67
911 C2 Cabrio TL 5G*	1992	3.6	184	250	1420	7.72	5.68
911 SC 3.0	1981/83	3.0	150	204	1160	7.73	5.69
911 Carrera 4 A*	1989/93	3.6	184	250	1450	7.88	5.80
911 C2 Cabrio TL Tip*	1992	3.6	184	250	1450	7.88	5.80
911 Carrera TL with cat. converter	1987/88	3.2	160	217	1260	7.88	5.81
911 Carrera with cat. converter	1985/86	3.2	152	207	1210	7.96	5.85
911 S	1969	3.0	125	170	995	7.96	5.85
911 S	1974/75	2.7	129	175	1075	8.33	6.14
911 SC	1980	3.0	138	188	1160	8.40	6.17
911 E	1972/73	2.4	121	165	1050	8.67	6.36
911 S	1967/68	2.0	118	160	1030	8.73	6.43
911 SC	1978	3.0	132	180	1160	8.79	6.44
911 E	1970/71	2.2	114	155	1020	8.94	6.58
911	1976	2.7	121	165	1120	9.20	6.79
911	1974/75	2.7	110	150	1075	9.77	7.17
911 E	1969	2.0	103	140	1020	9.90	7.29
911 T	1967/69	2.0	81	110	1020	10.20	9.27

Key: : A = all-wheel drive, C2 = Carrera 2, C4 = Carrera 4, TL = Turbo Look, 5G = with 5-speed transmission